# WOMEN'S MENTAL HEALTH ISSUES ACROSS THE CRIMINAL JUSTICE SYSTEM

**Rosemary L. Gido**

**Lanette P. Dalley**

PEARSON

Prentice
Hall

Upper Saddle River, New Jersey
Columbus, Ohio

**Library of Congress Cataloging-in-Publication Data**

Women's mental health issues across the criminal justice system / Rosemary L. Gido,
Lanette Dalley [editors].
    p. cm.
ISBN-13: 978-0-13-243535-2
ISBN-10: 0-13-243535-7
1. Women prisoners--United States. 2. Women prisoners—Mental health services
—United States. 3. Female offenders—United States. 4. Female offenders
—Rehabilitation—United States. I. Gido, Rosemary L. II. Dalley, Lanette.
HV9471.W68 2008
365'.66720820973—dc22                                                2008007579

**Editor in Chief:** Vern Anthony
**Acquisitions Editor:** Tim Peyton
**Editorial Assistant:** Alicia Kelly
**Director of Marketing:** David Gesell
**Marketing Manager:** Adam Kloza
**Senior Marketing Assistant:** Alicia Dysert
**Production Manager:** Wanda Rockwell
**Creative Director:** Jayne Conte
**Cover Design:** Bruce Kenselaar
**Cover Illustration/Photo:** Getty Images, Inc.
**Full-Service Project Management/Composition:** Abhinav Mathur/Aptara, Inc.
**Printer/Binder:** RR Donnelly/Harrisonburg

Credits and acknowledgments borrowed from other sources and reproduced, with permission, in this text-
book appear on appropriate page within text.

Pearson Education Ltd., London
Pearson Education Singapore, Pte. Ltd
Pearson Education Canada, Inc.
Pearson Education–Japan

Pearson Education Australia PTY, Limited
Pearson Education North Asia Ltd., Hong Kong
Pearson Educación de Mexico, S.A. de C.V.
Pearson Education Malaysia, Pte. Ltd.
Pearson Education Upper Saddle River, New Jersey

10 9 8 7 6 5 4 3 2 1
ISBN 13: 978-0-13-243535-2
ISBN 10:      0-13-243535-7

# DEDICATION

*This book is dedicated to my wonderful family—my husband, Jack; my sons, Stephen and Jeffrey; my "daughters," Wendy and Teresa; and our brilliant grandchildren, Sophie, Meghan, Allison, Alex, and Mathew.*

Rosemary Gido

*To my twin daughters, Miranda and Sophia, who make life worthwhile and to my husband, Lynn, who shares the same vision for social justice.*

Lanette Dalley

# CONTENTS

☙

## CHAPTER 4  The Challenges of Policing the Mentally Ill: An Exploration of Gendered and Ungendered Perspectives    71

**Mary Dodge**
**Terri Schreiber**

## CHAPTER 5  Improving Police Interactions with the Mentally Ill: Crisis Intervention Team (CIT) Training    84

**Laura Ketteler**
**Mary Dodge**

**Lanette P. Dalley**
**Vicki Michels**

**Andrew Harris**
**Arthur J. Lurigio**

# FOREWORD

### Roslyn Muraskin

Female offenders have always been a forgotten and neglected population. The disregard and mistreatment of female offenders becomes even more glaring when we examine the treatment of mentally ill female offenders throughout the criminal justice system. Similar to mentally ill persons in the U.S. general population, mentally ill female offenders have also been misunderstood, feared, and stigmatized. Although female offenders also bear the additional stigma of criminal labeling, the criminal justice system has rarely acknowledged the harsh and profound consequences of this dual status.

In recent years, professionals in the criminal justice system have begun to focus on the needs of mentally ill female offenders. This is a result of the growing number of mentally ill female offenders in the criminal justice system as compared to mentally ill male offenders. According to the Bureau of Justice Statistics (BJS, 2002 and 2004), female offenders have consistently higher rates of mental health problems than male inmates (i.e., federal prisons: 61% of females and 44% of males; state prisons: 73% of females and 55% of males; local jails: 75% of females and 63% of males).[1] Yet, gender-specific treatment policies and program models have not been widely designed and disseminated. In addition, criminal justice professionals, including police officers, probation officers, and correctional officers who acknowledge their lack of knowledge and skills in dealing with these women, point out that there is little if any funding for specialized training programs. Thus, the women continue to be invisible to society, at least until they commit another crime.

As the research presented in this book illustrates, mentally ill female offenders are extremely difficult to manage—from their first contact within the system usually involving the police—to ultimately being warehoused in prison until their release. They bring with them not only their chronic mental illnesses but also a variety of other complex and often overwhelming problems. These women typically have persistent addictions to drugs and/or alcohol, often the result of attempting to self-medicate their mental illnesses. Addiction for many of them is the driving force in their lives, which results in their committing drug-related crimes. Coupled with these issues of substance abuse, justice-related girls and women have often experienced a variety of traumas, either as adults or children, and socio-economic deprivations related to homelessness, unemployment, and single parenthood. It is also not uncommon for girls and women in the justice system to exhibit suicidal ideations and self-harming behaviors and to be lacking in decision-making and coping skills. The compounding of these problems too often results in repeated arrests and inappropriate "placements."

---

[1]Bureau of Justice Statistics. Survey of Inmates in State and Federal Correctional Facilities, 2004, and the Survey of Inmates in Local Jails, 2002.

Given that there are few studies of mentally ill female offenders, this book provides a significant contribution to our knowledge and understanding of their needs across the major criminal justice system components—law enforcement, courts, and corrections. Police officers typically face frustration over the lack of coordination with mental health professionals and the limited options available in dealing with this population. Until recently, courts did not have the flexibility to incorporate treatment as part of sentencing. The general movement across the United States to establish mental health courts offers a model that needs a greater focus on female offenders.

Similarly, few jails and prisons have established gender-appropriate treatment and models of best practice of care. The majority of imprisoned mentally ill women and girls require treatment for their mental illnesses, trauma, and addictions; education on ways to cope with their emotional problems and addictions; vocational and life skills training; and parenting programming. Even more critical, where are the model post-release programs to provide "safety nets" for them when they attempt to reenter and reintegrate into their communities? These programs would provide interventions at critical points to prevent their entering the criminal justice system once again.

Clearly, as the studies in this book document, there are serious repercussions for the lack of interest, care, and treatment of mentally ill female juvenile and adult offenders. Therefore, a special focus throughout the book is the examination of the elements of effective gender-responsive treatment and recommendations in terms of best practices for women and girls.

The response of the criminal justice system to mentally ill female offenders must be one that will have a positive effect on these individuals and allow them to reenter society as productive citizens. The public and government policy makers at all levels need to be educated, as do professionals within the system. This is a growing population that will not disappear. In fact, unless appropriate steps are taken, these women and girls will continue to fall into society's abyss.

## References

Shipley, S. (2007). Perpetrators and victims: Maternal filicide and mental illness. In R. Muraskin (Ed.), *It's a crime: Women and justice* (4th ed.). Upper Saddle River, NJ: Prentice Hall.

# ACKNOWLEDGMENTS

We wish to acknowledge the "vision" of Roslyn Muraskin who suggested that we write this book. She truly saw the need to address the issues that render mentally ill female offenders "invisible." We are indebted to the authors for their scholarship and commitment to giving mentally ill women and girl offenders a voice.

Thanks again to the Prentice Hall "family" for their support in this endeavor.

Rosemary L. Gido, Ph.D. and Lanette P. Dalley, Ph.D.

# ABOUT THE AUTHORS/EDITORS

**Bruce A. Arrigo, Ph.D.** is a Professor of Crime, Law, and Society in the Department of Criminal Justice at the University of North Carolina–Charlotte. He has written extensively in the areas of law, psychology, and crime, as well as criminology and ethics. A selected recent book is *Ethics, Crime, and Criminal Justice* (Prentice Hall, 2008). He was the 2007 Bruce Smith Sr. Award Recipient for Distinguished Research by the Academy of Criminal Justice Sciences.

**David P. Bernstein, Ph.D.** is an Associate Professor of Psychology at the University of Maastricht in the Department of Clinical Psychological Services. He is Past President of the Association for Research on Personality Disorders and Vice President of the International Society for the Study of Personality Disorders. He is the lead investigator on a multicenter randomized clinical trial of the effectiveness of Schema Focused Therapy funded by The Netherlands Ministry of Justice. He is the author of more than 70 peer-reviewed articles and book chapters and the Childhood Trauma Questionnaire.

**Kristie R. Blevins, Ph.D.** is an Assistant Professor of Criminal Justice at the University of North Carolina–Charlotte. Her research interests include correctional rehabilitation, victimization, and occupational attitudes of employees in the criminal justice system. She recently served as Co-Editor and Contributing Co-Author of *Taking Stock: The Status of Criminological Theory*. She is currently involved in research examining lifetime drug use among a sample of jail inmates.

**Barbara E. Bloom, Ph.D.** is an Associate Professor in the Department of Criminology and Criminal Justice Studies at Sonoma State University and Co-Director of the Center for Gender and Justice. She is the recipient (with Barbara Owen) of the American Society of Criminology Division on Women and Crime 2006 Saltzman Award for Contributions to Practice, recognizing her professional accomplishments in increasing the quality of justice and level of safety for women.

**Rebecca J. Boyd** is a doctoral candidate in the Department of Criminology at Indiana University of Pennsylvania. She received her M.A. degree in Applied Sociology and Criminal Justice from Old Dominion University in 2003. Her current research interests include developmental science and the risk factor paradigm: juvenile delinquency and justice policy, quantitative research methods, and criminological theory testing.

**Nahama Broner, Ph.D.** is a Senior Research Psychologist at Research Triangle Institute (RTI) International and Adjunct Associate Professor at New York University. Her research focuses on the effectiveness of diversion and reentry models, services, characteristics, and health risks of criminal justice populations with mental and addictive disorders and transfer of knowledge between science and practice.

**Henry H. Brownstein, Ph.D.** is a Senior Vice President and Director of the Substance Abuse, Mental Health, and Criminal Justice Studies Department at NORC at the University of Chicago. Previous positions include: Director, Drugs and Crime Division, National Institute of Justice; Professor and Graduate Program Director, University of Baltimore; Director, Statistical Analysis Center, NYS Division of Criminal Justice Services.

**Stephanie Covington, Ph.D.** is a clinician, author, organizational consultant, and lecturer. Recognized for her pioneering work in the area of women's issues, she specializes in the development of gender-responsive services for women and girls. She is the Co-Director of the Center for Gender and Justice in La Jolla, CA.

**Lanette P. Dalley, Ph.D.** is an Associate Professor in the Social Work and Criminal Justice Programs at the University of Mary, Bismarck, North Dakota. Her publications and studies focus on female prisoners and their children. In addition to her doctorate in criminology, she earned an M.S.W. from Washington University–St. Louis, Missouri. She is a licensed clinical social worker and has previously served as a juvenile probation officer.

**Mary Dodge, Ph.D.** is an Associate Professor and Director of the Criminal Justice Programs at the Graduate School of Public Affairs, University of Colorado at Denver and Health Sciences Center. Her research interests include white-collar crime with an emphasis on gendered varieties, fraud in assisted reproductive technology, women in the criminal justice system, and policing. She is co-editor with Gilbert Geis of *Lessons of Criminology* and co-author with Gilbert Geis of *Stealing Dreams: A Fertility Clinic Scandal*.

**Rosemary L. Gido, Ph.D.** is a Professor in the Indiana University of Pennsylvania Department of Criminology. She is Editor of *The Prison Journal* and *Turnstile Justice: Issues in American Corrections* (Prentice Hall, 2nd Edition, 2002). The former Director of the Office of Program and Policy Analysis, New York State Commission of Correction, she directed the first national prison-based study of HIV/AIDS in the New York State Prison System. She received the Academy of Criminal Justice Sciences 2005 Corrections Section Award for Outstanding Contributions to Corrections.

**Anthony J. Harris, Ph.D.** is an Assistant Professor in the Department of Criminal Justice and Criminology at the University of Massachusetts–Lowell. He has held senior-level management positions in human services, criminal justice, and policy-making agencies in Massachusetts and New York City.

**Phyllis Harrison Ross, M.D.** is a nationally recognized expert in forensic psychiatry and correctional medicine. She formerly served as President of the Medical Board, Staff Associate Medical Director, and Director of the Department of Psychiatry and Community Mental Health Center at Metropolitan Hospital Center in Bronx, New York. She is currently Emeritus Professor of Clinical Psychology at New York Medical Center, Metropolitan Hospital. She serves by governor's appointment on the Correctional Medical Review Board that oversees correctional health care in New York prisons and jails.

**Stephanie W. Hartwell, Ph.D.** is an Associate Professor of Sociology and Criminal Justice and the Director of the Graduate Program in Applied Sociology at the

University of Massachusetts–Boston. She is a research fellow at the Center for Mental Health Services at the Department of Psychiatry at U Mass Medical School and affiliated with the Massachusetts Department of Mental Health, Division of Forensic Services. She publishes widely on multiproblem populations and the organization of services and institutions arranged to address their needs.

**Janice Joseph, Ph.D.** is a Professor in the Criminal Justice Program at Richard Stockton College of New Jersey. She is the Editor of the *Journal of Ethnicity in Criminal Justice*. She has published books and articles on delinquency, gangs, domestic violence, stalking, sexual harassment, and minorities and crime. She has held a variety of leadership positions in the Academy of Criminal Justice Sciences.

**Laura Ketteler, M. A.** recently received her Master's Degree in Criminal Justice from the University of Colorado–Denver. She plans to continue her career in the field of criminal justice.

**Sarah Kopelovich, M.A.** is a doctoral student in clinical forensic psychology at John Jay College of Criminal Justice, City University of New York. She received her Master of Arts degree in forensic psychology from John Jay College of Criminal Justice.

**Sandra Langley, Ph.D.** is a research consultant who specializes in applied measurement, design, and data analysis. She holds a Ph.D. in Measurement, Evaluation and Statistics from Teachers College, Columbia University. Her substantive work involves a variety of social issues, including violence, sexuality education, and public school reform.

**James E. Lawrence, M.A.** is the Director of Operations of the New York State Commission of Correction, the Executive Department agency responsible for the oversight of all of New York's state and local correctional facilities. He has been active in the field of prisoner mortality and correctional health for the past 30 years, first as forensic medical investigator, then for 10 years as the Director of the New York State Correction Medial Review Board.

**Arthur J. Lurigio, Ph.D.** is the Associate Dean for Faculty in the College of Arts and Sciences and a Professor of Criminal Justice and Psychology at Loyola University–Chicago. He is a member of the Graduate Faculty and Director of the Center for the Advancement of Research, Training, and Education (CARTE) at Loyola University–Chicago, and a Senior Research Advisor at Illinois Treatment Alternatives for Safe Communities (TASC). In 2003, Dr. Lurigio was named faculty scholar, the highest honor bestowed on senior faculty at Loyola University.

**Damon Mayrl, M.A.** is a Ph.D. candidate in the Department of Sociology at the University of California, Berkeley. His research interests include political sociology, the sociology of punishment, and the sociology of religion. From 2000 to 2002, he was a Research Associate on the SAMHSA Jail Diversion Research Project at New York University and RTI. His current research compares the changing role of religion in Australian and American education between 1830 and 1980.

**Vicki J. Michels, Ph.D.** is the Director of Addiction Studies at Minot State University, Minot, North Dakota. She is a practicing licensed psychologist and researches treatment outcomes and alcohol effects.

**Karen Orr, LICSW**, is a social worker and manager for the Massachusetts Department of Mental Health's Forensic Division. She is also an Adjunct Professor at Merrimack College in Andover, MA.

**Judith A. Ryder, Ph.D.** is an Assistant Professor in the Sociology and Anthropology Department, St. John's University. She is a Research Fellow at the Center for Community and Urban Health and previously served as Senior Project Director, Institute on Trauma and Violence, National Development and Research Institutes (NDRI). Her research interests include correctional policy and female offenders.

**Terri L. Schreiber** is a Ph.D. candidate at the University of Colorado. Having interests that span both the private and public sector, she holds Master's Degrees in Business Administration and Public Administration. An active community volunteer, she became an advocate for the Chronically Mentally Ill where she was introduced to the issue of policing and the mentally ill.

**Philip M. Stinson** is a Ph.D. candidate in Criminology at Indiana University of Pennsylvania. He holds a J.D. from the University of the District of Columbia and is currently the managing editor of *Criminal Justice Policy Review*. His research interests include police crime/misconduct, delinquency and mental health, and prisoner reentry issues.

**Nancy Wolff, Ph.D.** is a Professor of Public Policy in the E. J. Bloustein School of Planning and Public Policy at Rutgers University and the Director of the Center for Mental Health Services and Criminal Justice Research in the Institute for Health, Health Care Policy, and Aging Research. Her research focuses on issues related to measuring the societal costs of interventions for persons with mental illness, designing cost-effectiveness analyses, and modeling and analyzing intersystem dynamics.

# INTRODUCTION
# THE MENTAL HEALTH NEEDS OF FEMALE OFFENDERS ACROSS THE CRIMINAL JUSTICE SYSTEM

## Rosemary L. Gido

## THE INVISIBILITY OF MENTALLY ILL FEMALE OFFENDERS

Over the past 15 years, the term *invisible* has been used by criminologists to describe both juvenile and adult female offenders across the U.S. criminal justice system (Belknap, 1996; Chesney-Lind, 2006; Covington, 2002; Gido, 1992). Even as rates of arrest, conviction, and incarceration have increased dramatically for adolescent girls and adult women, the criminal justice system has been slow to respond to "craft a system (not simply prisons) that responds to the issues presented by women offenders" (Chesney-Lind, 2003, p. 6).

The source of girls and women offenders' invisibility is variously traced to gender and racial bias (Young & Reviere, 2006), the lack of training of criminal justice personnel in gender differences and understandings, the lack of programming for girls and women in correctional facilities and community placements, and the continued utilization of "genderless" treatment, assessment, and service models that are, in fact, *male oriented* (Covington, 2002, p. 1).

Only in the last decade have researchers and policy makers called for *gender-specific programming* (Bloom & Covington, 2002), based on the documented factors that characterize the lives of justice-involved women and girls—economic marginality; personal and family histories of sexual, emotional, and physical abuse and neglect; and interpersonal violence (Kruttschnitt & Garner, 2003).

Yet, lost in all these discussions are the *most invisible* of females in the justice system—*mentally ill adolescent girl and women offenders* (Criminal Justice/Mental Health Consensus Project, 2002). When we dare to look at or ask who they are and what is at the root of their invisibility, we find:

- 74% of adolescent girls in detention, compared to 66% of boys in detention, meet the criteria for a mental disorder (Teplin, 2002; Veysey, 2003, p. 1).
- Girls in detention are more likely than boys to exhibit a co-occurring substance abuse dependency and second psychiatric diagnosis (Veysey, 2003, p. 2).

- Girls known to the criminal justice system manifest high rates of major depression, anxiety disorders, and borderline personality disorders—all linked to histories of sexual and physical abuse and neglect (Veysey, 2003, pp. 2–3).
- Adult women coming before the courts are also most likely to present with co-occurring substance abuse and mental disorders. Most have been victims of physical and sexual trauma, exacerbated by dysfunctional adult relationships, poor medical care histories, and child care issues impacting their recovery (Hills, 2004, pp. 2–6).
- Compared to male inmates, female inmates are more likely to have a serious mental illness (SMI) (Teplin et al., 1996)

This book is thus dedicated to giving mentally ill female offenders a face and a voice. The chapters are organized according to the subsystems of the U.S. criminal justice system, highlighting mental health research and policy issues, and focusing on impediments to treatment and service delivery, as well as model programs, assessments, and intervention processes that offer hope within and across the system.

## THE MENTAL HEALTH NEEDS OF FEMALE OFFENDERS ACROSS THE CRIMINAL JUSTICE SYSTEM

### THE JUVENILE JUSTICE SYSTEM

Despite a renewed emphasis on addressing the inadequacies of the juvenile justice system for girls and its failure to address their special needs with specific programming (Acoca, 1999; *Girls Study Group*, 2007; Sharp & Simon, 2000), much needs to be done to address the barriers that result in mentally ill adolescent girls being one of the most neglected groups in the U.S. criminal justice system. Rebecca Boyd, in Chapter 1, identifies current and entrenched systemic and interagency barriers to the availability and delivery of quality gender-responsive mental health services for female juvenile offenders. She offers five recommendations for policy and programming change.

Focusing on one of Boyd's policy recommendations—better mental health screening and assessment for girls, Phil Stinson's research study in Chapter 2 compares results using the Massachusetts Youth Survey Instrument with two groups, detained and nondetained boys and girls. The study finds girls at age 15 to present with the highest percentage of suicide ideation at intake and higher scores on the traumatic experiences scale than boys. These findings confirm that at the time of intake, girls are more likely than boys to be at risk for more serious unmet mental health needs (Fishbein et al., 2006; Ruffolo et al., 2004).

Trauma exposure is one of the key documented factors in juvenile female offenders' needs for mental health services. In Chapter 3, Judith Ryder, Sandra Langley, and Henry Brownstein offer a comprehensive review of the definition and measurement of trauma. The authors illustrate how combined methods of assessment facilitate a better understanding of the nature and prevalence of trauma as identified by the girls themselves.

## LAW ENFORCEMENT

In Chapter 4, Mary Dodge and Terri Schreiber discuss the dramatic changes that have occurred in "policing the mentally ill." Law enforcement departments at local, state, and national levels were unprepared as the 1960s deinstitutionalization movement created a climate of "criminalization of the mentally ill" and became the standard for dealing with disturbed individuals engaged in misdemeanor and felony offenses. Specific to gender, the entrance of women into police patrol officer roles raised the question of how they compare with male officers in dealing with mentally disordered individuals. Dodge and Schreiber offer insights into this question with exploratory research examining differences in gendered interactions between police officers and the mentally ill.

Laura Ketteler and Mary Dodge provide a "case" from Colorado in the emergence of Crisis Intervention Training (CTI) in Chapter 5. Intended to prevent the use of deadly force in police encounters with the mentally ill, the authors offer insights into CTI training generally and its role in giving female command officers a voice in law enforcement.

## MENTAL HEALTH COURTS

Specialty diversion courts for the mentally ill, termed *mental health courts*, have grown rapidly since their introduction in 1997. One of the most "cited" of these courts, the Brooklyn Mental Health Court, had a high one-year retention rate (84%) and a successful outcome evaluation, based on meeting its goals of linking mentally ill offenders with mental health treatment and services, after 28 months of operation (O'Keefe, 2007). However, there is, overall, limited information on females in mental health courts.

Janice Joseph, in Chapter 6, summarizes the purpose, characteristics, and processes of these courts. Finding the system lacking in its dealings with female offenders, she offers a femicentric approach as an analytic tool to examine the heterogeneous and diverse populations of women served by these courts. The chapter also presents an integrated model of service delivery for women with multiple disorders as well as policy implications and issues for future research.

## JAILS

In U.S. history, jails have been referred to as a "dumping ground for . . . society's problems (Moynahan & Stewart, 1980, p. 104). Over the past 20 years jails have become even more overcrowded and underresourced as a result of the "War on Drugs," mandatory minimum sentencing laws, and the increased number of parole violators (Gido & Alleman, 2002). More than half of all U.S. jail and prison inmates have a mental health problem (James & Glaze, 2006).

Emphasizing the high jail incarceration rates of poor and minority women, Phyllis Harrison-Ross and James Lawrence address the disproportionate representation of women with mental disorders in U.S. jails in Chapter 7. With anxiety and depression the most prevalent health problem, the authors illustrate the catastrophic results of breakdowns in jailed women's mental health care with three actual case studies. A model for case finding, mental health assessment, crisis intervention, and continuity of care is recommended.

Echoing Harrison-Ross's and Lawrence's discussion of post-traumatic stress disorder (PTSD) in jailed women, Nahama Broner, Sarah Kopelovich, Damon Mayrl, and David Bernstein report in Chapter 8 on research they conducted on the impact of childhood trauma on jailed adults with co-occurring mental and addictive disorders. They find that women were twice as likely as men to experience more severe degrees of sexual and emotional abuse and neglect in conjunction with physical neglect. Being female and abused significantly contributed to a clinical risk for violent recidivism. The study supports the need to integrate trauma screening, risk assessment, and treatment into interventions.

### PRISONS

Much of the emphasis in research and policy discussions in the last decade has been the impact of the U.S. "incarceration boom" on imprisoned female offenders who are typically poor, women of color, unemployed, and the parent of a young child (Joseph, 2001; Kruttschnitt et al., 2000; Young & Reviere, 2006).

Barbara Bloom and Stephanie Covington (2002) have been leaders in this policy discussion. Here, in Chapter 9, they discuss the mental health needs of women in the U.S. correctional system. Like many of the authors in this book, Bloom and Covington stress the connection between trauma and mental illness in the lives of these women. The chapter offers recommendations for correctional program content to develop gender responsive mental health services to women offenders.

Chapter 10 summarizes research by Lanette Dalley and Vicky Michels in a North Dakota correctional facility for women. The study confirms the national profile of deficits in treatment and programming for women with co-occurring disorders. Sixty-two percent of the female offenders scored in the "at risk" range in terms of the numbers of symptoms, their intensity, and depth of their psychological distress. More than half had chronic medical problems, and 55% needed treatment for drug addiction. Recommendations are offered to the prison administration for in-prison and post-release programming for the women and their children.

Chapter 11 recognizes the challenges to the criminal justice system to meet the needs of Persons with Serious Mental Illness (PSMIs) in prisons (Lurigio & Swartz, 2000). Arthur Lurigio and Andrew Harris offer three unique contributions to state-of-the-art-research on PSMIs. First, they delineate the role of courts, accrediting bodies, and professional associations in defining the parameters of minimally adequate mental health services in prison. Second, a "best practice" approach to the planning and implementation of effective systems of care and intervention for mentally ill women inmates is presented. Third, the authors address the key issue of resources and the public health and public safety imperatives of sufficiently investing in systems of care.

### REENTRY

As the tides of the incarcerated flood back into U.S. communities (Petersilia, 2003: Travis, 2005), the reentry needs of female mentally ill offenders and girls are not being met. In Chapter 12, Stephanie Hartwell and Karin Orr present data updating their previous research in gender differences of 1,245 mentally ill offenders post-prison release by the Massachusetts Department of Mental Health Forensic Transition Team. Although female offenders with mental illness were more likely than males to be engaged in services post-release, they were also more likely to be "lost in follow up" and recidivate to prison. The authors note that these returning women are typical of today's returning mentally ill female offender—single, unemployed, mothers, with criminal history and psychiatric problems. They also face common impediments to reintegration—housing, employment, health services, and specialty treatment and case management for their unique needs.

Similarly, in Chapter 13, Nancy Wolff clearly outlines the overall gendered pathway difficulties of mentally ill women offenders returning to their home communities post-release. Based on two of her research studies of reentering mentally ill women offenders and interviews with women about to leave prison, she recommends a reentry strategy based on empowerment, reintegration, and recovery, each with elements of information, skill-building, resources, and support. The chapter ends with recommendations for getting reentry right for women leaving prison.

### POLICY

Finally, in Chapter 14, Kristie Blevins and Bruce Arrigo strongly challenge the justice and mental health systems for their failure to deliver programming based on the gendered interests of women. With illustrations from the "case" of Eileen Wuornos, the authors demonstrate how both systems missed the opportunity to treat her during her frequent contacts with the criminal justice system. At issue is the extent to which both systems function to maximize (or not) desistance from crime and community reintegration efforts. Blevins and Arrigo sketch the ethical limits of current programming, arguing that both failure and abandonment more aptly characterize systemic strategies in place to assist female offenders with mental health issues.

## References

Acoca, L. (1999). *Investing in girls: A 21st century strategy: Characteristics of girls at risk of entering or involved with the juvenile justice system.* Oakland, CA: National Council on Crime and Delinquency.

Belknap, J. (1996). *Invisible woman: Gender, crime and justice.* Belmont, CA: Wadsworth Publishing Company.

Bloom, B., & Covington, S. (2002). *Gender-responsive strategies: Research practices and guiding principles for women offenders.* Washington, DC: National Institute of Corrections.

Chesney-Lind, M. (July, 1999). Challenging girls' invisibility in juvenile court. *The Annals, 564,* 185–202.

Chesney-Lind, M. (2003). Reinventing women's corrections: Challenges for contemporary feminist criminologists and practitioners. In S. F. Sharp (Ed.), *The incarcerated woman: Rehabilitative programming in women's prisons* (pp. 3–14). Upper Saddle River, NJ: Prentice Hall.

Chesney-Lind, M. (2006). From invisible to incorrigible, the demonization of marginalized women and girls. *Crime, Media, Culture, 2*(1), 29–47.

Covington, S. S. (January, 2002). *From prison to home: the effect of incarceration and reentry on children, families, and communities.* Washington, DC: U.S. Department of Health and Human Services, The Urban Institute (Working Paper from Conference).

*Criminal Justice/Mental Health Consensus Project.* (2002). Lexington, KY: Council of State Governments.

Fishbein, D., Winn, D. M, Miller-Johnson, S., & Dakof, G. (January 2006). *Presentation from the Girls Study Group.* Retrieved September 3, 2007, from http://www.girlsstudygroup.rti.org

Gido, R. (1992). Invisible women: The status of incarcerated women with HIV/AIDS. *The Justice Professional, 7*(1), pp. 25–33.

Gido, R. (2002). Turnstile justice: American corrections in the new millennium. In R. Gido & T. Alleman (Eds.), *Turnstile justice: Issues in American corrections* (pp. 1–5). Upper Saddle River, NJ: Prentice Hall.

*Girls Study Group.* (2007). Retrieved September 3, 2007, from http://www.girlsstudygroup.rti. org

Hills, H. (April, 2004). *The special needs of women with co-occurring disorders diverted from the criminal justice system.* Washington, DC: The National GAINS Center and the Tapa Center for Jail Diversion.

James, D. J., & Glaze, L. (September, 2006). *Mental health problems of prison and jail inmates.* Washington, DC: Bureau of Justice Statistics.

Joseph, J. (March, 2001). Female offenders: Imprisonment and re-integration. *The Prison Journal* (Special Issue), *81*(1).

Kruttschnitt, C., and Gartner, R. (2003). Women's imprisonment. In M. Tonry (Ed.), *Crime and justice: A review of research*, Vol. 30 (pp. 1–81). Chicago: University of Chicago Press.

Kruttschnitt, C., Gartner, R., & Miller, A. (2000). Doing her own time: Women's response to prison in the context of the old and new penology. *Criminology, 38*(3), pp. 681–717.

Lurigio, A., & Swartz, J. (2000). *Criminal justice 2000: Changing the contours of the criminal justice system to meet the needs of persons with serious mental illness.* Vol. 3. Washington DC: National Institute of Justice.

Moynahan, J. M., & Stewart, E. K. (1980). *The American jail: Its growth and development.* Chicago: Nelson-Hall.

O'Keefe, K. (2007). The Brooklyn mental health court: Implementation and outcomes. In G. Berman, M. Rempel, & R. V. Wolf (Eds.), *Documenting results: Research on problem-solving justice* (pp. 281–318). New York: Center for Court Innovation.

Petersilia, J. (2003). *When prisoners come home: Parole and prisoner reentry.* New York: Oxford University Press.

Ruffolo, M. C., Sarri, R., & Goodkind, S. (2004). Study of delinquent, diverted, and high-risk adolescent girls: Implications for mental health intervention, *28*(4), pp. 237–244.

Sharp, C., & Simon, J. (2000). *Girls in the justice system: the need for more gender-responsive services..* Washington DC: Child Welfare League of America.

Teplin, L. A., Abram, K., & McClelland, G. M. (1996). Prevalence of psychiatric disorders among incarcerated women. *Archives of General Psychiatry*, 53, (pp. 505–512).

Travis, J. (2005). *But they all come back: Facing the challenges of prisoner reentry.* Washington, DC: The Urban Institute Press.

Veysey, B. M. (July, 2003). *Adolescent girls with mental health disorders involved in the juvenile justice system* (Research and Program Brief). Washington, DC: National Center for Mental Health and Juvenile Justice.

Young, V. D., & Reviere, R. (2006). *Women behind bars: Gender and race in U.S. prisons.* Boulder, CO: Lynne Rienner Publishers.

# CHAPTER 1

# MEETING THE MENTAL HEALTH NEEDS OF FEMALE JUVENILE OFFENDERS:

## Where Are We Now, and Where Do We Go from Here?

∿

## Rebecca J. Boyd

### ABSTRACT

Meeting the mental health needs of female juvenile offenders can impact their recidivism, longevity, and engagement in other problem behaviors such as self-mutilation, attempted suicide, and substance abuse. Moreover, the provision of gender-responsive services, programs, and treatment enhances the current and future quality of these girls' lives. Drawing on current research, this chapter discusses major systemic and interagency barriers to the availability and delivery of quality gender-responsive mental health services. Recent efforts to establish and make available gender-responsive programming and treatment are also highlighted. Policy recommendations for juvenile justice and mental health systems are offered, as well as potential lines of future empirical inquiry.

Ever since the conception of the juvenile court in the late 1800s, the American juvenile justice system has approached issues of juvenile behavioral modification, treatment, and rehabilitation from a male-oriented perspective. Theories of juvenile delinquency, model delinquency intervention programs and initiatives, and general juvenile justice policy have tended to be based on the experiences of male delinquents and their interaction with the larger society.

There appear to be two major reasons for this gender disparity. First, most juvenile crime is committed by males, and the types of crime these male youth commit are of a more violent nature than that committed by their female counterparts (Chesney-Lind & Sheldon, 1992; Poe-Yamagata & Butts, 1996). Second, the disproportionate number of males in the juvenile justice system explains why research has traditionally focused on male juvenile offenders and the differences between them and nondelinquent males. Further, male delinquency program implementation and delivery stemming from such studies have traditionally offered little knowledge concerning what programs and services may be effective in reducing female juvenile offender recidivism and addressing their needs. As a result, there is a disjuncture between what we know about adolescent male offenders and female juvenile offenders.

Justice-involved adolescent females have typically been pigeonholed into services and treatment largely directed toward intervening in the delinquent pathways of their justice-involved male counterparts (Chesney-Lind & Sheldon, 1992). As a result, female juvenile offenders have been underserved as their needs, particularly those pertaining to mental health, have gone unmet.

The inattention to the needs of female juvenile offenders and calls for correction were raised at the federal level more than 30 years ago. The first major piece of federal legislation that had a direct impact on female juvenile offenders was the Juvenile Justice and Delinquency Prevention (JJDP) Act of 1974 (42 U.S.C. 5601 et. seq.). After enactment, state receipt of federal funding for juvenile justice systems was contingent on meeting two federal mandates: deinstitutionalization of all status offenders (of which many were female) and the separation of adult and juvenile offenders. Also mandated, and outlined in Section 223(a)(16) of the Act, was state adherence to the assistance of all youth in the juvenile justice system, including females, minorities, and those with emotional and physical problems. The concern with female juvenile offenders was echoed a year later with the Law Enforcement Assistance Administration's (LEAA) release of *The Report of the LEAA Task Force on Women* (LEAA, 1975). In response to the lack of services female juvenile offenders received in the 1960s and 1970s and the disproportionate number of females charged with status offenses, the LEAA called for a comprehensive approach for studying the characteristics of female juvenile offenders and identifying and meeting their needs.

By 1992, the JJDP Act was reauthorized three times, two of which were intended to directly impact the mental health needs of female juvenile offenders. The first reauthorization in 1977, under President Carter's administration, allowed for an increase in federal funding to states and localities in order to meet the act's mandated requirements. Funding was allocated under the agreement to require state juvenile justice systems to assess their respective populations of female juvenile offenders, determine their level of need, and provide gender-responsive programs to address these needs.

In response to the increase in juvenile crime in the late 1980s and early 1990s, the JJDP Act was reauthorized a third time in 1992. This particular reauthorization was the first time in American juvenile justice history that the federal government took specific action to decrease the gender gap in juvenile justice services, programs, and treatment (Community Research Associates, 1998). Action was taken on several important fronts. First, Federal Formula Grants to states were made contingent upon statewide analyses of juvenile justice systems in terms of gender gaps in service availability and delivery. These analyses included an assessment of female juvenile offenders' needs and the services available to meet them. States also were required to formulate strategic plans concerning how female-oriented services (e.g., mental health, delinquency prevention, substance abuse prevention) were to be made available and delivered (Community Research Associates, 1998). Second, the JJDP Act was expanded to include a new section, State Challenge Activities. This additional section of the legislation enabled states to apply for federal Challenge grants to address one of ten critical juvenile justice issues.

Of the ten activities, three (Activities A, E, I) included those related to enhancing mental health services for juvenile offenders. Activity E is specifically geared toward decreasing gender bias in juvenile offender placement and treatment. Under this funding category, states are required to establish policies and programs that ensure female juvenile offenders have access to quality physical and mental health services, general and occupational education, and vocational training (Hsia & Beyer, 2000; Iowa Commission on the Status of Women, 1999). Of the states that applied for Challenge grants in the 1990s, more states applied for funding under Activity E than any other activity category (Community Research Associates, 1998). A third line of action tied to the 1992 reauthorization of the JJDP Act had a direct impact on female juvenile offenders. The General Accounting Office was mandated to conduct a national study on the degree to which gender bias existed in state juvenile justice systems.

Perhaps partly a result of the 1992 reauthorization's emphasis on decreasing gender disparity, a nationwide focus on the needs of female juvenile offenders has gained momentum. Since the mid 1990s, the Office of Juvenile Justice and Delinquency Prevention (OJJDP) has established planning committees, sponsored conferences centered on female juvenile offenders, conducted juvenile justice training sessions on how to implement gender-responsive programs, reviewed new gender-specific programs, and provided informational and technical assistance to states in establishing and maintaining gender-responsive services (Community Research Associates, 1998). Additional federal grants designed specifically for gender-responsive programming have also been made available through OJJDP. Examples include the "Comprehensive Community-Based Services for At-Risk Girls and Adjudicated Juvenile Female Offenders" and the "Training and Technical Assistance Program to Promote Gender-Specific Programming for Female Juvenile Offenders and At-Risk Girls" (Community Research Associates, 1998). Gender-responsive training sessions, educational programs, training tools, protocols, curriculums, and publication material outlining innovative strategies and gender-responsive initiatives also have increased in recent years (see, e.g., Acoca, 1999; Budnick & Shields-Fletcher, 1988; Daniel, 1999; Greene, Peters, & Associates, 1998). National conferences, specifically devoted to the issue of gender-responsive programming in the juvenile justice system, have been held and sponsored by various national organizations, including the American Correctional Association and Girls Incorporated (Budnick & Shields-Fletcher, 1998; Community Research Associates, 1998). Moreover, special reports devoted to examining the lives and behaviors of female juvenile offenders, their offending patterns, and their mental health needs have emerged (see American Bar Association and National Bar Association [ABA/NBA], 2001; Bergsmann, 1989; Community Research Associates, 1998; National Institute of Justice, 1998; Poe-Yamagata & Butts, 1996; Streffensmeier, 1993).

There has always been some degree of interest in female delinquency research (see, e.g., Bergsmann, 1989; Bracey, 1983; Cernkovich & Giordano, 1987; MacVicar & Dillion, 1980; McCormack, Janus, & Burgess, 1986; Silbert & Pines, 1981; Vedder & Somerville, 1970; Zedner, 1991). However, it was not until the late 1990s that research in this area increased steadily. Particular attention began to be paid to understanding female juvenile delinquency characteristics (see, e.g., Belknap, Holsinger, & Dunn, 1997; Schoen, Davis, Collins, Greenberg, Des Roches, & Abrams, 1997; Veysey, 2003) and the factors contributing to their delinquency (Booker, 2000; Chandy, Blum, & Resnick, 1996; Hoyt & Scherer, 1998; Hubbard & Pratt, 2002). Moreover, research outlined a number of important correctional and treatment recommendations for gender-responsive programs and services to effectively address the mental health needs of female juvenile offenders while simultaneously reducing recidivism and entrenchment in the justice system (see, e.g., Bloom & Covington, 1998; Chesney-Lind & Sheldon, 1992; Gender-Specific Programming for Girls Advocacy Committee, 1998; Greene, Peters, & Associates, 1998; Prescott, 1997).

Findings from studies conducted from the mid 1990s to the present echo some of the same concerns of the LEAA in 1975. Specifically, studies revealed four particularly striking gender differences in offense and offender characteristics and juvenile justice programming and services. First, although particular types of violent crime have increased among adolescent females, juvenile female offenders continue to commit a disproportionate number of status and minor delinquency offenses (Snyder & Sickmund, 2006). Second, although most male and female juvenile offenders enter the system from lower-income, urban environments, the experiences of these youth appear clearly demarcated by gender. Specifically, female offenders are disproportionately victims of physical, sexual, and emotional abuse, and many have histories of self-destructive behavior (Dembo, Williams, & Schmeidler, 1993). Third, as compared to their male counterparts, female juvenile offenders have significantly higher rates of both major and minor mental health problems and disorders (Haapanen & Steiner, 2003), all of which may stem from their differential exposure to trauma and victimization. Fourth, male-oriented juvenile justice services, programs, and treatment do not appropriately and adequately address the mental health needs of female juvenile offenders. As a result, many of these adolescent females are left to cope with their mental health issues in limited and dysfunctional ways, including, in many instances, engaging in the same self-destructive and delinquent behavior that initially brought them into contact with the juvenile justice system.

The purpose of this chapter is to advance scholarly and practitioner knowledge concerning the major systemic and interagency barriers that hinder juvenile justice systems from providing gender-responsive mental health services and treatment to juvenile female offenders. The increase in female delinquency in recent years underscores the importance of examining and understanding various risk factors that contribute to this type of antisocial behavior, particularly self-abuse and mental health disorders. A brief discussion concerning recent efforts to provide gender-responsive mental health services serves as a springboard for an in-depth examination of major systemic and interagency barriers that hinder this effort. Juvenile justice policy recommendations and directions for future empirical inquiry are offered.

## FEMALE DELINQUENCY AS A GROWING PROBLEM

Historically, female delinquents have been overlooked and underresearched because their offenses were perceived as less serious than their male counterparts (Alderden, 2002). Over the past 20 years, a gender shift has occurred in the juvenile justice system. Although male offenders continue to outnumber female offenders and adolescent males commit more index crimes than adolescent girls, female juvenile offending patterns have changed. Not only has the sheer number of females in the juvenile justice system increased, but female adolescents are increasingly arrested for assault-type crimes, and the average age of initiation into the juvenile justice system has dropped in recent years (Snyder & Sickmund, 2006).

## ARRESTS

Between the late 1980s and early 1990s, the number of adolescent females entering juvenile justice systems increased significantly. Female juvenile arrests increased 23% between 1989 and 1993, compared to an 11% increase in male juvenile arrests (Poe-Yamagata & Butts, 1996). By 1993, 25% of youth arrested were female. Between 1981 and 1997, the female violent crime arrest rate increased by 103%, whereas the similar arrest rate for juvenile males increased only 23% (Acoca, 1999). The increase in female arrests for aggregated assault observed in the late 1980s continued well into the 1990s. Between 1991 and 2000, this rate increased 44% while juvenile male arrests for aggregated assault during this time period declined 16%.

By 2000, females constituted 28% of all juvenile arrests compared with 19% in 1990 (Community Research Associates, 1998; Snyder, 2002). Arrest statistics from 2000 also bore out the fact that adolescent females were starting to enter the juvenile justice system at younger ages. Twenty-two percent of adolescent males arrested in 2000 were younger than 15 years, compared to 35% of females in this age group (Federal Bureau of Investigation, 2000).

The most recently published juvenile arrest and court processing statistics (Snyder & Sickmund, 2006) allow for an examination of current trends. Between 1994 and 2003, the female juvenile violent crime rate declined by only 3% while similar male arrests dropped 22%. Changes in arrest rates between 1980 and 2003 for females between 10 and 12 years of age provide additional evidence that adolescent females are entering the juvenile justice system at progressively younger ages. Whereas the arrest rate for males between ages 10 and 12 years declined 20%, the arrest rate for females in this age group increased 22% (Snyder & Sickmund, 2006). An examination of changes in offense behavior among this subpopulation of females provides some alarming insights. Not only are adolescent females engaging in more assaultive-type behavior in the twenty-first century than in the 1980s, but the number of young girls engaging in these crimes has increased dramatically. For example, the arrest rate of 10- to 12-year-old females between 1980 and 2003 increased 284% for simple assault; 244% for disorderly conduct; 186% for aggravated assault and sex offenses, respectively; and 143% for drug abuse violations (Snyder & Sickmund, 2006, p. 131).

## CUSTODY

Today, more adolescent females are held in custody than ever before, and more are held for status offenses. Between 1991 and 2003, the custody rate for this population increased 52%, and by 2003, females constituted 15% of detained youth. Of those held in 2003, 40% were charged with status offenses whereas 14% were charged with delinquent offenses (Snyder & Sickmund, 2006). Adolescent females also were held in custody for status offenses at significantly higher rates than their male counterparts.

Detainment and commitment have also increased substantially since the early 1990s. In fact, detainment increased 98% and commitment increased 88% between 1991 and 2003. Of those females held in juvenile facilities in 2003, almost 50% were held in detention centers. Approximately 22% of these females were 14 years and younger (Snyder & Sickmund, 2006).

## EXPLAINING TRENDS

Several explanations have been offered for the decline in the juvenile justice gender gap over the past 20 years. Due to the fact that an increase in female adolescent assaultive behavior has increased, and not all types of violent behavior have, it is unlikely that adolescent females are simply becoming more violent (Snyder & Sickmund, 2006). On the contrary, it appears that a change in a number of policies have contributed, in part, to an increase in the number of female juveniles being formally and informally processed through the juvenile justice system (Chesney-Lind, 1997; Sharp & Simon, 2004).

Since the late 1980s, the punishment philosophy that underlies the juvenile justice system has become more conservative in nature, resulting in an increase in punitive sanctioning (Feld, 1998; Myers, 2005; Torbet et al., 1996). For example, the 1980 amendment to the JJDP Act of 1964 enables status offenders to be processed as delinquents if court orders or proceedings are violated. Some argue that this amendment has led to the increased use of "bootstrapping" among female juvenile offenders (see ABA/NBA, 2001; Chesney-Lind & Sheldon, 1992).

Other researchers contend the number of girls involved in gang activity and substance abuse, both risk factors for delinquency, has increased (Hagedorn & Moore, 2001; Owen & Bloom, 2000; Sharp & Simon, 2004). Empirical correlations have been found between substance abuse and adolescent fighting (National Center on Addiction and Substance Abuse, 2003) and female gang involvement and property, drug, and status offenses (Chesney-Lind, 1997; Hagedorn & Moore, 2001).

A third major explanation centers on welfare reform and the disruption of Medicaid benefits. With the increased push for "welfare-to-work," the number of families with any type of health insurance has decreased. Although welfare reform successfully moved families to the workforce, many could not afford to pay for various benefits, including copayments for health insurance (Heymann & Earle, 1996). As a result, many children, previously covered by Medicaid while on welfare, do not have health insurance and are now less likely to be diagnosed with various illnesses, including mental health disorders (Acs & Loprest, 2001; Tout, Scarpa, & Zaslow, 2002). The increased use of managed care systems, which dominate the private health insurance industry, has allowed increased control over public health insurance, including Medicaid (Frank, 2000; Iglehart, 1996). With increased restrictions on what mental health disorders are covered, many mentally ill youth are not having their needs met. Some researchers contend the juvenile justice system increasingly has been used as a "dumping ground" for many of these youth, because the juvenile justice system appears to be one of the only readily accessible avenues by which the mental health status of youth may be screened, assessed, and potentially treated (Boesky, 2003; Redding, 2000; Virginia Commission on Youth, 1996).

# FEMALE RISK FACTORS FOR DELINQUENCY

Risk factors are typically defined as conditions identified in an individual, or elements and circumstances in the environment, that increase the probability of engaging in antisocial, problem behaviors (Howell & Hawkins, 1998). Risk factors that place youth at risk for delinquency or contribute (directly or indirectly) to their delinquent behavior have been the focus of detailed and rigorous study since the mid-1980s (see, e.g., Catalano, Park, Harachi, Haggerty, Abbott, & Hawkins, 2005; Hawkins, Catalano, & Miller, 1992; Hawkins & Weis, 1985; Pollard, Hawkins, & Arthur, 1999). Similar to males, females who enter the juvenile justice system tend to be exposed to multiple risk factors that span individual, peer, family, school, and community levels of interaction.

Many risk factors have been empirically linked to delinquency. Regardless of gender, youth who have favorable attitudes toward delinquency and antisocial behavior, and who are impulsive and rebellious, have an increased chance of engaging in delinquent behavior (Catalano et al., 2005; Colder & Stice, 1998). Risk factors found at the peer level of interaction include associating with friends that engage in delinquent behavior and/or hold favorable attitudes toward delinquency (Akers, Krohn, Kaduce, & Radosevich, 1979; Warr & Stafford, 1991). Major family risk factors include a family history of criminal and substance abuse involvement, permissive parental attitudes concerning antisocial and delinquent behavior, family conflict, low family bonding, and poor parental management (Garnier & Stein, 2002; Glueck & Glueck, 1959; Gottfredson & Hirschi, 1990). School risk factors include poor school performance and low commitment to school (Hawkins, Smith, Hill, Kosterman, Catalano, & Abbott, 2003; Hirschi, 1969), and community-level risk factors include low neighborhood attachment, community disorganization, and community norms that favor antisocial and criminal behavior (Liska & Reid, 1985; Loeber, 1990).

Although many of the risk factors for female delinquency are the same as those for male delinquency (Hubbard & Pratt, 2002), several distinctive risk factors are endemic to females. These substantially raise their risk of engaging in antisocial, delinquent, and self-destructive behaviors.

### ABUSE

Compared to adolescent males, female juveniles have a higher probability of being exposed to one particular type of individual risk factor—abuse (physical, sexual, or emotional). Females who have been victimized physically, sexually, or emotionally run a significantly high risk of engaging in a variety of antisocial behaviors, including self-mutilation, substance abuse, and delinquency (Prescott, 1998). As research bears out, the majority of adolescent females involved in the juvenile justice system have been physically, sexually, and/or emotionally abused (Dembo et al., 1993; Widom & Maxfield, 2001). Widom and Maxfield's (2001) longitudinal study found that youth who are abused have a 59% increased chance of being arrested as a juvenile, and adolescent female victims of abuse have a 73% increased risk of being arrested for drug and nonviolent property offenses. Compared to adolescent girls who have not been abused or neglected, Widom and Maxfield also found that abused and/or neglected females are 2 times as likely to be arrested as a juvenile, 2 times as likely to be arrested during adulthood, and 2.4 times as likely be arrested for a violent offense. Exposure to physical, sexual, and emotional abuse also substantially increases the risk of various types of mental disorders, a second type of risk factor that poses a unique threat to the behavior and quality of life of female juvenile offenders.

## MENTAL ILLNESS

Rates of mental health disorders appear to be increasing among youth in the United States, particularly adolescent females (Coiro, Zill, & Bloom, 1994; Kelleher, McInerny, Gardner, Childs, & Wasserman, 2000). Mental illness among adolescent females serves as a risk factor for various types of problem behaviors, including delinquency, attempted suicide, self-mutilation (e.g., cutting), teenage pregnancy, and substance abuse (Girls Incorporated, 1996; Miller, 1994; Miller, Trapani, Fejes-Mendoza, Eggleston, & Dwiggins, 1995).

Of male and female delinquents and nondelinquents, female juvenile offenders have the highest rates of mental disorders (see, e.g., Cauffman, Feldman, Waterman, & Steiner, 1998; Haapanen & Steiner, 2003; Marsteller et al., 1997; Oregon Youth Authority, 2002; Texas Juvenile Probation Commission, 2003). Results of epidemiological studies examining the prevalence of one or more mental disorders among juvenile-involved females indicate it is not uncommon for 70% (or even 80%) of females to be diagnosed with one or more mental health disorders (Patino, Ravoira, & Wolf, 2006; Teplin, Abram, & McClelland, 2002; Timmons-Mitchell et al., 1997).

It is important to note that exposure to abuse may interact with normal psychological symptomatology to produce mental health disorders, and this interaction may increase the probability of adolescent females engaging in antisocial and delinquent behavior. Adolescent females are biologically different than their male counterparts, and they typically experience some depression and a decrease in self-esteem during puberty (Allgood-Merten, Lewinsohn, & Hops, 1990; Miller et al., 1995; Pipher, 1994). In essence, it is not atypical for adolescent girls to possess a small degree of psychological symptomatology during the early teen years (Pipher, 1994; Sharp & Simon, 2004). What is not normal, however, is exposure to trauma and victimization. When an adolescent female's pubertal experience includes trauma and victimization, already lowered self-esteem and increased depression are compounded and aggregated. Researchers contend that these inflated levels of depression and anxiety, and lowered self-esteem, contribute to the onset of inward (i.e., substance abuse, self-mutilation, and attempted suicide) and outward (i.e., running away, truancy, fighting, and assault) destructive and antisocial behaviors (Chesney-Lind & Sheldon, 1992; Sharp & Simon, 2004).

## TYPICAL FEMALE JUVENILE OFFENDER

Female juvenile offenders share many of the same characteristics, enter the justice system from similar types of environments, and typically have been exposed to many of the same risk factors. On average, female juvenile offenders are between 14 and 16 years of age, are of a racial or ethnic minority, and have academic problems (Greene, Peters, & Associates, 1998). Most have been exposed to various individual- and family-level risk factors, including one or more types of abuse at the hands of someone they know; maltreatment; and parental conflict (Bloom, Owen, Covington, & Raeder, 2002; Booker, 2000; Greene, Peters, & Associates, 1998; McCabe, Lansing, Garland, & Hough, 2002). Most enter the juvenile justice system from disorganized, inner-city, low-income neighborhoods, and they cope with one or more types of mental disorders, particularly depression, post-traumatic stress disorder, suicidal ideation, and mood and eating disorders (Greene, Peters, & Associates, 1998; Haapanen & Steiner, 2003; Teplin et al., 2002). Many have very low levels of self-esteem and have engaged in other types of problem behaviors, including substance abuse, self-mutilation (e.g., cutting), early sexual activity, and attempted suicide (Booker, 2000; Brent, 1995; Ziemba-Davis, Garcia, Kincaid, Gullins, & Myers, 2004).

## BARRIERS TO MEETING MENTAL HEALTH NEEDS

### CONTEMPORARY INITIATIVES

Juvenile offenders with mental health problems need access to four particular types of services. These youth must have access to medication, emergency mental health services, screening and evaluation, and therapy, at a minimum (Goldstrom, Jaiquan, Henderson, Male, & Manderscheid, 2001). To effectively address the mental health needs of female juvenile offenders, emergency services, screening, evaluation, and therapy must be gender-responsive.

In recent years, various states and localities have taken advantage of grant funding and blueprint program models, reallocated budgets, and trained personnel to enhance the provision of gender-responsive mental health services. Explicit efforts have been made to (a) enhance information sharing and increase collaboration between agencies, (b) train juvenile justice officials and line workers on mental health issues endemic to females, (c) provide early mental health intervention programming, (d) mandate the use of reliable mental health screening instruments, and (e) establish mental health courts and diversion programs for juveniles with serious mental health disorders (see, e.g., Cocozza & Skowyza, 2000; Council of State Governments, 2002; Texas Juvenile Probation Commission, 2003). A sampling of gender-responsive programs and initiatives that have emerged in recent years include:

- San Diego's Working to Insure and Nurture Girls Success (WINGS) (Burke, Keaton, & Pennell, 2003)
- Alameda County's (California) Department of Juvenile Probation's special girls' unit (Howell, 2003)
- California's System of Care program (Hartney, Wordes, & Krisberg, 2002)
- Milwaukee (Wisconsin) Wrap Around program (Kamradt, 2002)
- Montgomery County's (Maryland) information sharing program (Council of State Governments, 2002)
- Cook County, Illinois, gender-responsive programming and treatment (Sherman, 1999)

Although recent efforts have been made to meet the mental health needs of female juvenile offenders, much work remains to be done. Recent statewide assessments of juvenile justice systems indicate that a significant number of justice-involved females in the United States continue to cope with their mental health issues without adequate and/or professional help (see, e.g., Alderden & Perez, 2003; Goldstrom et al., 2001; Hartney, McKinney, Eidlitz, & Craine, 2003; Patino & Krisberg, 2005; Patino et al., 2006; Texas Juvenile Probation Commission, 2002; Ziemba-Davis et al., 2004). Some states are just beginning to document the numbers of females processed through their systems, let alone assess their mental health needs and attempt to address them (see, e.g., Alderden, 2002).

There is a paucity of information on the impact (outcome evaluations) of gender-responsive services and programs. Of the studies that have been conducted, the majority have examined either the degree of mental health need among juvenile female offenders *or* the availability of gender-responsive mental health services in the juvenile justice system. Very few studies have systematically and simultaneously assessed both issues in an effort to determine the extent to which a disjuncture exists between the two (see, e.g., Patino et al., 2006). What follows is a discussion of the major systemic and interagency barriers identified by research as hindering the availability of gender-responsive mental health services to female juvenile offenders.

## SYSTEMIC BARRIERS

Six factors inherent in the organization of the juvenile justice system serve as significant barriers to the establishment, availability, and effective delivery of female-oriented mental health services, programs, and treatment. These barriers center on issues related to resources; mental health screening, assessment, and diagnosis; caseload management; programming and treatment; education and training; and justice system culture.

### Resources

The lack of availability and inadequacy of female facilities, staffing, and funding are recurrent themes in most of the research reviewed. Results from three studies indicate that facility overcrowding is an issue and there is a lack of female facilities available (Belknap et al., 1997; Boddy Media Group, 1997; Texas Juvenile Probation Commission, 2002). Female juvenile offenders are typically confined to overcrowded detention facilities (which may exacerbate existing mental health problems) where mental health treatment services are often limited. Efforts to alleviate overcrowding have resulted in some female offenders being placed in treatment programs and facilities that are inappropriate for their needs (Boddy Media Group, 1997). In many Texas juvenile justice systems, male and female juvenile offenders are housed together and several counties have male-only facilities (Texas Juvenile Probation Commission, 2002). Placing females in appropriate facilities is problematic due to the lack of facilities equipped to handle their various needs.

Numerous studies have found that staff turnover and shortages pose a serious barrier to providing gender-responsive services to female juvenile offenders (Hartney et al., 2003; Patino & Krisberg, 2005; Patino et al., 2006; Texas Juvenile Probation Commission, 2003; Ziemba-Davis et al., 2004). One possible reason to explain staff turnover and shortages is the difficulty involved in finding staff willing to work with female juvenile offenders who have a multitude of physical and mental health problems (Ziemba-Davis et al., 2004). Approximately 61% of probation departments and the majority of mental health directors surveyed in Hartney et al.'s (2003) research reported that the number of staff is inadequate to handle the large volume of juveniles that come into the system with mental health issues. Inadequate mental health staffing appears to also be an issue in Florida detention centers (Patino & Krisberg, 2005).

Inadequate funding appears to serve as a barrier. Patino et al.'s (2006) comprehensive assessment found that low levels of funding was identified by juvenile justice officials as the most significant barrier to the provision of mental health services to juvenile offenders. Inadequate funding also was cited as hindering the establishment of long-term treatment programs, aftercare, and specialized services (Belknap et al., 1997; Hartney et al., 2003; Redding, 2000; Texas Juvenile Probation Commission, 2002; Ziemba-Davis et al., 2004); transitional services (Owen & Bloom, 1997); and early intervention programs and services (Hartney et al., 2003).

### Mental Health Screening, Assessment, and Diagnosis

Several studies indicate that mental health screening and assessment procedures and instruments are not gender-responsive (Hartney et al., 2002; Patino et al., 2006; Texas Juvenile Probation Committee, 2002). Juvenile justice officials from several small and medium California counties indicated that assessment results go "largely unrecorded" because these systems lack access to automated database systems (Hartney et al., 2002, p. 17). In Texas, fewer than 5% of the 123 probation departments surveyed indicated using gender-responsive procedures (Texas Juvenile Probation Commission, 2002).

Systems that do not employ gender-specific or -responsive assessment, screening, and diagnostic instruments, or use instruments that are unreliable, are more apt to misdiagnose mental health disorders (Cocozza & Skowyra, 2000). As pointed out by Wasserman, Ko, and McReynolds (2004), accurate diagnosis is crucial because it "drives mental health treatment" (p. 2). It is hardly possible to address the mental health needs of female juvenile offenders if they are misdiagnosed and potentially set up to experience additional mental health issues. Although only one study indicated this is a problem, it is worth noting that the majority of those surveyed felt misdiagnosis was occurring in their respective jurisdictions. Specifically, 85% of attorneys, 64% of judges, and 54% of defense counsel surveyed by Girls Justice Initiative (2003) felt that both male and female juvenile offenders were being misdiagnosed for mental health problems.

### Caseload Management

Allocating mental health practitioners to handle the cases of mentally ill juvenile offenders, or integrating their active input into decisions made, enables individual, quality attention to be paid to meeting the needs of these offenders. Case management teams have been established in some jurisdictions to ensure that adequate attention is paid and quality service is delivered. These case management teams typically comprise juvenile justice line workers (probation officers, corrections staff) and mental health practitioners who handle the cases of all mentally ill juvenile offenders. All team members have special training in adolescent mental health, and they work only with mentally ill juvenile offenders. This type of case management approach has proven effective in detention centers, but not enough facilities are using this strategy. Goldstrom et al.'s (2001) national study of the state of confinement and services in detention centers found that only 27% of detention centers devote special teams or managers to the case management of juvenile offenders with mental health needs. Of these detention centers, only 25% had mental health providers that aided in case management. The majority of detention centers delegate case management to juvenile justice officials, such as corrections staff. In Texas, only 3 of 123 probation departments surveyed reported maintaining specialized female offender caseloads (Texas Juvenile Probation Commission, 2002).

### Programming and Treatment

Limited (or lacking) gender-responsive mental health programming and treatment serves as both an indicator that the mental health needs of female juvenile offenders are not being met *and* a barrier to meeting these needs. It is hardly possible to meet the needs of these offenders when the services required are inadequate or simply not available. A clear consensus echoed by juvenile justice officials in numerous studies is the concern that the number of gender-responsive programs and services for female juvenile offenders is either lacking or inadequate (Alderden & Perez, 2003; Belknap et al., 1997; Goldstrom et al., 2001; Hartney et al., 2003; Owen & Bloom, 1997; Patino & Krisberg, 2005; Patino et al., 2006; Redding, 2000; Texas Juvenile Probation Commission, 2002; Ziemba-Davis et al., 2004). Only two Florida counties surveyed in Patino and Krisberg's (2005) study reported using gender-responsive group counseling.

Mental health services provided at particular stages of case processing are crucial for improving the mental health status of female juvenile offenders. Assessment, screening, and diagnosis are particularly important early on in the pre-dispositional stage, whereas mental health treatment is crucial at the post-dispositional stage. The sheer number and quality of mental health services (regardless of gender-responsiveness) in detention and other pre-dispositional confinement facilities is a serious concern. As of 2000, few mental health services were provided in Virginia detention facilities (Redding, 2000). As of 2002, more than 50% of both medium and large California counties surveyed by Hartney et al. (2003) reported providing few mental health services in detention facilities. Patino and Krisberg's (2005) study of Florida detention facilities found that 85% of detention centers provided only emergency mental health services, 71% provided screening, 57% evaluation, 43% therapy, and only 19% of females who needed substance abuse treatment received it.

The number and quality of gender-responsive post-dispositional treatment services for mentally ill juvenile offenders also is a concern. There appears to be an inadequate number of aftercare treatment programs for females released back into the community (Alderden & Perez, 2003; Boddy Media Group, 1997; Hartney et al., 2003; Patino et al., 2006; Redding, 2000; Ziemba-Davis et al., 2004), an inadequate number of transitional living centers (Alderden & Perez, 2003), and the quality and amount of follow-up care has been questioned (Patino et al., 2006). Moreover, there appears to be a lack of mental health community services for all juvenile offenders, particularly nonviolent and status offenders (Patino et al., 2006; Redding, 2000). Mental health services for juvenile offenders residing in rural jurisdictions are limited (Texas Juvenile Probation Committee, 2003), and not enough culturally sensitive programming is being provided (Hartney et al., 2003). Results from an assessment of Iowa's juvenile justice systems found that female juvenile offenders were provided male-oriented programming that juvenile justice officials recognized as ineffective (Boddy Media Group, 1997).

Several reasons for the lack of quality gender-responsive programming have been offered. Probation officers in Texas cited the small number of institutionalized female juvenile offenders and their small numbers relative to males as reasons why female-oriented services are not provided. Another reason is the lack of specialized services available in rural jurisdictions. Many juvenile justice systems must utilize community mental health services, and in many rural areas in the United States, these services simply do not exist. According to some juvenile justice officials, low numbers of female delinquents, coupled with resource problems, makes the establishment of gender-responsive services not a cost-effective venture (see, e.g., Texas Juvenile Probation Commission, 2002).

### Education and Training

Mental health training and education are fundamental components of delivering effective mental health services. All key participants in the juvenile court process (prosecutors, defense counsel, judges, probation officers, and court staff) and those who work with juvenile offenders need to receive training on the mental health needs of female juvenile offenders. In addition, training and education needs to include information about differences in male and female psychosocial development and behavior. It is important for juvenile justice and mental health officials to identify symptoms of mental illness and correctly interpret the behavior.

### Justice System Culture

Survey and interview results from the recent literature indicate that some of the attitudes of juvenile justice officials may serve as barriers to meeting the mental health needs of female juvenile offenders (Hartney et al., 2003; Redding, 2000; Texas Juvenile Probation Commission, 2002; Ziemba-Davis et al., 2004). Several probation officers in Texas indicated that their complacent attitude concerning the need to meet the mental health needs of female offenders is due, in part, to the fact that juvenile male referrals far outnumber that of females (Texas Juvenile Probation Committee, 2002). Moreover, many of the Texas probation officers surveyed felt that the level of services was adequate for female offenders. Results from the Texas study confirm that this is not the case in most Texas jurisdictions (Texas Juvenile Probation Commission, 2002, p. 39). Survey respondents in Redding's (2000) Virginia study indicated that the judiciary in their jurisdictions had little knowledge of the degree to which justice-involved youth have mental health problems. Moreover, the general sentiment among many officials is that there is not a problem that needs to be addressed. The low level of importance placed on meeting the mental health needs of female juvenile offenders, and juvenile offenders in general, also was found in Hartney et al.'s (2003) study of juvenile justice systems in California. Ziemba-Davis et al. (2004) found that gender-responsive programming is not a high priority in the Indiana counties surveyed. In fact, most juvenile justice staff interviewed did not know what "gender-responsive" programming was.

## INTERAGENCY BARRIERS

A review of the literature indicates that three factors in the interaction of multiple agencies that work with female juvenile offenders serve as barriers to service availability. These barriers center on issues related to policies and procedures, collaboration and communication, and information sharing.

### Policies and Procedures

Two assessments of juvenile justice systems found that the lack of appropriate policies and procedures provide challenges for making services available to juvenile offenders. Redding's (2000) study found that record sharing was hindered by the lack of policies and procedures concerning how this activity should occur between the juvenile justice system, mental health, and social welfare agencies. The Texas Juvenile Probation Commission's (2003) assessment of Texas Special Needs Diversionary Programs found that jurisdictions that had successfully and fully implemented the program were those that had to completely rewrite policies and procedures. Of those policies and procedures that needed to be rewritten, some pertained to paperwork and how it needs to be handled between agencies, how and by whom programs are delivered, and how communication between the juvenile justice, mental health, and social service systems should be conducted.

### Collaboration and Communication

Unlike the adult criminal justice system, the juvenile justice system is inextricably tied to community agencies and social services. Not only does the juvenile justice system depend on these agencies for supplemental services and aid, but many of the juvenile offenders, themselves, are involved in multiple systems. An assessment of the Illinois juvenile justice system found that 45% of justice-involved females were involved in both the juvenile justice and social service systems (Alderden & Perez, 2003). Four of the studies and assessments reviewed found that poor collaboration existed between juvenile justice systems and community organizations, including mental health, social services, and schools (Hartney et al., 2003; Redding, 2000; Patino et al., 2006; Ziemba-Davis et al., 2004). Two indicated low levels of communication between agencies (Belknap et al., 1997; Texas Juvenile Probation Commission, 2003).

Increased collaboration between agencies in Indiana was cited by juvenile justice line workers as a component necessary for establishing case management and treatment plans, reducing the duplication of services, enhancing service delivery, and improving contact with youth (Ziemba-Davis et al., 2004). Hartney et al.'s (2003) assessment of California juvenile justice systems highlights how fragmented services are often a product of poor service integration and collaboration. Many probation department respondents reported that the lack of integration between community mental health and substance abuse agencies contributed to the fragmentation of treatment for juvenile offenders with co-occurring disorders (Hartney et al., 2003).

Delayed communication also appears to be an interagency barrier to the delivery of mental health treatment. Probation officers in Texas reported that delayed communication between managed healthcare systems made service provision through the Texas Special Needs Diversionary Program challenging. Often, the participation of juvenile offenders in treatment was delayed because communication between the two systems was too slow (Texas Juvenile Probation Commission, 2003).

### Information Sharing

Agencies that do not share or are slow to share information concerning available resources and services, and information pertinent to the mental or developmental capacity of offenders, are not collaborating toward reaching system goals. When this occurs, the needs of female juvenile offenders are either compromised or simply not met. The level and type of information sharing between agencies is often contingent on the type of information systems used (Hartney et al., 2003), privacy and confidentiality provisions (Goldstrom et al., 2001; Redding, 2000), and the number of youth involved in multiple systems, which tends to congest and complicate information-sharing capacities (Goldstrom et al., 2001). Although confidentiality policies are meant to protect the privacy of juvenile offenders, and rightly so, one significant drawback is that vital mental health information cannot be shared between agencies. Some states, like Virginia, have confidentiality provisions built into state codes that preclude relevant agencies from sharing and transferring vital mental health information (Redding, 2001). Privacy and confidentiality provisions were cited by juvenile justice and mental health officials in Goldstrom et al.'s (2001) national study as the most significant barrier to interagency information sharing.

## CONCLUSION

Adolescent males and females appear to enter the juvenile justice system with different sets of issues and problems. A significant proportion of female juvenile offenders are victims of abuse and maltreatment, and their problem behaviors appear related to abusive relationships and family life (Dembo et al., 1993). Many of these adolescents also have mental health disorders, including anxiety, depression, and post-traumatic disorder. These disorders require immediate professional attention and gender-responsive services, programs, and treatment. With ever-increasing numbers of females involved in the juvenile justice system, the issue of meeting their mental health needs has become all the more pressing.

The purpose of this chapter was to present a synopsis of the various barriers to mental health service availability. A review of the literature indicates that few assessments of the disjuncture between mental health service need and availability have been conducted. A number of studies do provide some insight into factors that hinder mental health service availability and delivery.

### Current State of Knowledge

Efforts have been made to address the mental health needs of female juvenile offenders in recent years, but not enough is being done. The few studies that have examined the disjuncture between gender-responsive mental health service availability and need among female juvenile offenders indicate that such a disjuncture does exist (e.g., Patino et al., 2006). In some jurisdictions, limited and/or inadequate mental health services are being provided. Other jurisdictions offer no gender-responsive services whereas still others provide juvenile female offenders with male-oriented programming and treatment.

Various systemic and interagency factors appear to hinder efforts to establish, maintain, and make available gender-responsive mental health services. Major systemic barriers identified include inadequate funding, staff turnover and shortages, the lack of gender-responsive assessment procedures and instruments, and misdiagnosis of mental health problems. Also impeding efforts to make available and/or deliver gender-responsive services is the lack of specialized caseload practices, an inadequate number of gender-responsive programs and pre- and post-dispositional mental health treatment, inadequate mental health education and training for juvenile justice officials, and low recognition of the importance of female offender mental health. Major interagency barriers include the lack of policies and procedures that guide the implementation and successful maintenance of gender-responsive programming, poor collaboration and communication between systems, and low levels of information sharing.

### Policy and Research Recommendations

**Policy and Programming.**  Five implications related to policy and programming flow from this review. First, more interagency collaboration, information sharing, and training should be conducted (Hubner & Wofson, 2000). Many justice-involved girls are involved in multiple systems. In an effort to avoid duplicating or providing fragmented services, collaboration among community mental health services, school systems, social services, and juvenile justice systems is crucial. As aptly stated by Goldstrom et al. (2001), juvenile offenders, regardless of gender, "cannot be placed at the doorstep of any one agency or system."

Second, mental health screening and needs assessments must be conducted. Mental health screening and assessment must be done as early in the stages of case processing as possible. In order to effectively address mental health needs, it is essential that screening be conducted upon intake and admission to any and all facilities as promulgated by the National Commission on Correctional Healthcare's (NCCHC) voluntary standards for juvenile justice systems. Qualified mental health professionals must assess juveniles using screening instruments evidenced as reliable. Numerous screening instruments are suitable, most notably the Massachusetts Youth Screening Instrument-2 (MAYSI-2; Grisso & Barhum, 2000). The mental health status of female juvenile offenders should be assessed through case processing, and numerous times in detention if youths are held there for extended periods of time. Two subgroups of the female juvenile offender population must be identified—those who need immediate mental health services, such as females experiencing suicidal ideation, and those who require consistent mental health monitoring (Wasserman et al., 2004). More mental health needs assessments in female juvenile populations are needed, particularly in jurisdictions that have not yet completed one. Various recommendations on how to conduct a needs assessment and samples of survey instruments are available (see, e.g., Owen & Bloom, 2000).

Third, a review of the literature indicates that the increased use of diversion should be employed, as should the use of community-based outreach services. Aftercare also should be practiced. Community-based mental health services are very important from both a treatment and interventionist standpoint, and both aftercare and integration back into the community constitute two important components of the continuum of care. The increased use of diversion can decrease overpopulation in detention facilities. Overpopulation not only places a strain on facility resources, such as beds, but it also may exacerbate the existing mental health issues of both male and female juvenile offenders.

Fourth, juvenile detention and confinement facilities not accredited by a national correctional healthcare organization should consider working toward accreditation. Currently, the National Commission on Correctional Healthcare (NCCHC) leads the field in providing healthcare standards for adult and juvenile correctional facilities. Meeting a set of professional healthcare standards has the potential to save facilities, juvenile justice systems, litigation costs, and possibly the lives of some youth. According to the NCCHC (J. A. Stanley, personal communication, September 25, 2006), as of September 21, 2006, 55 of the 435 juvenile detention and/or confinement facilities in the United States were accredited by the NCCHC.

Fifth, both individual and cross-systems training should be conducted. Both are essential for delivering gender-responsive services effectively (Council of State Governments, 2002).

**Research and Evaluation.**   Six lines of future empirical inquiry are offered in an attempt to advance knowledge in this area. First, more gender-specific empirical research is needed that examines differences in the utility of various risk factors for explaining female delinquency and other problem behaviors (Prescott, 1998). Studies that examine the utility of protective factors for mediating the negative impact of risk factors on these behaviors also are encouraged.

Second, many of the barriers to the establishment, maintenance, and availability of gender-responsive services for female juvenile offenders need additional verification.

This is a relatively new area of research, and there is plenty of room for advancing knowledge. Third, and in a similar vein, more methodologically rigorous empirical studies are needed that employ statistical techniques capable of establishing causality. Although most studies reviewed used qualitative data collection methods (focus groups, interviews), quantitative survey methodologies, or both, the majority did not subject data to causal verification using statistical techniques.

Fourth, researchers interested in studying the degree of disjuncture between mental health service need and availability, or systemic and interagency barriers to service availability, should take a multi-method approach to data collection. Doing so will provide for a more comprehensive and holistic assessment. To examine both quantitative and qualitative aspects of the status of mental health services for female juvenile offenders, data may be obtained from surveys of juvenile justice officials; mental health providers and practitioners; female juvenile offenders, themselves; social service agencies; schools; policymakers; facility reports; well-designed interview protocols; focus groups; and site visits.

Fifth, systematic empirical research is needed that identifies model programs and effective program components. Such knowledge can be added to the growing repertoire of blueprint programs and best-practice strategies. The Girls Study Group (2006) is currently leading this effort, but more work in this area will serve to advance knowledge. Also needed are more implementation and outcome evaluations of current gender-responsive interventions.

Sixth, as pointed out by Alderden (2002), there is a paucity of empirical research that examines the impact of mental health services on female recidivism, mental health status, substance use and abuse, self-esteem, and school performance. Longitudinal research examining these outcome measures will provide important information concerning what does and does not work in reducing recidivism and enhancing mental health, life skills, and quality of life among mentally disordered female juvenile offenders.

## References

Acoca, L. (1999). Investing in girls: A 21st century strategy. *Juvenile Justice, 6,* 3–13.

Acs, G, & Loprest, P. (2001). *Final synthesis report of findings from ASPE's Leavers' Grants.* Washington, DC: Urban Institute.

Akers, R. L., Krohn, M. D., Kaduce, L. L., & Radosevich, M. (1979). Social learning and deviant behavior: A specific test of a general theory. *American Sociological Review, 44,* 635–655.

Alderden, M. (2002). *Understanding and addressing female delinquency in Illinois.* Chicago: Illinois Criminal Justice Information Authority.

Alderden, M., & Perez, A. (2003). *Female delinquents committed to Illinois Department of Corrections: A profile.* Chicago: Illinois Criminal Justice Information Authority.

Allgood-Merten, B., Lewinsohn, P. M., & Hops, H. (1990). Sex differences and adolescent depression. *Journal of Abnormal Psychology, 99,* 55–63.

ABA/NBA, American Bar Association and National Bar Association. (2001). *Justice by gender: The lack of appropriate prevention, diversion and treatment alternatives for girls in the justice system.* Washington, DC: Authors.

Belknap, J., Holsinger, K., & Dunn, M. (1997). Understanding incarcerated girls: The results of a focus group study. *Prison Journal, 77,* 381–404.

Bergsmann, I. (1989). The forgotten few: Juvenile female offenders. *Federal Probation, 53,* 73–78.

Bloom, B., & Covington, S. (1998, November). *Gender-specific programming for female offenders: What is it and why is it important?* Paper presented at the meeting of the American Society of Criminology, Washington, DC.

Bloom, B., Owen, B., Covington, S., & Raeder, M. (2002). *Gender-responsive strategies: Research, practice, and guiding principles for women offenders.* Washington, DC: Department of Justice.

Boddy Media Group. (1997). *Female juvenile justice report.* Des Moines, IA: Iowa Commission on the Status of Women.

Boesky, L. (2003). Mentally ill youths and the juvenile justice system: A primer on mental health disorders. *Juvenile and Family Justice Today, Winter,* 17–22.

Booker, A. L. (2000). *Female juvenile delinquency: Risk factors and promising interventions* (Juvenile Justice Fact Sheet). Charlottesville, VA: Institute for Law, Psychiatry, and Public Policy, University of Virginia.

Bracey, D. H. (1983). The juvenile prostitute: Victim and offender. *Victimology, 8,* 151–160.

Brent, D. A. (1995). Risk factors for adolescent suicide and suicidal behavior: Mental and substance abuse disorders, family environmental factors, and life stress. *Suicide and Life-Threatening Behavior, 25,* 52–63.

Budnick, K., & Shields-Fletcher, E. (1998). *What about girls?* (Fact Sheet No. 84). Washington, DC: Office of Juvenile Justice and Delinquency Prevention.

Burke, C., Keaton, S., & Pennell, S. (2003). *Addressing the gender-specific needs of girls: An evaluation of San Diego's WINGS program.* San Diego, CA: San Diego's Regional Planning Agency.

Catalano, R. F., Park, J., Harachi, T. W., Haggerty, K. P., Abbott, R. D., & Hawkins, J. D. (2005). Mediating the effects of poverty, gender, individual characteristics, and external constraints on antisocial behavior: A test of the social development model and implications for life-course theory. In D. B. Farrington (Ed.), *Developmental and life-course theories of offending* (pp. 93–123). New Brunswick, NJ: Transaction Publishers.

Cauffman, E., Feldman, S., Waterman, J., & Steiner, H. (1998). Posttraumatic stress disorder among female juvenile offenders. *Journal of the American Academy of Child and Adolescent Psychiatry, 37,* 1209–1217.

Cernkovich, S., & Giordano, P. (1987). Family relationships and delinquency. *Criminology, 25,* 295–319.

Chandy, J. M., Blum, R. W., & Resnick, M. D. (1996). Gender-specific outcomes for sexually abused adolescents. *Child Abuse and Neglect, 20,* 1219–1231.

Chesney-Lind, M. (1997). *The female offender: Girls, women, and crime.* London: Sage.

Chesney-Lind, M., & Sheldon, R. G. (1992). *Girls, delinquency, and juvenile justice.* Pacific Grove, CA: Brooks/Cole.

Cocozza, J. J., & Skowyra, K. R. (2000). Youth with mental health disorders: Issues and emerging responses. *Juvenile Justice, 7,* 3–13.

Coiro, M. J., Zill, N., & Bloom, B. (1994). *Health of our nation's children* (Vital and Health Statistics Series No. 10). Washington, DC: U.S. Government Printing Office.

Colder, C. R., & Stice, E. (1998). A longitudinal study of the interactive effects of impulsivity and anger on adolescent problem behavior. *Journal of Youth and Adolescence, 27,* 255–274.

Community Research Associates. (1998). *Juvenile female offenders: A status of the states report.* Washington, DC: Office of Juvenile Justice and Delinquency Prevention.

Council of State Governments. (2002). *Criminal Justice/Mental Health Consensus Project.* Lexington, KY: Author.

Daniel, M. D. (1999). The female intervention team. *Juvenile Justice, 6,* 14-20.

Dembo, R., Williams, L., & Schmeidler, J. (1993). Gender differences in mental health needs among youths entering a juvenile detention center. *Journal of Prison & Jail Health, 12,* 73–101.

Federal Bureau of Investigation. (2000). *Crime in the United States.* Washington, DC: U.S. Government Printing Office.

Feld, B. C. (1998). Abolish the juvenile court: Youthfulness, criminal responsibility, and sentencing policy. *The Journal of Criminal Law & Criminology, 88,* 68–136.

Frank, R. G. (2000). The creation of Medicare and Medicaid: The emergence of insurance markets for mental health services. *Psychiatric Services, 51,* 465–468.

Garnier, H. E., & Stein, J. A. (2002). An 18-year model of family and peer influences on adolescent drug use and delinquency. *Journal of Youth and Adolescence, 31,* 45–56.

Gender-Specific Programming for Girls Advocacy Committee. (1998). *Guiding principles for promising female programming.* Washington, DC: Office of Juvenile Justice and Delinquency Prevention.

Girls Incorporated. (1996). *Prevention and parity: Girls in juvenile justice report.* Indianapolis, IN: Girls Incorporated National Resource Center and the Office of Juvenile Justice and Delinquency Prevention.

Girls Justice Initiative. (2003). *Girls in the juvenile justice system: Perspectives on services and conditions of confinement.* Washington, DC: Author.

Girls Study Group. (2006). *Girls Study Group: Spring/Summer 2006 update.* Retrieved October 2, 2006, from: http://girlsstudygroup.rti.org/GSG_Update_2006_Spring_Summer.pdf

Glueck, S., & Glueck, E. (1959). *Predicting delinquency and crime.* Cambridge, MA: Harvard University Press.

Goldstrom, I., Jaiquan, F., Henderson, M., Male, A., & Manderscheid, R. W. (2001). The availability of mental health services to young people in juvenile justice facilities: A national survey. In R. W. Manderscheid & M. J. Henderson (Eds.), *Mental health, United States, 2000* (Report No. SMA01-3537). Rockville, MD: Substance Abuse and Mental Health Services Administration, Center for Mental Health Services. Retrieved May 4, 2006, from http://www.mentalhealth.samhsa.gov/publications/allpubs/SMA01-3537.chapter18.asp

Gottfredson, M., & Hirschi, T. (1990). *A general theory of crime.* Palo Alto, CA: Stanford University Press.

Greene, Peters, & Associates. (1998). *Guiding principles for promising female programming: An inventory of best practices.* Washington, DC: Office of Juvenile Justice and Delinquency Prevention.

Grisso, T., & Barhum, R. (2000). *Massachusetts Youth Screening Instrument-2 (MAYSI-2).* Worchester, MA: University of Massachusetts Medical School.

Haapanen, R., & Steiner, H. (2003). *Identifying mental health treatment needs among serious institutionalized delinquents using paper-and-pencil screening instruments.* Sacramento, CA: California Youth Authority.

Hagedorn, J., & Moore, J. (2001). *Female gangs: A focus on research.* Washington, DC: Office of Juvenile Justice and Delinquency Prevention.

Hartney, C., McKinney, T., Eidlitz, L., & Craine, J. (2003). *A survey of mental health care delivery to youth in the California juvenile justice system: Summary of findings* (NCCD Focus Report). Oakland, CA: National Council on Crime and Delinquency.

Hartney, C., Wordes, M., & Krisberg, B. (2002). *Healthcare for our troubled youth: Provision of services in the foster care and juvenile justice systems of California.* Oakland, CA: National Council on Crime and Delinquency.

Hawkins, J. D., Catalano, R., & Miller, J. (1992). Risk and protective factors for alcohol and other drug problems in adolescence and early adulthood: Implications for substance abuse prevention. *Psychological Bulletin, 112,* 64–105.

Hawkins, J. D., Smith, B. H., Hill, K. G., Kosterman, R., Catalano, R. F., & Abbott, R. D. (2003). Understanding and preventing crime and violence. In T. P. Thornberry & M. D. Krohn (Eds.), *Taking stock of delinquency: An overview of findings from contemporary longitudinal studies* (pp. 255–312). New York: Kluwer Academic/Plenum.

Hawkins, J. D., & Weis, J. G. (1985). The social development model: An integrated approach to delinquency. *Journal of Primary Prevention, 6,* 73–97.

Heymann, S. J., & Earle, A. (1999). The impact of welfare reform on parents' ability to care for their children's health. *American Journal of Public Health, 89,* 502–505.

Hirschi, T. (1969). *Causes of delinquency.* Berkeley: University of California Press.

Howell, J. (2003). *Preventing and reducing juvenile delinquency: A comprehensive framework.* Thousand Oaks, CA: Sage.

Howell, J., & Hawkins, J. D. (1998). Prevention of youth violence. In *Crime and justice, Youth violence* (Vol. 24, pp. 263–315). Chicago: University of Chicago Press.

Hoyt, S., & Scherer, D. G. (1998). Female juvenile delinquency: Misunderstood by the juvenile-justice system, neglected by social science. *Law and Human Behavior, 22,* 81–107.

Hsia, H. M., & Beyer, M. (2000). *System change through State Challenge Activities: Approaches and products* (NCJ 177625). Washington, DC: Office of Juvenile Justice and Delinquency Prevention.

Hubbard, D. J., & Pratt, T. C. (2002). A meta-analysis of the predictors of delinquency among girls. *Journal of Offender Rehabilitation, 34,* 1–13.

Hubner, J., & Wofson, J. (2000). *Handle with care: Serving the mental health needs of young offenders.* Washington, DC: Coalition for Juvenile Justice.

Iglehart, J. K. (1996). Managed care and mental health. *New England Journal of Medicine, 334,* 131–135.

Iowa Commission on the Status of Women. (1999). *Providing gender-specific services for adolescent female offenders: Guidelines and resources.* Des Moines, IA: Iowa Department of Human Rights.

Juvenile Justice and Delinquency Prevention Act of 1974. 42 U.S.C. 5601 et. seq.

Kamradt, B. (2002). *Funding mental health services for youth in the juvenile justice system: Challenges and opportunities* (NCMHJJ Research and Program Brief). Delmar, NY: National Center for Mental Health and Juvenile Justice.

Kelleher, K. J., McInerny, T. K., Gardner, W. P., Childs, G. E., & Wasserman, R. C. (2000). Increasing identification of psychosocial problems: 1979–1996. *Pediatrics, 105,* 1313–1321.

LEAA, Law Enforcement Assistance Administration. (1975). *The Report of the LEAA Task Force on Women.* Washington, DC: U.S. Department of Justice.

Liska, A. E., & Reid, M. D. (1985). Ties to conventional institutions and delinquency: Estimating reciprocal effects. *American Sociological Review, 50,* 547–560.

Loeber, R. (1990). Development and risk factors of juvenile antisocial behavior and delinquency. *Clinical Psychology Review, 10,* 1–41.

MacVicar, K., & Dillion, M. (1980). Childhood and adolescent development of 10 prostitutes. *Journal of the American Academy of Child Psychiatry, 19,* 14–59.

Marsteller, F., Brogan, D., Smith, I., Ash, P., Daniels, D., Rolka, D., et al. (1997). *The prevalence of substance use disorders among juveniles admitted to regional youth detention centers operated by the Georgia Department of Children and Youth Services.* Atlanta, GA: Georgia Department of Children and Youth Services.

McCabe, K., Lansing, A., Garland, A., & Hough, R. (2002). *Gender differences among adjudicated delinquents* (Research Brief, Vol. 2, No. 2). San Diego, CA: Child and Adolescent Services Center.

McCormack, A., Janus, M., & Burgess, A. (1986). Runaway youth and sexual victimization: Gender differences in an adolescent runaway population. *Child Abuse and Neglect, 10,* 387–395.

Miller, D. (1994). Exploring gender differences in suicidal behavior among adolescent offenders: Findings and implications. *Journal of Correctional Education, 45,* 134–138.

Miller, D., Trapani, C., Fejes-Mendoza, K., Eggleston, C., & Dwiggins, D. (1995). Adolescent female offenders: Unique considerations. *Adolescence, 30,* 429–435.

Myers, D. (2005). *Boys among men: Trying and sentencing juveniles as adults.* Westport, CT: Praeger.

National Center on Addiction and Substance Abuse. (2003). *The formative years: Pathways to substance abuse among girls and young women ages 8–22.* New York: Author.

National Institute of Justice. (1998). Female juvenile offenders. In National Institute of Justice (Ed.), *Women in criminal justice: A twenty-year update* (pp. 19–39). Washington, DC: U.S. Department of Justice, Author.

Oregon Youth Authority. (2002). *Mental health and female offenders in the custody of the Oregon Youth Authority.* Portland, OR: Author.

Owen, B., & Bloom, B. (2000). *Profiling the needs of young female offenders: Instrument development and pilot study–Final report* (NCJ 182737). Washington, DC: U.S. Department of Justice, National Institute of Justice.

Patino, V., & Krisberg, B. (2005). *Reforming juvenile detention in Florida.* Oakland, CA: The National Council on Crime and Delinquency.

Patino, V., Ravoira, L., & Wolf, A. (2006). *A rallying cry for change: Charting a new direction in the State of Florida's response to girls in the juvenile justice system.* Oakland, CA: National Council on Crime and Delinquency.

Pipher, M. (1994). *Reviving Ophelia: Saving the selves of adolescent girls.* New York: G. P. Putnam's Sons.

Poe-Yamagata, E., & Butts, J. (1996). *Female offenders in the juvenile justice system: Statistics summary* (NCJ 160941). Washington, DC: Office of Juvenile Justice and Delinquency Prevention.

Pollard, J. A., Hawkins, J. D., & Arthur, M. W. (1999). Risk and protection: Are both necessary to understand diverse behavioral outcomes in adolescence? *Social Work Research, 23,* 145–158.

Prescott, P. (1997). *Adolescent girls with co-occurring disorders in the juvenile justice system.* Delmar, NY: Policy Research Associates, Inc.

Prescott, L. (1998). *Improving policy and practice for adolescent girls with co-occurring disorders in the juvenile justice system.* Delmar, NY: Policy Research Associates, Inc.

Redding, R. (2000). *Barriers to meeting the mental health needs of offenders in the juvenile justice system.* Charlottesville, VA: Institute of Law, Psychiatry, & Public Policy, University of Virginia.

Schoen, C., Davis, K., Collins, K. S., Greenberg, L., Des Roches, C., & Abrams, M. (1997). *The Commonwealth Fund Survey of the health of adolescent girls.* New York: The Commonwealth Fund.

Sharp, C., & Simon, J. (2004). *Girls in the juvenile justice system: The need for more gender responsive services.* Washington, DC: Child Welfare League of America.

Sherman, F. T. (1999). The Juvenile Rights Advocacy Project: Representing girls in context. *Juvenile Justice, 6,* 29–31.

Silbert, M., & Pines, M. (1981). Sexual child abuse as an antecedent to prostitution. *Child Abuse and Neglect, 5,* 407–411.

Snyder, H. N. (2002). *Juvenile arrests 2000.* Washington, DC: Office of Juvenile Justice and Delinquency Prevention.

Snyder, H. N., & Sickmund, M. (2006). *Juvenile offenders and victims: 2006 national report* (NCJ 212906). Washington, DC: Office of Juvenile Justice and Delinquency Prevention.

Streffensmeier, D. (1993). National trends in female arrests, 1960–1990: Assessment and recommendations for research. *Journal of Quantitative Criminology, 9,* 414–441.

Teplin, L. A., Abram, K. M., & McClelland, G. M. (2002). Psychiatric disorders in youth in juvenile detention. *Archives of General Psychiatry, 59,* 1133–1143.

Texas Juvenile Probation Commission. (2002). *Female juvenile offenders: Services in Texas.* Austin, TX: Author.

Texas Juvenile Probation Commission. (2003). *Mental health and juvenile justice in Texas*. Austin, TX: Author.

Timmons-Mitchell, J., Brown, C., Schultz, C., Webster, S., Underwood, L., & Semple, W. (1997). Comparing the mental health needs of female and male incarcerated juvenile delinquents. *Behavioral Sciences and the Law, 15,* 195–202.

Torbet, P., Gable, R., Hurst, H., Montgomery, I., Szymanski, L., & Thomas, D. (1996). *State responses to serious and violent juvenile crime* (Report No. NCJ 161565). Washington, DC: Office of Juvenile Justice and Delinquency Prevention.

Tout, K., Scarpa, J., & Zaslow, M. (2002). *Children of current and former welfare recipients: Similarly at risk*. Washington, DC: Child Trends.

Vedder, C. B., & Somerville, D. B. (1970). *The delinquent girl*. Springfield, IL: Charles C. Thomas.

Veysey, B. (2003). *Adolescent girls with mental health disorders involved with the juvenile justice system* (NCMHJJ Research and Program Brief). Delmar, NY: National Center for Mental Health and Juvenile Justice.

Virginia Commission on Youth. (1996). *The study of juvenile justice system reform*. House Document No. 37. Richmond, VA: Commonwealth of Virginia, Virginia General Assembly.

Warr, M., & Stafford, M. (1991). The influence of delinquent peers: What they think or what they do? *Criminology, 4,* 851–866.

Wasserman, G. A., Ko, S. J., & McReynolds, L. S. (2004). *Assessing the mental health needs of youth in juvenile justice settings* (NCJ 202713). Washington, DC: Office of Juvenile Justice and Delinquency Prevention.

Widom, C. S., & Maxfield, M. (2001). *An update on the "cycle of violence."* Washington, DC: National Institute of Justice, Office of Justice Programs.

Zedner, L. (1991). Women, crime, and penal responses: A historical account. *Crime and Justice, 14,* 307–362.

Ziemba-Davis, M., Garcia, C. A., Kincaid, N. L., Gullans, K., & Myers, B. L. (2004). *What about girls in Indiana's juvenile justice system?* Indianapolis, IN: Indiana Research Justice Institute.

# CHAPTER 2

# MENTAL HEALTH SCREENING AS INTAKE TRIAGE FOR JUVENILE GIRL OFFENDERS:

## A MAYSI-2 Comparison of Nondetained and Detained Youth

**Philip Matthew Stinson, Sr.**

## ABSTRACT

Recent investigation reports have concluded that many juvenile detention centers are improperly used to warehouse children with unmet mental health needs. This chapter examines the prevalence rates of unmet mental health needs of nondetained court-involved children at time of intake to the delinquency system, in comparison to a group of children detained in juvenile detention centers awaiting delinquency adjudication. A self-report instrument, the Massachusetts Youth Screening Inventory–Version 2 ("MAYSI-2"), is used for assessment. As to girls, the findings are significant. A high prevalence of girls enter the delinquency system with a manifestation of suicide ideation at intake. Girls at age 15 present with the highest prevalence of suicide ideation at intake, and girls of all ages present with a higher prevalence of suicide ideation than like-age boys. Likewise, girls scored higher on the traumatic experiences scale than boys. These findings confirm that at time of intake to the delinquency system, girls are more likely than boys to be at risk for having intense unmet mental health needs. Finally, the results of this study support the proposition that there should be mandatory mental health screening of all children—especially girls—at intake to the delinquency system.

## INTRODUCTION

Numerous studies have attempted to determine the prevalence of disability in the juvenile delinquency system (e.g., Leone, Zaremba, Chapin, & Iseli, 1995). Most of them have studied youth who are incarcerated at juvenile detention centers or other residential placements (e.g., Foley, 2001; Leone, 1994; Quinn, Rutherford, & Leone, 2001; Rutherford, Bullis, Anderson, & Griller-Clark, 2002; Snyder & Sickmund, 1995). Few have attempted to determine the prevalence of disability for children entering the juvenile delinquency system who are not incarcerated pending delinquency adjudication and disposition, and none have made a between-group analysis of prevalence in detained and nondetained youth at time of intake to the juvenile delinquency system. One recent study examined gender differences in psychiatric disorders at juvenile probation intake and found that "among youths with conduct disorders, girls demonstrated an elevated risk for co-occurring anxiety or affective disorder" (Wasserman, McReynolds, Ko, Katz, & Carpenter, 2005, p. 000).

Recent investigation reports have concluded that many juvenile detention centers in the United States are improperly used to warehouse youths with unmet mental health needs, including but not limited to children with mental disorders, serious emotional disturbances, and substance abuse disorders. This research examines the prevalence rate of unmet mental health needs of court-involved children at time of intake to the juvenile delinquency system. The study of prevalence of mental health disorders and other disabilities in the juvenile delinquency system is important for three reasons: (a) juvenile justice agencies have a custodial treatment obligation for children and youth in their custody, (b) juveniles enjoy due process rights under the law, and (c) to protect the public safety by way of "identification, management, and treatment of adolescents who manifest mental disorders" (Grisso, 2004, p. 000). The use of the MAYSI-2 instrument as a gateway screening assessment for all juveniles upon intake to the juvenile delinquency system, whether detained or not pending adjudication, is beneficial in achieving these purposes.

## THE JUVENILE DELINQUENCY INTAKE PROCESS

Although the processes vary from state to state and statutory exceptions for serious crimes are often handled in adult criminal courts, juveniles who are arrested in the United States are typically processed through the juvenile justice system. This process commences with an intake where decisions are made as to whether the case should be handled informally or formally. The criteria for detention of juveniles (at time of arrest or upon intake to the juvenile delinquency system), pending a youth's delinquency adjudication hearing, vary widely from state to state. As such, comparisons based on pre-adjudication detention status alone are difficult and, perhaps, misleading.

In 1998, 57% of all delinquency cases in the United States were formally processed through the juvenile court systems in the states (U.S. Department of Justice, 2003). The remaining 43% of delinquency cases nationwide in 1998 were disposed of informally: about 19% of all delinquency cases were dismissed at intake (often for a lack of legal sufficiency), and another 24% were processed informally (Stahl, 2001). Likewise, in 1999, 57% of all delinquency cases in the United States were formally processed, whereas about 17% were dismissed at intake, and 26% were processed informally (Stahl, 2003). As such, research to date has not tracked or accounted for the 43% of all children entering the juvenile delinquency system when attempting to determine the prevalence of disability within delinquency. This is due to the fact that research has typically relied upon data regarding only those youth who were detained as a result of their arrest.

Recent research by the U.S. Department of Justice (2003) indicates that other considerations regarding age, gender, and race are relevant in a discussion of the intake decision-making process:

- In each year between 1989 and 1998, delinquency cases involving juveniles age 16 or older were more likely to be petitioned than were cases involving younger juveniles.
- In 1998, 54% of delinquency cases involving children age 15 or younger were petitioned, compared with 61% of cases involving older youth.
- In 1998, juvenile courts were less likely to petition delinquency cases involving females (48%) than cases involving males (60%).
- In 1998, for girls, the cases most likely to be petitioned were those involving public order offenses (56%), whereas for boys, drug law violations were the most likely to be petitioned (65%).
- Delinquency cases involving Black juveniles were more likely to be petitioned than were cases involving White youth or youth of other races.
- In 1998, racial differences in the likelihood of petitioning were greatest for drug law violation cases: 81% of drug cases involving Black juveniles were petitioned, compared with 55% for both White juveniles and juveniles of other races.

## METHODS AND PROCEDURES

### METHODOLOGY

A survey form was used as an instrument to determine an indication of the prevalence of mental disability, emotional disturbance, and/or behavioral needs exhibited and self-reported by a sample of nonincarcerated and incarcerated children at time of intake to the juvenile delinquency system.

### SAMPLING

This research study is a secondary analysis of a dataset of 1,346 youth, each under the age of 18 at the time their underlying alleged delinquent offense(s) occurred, who were arrested and the subjects of juvenile delinquency complaints in the Commonwealth of Massachusetts during 1997. Of this sample, 266 of the youth (19.8%) were arrested but not detained or incarcerated pending a delinquency adjudication hearing in juvenile court, and 1,080 of the youth (80.2%) were arrested and incarcerated in secure detention pending a juvenile delinquency adjudication hearing. The data were collected in a study by Grisso et al. (2001) and provided by the National Youth Screening Assistance Project (NYSAP), Department of Psychiatry, University of Massachusetts Medical School, for the instant secondary analysis.

The probation sample includes 152 males (59.4%) and 104 (41.6%) females. The detention sample includes 629 males (58.2%) and 451 (41.8%) females. The ethnicity of the probation sample is 44.7% White, 17.7% Black, 5.6% Asian, 21.8% Hispanic, and 3.0% other, whereas the detention sample is 39.7% White, 29.4% Black, 3.6%

**TABLE 2.1** Demographic information

|  | *Probation* | *Detention* | *Total* |
|---|---|---|---|
| Subjects | *n* = 266 (19.8) | *n* = 1080 (80.2) | *n* = 1346 (100.0) |
| Boys | 152 (57.1) | 629 (58.2) | 781 (58.8) |
| Girls | 104 (39.1) | 451 (41.8) | 555 (41.2) |
| Missing | 10 (3.8) | 0 (0.0) | 10 (0.8) |
| Race |  |  |  |
| Asian | 15 (5.6) | 39 (3.6) | 54 (4.0) |
| Black | 47 (17.7) | 317 (29.4) | 364 (27.0) |
| Hispanic | 58 (21.8) | 247 (22.9) | 305 (22.7) |
| White | 119 (44.7) | 429 (39.7) | 548 (40.7) |
| Other | 8 (3.0) | 47 (4.4) | 55 (4.1) |
| Missing | 19 (7.1) | 1 (0.1) | 20 (1.5) |
| Age |  |  |  |
| *M* | 15.07 | 15.49 |  |
| *SD* | 1.450 | 1.209 |  |
| *Mdn* | 15[a] | 16[a] |  |
| Minimum | 9 | 7 |  |
| Maximum | 19 | 20 |  |
| Range | 9 | 13 |  |

[a]Median age is calculated by age in years at last birthday, and not by exact age at time of administration of the instrument.

*Note.* Frequency percentages are in parenthesis.

Asian, 22.9% Hispanic, and 4.4% other. The mean age of the probation sample is 15.07 years, with ages ranging from 9 years to 19 years. Age is recorded in the dataset by age in years at last birthday, and not by exact age at time of administration of the instrument. The mean age of the detention sample is 15.49 years, with ages ranging from 7 years to 20 years (see Table 2.1).

## SURVEY INSTRUMENT

The instrument used in this study is the Massachusetts Youth Screening Instrument – Second Version ("MAYSI-2") (Grisso and Barnum, 2003). The MAYSI-2 is a standardized, true-false, paper-and-pencil method, 52-item self-reporting inventory for screening youth ages 12–17 entering the juvenile delinquency system (e.g., at intake to probation or juvenile detention) or at intake to successive placements within the system (National Youth Screening Assistance Project, 2004). The instrument was designed for the purpose of alerting staff to potential mental health needs of youth entering the delinquency system and, specifically, to: (a) require no more than ten minutes to administer; (b) rely on youth self-report; (c) be easy to read; (d) require no special clinical expertise to administer, score, and interpret; (e) use very low cost materials; (f) be usable with a wide range of adolescents (by age, gender, and ethnicity); and (g) be amenable to development of age-and-gender-based norms, appropriate psychometric reliability, and validity (Grisso, Barnum, Fletcher, Cauffman, & Peuschold, 2001).

The instrument identifies problems in seven domains that are referred to herein as MAYSI-2 scales: Alcohol/Drug Use (8 items), Angry-Irritable (9 items), Depressed-

Anxious (9 items), Somatic Complaints (6 items), Suicide Ideation (5 items), Thought Disturbance (5 items), and Traumatic Experiences (5 items). The Thought Disturbance scale is calculated for boys only and the Traumatic Experience scale is gender-specific (Grisso et al., 2001). Scoring is based on the total number of positive responses recorded, and cutoff thresholds for clinically significant scores have been developed in previous studies (Grisso et al., 2001).

### Reliability and Validity

The MAYSI-2 has been found to have good psychometric properties as evaluated within a test theory framework (Cauffman, 2004). Test-retest reliability in Grisso and Barnum (2003) shows correlation coefficients on all of the MAYSI-2 scales ranging from .53 to .89 for boys (average = .74) and .66 to .85 for girls (average = .74), both of which are considered very good coefficients. The instrument has test-retest correlations in the same range as two self-reporting instruments that are widely used to assess troubled youth: the Millon Adolescent Clinical Inventory ("MACI") and Achenbach's Child Behavior Checklist – Youth Self-Report ("YSR") (Achenbach, 1991; Grisso and Barnum, 2003; Grisso et al., 2001). Reliability of the MAYSI-2 has been established in a replication study using a Mid-Atlantic sample from the Tidewater, Virginia, area that was predominantly Black youth (Archer, Vauter Stredny, Mason, & Arnau, 2004). Grisso and Barnum (2003) report that "studies are underway to determine the degree to which scores on the MAYSI-2 scales correspond to past and present behaviors, or other external criteria, to which the scales should be related." Grisso and Barnum (2003) note differences in the gender norms on most of the MAYSI-2 scales, whereby girls on average scored higher on all scales except the alcohol/drug use scale. Several plausible explanations for the higher average scale scores for girls as they relate to the instant study are discussed below.

### Purpose of the Instrument

The MAYSI-2 is not designed to identify clinical disorders as defined by DSM-IV criteria (Grisso et al., 2001). Rather, it is designed as a triage tool to identify youths who may be exhibiting signs of mental, emotional, and/or behavioral distress and in need of clinical intervention at time of intake to the juvenile delinquency system. MAYSI-2 scores are not intended to be an appropriate measure for judicial consideration as conclusive evidence of a psychiatric diagnosis of a child's mental disorder at delinquency adjudication or disposition.

### PROCEDURES

Statistical analyses of the dataset were performed using SPSS 13.0. Frequency determination on each independent variable was assessed by a split group analysis of the probation group versus the detention group. A cross-tabulation analysis was performed to address the relationship between the categorical variables. Each variable was assessed using chi-square analysis to determine whether differences between observed and expected frequencies were statistically significant. Additionally, the same analysis was rerun while controlling for race in the three largest categories represented in this study: Black, Hispanic, and White. For the purposes of this study, all $p$ values of less than .05 than the results are considered statistically significant. Thus, when there is less than a 1 in 20 probability that a certain outcome occurred by chance, then that result is considered statistically significant in this study.

**TABLE 2.2** Variable information

| Variable | Position | Measurement Level | Label/Comments |
|---|---|---|---|
| state | 1 | Scale | State/Jurisdiction |
| site | 2 | Ordinal | Specific Site |
| id | 3 | Scale | ID |
| gate | 4 | Ordinal | Facility type |
| age | 5 | Ordinal | Age in years at last birthday |
| gender | 6 | Ordinal | Gender |
| ethnic | 7 | Nominal | Ethnic |
| timein | 8 | Scale | Time in facility |
| maystime | 9 | Ordinal | Time in when MAYSI administered |
| q1–q52 | 10–61 | Ordinal | Questions on MAYSI-2 inventory |
| ai | 62 | Scale | angry-irritable |
| td | 63 | Scale | thought disorder |
| sc | 64 | Scale | somatic complaints |
| adu | 65 | Scale | alcohol/drug use |
| si | 66 | Scale | suicide ideation |
| te | 67 | Scale | traumatic experiences |
| da | 68 | Scale | depressed-anxious |
| aicaut | 69 | Scale | angry-irritable caution cut |
| aducaut | 70 | Scale | alcohol-drug caution cut |
| dacaut | 71 | Scale | depressed-anxious caution cut |
| sccaut | 72 | Scale | somatic caution cut |
| sicaut | 73 | Scale | suicide ideation caution cut |
| tdcaut | 74 | Scale | thought disorder caution cut |
| aiwarn | 75 | Scale | angry-irritable warning cut |
| aduwarn | 76 | Scale | alcohol-drug warning cut |
| daawrn | 77 | Scale | depressed-anxious warning cut |
| scwarn | 78 | Scale | somatic warning cut |
| siwarn | 79 | Scale | suicide ideation warning cut |
| tdwarn | 80 | Scale | thought disorder warning cut |

## RESULTS

As shown in Table 2.2, the dataset consists of 80 variables, including the 52 questions on the inventory, 18 variables recording scaled scores based on inventory responses, and 10 variables relating to other items, including demographic information, site locations, and case numbers. Several of the inventory questions are not incorporated into the scale scores, as discussed *infra*, but the variables were left on the MAYSI-2 inventory by Grisso et al. (2003), for possible future research and analysis purposes.

In many respects, the responses to the inventory items by those subjects in the probation group and those in the detention group are very similar. On 35 items (67.3%) there is no statistical significance to variation or differences in responses between the two groups. Statistical significance of $p < .05$ in the responses is present in 17 items (32.6%) on the inventory (see Table 2.3). Of these, 14 are used in scales for assessment

**TABLE 2.3**  Prevalence of differences in responses to items between the groups

| Variable Label/Comment | | Probation | Detention | $\chi^2(1)$ |
|---|---|---|---|---|
| q4[a] | problems concentrating/attention? | 109 ($n = 264$) | 366 ($n = 1075$) | 4.855* |
| q8 | really jumpy or hyper? | 100 ($n = 263$) | 262 ($n = 1076$) | 20.031* |
| q9 | seen things other people say not there? | 34 ($n = 265$) | 90 ($n = 1073$) | 4.988* |
| q10 | done things wish hadn't done when drunk or high? | 56 ($n = 262$) | 406 ($n = 1077$) | 24.847* |
| q12[a] | daydreaming too much in school? | 97 ($n = 265$) | 296 ($n = 1070$) | 8.173* |
| q18 | felt like hurting yourself | 47 ($n = 266$) | 133 ($n = 1075$) | 5.149* |
| q19 | parents or friends thought you drunk too much? | 13 ($n = 263$) | 202 ($n = 1073$) | 30.149* |
| q23 | gotten in trouble when been high or drinking? | 49 ($n = 262$) | 426 ($n = 1077$) | 40.030* |
| q24 | if yes, is this fighting? | 23 ($n = 254$) | 205 ($n = 958$) | 20.029* |
| q33 | used alcohol or drugs to help you feel better? | 49 ($n = 263$) | 356 ($n = 1076$) | 20.929* |
| q37 | been drunk or high at school | 53 ($n = 264$) | 404 ($n = 1072$) | 29.192* |
| q40 | used alcohol and drugs at the same time? | 62 ($n = 264$) | 518 ($n = 1075$) | 52.670* |
| q41 | hard to feel close to people outside family? | 60 ($n = 264$) | 328 ($n = 1071$) | 6.409* |
| q45 | so drunk/high that couldn't remember what happened? | 34 ($n = 263$) | 310 ($n = 1075$) | 28.002* |
| q49 | been badly hurt or in danger of getting hurt/killed? | 81 ($n = 263$) | 470 ($n = 1071$) | 14.914* |
| q50[b] | been raped, or been in danger of getting raped? | 29 ($n = 262$) | 213 ($n = 1076$) | 10.831* |
| q52 | seen someone severely injured or killed? | 106 ($n = 262$) | 598 ($n = 1073$) | 19.709* |

$* p < .05$

[a]Item not assigned to scales.

[b]Item excluded from scales for boys only.

and triage purposes. There is no statistical significance between the groups on the angry-irritable, depressed-anxious, somatic complaints, and thought disturbances scales.

## ATTENTION AND CONCENTRATION

Three of the MAYSI-2 inventory items where statistical significance is present between the two groups are items not incorporated into MAYSI-2 scales (question 4, question 12, and question 50). Interestingly, two of these items relate to self-reported attention and concentration issues, where the probation group reports higher incidence of problems concentrating or paying attention, as well as higher incidence of daydreaming too much in school. One item, question 4, asks, "Have you had a lot of problems concentrating or paying attention?" A second item, question 12, asks, "Have you been daydreaming too much in school?" A third item of statistical significance, question 8, incorporated into the angry-irritable scale, also potentially relates to the issue of attention, asking, "Have you been real jumpy or hyper?" The probation group indicates a considerably higher prevalence of self-reported attention difficulties than the detention group on all three items, with a statistical significance of $p < .05$. However, when controlling for race, we find statistical significance only in the difference in prevalence of self-reported problems concentrating and paying attention (question 4) as to the Black youth. Likewise, when controlling for race, we find statistical significance only in the difference in prevalence of self-reported feelings of being "really jumpy or hyper" (question 8) as to the White youth.

**TABLE 2.4** Rape-related item by age and gender

|        |                                                                 | *Probation* | *Detention* |
|--------|-----------------------------------------------------------------|-------------|-------------|
|        |                                                                 | $n = 262$   | $n = 1076$  |
| q50    | been raped, or been in danger of getting raped?                 | 29 (10.9)   | 213 (19.7)  |
| Summary | Boys 36 (4.6) ($n = 778$)<br>Girls 204 (36.8) ($n = 550$)       | 5 (3.3)<br>22 (21.2) | 31 (4.9)<br>182 (40.9) |
| Age 12 | Boys<br>Girls                                                    | ns<br>ns    | ns<br>2 (25.0) |
| Age 13 | Boys<br>Girls                                                    | 1 (14.3)<br>1 (11.1) | ns<br>15 (42.9) |
| Age 14 | Boys<br>Girls                                                    | 1 (4.2)<br>4 (16.7) | ns<br>28 (38.4) |
| Age 15 | Boys<br>Girls                                                    | 1 (2.2)<br>5 (20.0) | 5 (3.7)<br>38 (30.9) |
| Age 16 | Boys<br>Girls                                                    | 3 (8.1)<br>5 (20.0) | 18 (6.6)<br>67 (46.2) |
| Age 17 | Boys<br>Girls                                                    | ns<br>5 (50.0) | 4 (3.3)<br>30 (47.6) |
| Age 18 | Boys<br>Girls                                                    | ns<br>ns    | ns<br>2 (100.0) |

*Note.* Frequency percentages are in parenthesis.

## RAPE AND DANGER OF RAPE

Another inventory item that is not an item incorporated in a MAYSI-2 scale (as to boys only) and where we find a statistical significance of $p < .05$ is the item "Have you ever been raped, or been in danger of getting raped?" (see Table 2.4). Here, we find that 10.9% of the youth in the probation group and 19.7% of the youth in the detention group self-report that they have either been raped or been in danger of getting raped. Although no information is included in the dataset as to the circumstances or location of sexual victimization, we do know that 71.1% of the detention group were administered the instrument within 6 hours of admission to a juvenile detention center, and 99.0% by the 14th day following admission. When we look at gender, 21.2% of the girls in the probation group and 40.9% of the girls in the detention group report that they have been raped or in danger of getting raped. The prevalence for boys is much lower: 3.3% of the boys in the probation sample and 4.9% of the detention sample report that they have either been raped or been in danger of getting raped. None of the children under the age of 12 ($n = 6$) reported having been raped or in danger of getting raped. The second largest age sample for girls in the detention group, age 16, yielded the highest prevalence of having been raped or in danger of getting raped, at 46.2%. Overall, 4.6% of all boys and 36.8% of all girls in the sample report that they have been raped or been in danger of getting raped. When controlling for race, however, we find statistical significance of $p < .05$ only in the difference between prevalence in the probation group and the detention group as to White youth on this item, and not when controlling for race as to the Black or Hispanic youth.

**TABLE 2.5** Prevalence of scores in the suicide ideation caution range

| Scale | Label | Yes to Questions on Scale | Probation | Detention | $\chi^2(1)$ |
|-------|-------|---------------------------|-----------|-----------|-------------|
| sicaut | suicide ideation caution | | $n = 265$ | $n = 1071$ | 4.563* |
| | cut | 2 and higher | 71 (26.7) | 222 (20.6) | |

\* $p < .05$

*Note.* Frequency percentages are in parenthesis.

## SUICIDAL IDEATION

The difference in prevalence of children in the probation sample versus those in the detention sample scoring in the caution range on the suicide ideation scale is statistically significant with a $p < .05$. This is not the case, however, on the suicide ideation warning scale, where $p < .639$. Five of the inventory questions are included in the category of suicide ideation:

q11     Have you wished you were dead?
q16     Have you felt like life was not worth living?
q18     Have you felt like hurting yourself?
q22     Have you felt like killing yourself?
q47     Have you given up hope for your life?

Subjects responding in the affirmative with "yes" answers on this scale to two or more of these questions are included in the caution cut, whereas subjects responding with "yes" answers to three or more questions are included in the warning cut. Here, 26.7% of the probation sample scored in the caution range on the suicide ideation scale, whereas only 20.6% of the detention sample scored in the same range (see Table 2.5).

Of the subjects scoring in the suicide ideation caution range, 13.2% are boys, and 33.9% are girls. The highest prevalence by age on the suicide ideation caution range is girls age 15, where 52.0% of the 15-year-old girls in the probation sample and 36.6% of the 15-year-old girls in the detention sample scored in this range. Overall, however, gender on this item is not statistically significant alone in terms of comparing the probation group to the detention group (see Table 2.6). When controlling for race on items related to suicide ideation, the difference in prevalence of youth in the probation sample versus those in the detention sample scoring in the caution range and the warning range on the suicide ideation scale is statistically significant with a $p < .05$ as to the Black youth. This is not the case when controlling for race as to either the White or Hispanic youth, where no such statistical disparity is found.

## ALCOHOL AND DRUG USAGE

All eight items on the MAYSI-2 inventory have a statistical significance of $p < .05$ relating to alcohol and drug usage when comparing the detention group to the probation group, whereby the detention group self-reports higher incidence of alcohol and drug usage:

q10     Have you done anything you wish you hadn't when you were
        drunk or high?

**TABLE 2.6** Suicide ideation caution cut by age and gender

| | | *Probation* | *Detention* |
|---|---|---|---|
| | | $n = 265$ | $n = 1071$ |
| Summary | Boys 103 (13.2) ($n = 777$) | 26 (25.2) | 77 (74.8) |
| | Girls 188 (33.9) ($n = 549$) | 43 (22.9) | 145 (77.1) |
| Age 12 | Boys | 2 (66.7) $n = 3$ | ns |
| | Girls | 3 (50.0) $n = 6$ | ns |
| Age 13 | Boys | 1 (14.3) $n = 7$ | ns $n = 20$ |
| | Girls | 8 (33.3) $n = 9$ | 9 (25.7) $n = 35$ |
| Age 14 | Boys | 4 (16.7) $n = 24$ | 10 (15.4) $n = 65$ |
| | Girls | 8 (33.3) $n = 24$ | 22 (30.1) $n = 73$ |
| Age 15 | Boys | 9 (20.0) $n = 45$ | 13 (9.6) $n = 136$ |
| | Girls | 13 (52.0) $n = 25$ | 45 (36.6) $n = 123$ |
| Age 16 | Boys | 4 (10.8) $n = 37$ | 36 (13.1) $n = 274$ |
| | Girls | 9 (36.0) $n = 25$ | 46 (31.7) $n = 145$ |
| Age 17 | Boys | 4 (20.0) $n = 20$ | 13 (10.7) $n = 122$ |
| | Girls | 3 (30.0) $n = 10$ | 21 (33.3) $n = 62$ |
| Age 18 | Boys | 1 (25.0) $n = 4$ | 1 (33.3) $n = 3$ |
| | Girls | ns | ns |
| Age 19 | Boys | ns | 1 (33.3) $n = 3$ |
| | Girls | 1 (100.0) $n = 1$ | ns |

*Note.* Frequency percentages are in parenthesis.

q19     Have your parents or friends thought you drink too much?
q23     Have you gotten in trouble when you've been high or have been drinking?
q24     If yes to q23, has the trouble been fighting?
q33     Have you used alcohol or drugs to help you feel better?
q37     Have you been drunk or high at school?
q40     Have you used alcohol and drugs at the same time?
q45     Have you been so drunk or high that you couldn't remember what happened?

The alcohol-drug caution scale includes subjects who answer in the affirmative to four or more of these items, whereas the alcohol-drug warning scale includes subjects who answer seven or more of the above items in the affirmative. The detention group has a high prevalence of self-reported alcohol and drug usage compared to the probation group on both the alcohol-drug caution scale and the alcohol-drug warning scale. On items relating to alcohol and drug use, 35.5% of the detention sample scored in the alcohol-drug caution range, whereas only 14.3% of the probation sample scored in the same range. Likewise, 10.7% of the detention sample scored in the alcohol-drug warning range, whereas only 3.0% of the probation sample scored in that range.

Both the probation and detention groups scored comparably as to the prevalence of alcohol and drug use when we look at the frequency of one self-reported affirmative answer to items in the alcohol-drug related questions, where 12.0% of the probation sample and 12.8% of the detention sample answered in the affirmative to one item each. Similarly, 10.5% of both the probation sample and 10.5% of the detention sample answered in the affirmative to two items in the alcohol-drug related questions. When controlling for race on items related to self-reported alcohol and drug use, the difference in prevalence of children in the probation sample versus those in the detention sample scoring in the caution range and the warning range on the alcohol-drug scale is statistically significant with a $p < .05$ as to the White and Hispanic youth. This is not the case when controlling for race as to the Black youth for questions regarding self-reported alcohol and drug use, where no such statistical disparity is found.

When controlling for race, the detention group has a high prevalence of self-reported alcohol and drug usage compared to the probation group on both the alcohol-drug caution scale and the alcohol-drug warning scale as to Hispanic youth. On items relating to alcohol and drug use, 31.5% of the Hispanic detention sample scored in the alcohol-drug caution range, whereas only 7.0% of the probation sample of Hispanic youth scored in the same range. Likewise, 8.9% of the detention sample of Hispanic youth scored in the alcohol-drug warning range, whereas none (0.0%) of the Hispanic probation sample scored in that range. The detention group has a prevalence of self-reported alcohol and drug usage compared to the probation group on both the alcohol-drug caution scale and the alcohol-drug warning scale when controlling for race as to White youth. On items relating to alcohol and drug use, 21.5% of the detention sample of White youth scored in the alcohol-drug caution range, whereas 27.4% of the probation sample of White youth scored in the same range. Finally, 16.4% of the detention sample of White youth scored in the alcohol-drug warning range, whereas 5.1% of the probation sample of White youth scored in that range.

## TRAUMATIC EXPERIENCES

There is a statistical significance of $p < .05$ on the prevalence of traumatic experiences scale when comparing the probation group to the detention group, whereby the detention group self-reports a higher incidence of having personally experienced traumatic events (see Table 2.7). The items included in the MAYSI-2 scale for traumatic experiences

**TABLE 2.7** Prevalence of traumatic experiences

| Scale | Label | Yes to Questions on Scale | Probation | Detention | $\chi^2(1)$ |
|-------|-------|---------------------------|-----------|-----------|-------------|
| te | traumatic experiences | | $n = 264$ | $n = 1075$ | 20.181* |
| | | none | 69 (25.9) | 193 (17.9) | |
| | | 1 | 54 (20.3) | 219 (20.3) | |
| | | 2 | 58 (21.8) | 199 (18.4) | |
| | | 3 | 46 (17.3) | 206 (19.1) | |
| | | 4 | 20 (7.5) | 173 (16.0) | |
| | | 5 | 17 (6.4) | 85 (7.9) | |

\* $p < .05$

*Note.* Frequency percentages are in parenthesis.

differ slightly for boys and girls, although both the boys' scale and the girls' scale each include five items:

**GIRLS:**

q48    Have you ever in your whole life had something very bad or terrifying happen to you?

q49    Have you ever been badly hurt, or been in danger of getting badly hurt or killed?

q50    Have you ever been raped, or been in danger of getting raped?

q51    Have you had a lot of bad thoughts or dreams about a bad or scary event that happened to you?

q52    Have you ever seen someone severely injured or killed (in person—not in movies or on TV or the Internet)?

**BOYS:**

q46    Have people talked about you a lot when you're not there?

q48    Have you ever in your whole life had something very bad or terrifying happen to you?

q49    Have you ever been badly hurt, or been in danger of getting badly hurt or killed?

q51    Have you had a lot of bad thoughts or dreams about a bad or scary event that happened to you?

q52    Have you ever seen someone severely injured or killed (in person—not in movies or on TV or the Internet)?

In the probation group, 74.1% of the subjects self-report affirmative answers to one or more of the items on the traumatic experiences scale, whereas 82.1% of the detention group self-report affirmative answers to one or more of the items on the traumatic experiences scale. With respect to multiple traumatic experience affirmative answers, 7.5% of the probation group and 16.0% of the detention group answered "yes" to four of the scale items, and 6.4% of the probation group and 7.9% of the detention group answered "yes" to all 5 items.

When we look at gender, 64.3% of the boys in the probation group and 72.1% of the girls in the probation group self-report affirmative answers to one or more of the items on the traumatic experiences scale, whereas 80.6% of the boys and 84.3% of the girls in the detention group self-report affirmative answers to one or more of the items on the traumatic experiences scale. With respect to multiple traumatic experience affirmative answers, 5.9% of the boys and 8.7% of the girls in the probation group, and 13.7% of the boys and 19.3% of the girls in the detention group, answered "yes" to 4 of the scale items. Also, 7.9% of the boys and 4.8% of the girls in the probation group, and 4.8% of the boys and 11.5% of the girls in the detention group, answered "yes" to all 5 items on the scale (see Table 2.8). When controlling for race on items related to traumatic experiences, the difference in prevalence of youth in the probation group versus those in the probation group, whereby the detention group self-reports a higher incidence of having personally experienced traumatic events, is statistically significant with a $p < .05$ as to the Black youth, not as to the White and Hispanic youth. Last, two items on the MAYSI-2 are found in this study as to Black youth, when controlling for race, with a statistical significance of $p < .05$ in the prevalence of differences in responses to

**TABLE 2.8** Traumatic experiences by gender

| Yes to Questions on Scale | Gender | Probation | Detention |
|---|---|---|---|
| | | $n = 254^a$ | $n = 1075$ |
| none | Boys | 39 (35.7) | 122 (19.4) |
| | Girls | 29 (27.9) | 71 (15.7) |
| 1 | Boys | 31 (20.4) | 139 (22.1) |
| | Girls | 20 (19.2) | 80 (17.7) |
| 2 | Boys | 29 (19.1) | 120 (19.1) |
| | Girls | 24 (24.0) | 79 (17.5) |
| 3 | Boys | 31 (20.4) | 126 (20.0) |
| | Girls | 15 (14.4) | 80 (17.7) |
| 4 | Boys | 9 (5.9) | 86 (13.7) |
| | Girls | 9 (8.7) | 87 (19.3) |
| 5 | Boys | 12 (7.9) | 33 (5.2) |
| | Girls | 5 (4.8) | 52 (11.5) |

[a]Missing values by gender account for disparity with $n = 264$ in Table 2.1.

*Note.* Frequency percentages are in parenthesis.

items between the probation group and the detention group, that do not appear in any other statistical analysis:

q25  Have other people been able to control your brain or your thoughts?

q46  Have people talked about you a lot when you're not there?

## ANALYSIS AND DISCUSSION

### ATTENTION-RELATED SURVEY ITEMS

As a group, the nondetained probation group scored higher on all three items on the MAYSI-2 instrument relating to attention deficits. Although the mean age is slightly lower in the probation group, 15.07 years old versus 15.49 years old in the detention group, that alone does not explain the difference. Nor does the median age, which is 15 years old for the probation group and 16 years old for the detention group. Likewise, the detention group subjects were each administered the instrument within hours of intake to the facility, so it is doubtful that their physical surroundings in a structured and rigid environment is a valid consideration. The extent is unknown, however, as to whether pharmacological interventions may play a role, because the dataset does not include information relating to prescription medications and any related impact on attention issues.

Statistically significant disparities exist in prevalence between the probation group and the detention group on items relating to attention deficits. When controlling for race, none of the race categories—Black, Hispanic, and White youth—exhibited statistically significant differences in prevalence on all of the attention-related items on the MAYSI-2. There is a statistically significant difference in responses to items of the probation group and the detention group for the Black youth as to the question "Have you had a lot of problems concentrating or paying attention?" This does not hold true, however, for the White youth when the analysis is run controlling for race. The inverse is true as to the question "Have you been really jumpy or hyper?" Here, we find a statistical significance of $p < .05$ in the prevalence of differences in responses to items between the probation group and the detention group for the White youth, but not for the Black youth. No statistically significant differences in prevalence on any of the items relating to self-reported attention-deficit issues exist as to the Hispanic youth between the probation and detention groups when controlling for race.

It is possible that youth of different ethnic groups—Black, Hispanic, and White, for example—interpret the instrument questions differently, thus perhaps nullifying the validity of the responses, at least as to the scale scores (Grisso, 2004). Although Grisso (2004) maintains that such is not the case due to any inherent design flaw in the MAYSI-2 instrument, it does seem a plausible explanation for the disparities as to race found herein. Indeed, Grisso and Barnum (2003) acknowledge that there are differences in MAYSI-2 mean scores between ethnic groups found in the norms studies, and offer possible reasons: (a) group differences in willingness to disclose information; (b) differences in the ways that youth perceive or understand the meanings of the items, based on their differences in cultural backgrounds; (c) differences in the system's response to youths of various ethnic groups, such that the types of youths who enter the juvenile justice system are different for one ethnic group than for another; and/or (d) actual differences between the ethnic groups (i.e., not specific to detained delinquent samples) in the prevalence of mental or emotional condition questions.

The MAYSI-2 does not include a scale relating to hyperactivity or attention-deficit issues. Nor is the instrument designed to diagnose anything, including ADD/ADHD (Attention-Deficit Disorder/Attention-Deficit Hyperactivity Disorder) or otherwise. It does, however, serve as an assessment tool whereby high scores on the three attention-related self-report items may indicate the necessity for additional screening, assessment, and psychoeducational or psychiatric diagnosis. Additional research is warranted to address the issue of high prevalence of self-reported attention deficits by nondetained youth entering the juvenile delinquency system, with special consideration attention to racial demographics.

**RAPE SURVEY ITEM**

A disproportionately high number of youth in the detention group answered that they had either been raped, or were in danger of getting raped. In part, this may simply be explained by the fear factor of being incarcerated, many for the first time, in a threatening institutional jail-like setting. Certainly, pop culture presents an image of prison as being a place where people get raped. Perhaps many of the subjects who answered "yes" to this inventory item were voicing their concerns and fears that they don't feel safe in the juvenile detention center. Also, it is worthy of note that the MAYSI-2 was administered to most of the youth within hours of intake to the detention center, before most were acclimated to the environment and before they would have had an opportunity to develop a sense of security and level of comfort in their new surroundings. The MAYSI-2 inventory item, question 50, reads, "Have you ever been raped, or been in fear of getting raped?" As such, the responses of the subjects in the sample are not limited to instances of sexual assault while incarcerated in detention, but, rather, refer to life experiences.

Also, as Grisso and Barnum (2003) note, a disproportionately high prevalence of juvenile offenders have a history of sexual victimization. The prevalence of affirmative responses to the rape item on the MAYSI-2 inventory may simply be an acknowledgment of that societal problem. This issue is also addressed *infra* in the discussion relating to the prevalence of self-reported history of traumatic experiences by the youth in this study. One recent study found that, when compared with girls who have not been neglected and abused, the neglected and abused girls were nearly twice as likely to be arrested as juveniles (20.0% versus 11.4%) (Spatz Widom, 2000). Another study found that "almost half of all women in jails and prisons had been physically or sexually abused before their imprisonment—a much higher rate than reported for the overall population" (Harlow, 1999, p. 000). The instant findings as they relate to girls in the juvenile delinquency system suggest a similar phenomenon. Further research is warranted to address the prevalence and correlation of sexual abuse of girls and juvenile delinquency.

## SUICIDE IDEATION SURVEY SCALE

The probation sample in this study presents with a higher prevalence of suicide ideation in the caution range on the MAYSI-2 suicide ideation scale than does the detention sample of youth at intake to the juvenile delinquency system. Grisso and Barnum (2003) suggest that this disparity may reflect a selective factor whereby those youth presenting as suicidal at intake may typically be diverted to placement within the mental health system and are less likely to be incarcerated at a juvenile detention center upon such manifestation of mental health needs. This does not, however, explain the high prevalence of girls entering the juvenile delinquency system with a manifestation of suicide ideation at intake. Girls at age 15 present with the highest prevalence of suicide ideation at intake, and girls of all ages present with a higher prevalence of suicide ideation than like-age boys in both the probation sample and the detention sample. Further research is warranted to address the apparent high prevalence of unmet significant mental health needs of girls—particularly manifestation of suicide ideation—upon intake to the juvenile delinquency system in comparison to similarly situated boys at intake.

When controlling for race, the Black youth were the only ethnic group where a statistical significance of $p < .05$ in the prevalence of differences in responses to items between the probation group and the detention group is found on both the suicide ideation caution range scale and the suicide ideation warning range scale. The findings are not especially relevant, in that in both instances the percentages of Black youth self-reporting suicide ideation in both the probation and detention groups are lower than when the statistical analysis is performed without race as a control. In fact, the suicide rate in the United States is considerably higher for White male juveniles than that of Black male juveniles, both of which are higher than the suicide rate for White female juveniles, which is higher than that of Black female juveniles (Snyder & Swahn, 2004). The suicide rate, however, for Native American juveniles (57 per 1 million) is almost twice the rate for White juveniles (Snyder & Swahn, 2004).

## ALCOHOL-DRUG SURVEY SCALE

The prevalence of alcohol and/or drug abuse is significantly higher in the detention group than in the probation group. Grisso and Barnum (2003) suggest that the "significantly lower score for the intake probation youths is probably due to the fact that they were considerably younger than the detention youth." The mean age of 15.07 in the probation group, however, is *not* significantly lower than the mean age of 15.49 in the detention group. The average age difference between the members of the two groups is less than six months and, typically, youth in that age frame are in the 10th grade at school. Likewise, the median age of 15 years old for the probation group and 16 years old for the detention group should not result in such disparity between the groups. Both groups were similar in reporting affirmative answers to one question on the alcohol-drug scale: 12.0% for the probation group and 12.8% for the detention group.

The differences between ethnic groups in self-reported alcohol and drug use are striking. This is especially so when we look at the prevalence of affirmative responses of White youth in the probation group as to alcohol-drug items and scale alcohol-drug scores on the MAYSI-2 in the caution and warning range. Here, the prevalence is significantly higher for White youth in the probation sample than that found when controlling for race as to either the Black or Hispanic youth, as well as for the entire sample when the analysis is performed without consideration for ethnicity. When controlling for race, the detention group has a high prevalence of self-reported alcohol and drug usage compared to the probation group on both the alcohol-drug caution scale and the alcohol-drug warning scale as to Hispanic youth. It is unclear as to why the differences in prevalence between the probation group and the detention group are statistically significant as to the Hispanic and White youth when controlling for race in the analysis, but not for Black youth. Additional research is warranted to address whether there is a racial disparity in the prevalence of drug and alcohol abuse by youths entering the juvenile delinquency system.

According to the White House Office of National Drug Control Policy (ONDCP) (2003), 10.4% of 8th grade students, 20.8% of 10th grade students, and 25.4% of 12th grade students reported past-month use of an illicit drug. Here, the issue is not mere alcohol and drug usage that is strikingly different but, rather, the extent of self-reported alcohol/drug problems that are prevalent in the detention group in comparison to the probation group. This is consistent with the fact that in 1998, 23% of all juvenile delinquency cases involving detention in the United States were drug-related cases (ONDCP, 2003). We do not know whether alcohol and/or drugs played a part in the commission of offenses and arrests of the youth in our study, nor do we know the nature and degree of the offenses and charges against any of the subjects, because that information is not collected with the MAYSI-2 instrument. It may well be that many of the youth in the probation group sample were not incarcerated at time of arrest or upon intake into the juvenile delinquency system because their offenses were of a less severe nature and degree than those youth in the detention group. These differences— together with other considerations that resulted in a decision to not incarcerate at intake pending delinquency adjudication—may explain the disparity in the prevalence of alcohol-drug issues between the two groups in the sample. Likewise, it is difficult to know whether the subjects in this study were truthful in their self-reported responses on the MAYSI-2, or whether they lied or answered with the responses that they thought the person administering the inventory to them wanted to hear.

## TRAUMATIC EXPERIENCES SURVEY SCALE

We start with an assumption that the prevalence of traumatic experiences is higher in the juvenile delinquency population than in the general population of youth because of the disproportionate history of "child abuse, sexual victimization, and exposure to other serious and disturbing violence in their families and communities, which can have compelling emotional consequences" (Grisso & Barnum, 2003). Additionally, the instant research study indicates that the prevalence of self-reported traumatic experiences is significantly higher in the detention group than in the probation group sample. We do not know the nature and degree of the charges against the subjects in the sample, nor does this study address the intake decision-making processes and criteria that may have led to the disproportionate findings in the detained youth versus the nondetained youth in the sample.

Girls scored higher on the traumatic experiences scale than boys in both the probation group and detention group samples. The likely reasons for this gender-based disparity are outside the scope of this research study. These findings support the proposition that there may be a "greater prevalence of emotional disturbances among delinquent girls than among delinquent boys in juvenile justice settings" (Grisso & Barnum, 2003; Hennessey, Ford, Mahoney, Ko, & Siegfried, 2004). As discussed *supra*, further research is warranted to address the apparent high prevalence of unmet significant mental health needs of girls *entering* the juvenile delinquency system. Detention of girls with post-traumatic stress disorder may exacerbate the problem because "the detention experience may result in re-traumatization and/or re-victimization" (Hennessey, Ford, Mahoney, Ko, & Siegfried, 2004, p. 5).

It is unclear as to why the differences in prevalence between the probation group and the detention group are statistically significant as to the Black youth when controlling for race in the analysis, but not as to Hispanic or White youth in self-reported traumatic experiences on the MAYSI-2 in this study. Perhaps, for some unknown cultural reason, the Black youth inherently give different meaning than Hispanic and White youth as their understanding of the questions on the MAYSI-2 instrument, thus resulting in the disparity between ethnic groups of juveniles. Additional research is warranted to address whether there is a racial disparity in the prevalence of self-reported traumatic experiences by youths entering the juvenile delinquency system and, if so, why that is the case.

## USE OF PRE-ADJUDICATION DETENTION IN MASSACHUSETTS

Some of the instant results, which varied from the hypothesis and anticipated results of the study, may be explained by the differences in delinquency statutes, differences in criteria and use of pre-adjudication detention in the various states, and/or the disparity in the availability and use of social services resources, including mental health treatment services, in the various states. For example, in Massachusetts, children as young as age 7 can be processed through the juvenile court system and adjudicated delinquent, whereas in Pennsylvania children under the age of 10 are subject to delinquency proceedings. Children as young as age 7 can be detained pending an adjudication hearing in Massachusetts, but must be at least age 14 to be held in a secure juvenile detention center pending delinquency adjudication. In Pennsylvania, a child as young as age 10 can be held in a secure juvenile detention center pending adjudication.

Alternatives to secure detention seem to be more readily available in Massachusetts than in other states, as does the provision of community-based mental health services. It appears that Massachusetts is, thus, less likely than other states, such as New Jersey, to warehouse juveniles who are in need of mental health services in secure juvenile detention centers for want of other viable alternative placement and treatment options (e.g., New Jersey Office of Child Advocate, 2004; Waxman, 2004). Also, it is possible that the "gatekeeper" function of the clerk-magistrate in Massachusetts may serve as an impetus for the provision of mental health services for juveniles at the juvenile court intake process, perhaps in lieu of entry into the system by way of issuance of a juvenile delinquency complaint.

## SUMMARY OF RESULTS

As a group, the nondetained probation group scored higher on all of the MAYSI-2 items relating to attention deficits. When controlling for race, however, there is no statistical significance in differences in prevalence on all of the items as a group, but there are differences as to individual inventory items. It is possible that cultural differences account for differences between ethnic groups, such as how the instrument questions are interpreted.

A disproportionately high number of youth in the detention group answered that they had either been raped, or were in danger of getting raped. This may be a manifestation of the disproportionately high prevalence of juvenile offenders having a history of sexual victimization. The probation sample in this study presents with a higher prevalence of suicide ideation in the caution range on the MAYSI-2 suicide ideation scale than does the detention sample of youth at intake to the juvenile delinquency system. Girls at age 15 present with the highest prevalence of suicide ideation at intake, and girls of all ages present with a higher prevalence of suicide ideation than like-age boys in both the probation sample and the detention sample.

The prevalence of alcohol and/or drug abuse is significantly higher in the detention group than in the probation group. When controlling for race, the prevalence of affirmative responses is significantly higher for White youth in the probation group on alcohol-drug items and with the MAYSI-2 drug-alcohol scale scores in the caution and warning range than for those in the other ethnic groups. Also, when controlling for race, there is a high prevalence of self-reported alcohol and drug usage in the detention group and compared to the probation group on both the alcohol-drug caution scale and the alcohol-drug warning scale as to Hispanic youth.

As to the MAYSI-2 traumatic experiences scale, the prevalence of self-reported traumatic experiences is significantly higher in the detention group than in the probation group. Girls scored higher on the traumatic experiences scale than boys in both the probation group and detention group samples. When controlling for race on items relating to traumatic experiences, the difference in prevalence between the probation and detention groups is statistically significant only as to the Black youth, whereby the Black youth in detention self-report a significantly higher incidence of having experienced traumatic events than that reported by Black youth in the probation group.

## LIMITATIONS

The MAYSI-2 has inherent limitations because it is a self-report instrument. It identifies only symptom domains in need of further psychiatric assessment and may produce both false positives and false negatives (Cauffman, 2004). Additionally, the sample analyzed in this study includes only court-involved youth and does not include any sample of youth not facing delinquency charges. As such, the findings may be limited in scope.

As Cauffman (2004) notes, without a comparison group of nondelinquent youth, only indirect comparisons based on previous studies can be made. The use of screening instruments such as the MAYSI-2 have inherent limitations. This instrument is not meant to be used to diagnose mental health disorders. It does, however, provide a triage device for use by staff in making detention, referral, treatment, and placement decisions pending adjudication. The instant study lacks information about the subjects relating to medical, social, and school history and is limited by the nature of the instrument as a self-reporting assessment.

## CONCLUSIONS, IMPLICATIONS, AND RECOMMENDATIONS

### Conclusions

Several conclusions can be drawn from the findings of the instant research, several of which are gender-specific as to girls' mental health needs at time of intake to the juvenile delinquency system:

- First, at time of intake to the juvenile delinquency system, in many respects no differences are found as to the unmet mental health needs of the nondetained youth versus the detained youth in certain areas (e.g., depression, anxiety, somatic complaints, anger, and thought disorders).
- Second, the prevalence of ADD/ADHD appears to be much higher in youth entering the juvenile delinquency system than that found in the general population of like-aged youth. The prevalence of self-reported attention difficulties is significantly higher among nondetained youth entering the juvenile delinquency system than among youth who are incarcerated upon intake.
- Third, the instant research supports the generally accepted proposition that the juvenile delinquency population has a higher prevalence of sexual victimization than the general population. The prevalence of self-reported past sexual victimization for boys and girls is higher among youth who are detained upon intake to the juvenile delinquency system than that of those youth who are not detained upon intake.
- Fourth, girls entering the juvenile delinquency system are far more likely than boys to exhibit suicide ideation, and, as a group, at time of intake, girls are more likely than boys to be at risk for having intense unmet mental health needs.
- Fifth, at time of intake to the juvenile detention system, nondetained youth are at significant risk for suicide, as indicated by self-reported suicide ideation. In fact, nondetained youth report a much higher prevalence of suicide ideation than do youth who are detained upon intake to the juvenile delinquency system.
- Sixth, the prevalence of self-reported alcohol and/or drug abuse is significantly higher among youth detained upon intake to the juvenile delinquency system than among youth who are not detained at time of intake. However, as to nondetained youth, the prevalence of self-reported alcohol-drug abuse is significantly higher for White and Hispanic youth at time of intake than that of Black youth entering the juvenile delinquency system.
- Seventh, the overwhelming majority of youth entering the juvenile delinquency system self-report a history of traumatic experiences in their lives. The prevalence

of self-reported traumatic experiences is significantly higher for youth who are detained upon intake to the juvenile delinquency system than that self-reported by youth who are not detained at time of intake.

### Policy Implications and Recommendations

In an effort to further determine the prevalence of mental health needs of youth at time of intake to the juvenile delinquency system, replication of this study in various jurisdictions is warranted, because the criteria for establishing personal jurisdiction of the juvenile delinquency system vary widely from one state to the next in the United States. There is also a lack of uniformity from state to state—and often from county to county within a state—in intake processes and pre-adjudication detention criteria. A multistate MAYSI-2 study of nondetained and detained youth at the intake level in urban, suburban, and rural areas would be beneficial for this purpose. Additional research is warranted to address the racial disparities in prevalence between ethnic groups on MAYSI-2 items and scales. Such research could be beneficial in determining whether differences in responses are the result of group differences in willingness to disclose information, cultural differences leading to perception or understanding of the meaning of instrument questions, differences in the response of the juvenile justice system to youth of various ethnic groups, and/or actual differences between the groups. In this regard, a MAYSI-2 study of youth entering the juvenile delinquency system on one or more Native American reservations, such as the Navajo reservation in Window Rock, Arizona, or the Hualapai reservation in Peach Springs, Arizona, is suggested as a venue for further research. Due to the small populations of these groups, and the delinquency population within these communities, a cross-tribal study could be facilitated through the Inter Tribal Council of Arizona, the Public Health Service, or the Bureau of Indian Affairs, so as to provide for a larger study sample.

The implications of the instant research study are relevant for juvenile justice practitioners, especially those working with youth at intake to the juvenile delinquency system and those working with youth in community-based settings during pre-adjudication stages of the juvenile delinquency system. It is clear that nondetained youth entering the juvenile delinquency system—both boys and girls—are at risk for significant unmet mental health needs. The prevalence of suicide ideation, for example, is significantly higher as to nondetained youth than youth who are detained pending delinquency adjudication hearings. The high prevalence of *nondetained* girls in this sample who scored high for suicide ideation (see Table 2.6), history of traumatic experiences (see Table 2.8), and history of sexual abuse (see Table 2.4) is of great concern and underscores the gender differences in the prevalence of mental health disorders in adolescent offenders. These findings are consistent with those of Wasserman et al. (2005) that at intake girls present with higher rates of internalizing disorders compared with boys, whereas boys are more likely to be diagnosed with externalizing disorders, such as conduct disorders and ADHD (e.g., Vincent & Grisso, 2005).

Mental health screening assessments, such as the MAYSI-2, should be an integral component of intake procedures for all youth entering the juvenile delinquency system, for both youth who are detained pending court proceedings and youth who are released to their parent(s) or other nonsecure community-based placement pending court proceedings (e.g., Skowyra & Cocozza, 2006). Use of mental health screening assessments serves as a useful triage device to determine whether further mental health assessment is warranted. Administration of the MAYSI-2 instrument may expose exigencies warranting additional mental health assessment leading to the delivery of community-based or in-patient mental health treatment for nondetained youth awaiting delinquency adjudication proceedings. In many instances, acute mental health needs may appropriately result in diversion from the juvenile delinquency system to the mental health system. Unfortunately, as was recently noted in a report on conditions of confinement in New York's juvenile facility for girls, oftentimes it is the case that "the usefulness of this preliminary assessment is undermined by the absence of specific facilities that could provide treatment tailored to girls' specific mental health problems and needs" (American Civil Liberties Union and Human Rights Watch, 2006, p. 93). That should never be so.

## References

Achenbach, T. (1991). *Manual for the Child Behavior Checklist.* Burlington: University of Vermont, Department of Psychiatry.

American Civil Liberties Union and Human Rights Watch. (2006). *Custody and control: Conditions of confinement in New York's juvenile prisons for girls.* New York: Author. Retrieved October 4, 2006, from http://hrw.org/reports/2006/us0906/us0906webwcover.pdf

Archer, R. P., Vauter Stredny, R., Mason, J. A., & Arnau, R. C. (2004). An examination and replication of the psychometric properties of the Massachusetts Youth Screening Instrument–Second Edition (MAYSI-2) among adolescents in detention settings. *Assessment, 11*(4), 290–302.

Cauffman, E. (2004). A statewide screening of mental health symptoms among juvenile offenders in detention. *Journal of the American Academy of Child and Adolescent Psychiatry, 43*(4), 430–439.

Foley, R. M. (2001). Academic characteristics of incarcerated youth and correctional educational programs. *Journal of Emotional and Behavioral Disorders, 9,* 248–259.

Grisso, T. (2004). *Double jeopardy: Adolescent offenders with mental disorders.* Chicago: University of Chicago Press.

Grisso, T., Barnum, R., Fletcher, K., Cauffman, E., & Peuschold, D. (2001). Massachusetts Youth Screening Instrument for mental health needs of juvenile justice youths. *Journal of the American Academy of Child and Adolescent Psychiatry, 40*(5), 541–548.

Grisso, T., & Barnum, R. (2003). *Massachusetts Youth Screening Instrument–Version 2: User's manual and technical report.* Sarasota, FL: Professional Resource Press.

Harlow, C. W. (1999). *Prior abuse reported by inmates and probationers.* Washington, DC: U.S. Department of Justice, Bureau of Justice Statistics, NCJ 172879.

Hennessey, M., Ford, J. D., Mahoney, K., Ko, S. J., & Siegfried, C. B. (2004). *Trauma among girls in the juvenile justice system.* Los Angeles: National Child Traumatic Street Network, Juvenile Justice Working Group. Retrieved October 4, 2006, from http://www.nctsn.org/nctsn_assets/pdfs/edu_materials/trauma_among_girls_in_jjsys.pdf

Leone, P. E. (1994). Education services for youth with disabilities in a state-operated juvenile correctional system: Case study and analysis. *Journal of Special Education, 28*(1), 43–58.

Leone, P. E., Zaremba, B. A., Chapin, M. S., & Iseli, C. (1995). Understanding the overrepresentation of youths with disabilities in juvenile detention. *District of Columbia Law Review, 3,* 389.

National Youth Screening Assistance Project. (2004). *About the MAYSI-2.* Worcester, MA: University of Massachusetts Medical School. Retrieved December 11, 2004, from http://www.umassmed.edu/nysap/MAYSI2/

New Jersey Office of Child Advocate. (2004). *Office of Child Advocate report: Juvenile detention center investigation: An examination of conditions of care for youth with mental health needs*. Retrieved December 11, 2004, from http://www.childadvocate.nj.gov/downloads/ FINAL_JJ_Mental_Health_Report_rev.pdf

Office of National Drug Control Policy. (2003). *Juveniles and drugs*. Washington, DC: Executive Office of the President, Office of National Drug Control Policy. Retrieved February 7, 2005, from http://www.whitehousedrugpolicy.gov/publications/factsht/juvenile/196879.pdf

Quinn, M., Rutherford, R. B., and Leone P. E. (2001). *Students with disabilities in correctional facilities*. ERIC EC Digest #E621. Arlington, VA: Educational Resources Information Center. Retrieved February 26, 2004, from http://ericec.org/digests.e621.html

Rutherford, R. B., Bullis, M., Anderson, C. W., & Griller-Clark, H. M. (2002). *Youth with disabilities in the correctional system: Prevalence rates and identification issues*. College Park, MD: National Center on Education, Disability, and Juvenile Justice.

Skowyra, K. R., & Cocozza, J. (2006). *Blueprint for change: A comprehensive model for the identification and treatment of youth with mental health needs in contact with the juvenile justice system*. Delmar, NY: National Center for Mental Health and Juvenile Justice. Retrieved September 18, 2006, from http://www.nicic.org/Library/021664

Snyder, H. N. & Sickmund, M. (1995). *Juvenile offenders and victims: A national report*. Washington, DC: U.S. Department of Justice.

Snyder, H. N., & Swahn, M. H. (2004, March). Juvenile Suicides, 1981–1998. *Youth Violence Research Bulletin*. Washington, DC: U.S. Department of Justice, Office of Justice Programs, Office of Juvenile Justice and Delinquency Prevention. Retrieved March 1, 2005, from http://ncjrs.org/html/ojjdp/196978/contents.html

Spatz Widom, C. (2000). Childhood victimization and the derailment of girls and women to the criminal justice system. In *Research on women and girls in the justice system*. Washington, DC: U.S. Department of Justice, Office of Justice Programs, National Institute of Justice. Retrieved February 8, 2005, from http://www.ncjrs.org/pdffiles1/nij/180973.pdf

Stahl, A. L. (2001). *Delinquency cases in juvenile courts, 1998*. Washington, DC: U.S. Department of Justice, Office of Justice Programs, Office of Juvenile Justice and Delinquency Prevention. Retrieved August 1, 2004, from http://www.ncjrs.org/pdffiles1/ojjdp/fs200131.pdf

Stahl, A. L. (2003). *Delinquency cases in juvenile courts, 1999*. Washington, DC: U.S. Department of Justice, Office of Justice Programs, Office of Juvenile Justice and Delinquency Prevention. Retrieved August 1, 2004, from http://www.ncjrs.org/pdffiles1/ojjdp/fs200302.pdf

United States Department of Justice. (2003). *Juvenile Court Statistics, 1998*. Washington, DC: U.S. Department of Justice, Office of Justice Programs, Office of Juvenile Justice and Delinquency Prevention. Retrieved August 1, 2004, from http://www.ncjrs.org/pdffiles1/ojjdp/ 193696.pdf

Vincent, G., & Grisso, T. (2005). A developmental perspective on adolescent personality, psychopathology, and delinquency. In T. Grisso, G. Vincent, & D. Seagrave (Eds.), *Mental health screening and assessment in juvenile justice* (pp. 22–43). New York: The Guilford Press.

Wasserman, G., McReynolds, L., Ko, S., Katz, L., & Carpenter, J. (2005). Gender differences in psychiatric disorders at juvenile probation intake. *American Journal of Public Health, 95,* 131–137.

Waxman, H. A. (2004). *Testimony of Rep. Henry A. Waxman, Hearings: "Juvenile Detention Centers: Are they warehousing children with mental illness?"* Government Affairs Committee, U.S. Senate, July 7, 2004. Washington, DC: U.S. Senate. Retrieved July 24, 2004, from http:// www.house.gov/reform/min/pdfs_108_2/pdfs_inves/pdf_health_mental_health_youth_ incarceration_july_2004_testimony.pdf

# CHAPTER 3
# "I'VE BEEN AROUND AND AROUND AND AROUND":
## Measuring Traumatic Events in the Lives of Incarcerated Girls

**Judith A. Ryder**

**Sandra Langley**

**Henry Brownstein**

## ABSTRACT

The need for mental health services is acute among juvenile female offenders. Often overlooked in the research but increasingly detained and incarcerated, justice-involved girls are at great risk for trauma exposure and highly vulnerable to its comorbid effects. Variability in how trauma is conceptualized and operationalized, however, has made it difficult to compare findings across studies and thereby develop effective programming that is empirically based and population-specific. In this chapter we review the ways in which trauma has been defined and measured in extant studies of girls in custody and suggest a classification of four approaches: studies that use (a) unstructured or semistructured interviews only, without a checklist of events; (b) inventories or checklists of events based on general population research (inventories that are population-specific); and (d) population-specific inventories in combination with open-ended questioning. We illustrate the unique strengths of the fourth approach, using data from a study of 51 girls adjudicated and remanded to custody for a violent offense. Population-specific inventories seek to encapsulate traumatic experiences unique to these girls' lives, whereas open-ended methods help identify events for such inventories and complement quantitative findings with context and depth. Combining methods facilitates a better understanding of the nature and prevalence of trauma as identified by girls themselves and contributes to more responsive mental health programming.

The trauma-delinquency web is insidious. Juveniles who experience psychological trauma are at increased risk of engaging in substance abuse, risky sexual behavior and criminal offending, and for developing symptoms of post-traumatic stress syndrome (PTSD) (Browne & Finkelhor, 1986; Dembo, Williams, Lavoie, & Berry, 1989; Gover & McKenzie, 2003; Smith, Leve, & Chamberlain, 2006; Smith & Thornberry, 1995). Each of these outcomes increases the likelihood of experiencing additional traumas, particularly among girls within the juvenile justice system. Compared to their male counterparts, girls in custody are at greater risk for trauma exposure overall and to certain types of trauma in particular, and they are highly vulnerable to its comorbid effects (Brosky & Lally, 2004; Dixon, Howie, & Starling, 2005). Further, the experience of being incarcerated can be traumatic in and of itself, and offenders with trauma histories are likely to have additional difficulties adjusting to confinement.

Scholars' understanding of the trauma-delinquency web among justice-involved girls, however, remains in its infancy for a variety of reasons. First, the study of trauma among the general population of children and adolescents, although burgeoning, is still relatively new, and the corresponding instruments and methods are not well established (Newman, 2002; Strand, Sarmiento, & Pasquale, 2005). In addition, because the preponderance of juveniles in the custodial population is male,[1] girls are rarely central to juvenile justice research, policy, or practice (e.g., Bloom, 2003).[2] Finally, although the prevalence of any mental health condition among adolescents in custody ranges from 44% to 85% (Golzari, Hunt, & Anoshiravani, 2006), there is a dearth of mental health treatment in juvenile justice facilities (Thomas, Gourley, & Mele, 2005; U.S. House of Representatives, 2004). Mental health services that *are* provided often fail to address trauma symptoms and even more rarely evaluate service outcomes (Greenwald, 2000).

In this chapter, we hope to contribute to this area of study through the examination and synthesis of research methods that have been used in extant studies of trauma among girls under custody. Specifically, we briefly review this emergent body of literature and present a typology of the primary measures and methods used. We provide an in-depth description from our own study of incarcerated girls to illustrate the unique strengths of combining two methods: trauma inventories and open-ended interviewing. Finally, we conclude that the study of trauma among incarcerated girls warrants the development of a population-specific trauma inventory to capture the traumatic experiences that are unique to the lives of these girls. We highlight the use of open-ended methods to identify events for such an inventory and to complement quantitative findings with context and depth.

---

[1]According to the most recent data, girls account for only 15% of all juveniles in official custody—18% of all detained juveniles and 12% of all committed juveniles. In 2003, in nearly all states females represented a relatively small proportion of juvenile offenders in residential placement. The four states with 10% or less are: Colorado (10%), Maryland (8%), New Jersey (8%), and Rhode Island (7%). In Vermont there were too few juveniles to calculate a reliable percentage. (Snyder and Sickmund, 2006, pp. 206–207.)

[2]One example of shifting priorities was the announcement in 2002 that the Office of Juvenile Justice and Delinquency Prevention (OJJDP) had cancelled funding for a National Girls Institute, even as it stated in the Federal Registrar (Final Program Plan for Fiscal Year 2002) that "OJJDP's commitment to . . . gender-specific programs for girls remains strong." The Institute was to be the first nationwide repository of information devoted to female delinquency and its prevention.

## BACKGROUND

Extensive empirical studies have established that there is a tremendous need for mental health services among juvenile offenders. The mental disorder rates of children and youth involved with the juvenile justice system are higher than those of youth in the general population and may be comparable to (or exceed) rates among youths treated in the mental health system (National Mental Health Association, 2004). Research indicates that approximately one-half of all youth in the juvenile justice system meet criteria for at least two mental health disorders (Marsteller et al., 1997; Teplin, Abram, McClelland, Dulcan, & Mericle, 2002). In response, national mental health advocates have called for major system and policy changes to address the disparity between the growing need and limited availability of appropriate mental health services for juvenile offenders (National Association of State Mental Health Program Directors, 2001).

The need for and availability of mental health services is especially acute among young female offenders (Golzari, Hunt, & Anoshiravani, 2006) who traditionally have been overlooked. Research has not kept pace with recent escalations in the number of girls held in custodial facilities, and some studies continue to refer to "youths" and "juvenile offenders" in ways that imply mixed gender samples, when in fact there are very few female subjects (or none at all) relative to the number of males. The findings of such studies are of minimal usefulness to those seeking to address the mental health needs of female juvenile offenders. Reflective of this general phenomenon are studies of adolescents' trauma histories that are either based on exclusively male samples (Ruchkin, Schwab-Stone, Koposov, Vermeiren, & Steiner, 2002; Steiner, Garcia, & Matthews, 1997; Wasserman, Ko, & McReynolds, 2004) or large male samples with a small number of females (Abrantes, Hoffmann, & Anton, 2005; Crimmins, Cleary, Brownstein, Spunt, & Warley, 2000). What is learned about adolescent male offenders may be applicable to females, but this cannot be assumed. Arguably, girls have a distinct profile of familial risk factors (Silverthorn & Frick, 1999), and there may be significant differences in how criminality and mental health are manifested in male and female adolescents (Alemagno, Shaffer-King, & Hammel, 2006; Hoyt & Scherer, 1998). Further research is needed to document and make visible the unique ways that trauma is experienced by girls in order to address implications for their mental health.

### TRAUMA IN THE CONTEXT OF FEMALE OFFENDERS' LIVES

Traumatic events are deeply upsetting and substantially change how one thinks and feels about the world (Herman, 1997). Traditionally considered an extreme subset of stressful life events (Dise-Lewis, 1988), traumatic events break through internal protective defenses and overwhelm normal coping mechanisms, often challenging basic assumptions such as fairness and safety, justice and predictability (Janoff-Bulman, 1992). These events may be indicative of a change in the environment or of ongoing conditions that are threatening or harmful.

Some conceptualizations of trauma, frequently based on the transactional definition of stress offered by Lazarus and Folkman (1984), hold that whether an event is perceived and processed as traumatic or not depends on the individual's perception, which may be influenced by a number of factors including severity and duration, context, personal characteristics, and the availability and effectiveness of social supports (Crimmins, Langley, Brownstein, & Spunt, 1997; Luthar & Zigler, 1991; McLeod &

Kessler, 1990). Although much research conceptualizes trauma as based on individuals' perceptions, frequently the corresponding measures of child and adolescent stressful and traumatic experiences do not systematically assess cognitive appraisals (Grant, Compas, Stuhlmacher, Thurm, McMahon, & Halpert, 2003, p. 448). This is often because of the variability of children's perceptions. Instead, many studies that assess stress generally, and trauma specifically, use a checklist, which is consistent with conceptualizations of trauma as an "objective" environmental event. Still other studies derive their definition of trauma from the American Psychiatric Association (1994), which states that a traumatic event contains both objective characteristics (i.e., "actual or threatened death, or serious injury, or a threat to the physical integrity of self or others") and the subjective response of the exposed person (i.e., "fear, helplessness or horror").

The impact of trauma can be exacerbated by the experience of multiple types or the repeated experience of a single type (Clausen & Crittenden, 1991). Herman (1997) argues that the study of a single traumatic incident is inadequate for understanding trauma among victims of violence, and Solomon and Heide (1999) propose a typology of trauma survivors that accounts for those who have experienced a single event, multiple events, or multiple and pervasive events beginning at an early age and continuing for years. Recently, Finkelhor, Ormrod, and Turner (2007) found polyvictimization to be a "powerful predictor of trauma symptoms" (p. 16) in a general population study of children ages 2–17. They suggest that the repetition of trauma can have an exponential, rather than additive, effect on adverse consequences, wearing down the ability to successfully address and cope with subsequent events. For many young women involved in the justice system, the accumulation of traumatic events may be likened to a chronic "condition" (Finkelhor, Ormrod, & Turner, 2007; Terr, 1990). Moreover, much research suggests that those who experience multiple traumas are more likely to exhibit poor functioning in academic performance, health, suicidal ideation, and suicide attempts (Giaconia et al., 1995) and to develop PTSD (Breslau, Chilcoat, Kessler, & Davis, 1999). Thus, depending on a number of factors, severely stressful and traumatic events may result in consequences detrimental to personality development and interpersonal relationships (e.g., Briere, 1992; Herman, 1997), with "varied and lasting" effects continuing into adulthood (Finkelhor, 1995).

## ADULT FEMALE OFFENDERS

Research on the nature and extent of traumatic life events among adult female offenders demonstrates the long-term effects of trauma's mental-health sequelae and is helpful to our understanding of trauma in girls' development. Adult female prisoners consistently report lifetime trauma exposure at rates that are much higher than those of women in the general population and among incarcerated men (McClellan, Farabee, & Crouch, 1997). There is strong evidence to suggest that women's exposure to trauma increases the risk for experiencing a number of disorders, including alcohol or drug abuse, depression, and PTSD (Horwitz, Widom, & White, 2001). In a study of female jail inmates, 62% reported childhood trauma, including sexual molestation, physical abuse, and neglect. Nearly three-fourths also reported either an alcohol or substance abuse problem, 25% reported current major depressive disorder, and 22% had current PTSD (Green, Miranda, Daroowalla, & Siddique, 2005). Cook, Smith, Tusher, and Raiford (2005) report that in a random sample of women in a Georgia prison, nearly all of the participants had experienced one traumatic event and 81% had experienced five or more.

Studies suggest that high rates of child abuse may be a factor in women's criminal offending (Zlotnick, 1997). For example, experiences of child abuse may precipitate running away; the subsequent development of PTSD and substance use are both associated with women's increased risk for criminality (Battle, Zlotnick, Najavits, Guittierrez, & Winsor, 2003; Maas-Robinson & Thompson, 2006). Using a prospective, matched cohort design, Widom (1989) demonstrated that abused or neglected girls were significantly more likely to have an adult arrest (16%) than were control females (9%). In a replication and extension of this work, English, Widom, and Brandford (2001) examined potential differences in the connections between child abuse (physical and sexual) and neglect and subsequent criminal behavior. Compared to the matched control group, abused and neglected females were nearly four times more likely to be arrested as a juvenile, twice as likely to be arrested as an adult, and nearly seven times more likely to be arrested as an adult for a violent crime. These prevalence rates paint a daunting picture, but there is also evidence of effective interventions to reduce symptoms of PTSD, anxiety, and depression and to raise the levels of self-efficacy among trauma-exposed female inmates (Carr, 2005; Valentine, 2000).

## ADOLESCENT GIRLS

Links between girls' problems and women's crimes are often closely interwoven and, yet, most of the scholarship on crime and gender over the past 30 years has focused on adult women, not girls (Zahn, 2006). Given the developmental differences between the two populations, we must be cautious when applying research findings about adults to the lives of girls (Odgers, Reppucci, & Moretti, 2005; Vincent & Grisso, 2005). The potential seriousness of the effects of trauma exposure, however, as well as the potential for effective interventions, dramatically underscores the need for additional research on females during the critical period of adolescence.

Although current findings are mixed as to whether girls are more likely than boys to be exposed to trauma overall, recent research with justice-involved youth confirms that *type* of traumatic experiences varies by gender (Blackburn, Mullings, Marquart, & Trulson, 2007). Further, trauma-exposed girls are more likely than their male counterparts to develop adverse outcomes, and there are gender differences in the types of outcomes experienced. For example, among those who are exposed, girls are more likely than boys to develop mental health problems as a result (Breslau, Davis, Andreski, & Peterson, 1991; Dembo, Schmeidler, Guida, & Rahman, 1998; Horowitz, Weine, & Jekel, 1995). Trauma is more strongly associated with involvement in serious delinquent activity in girls than in boys (Rivera & Widom, 1990; Wood, Foy, Goguen, Pynoos, & James, 2002). Female trauma victims are also more likely than males to develop drug problems and to be involved in drug-related crime (Harlow, 1999; Widom, Ireland, & Glynn, 1995).

Recent feminist discourse, in particular, attributes girls' delinquency to exposure to traumatic events, positing that childhood victimizations are a "pathway" to delinquent behavior (Gaarder & Belknap, 2002; Gilfus, 1992). For example, sexual abuse is a primary reason girls run away from home, and this status offense is frequently a girl's first encounter with the juvenile justice system, which may then criminalize the girl's actions (Arnold, 1990; Kaufman & Widom, 1999, Simkins & Katz, 2002; Whitbeck &

Simons, 1993). Among one sample of justice-involved adolescent girls, both chronicity and variety of traumas experienced predicted criminal offending and risky sexual behavior (Smith, Leve, & Chamberlain, 2006).

Analyses referencing justice system-involved girls and trauma include in-depth case studies (Robinson, 2007) as well as larger studies, many of which describe a specific set of maltreatment experiences, primarily child sexual and physical abuse and neglect (Acoca, 1998; Goodkind, Ng, & Sarri, 2006). For example, Gaarder and Belknap (2002) conducted in-depth interviews and reported persistent themes of "sexual and physical abuse, neglect and disorder in the family" among 22 juvenile girls bound over and sentenced to an adult prison (p. 509). In a survey of 162 young women convicted of felonies and incarcerated in the California Youth Authority, Owen and Bloom (1997) determined that approximately 85% of the sample indicated some type of physical, emotional, or sexual abuse or sexual attack at some time in their life.

Whereas some studies of trauma among incarcerated girls focus on discerning maltreatment, others measure trauma only in relation to PTSD symptoms, which are themselves explained by a range of biological, behavioral, cognitive, and cathartic theories (Strand et al., 2005; Valentine, 2000). An Australian study of incarcerated girls reported high levels of both trauma exposure and PTSD and also found that offenders with PTSD had experienced a greater number of traumas and reported more comorbid diagnoses than those without. Such evidence suggests that for some girls, both "trauma and PTSD may be predisposing factors for the development of other psychopathology" (Dixon, Howie, & Starling, 2005, p. 803), which may in turn increase exposure to subsequent traumatic events and justice system involvement. It is likely that without effective interventions, the complex and multiple mental health problems of justice-involved girls will persist into adulthood (Teplin et al., 2002).

As girls continue to comprise a growing percentage of all juvenile delinquency cases and residential placements, the need for research and empirically based interventions will become even more critical.[3] Given the youth of these offenders, as well as their physical location in custodial facilities, there is a tremendous opportunity to address girls' trauma-related needs early on, with the intention of redirecting trajectories toward a healthy future. Effective programming will depend, however, on a deep understanding of trauma that is empirically based and population-specific. To date, variability in how trauma is conceptualized and operationalized has inhibited our ability to compare findings across studies and thereby develop a working definition of trauma that is both specific and comprehensive. To begin to sort out some of the variation, we examine how studies of incarcerated girls generally define and measure trauma.

## TOWARD A TYPOLOGY OF TRAUMA

The intersection of trauma and child abuse and interpersonal violence is a relatively new area of study (Gold, 2000), particularly with child and adolescent subjects (Strand et al., 2005) and even more so when it comes to female juvenile offenders. A sizable

---

[3]The most current data indicate that the *number* of female delinquents in juvenile facilities has increased a dramatic 96%—from 6,457 in 1991 to 12,626 in 2003 (Snyder & Sickmund, 2006).

body of general knowledge has amassed over the past two decades but the interdisciplinary nature of trauma-related research has complicated how findings are shared and discussed and has contributed to the field's "methodological and conceptual confusion" (Jackson, Veneziano, & Ice, 2005, p. 472). To further the research pertaining to trauma and incarcerated girls, we present a typology of four primary approaches used to determine trauma among this population. We include data from our own study of 51 adjudicated girls to demonstrate the value of the fourth approach, which uses a combination of closed-ended checklists and semistructured open-ended interviews.

In the present review, we include studies of the nature and prevalence of trauma among girls under custodial supervision in the juvenile justice system. We conducted a computerized search of peer-reviewed literature for the period January 1997–January 2007. Because the trauma literature is extensive, reflecting a diverse and rapidly evolving field (Lerner, 1996, p. 3), we used four distinct databases: Criminal Justice Abstracts, PILOTS (Published International Literature on Traumatic Stress), Medline, and PsychInfo. In addition, we entered terms into Google Scholar. The following terms and combination of terms were used in the search: traumatic stress/trauma/mental health, girl(s)/adolescence/juvenile(s)/youth, and incarceration/detention/custody/corrections. We supplemented findings by crosschecking citations from the reference lists of identified documents. We further refined our pool of studies by including only those that were (a) based in the United States, (b) focused on female offenders in juvenile justice custody (not primarily treatment facilities), and (c) included more than one type of victimization or other traumatic event (e.g., not sexual abuse only). A few studies were excluded from our review because insufficient detail was provided to discern the instrumentation.

## FOUR APPROACHES TO MEASURING TRAUMA AMONG GIRLS IN CUSTODY

In seeking to understand the different approaches to measuring the trauma experiences of this population, we limited our review to studies that examined whether or not particular traumas were ever experienced by the respondent. Although some studies also measured PTSD, our interest was broader, given that "traumatic experiences can precipitate other conditions" [besides PTSD] including "disruptive behavior disorders, other internalizing disorders, some personality disorders, and physical illnesses" (Abram, Teplin, Charles, Longworth, McClelland, & Dulcan, 2004, p. 408). We focus on external, environmental events that objectively threaten the individual (Cohen, Kessler, & Gordon, 1995), while also recognizing that the occurrence of trauma may depend on the degree to which an individual perceives an event as threatening or harmful. This distinction is made because most measures do not systematically assess children's and adolescent's perceptions of events given that they are likely to vary with the juvenile's development (Grant et al., 2003). Some of the retained studies also assessed other variables related to each trauma experienced, such as the frequency or repetition of a particular type of trauma, earliest age at which each trauma was experienced, and persistent affective experiences related to a particular trauma.

The studies we examined fall into four major categories in terms of the approach used to measure trauma prevalence. The first grouping includes those that used only *unstructured or semi-structured interviews without presenting a systematic inventory of events*. For example, in their early work with justice-involved girls, Belknap, Holsinger, and Dunn (1997) conducted focus groups that included 11 general questions, which elicited a considerable amount of trauma-related responses. Questions included: "What happened that you got into trouble the first time?" "Who do you want attention from?" and "What changes would you like in your families and other places outside the system?" Among five key findings was the "significant impact of difficult and traumatic life and family experiences" including witnessing a father's killing, being sexually assaulted at school—and then taken into custody for a knife carried in self-defense, and being charged with a drug offense related to involvement with much older boyfriends.

Simkins and Katz (2002) generated a profile of girls held in detention in Philadelphia after reviewing court history files and conducting individual interviews. Interviewers did not systematically ask about specific traumas, but were instructed to pay particular attention to the girls' trauma histories (p. 1482). The interview protocol was not described in detail, but the authors report that 81% of the 40 girls in the study experienced some type of trauma: physical abuse (43%), sexual abuse (38%), neglect or abandonment (29%), and witnessing violence (38%). Representative of the last type and of this population, one girl stated "I've seen 2 people shot and killed. I've seen more than 10 people shot" (p. 1484). Findings from this group of studies employing unstructured or semistructured interviews reveal numerous traumatic events, but without the "prompting" of a checklist, other traumatic experiences may have been missed. Indeed, focus group observers (Belknap, Holsinger, & Dunn, 1997) reported reluctance on the part of the girls to speak about certain experiences, and Simkins and Katz (2002) note that girls often minimized or did not mention severe and chronic victimizations that were included in their official case files.

The second major approach to measuring trauma prevalence is characterized by the use of *general-population inventories* that include items that are conventionally considered traumatic and therefore tend to be the most frequently studied (e.g., sexual abuse, physical abuse, accidents, and disasters). In their study comparing female juvenile offenders and high school students, Dixon, Howie, and Starling (2004, 2005) utilized the PTSD Traumatic Events component of the K-SADS-PL (Schedule for Affective Disorders and Schizophrenia for School-Age Children—Present and Lifetime Version). This semistructured instrument asks whether the respondent ever experienced any of 10 traumatic events, or any additional traumas. The events listed are: car accident, other accident, fire, disaster, witness violent crime, victim of violent crime, confronted with traumatic news, witness domestic violence, physical abuse, and sexual abuse. Offenders had significantly more types of traumatic experiences, including higher levels of personal victimization, than did the comparison group. The items that offenders most frequently reported were witnessing violent crime (70%), being confronted with traumatic news (66%), and witnessing domestic violence (52%). This suggests that traumatic experiences among girls involved in the justice system were more far ranging than accidents, natural disasters, and child abuse.

Other examples of studies using structured and diagnostic inventories include Abram et al. (2004) and Lederman, Dakof, Larrea, and Li (2004). Abram et al. used the PTSD module of the DISC-IV (Diagnostic Interview Schedule for Children) to determine prevalence estimates of exposure to trauma among 366 female and 898 male juvenile detainees. Respondents were asked if they had ever experienced any of eight traumatic experiences and then, to assess PTSD, which event was "the most difficult for you in your entire life."[4] The most frequently reported trauma for females was seeing someone get hurt badly or killed (64%). Thinking they or someone else they were close to was going to be hurt very badly or die was the second most common trauma (49%) (and the most frequent precipitating experience for those with PTSD), followed by being threatened with a weapon (47%). Significantly more girls than boys were forced to do something sexual (30% versus 2%).

Lederman et al. (2004) do not specify the use of the DISC-IV in their study of 493 female detainees, but include nearly identical questions and add a ninth that asks if the respondent was ever attacked sexually or raped. Eighty-four percent reported significant trauma in their lives, the nature of which was "markedly violent" (p. 325). Similar to Abram et al. (2004), the most frequently reported experiences were witnessing a violent attack on somebody else (50%) and thinking that they or someone close to them would be killed or hurt badly (40%). Although these general population inventories were not designed specifically for the juvenile offender population, findings from this second group of studies demonstrate high rates of fear and violence and suggest that "exposure to trauma is a fact of life for delinquent youth" (Abram et al., 2004, p. 407), and specifically for girls.

A third approach to trauma measurement consists of studies that use a compendium of several structured instruments, which together provided a *population-specific inventory* of events experienced by justice-involved girls (Odgers, Reppucci, & Moretti, 2005). In a series of studies, Wood and colleagues created an extensive inventory that focused on violence exposure and psychological distress through the use of eight different item sources, including the Survey of Children's Exposure to Community, the Sexual Abuse Exposure Questionnaire, and the general distress and PTSD scales of the LASC-Rev. (Los Angeles Symptom Checklist-Revised-Adolescent, 1997). A sample of 100 incarcerated girls (Wood, Foy, Goguen, Pynoos, & James, 2002) reported high rates of exposure to dating and sexual violence, as well as significant community violence: a gun held to their head (58%), witnessing the homicide of a close friend or relative (56%), or tortured or physically mutilated (10%). Compared to female high school students, incarcerated girls reported significantly higher levels of direct victimization (i.e., 16% reported rape, sexual assault, and molestation compared to 6% of the high school students) and significantly more overall community violence exposure (Wood, Foy, Layne, Pynoos, & James, 2002). Given the delinquent girls' histories of victimization, the authors suggest that multiple forms of violence exposure be considered in future research.

Smith, Leve, and Chamberlain's (2006) aggregated instrumentation included diagnostic measures of PTSD (DISC) and eight experiential measures of trauma, including the Traumatic Stress Schedule and Childhood Sexual Experience Questionnaire. The traumatic experiences of the girls included assault (51%), the unexpected death of a loved one (32%), and robbery (15%). Other items of particular relevance to this

---

[4]The eight items are: Have you ever been: (a) in a situation where you thought you or someone close to you was going to be hurt very badly or die; (b) attacked physically or beaten badly; (c) threatened with a weapon; (d) forced to do something sexual that you did not want to do; (e) in a bad accident; (f) in a fire, flood, tornado, earthquake, or other natural disaster where you thought you were going to die or be seriously injured; (g) very upset by seeing a dead body/pictures of a dead body of someone you knew well; and (h) have you ever seen or heard someone get hurt very badly or be killed?

population were measured cumulatively wherein girls were asked whether, in every year of their lives, they had witnessed domestic violence (75%) and a parent's incarceration (64%). The girls also reported they had experienced 4 to 36 parental transitions, averaging more than one per year, and 77% reported experiencing at least one out-of-home placement prior to referral. The authors suggest that delinquent girls who have experienced high rates of trauma may benefit from trauma treatment even if they are not currently exhibiting PTSD symptoms (Smith, Leve, & Chamberlain, 2006, p. 351).

Gavazzi, Yarcheck, and Chesney-Lind (2006) used the Global Risk Assessment Device (GRAD) to assess 11 domains of risk, including traumatic events, among detainees. The authors specified, however, only one question from the trauma domain ("Have you witnessed domestic violence in your home?"). Girls scored significantly higher than boys on items related to traumatic events, suggesting the need for "the development of gender-sensitive assessment instruments for use with juvenile offenders" (p. 605).

Finally, a fourth approach is a combination of population-specific trauma inventories (including items that may be rare in the general population but normative among incarcerated populations) in conjunction with open-ended questions in semistructured interviews. These are exemplified by studies with only juvenile female offenders (Cauffman, Feldman, Waterman, & Steiner, 1998; Ryder, 2003, 2007), as well as both juvenile females and males (Crimmins, Brownstein, Spunt, Ryder, & Warley, 1998). In these studies, youth were asked about a number of traumatic events from a checklist, which were then investigated more deeply through open-ended questioning.

In their study of PTSD among 96 adolescent female offenders, Cauffman, Feldman, Waterman, and Steiner (1998) reported the incidence of trauma in two ways. First, overall exposure was assessed by asking respondents three questions: if they had ever been badly hurt or in danger of being hurt, ever raped or in danger of being raped, and ever seen someone severely injured or killed. In addition to the standardized questions, interviewers reported whatever traumatic experiences respondents spontaneously recalled in a PTSD interview (Psychiatric Diagnostic Interview-Revised, PTSD module). Interviewers did not systematically ask for an enumeration of all traumatic events, but grouped all responses into five categories: (a) being a victim of violence (e.g., victim of rape/molestation, physical assault/attack), (b) witnessing a violent act (e.g., seeing someone shot or stabbed), (c) participating in a violent act (e.g., their own committing offense), (d) other (e.g., being in a serious car accident), and (e) no mention of any trauma. Such a format provides space for a girl to speak of and elaborate on any other events that may come to mind, perhaps prompted by the three standard queries.

As an example of how questions in a checklist were further expanded in open-ended questioning, Ryder (2007) and Crimmins et al. (1998) asked respondents if they had ever experienced the death of a loved one, and if so, the earliest age when the death occurred, the lifetime frequency, and how upsetting the death was to them. The death of loved ones was very common, occurred when respondents were young, and considered extremely upsetting. In their narrative responses, the youth described in detail the context of these deaths, which were often violent. The combination of both formats of data collection provided a consistent measure as well as a fuller description of what had occurred and how the youth felt about the event. This approach is expanded upon in the following section.

# A STUDY OF VIOLENT OFFENDERS

This section analyzes data from interviews with 51 girls adjudicated for a violent offense and remanded to custody in an Office of Children and Family Services (OCFS) facility in New York State.[5] The data are derived from a larger National Institute on Drug Abuse (NIDA)-funded study that examined the relationship between drug trafficking and violence among adolescents (Crimmins et al., 1998). We use these data to illustrate how our Trauma Inventory, or checklist, of traumatic events, together with our open-ended questions, provided a thick understanding of the trauma in the lives of a group of incarcerated girls. Affording girls an opportunity to discuss in greater detail the events in their life aided in building rapport, which, in turn, provided us with a more nuanced understanding of the meaning and context of their affirmative responses to the Trauma Inventory. The combination of methods also generated spontaneous revelations, alerting us to additional events that should be included in future research with this population.

## SAMPLE AND INTERVIEW PROCEDURES

Respondents were young and primarily women of color. Age at the time of the interview ranged from 12 to 20 years old; the median age was 15 years.[6] The girls reported their race/ethnicity as: 59% Black, 18% Hispanic/Latina, 12% Multi/Biracial, and 12% White.[7] Education was measured by the last grade completed before custody; the median level for all respondents was 8th grade (ranging from 6th to 10th grade). The respondents were in the "deep end" of the justice system, having been adjudicated for assault ($n = 38, 75\%$) or robbery ($n = 13, 25\%$) and remanded to residential custody. Four of the girls had a child; one had two children.

Each girl participated in a semistructured interview that focused on the respondent's life prior to custody, including exposure to traumatic events. The interview schedule used a retrospective reconstruction approach to recalling past experiences. The interview included closed-ended items, such as the inventory of traumatic events, which is described below, and open-ended items such as "Please describe what your family life was like before you came to DFY."[8] These voluntary, one-on-one interviews were conducted with a trained interviewer January through August of 1996 in four OCFS residential facilities. With the teen's permission the interview was tape recorded. Respondents had the option to halt the interview at any time but none chose to do so.[9] Interviews lasted an average of 1½ hours; respondents received a certificate of participation and a copy was placed in their institutional file.

---

[5]All contacted girls participated in an interview ($n = 51$). Of the 64 not contacted, 58 were released, 4 were transferred to adult corrections, 1 was AWOL, and 1 OCFS staff was considered too unstable to participate.

[6]During the study young women age 18 and older residing in OCFS facilities were moved to the adult Department of Correctional Services.

[7]Respondents were asked to specify race or ethnic background. Ten categories were offered as probes and responses were recoded: Black, Hispanic/Latina, White, and Biracial/Multiracial.

[8]The New York State Division for Family and Youth. Subsequent to conducting the interviews in 1998, DFY and certain children's programs administered by the Department of Social Services were merged to form the Office of Children and Family Services.

[9]The girls were told that some questions might cause them to recall stressful or painful events and were informed that counseling services were available should they desire them as a result of the interview.

## A RANGE OF TRAUMATIC EXPERIENCES

The trauma literature has focused little attention on juvenile offenders' perceptions of their victimization experiences. Prior to measuring the extent of trauma among our sample of incarcerated youth, we sought to ascertain, through a series of pilot tests, the range of possible traumatic experiences of urban youth (Crimmins et al., 1998). We compiled an inventory of 23 items and included an "other" category. For all events that had occurred, respondents were asked the earliest age of occurrence and the lifetime frequency of occurrence.[10] The girls were also asked to rank each event on a Likert scale in terms of how upsetting the particular event was to them (i.e., not at all upsetting, a little upsetting, somewhat upsetting, very upsetting, and extremely upsetting).

Table 3.1 shows the prevalence of the Trauma Inventory items, generally grouped by three domains: domestic, community, and other. These are further divided by loss, experienced violence, and witnessed violence. Columns indicate the actual number and percentage of girls who reported that an event had ever occurred, and the median for earliest age of occurrence, lifetime frequency of occurrence, and how upsetting the event was, including the range. The total number of traumatic lifetime events experienced by the 51 girls ranged from 2 to 18, with an average of 9.[11]

The young women reported directly experiencing and also witnessing many and varied traumatic events in their homes. More than three-fifths (69%) reported that a family member had kicked, bitten, or hit them, or burned or scalded them (18%). Almost half (47%) had witnessed someone being kicked, bitten or hit; one-fifth (20%) had witnessed someone burned or scalded, and 18% reported witnessing someone being shot or stabbed, all inside their home. Sixty-one percent reported being awakened by gunfire. When asked if anyone in their "family ever bother[ed] you sexually or forced you to have sex against your will," one-fourth (26%) answered affirmatively, and 16% had witnessed such acts against a family member. More than one-fourth of the girls (26%) said a stranger or acquaintance had bothered them sexually or forced them to have sex against their will. Over one-fifth (22%) reported that *both* family members and strangers/acquaintances had sexually bothered or coerced them. Relative to other events, sexual abuse was reported by a small number of the girls; however, the median frequency of *family* sexual abuse was among the highest (4, "very upset") and the earliest median ages were among the youngest (6–13 years old). The median levels of how upsetting family sexual abuse were to the girls were also high (5 and 4.5). Indicators of exposure to community violence include being kicked, bitten, or hit by an acquaintance or stranger (65%); being mugged (18%); and witnessing someone being shot or stabbed outside the home (61%). By the median age of 12 1/2 years, 51% of the girls in this study had witnessed at least one killing.

In addition to violence, the girls experienced substantial losses before the age of 12. More than 82% reported the death of at least one loved one, and over three-fourths (77%) experienced the serious illness or injury of a loved one. Many of the girls' parents had separated or divorced (63%),[12] and more than one-fifth (22%) had lost their

---

[10]Frequencies were recorded on an ordinal scale, e.g., 1=Once, 2=Couple, 3–4=Few, 5–7=Several.

[11]It is important to note that this refers to the number of trauma items that the girls *reported* ever experiencing, not the actual number of events they experienced.

[12]An additional 12% said their parents "were never together."

**TABLE 3.1**  A Traumatic Events Inventory

| | | Ever occurred* % | Earliest age (Median) | Frequency (Median number of times experienced) | How upsetting** (Median rating) |
|---|---|---|---|---|---|
| **Domestic** — Inside home; involving family | **Loss** — Death of a loved one | 82 | 10 | 2 | Extremely |
| | Serious injury/illness of loved one | 77 | 12 | 2 | Very |
| | Parents separated or divorced | 63 | 3 | 1 | Not at all |
| | Lost home | 22 | 7 | 1 | Somewhat |
| | **Experience violence** — Kicked, bitten, or hit | 69 | 8 | 6 | Very |
| | Awakened by gunfire | 61 | 11 | 7 | A little |
| | Sexually bothered/forced sex | 26 | 7 | 4 | Extremely |
| | Burned or scalded | 18 | 5 | 1 | Somewhat |
| | **Witness violence** — Witness kicked, bitten, or hit | 47 | 8 | 6 | Very |
| | Witness burning or scalding | 20 | 11 | 1 | Very/somewhat |
| | Witness shooting or stabbing | 18 | 12.5 | 1 | Somewhat |
| | Witness someone sexually bothered/forced sex | 16 | 6 | 3 | Extremely/very |
| **Community** — Outside home; involving acquaintance or stranger | **Experience violence** — Kicked, bitten or hit | 65 | 10 | 7 | Somewhat |
| | Sexually bothered/forced sex# | 26 | 13 | 2 | Extremely |
| | Shot or stabbed# | 24 | 13.5 | 2 | Extremely/very |
| | Mugged | 18 | 13 | 1 | A little |
| | Burned or scalded | 14 | 13 | 1 | A little |
| | **Witness violence** — Witness shooting or stabbing | 61 | 13 | 3 | A little |
| | Witness a killing# | 51 | 12.5 | 3 | Extremely |
| ***Other*** | Accident; hospital treatment | 41 | 12 | 1 | Very upsetting |
| | Fire or explosion | 31 | 8 | 2 | A little |
| | Any other upsetting event## | 28 | 13 | 1 | Extremely |
| | Serious physical illness | 20 | 7.5 | 2 | Somewhat/very |
| | Kidnapped | 2 | 15 | – | Extremely |

*Actual numbers range from 44–51 because of missing data.    **1 = Not at all upsetting; 2 = A little upsetting; 3 = Somewhat upsetting; 4 = Very upsetting; 5 = Extremely upsetting.    #Question did not specify whether event was domestic- or community-related.    ##Other events included being locked up, death of a pet, loss of best friend.

home. In addition, many of the girls had been injured or sick: 41% reported an accident requiring hospital treatment, 24% had been stabbed or shot, and 20% had been seriously ill.

We also asked respondents if there were any other events that were not mentioned that they found upsetting. If they said "yes," we prompted them to "tell me what happened." Over one-fourth (28%) of the girls mentioned other events, including "getting locked up," the death of a pet, and being separated from a best friend. When asked to assess the degree to which this event upset them, the girls' median level was "extremely upsetting." Finally, of all the events talked about, 46% reported that the death of a loved one was the most upsetting; 10% said it was the illness or injury of a loved one.

## NARRATIVE DATA

A primary way that people make sense of experiences, especially traumatic ones, is to put them in a narrative form that moves "reality" into the "intensely human realm of value" (Cronon, 1992, p. 1349). Narrative analysis assumes an interpretive perspective and is useful when, as in the current study, girls were prompted to "tell me what happened" or they spontaneously responded to a close-ended question with a rendition of a complex story. For example, a question on the Trauma Inventory asked, "Have you ever lost your home?" which was followed by asking the girl's age when this first happened, the number of occurrences, and how upsetting was the event. The girls' narrative responses, however, describe the context of the loss, providing details of family evictions, being thrown out of the house by a parent or other caregiver, the destruction of the home (e.g., fire), and numerous placements in mental health and correctional facilities. The narrative data generated by a subsample of girls ($n = 24$) were imported into N5, a qualitative research software program designed to assist in a theoretical understanding of text.[13] A grounded theory approach, in which data were constantly compared and contrasted, sought to discern patterns in the respondents' narratives. Although the data-driven categories of violence and loss overlap with some of the Trauma Inventory events, there is a marked difference in the nature of the responses in the narrative descriptions. It is here that we begin to confront the lived experiences of trauma.

## HOME AND COMMUNITY VIOLENCE

Violence was pervasive, both within the girls' homes and in their communities. For them, the family home was a significant source of danger, especially in terms of physical and sexual abuse and exposure to intimate partner violence. Open-ended questions such as "Who did you mostly live with?" and "Please describe what your family life was like" elicited violent narratives, much of which was associated with adults fighting one another verbally and physically, situations dangerous to the safety of children in the home (Mitchell & Finkelhor, 2001). A verbal exchange could quickly escalate: "My mother was cooking and she had a boyfriend . . . they got into an argument and she went to throw a pot and he kind of smacked it, and it fell all over her." One girl told of

---

[13]The qualitative analyses of traumatic events are based on narratives from 24 interviews; the other interviews were lost in the attack on the World Trade Center in 2001. Analyses of demographic characteristics indicate that the surviving group of 24 is similar to the sample of 51 from which it came.

how her mother "used to wreck his house [stepfather's], cuz he's got money hiding in the house" and in retaliation the stepfather beat the girl and her mother and threatened them with a gun.

In some instances, violence was the method for enforcing discipline, and the girls often described the acts as appropriate. For example, one 14-year-old claimed that because she "caught an attitude" when she disagreed with rules, her grandmother would chase her, and hit her with a large wooden stick: "She beat me, but I deserved it. She wouldn't do it just to beat me." Others stated that beatings and fistfights were "for my own good though" because "I was messing up"; "I was one of them kids you had to . . . 'cuz, I used to do very stupid things"; or because a father could tolerate only so much before he would "have to hit" his daughter and pin her to the wall by the throat. Respondents also described being sexually assaulted in their homes and witnessing similar assaults on siblings, cousins, and mothers. The few girls who described reporting their sexual victimization to adults in their lives said they were ignored, punished, or accused of lying.

As indicated on the Trauma Inventory, two of the most prevalent indicators of community violence were being "awakened by gunfire" and "witnessing someone being shot or stabbed outside the home." In response to open-ended questions about their neighborhood, and in spontaneous commentaries, the girls provide disturbing detail and context for these events. They knew, for example, not to look out the window from a low floor and that Plexiglas was installed "because they shoot there." They knew to call up to the apartment for someone to meet them at the elevator, and they knew to stay inside after 10 p.m. to avoid gunfights. Despite these precautions, Jennifer[14] explained that violence was "all over" so that even if one was not directly involved, the evidence was there for everyone: "You hear a lot of gunshots, you see the aftereffects when somebody get shot . . . you could be driving by and you see somebody laying there, [and wonder] what happened? They just got shot, or they just [gat] stabbed, they just got in a fight." Shootings were often lethal, and many times the girls knew the victim, the perpetrator, or both. For example, Natalie often accompanied her father on drug-dealing rounds in the neighborhood. She "used to see him shoot people and kill them" and described being with him when he committed the murder for which he was currently incarcerated.

In addition to the general threat of community violence, the young women described incidents where they had been personally threatened. They were jumped at school, robbed, threatened by other girls in disputes over boys, and held at gunpoint by boys demanding sex. Guns were involved in much of the community violence, particularly in the context of drug-dealing activities where arguments over turf, product quality, or money were often "resolved" through gunfire. As one girl noted, however, "You can get shot over the stupidest things. If you take somebody's bike, you're putting your life in jeopardy 'cuz they will shoot you over a bike or a dollar."

## CHILDHOOD LOSSES

As the girls answered our questions about traumatic events and talked about violence in their homes and communities, they also introduced and elaborated on themes of

---

[14]Pseudonyms are used throughout.

loss. These unprompted narratives revealed multiple losses, many of which occurred in violent or socially stigmatized contexts (e.g., homicide, AIDS, drug overdose). Four types of loss were inductively derived from the data: death of a loved one, physical absence, psychological unavailability, and loss of home (Ryder, 2003). Gayle's story demonstrates how closely the four categories are actually intertwined. Her father died before she was born (death of a loved one), and her mother often left her alone outside while the mother did drugs with friends in the house (psychological unavailability). Eventually her mother was "busted" for selling drugs: "She went to jail for like two years (physical absence), and they put me in the foster home (loss of home) and I couldn't get no contact with my mother."

### Death of a Loved One
Most of the girls (82%) indicated on the Trauma Inventory that they had experienced at least one death, and that the deaths were extremely upsetting. The narratives augment this data through descriptions of the loss as well as the girls' emotional responses. Although many of the girls experienced the deaths from disease and accidents as violent events, several of the young women also experienced the particular violence of a homicide. Believing that her uncle's death "had something to do with drugs," Christine recalled "... seeing that he was running down the block, and somebody was chasing him with a gun and they shot him in his head and he fell to the ground. It upset me 'cuz I seen him on the floor bleeding." Elena's younger brother was stabbed to death by a neighborhood boy in the course of a "common" fight: "I was getting ready to take him to the movies" and while he waited outside on the street "some guy did something to him . . . and they just started fighting and the boy must of started stabbing him in the chest." She ran downstairs but "he was just having, it was, like—blood." She described the horror of trying to "keep pressuring him so the blood wouldn't come out" and blamed herself for not preventing or intervening in the fight.

### Physical Absence
Death, as devastating and complete as it is, was unfortunately only one type of loss common to the young women. They also suffered the loss of loved ones who, though alive, were physically absent from their lives. Such absences included situations where parents or primary caregivers were hospitalized, divorced or separated, incarcerated, or living in another country. As indicated from the Trauma Inventory, three-fourths of the girls said their parents were divorced, separated, or "never really together." Jennifer's situation was not atypical: she was six when her parents divorced, and her mother "she wasn't never really ever there 'cuz she was either locked up or I was locked up." Another 16-year-old said her mother had a problem with drugs and thus, ". . . lived place to place, Manhattan and Brooklyn. Place to place. She didn't see me, but it was a close relationship, like if I would see her we would talk . . . . She'll come see me like every six months."

### Psychological Unavailability
In contrast to death or other physical absences were circumstances in which parents or primary caregivers were present but emotionally unavailable. This may have been because of addiction, illness, or disability, or the distractions of attending to other children, work, or personal problems. The girls frequently described adults who appeared incapable or unwilling to emotionally nurture them. Gina's mother was physically absent during much of her life because of a substance abuse problem, and

her grandmother and aunt felt emotionally unavailable to her: "I would want to go outside and do something that like a mother would do with you, but my grandmother wouldn't want to go outside or play cards with me . . . . [My aunt] worked at night so she sleeps in the daytime. So, sometimes she was tired. My grandmother watched soap operas and my aunt slept and I be outside, running the streets." Marcella depicts a home where "there was like nobody I could really talk to" because her mother was alcoholic and the two "didn't have a lot of communication." From the time she was 10 years old Marcella had struggled almost single-handedly to care for her mother, who was confined to a wheelchair, and to control her mother's substance use and attempts at self-harm. While describing her efforts to protect her mother ("grabbing pills outta her hand, knives and stuff"), Marcella segued into a story of sexual assault in her home by one of her mother's friends. Consumed by her own concerns, the mother was unaware and thus unavailable to protect her. Marcella later filed charges on her own, but never went to court because "I didn't have nobody to take me."

### Loss of Home

More than one-fifth of the respondents indicated on the Trauma Inventory that they had lost their home. The girls told of being evicted by landlords, or forced to move because their buildings were unlivable. One girl described her apartment building as "always on fire" because "every crackhead that had a lighter came to that building to shoot up—to smoke and they kept dropping lighters and stuff." Eventually, someone burned a hole in her apartment's ceiling and her family had to move out. In another case, Lisa explained that the extensive drug use and related violence in her Bronx neighborhood was "how come we be moving," searching for a safe place to stay. Although closed-ended interview items were used to establish that one-quarter (24%) of the girls had been in foster care, we did not anticipate the need to ask about other types of out-of-home placements when designing the interview schedule. In fact, nearly all of the young women revealed in the narrative data that they had spent time in other out-of-home placements. Generally, they could not remember where their placements had been, only barely distinguishing between foster families and institutions such as group homes, psychiatric evaluation centers, and juvenile justice facilities. The differences seemed unimportant—what the girls did describe was being without a home base and the disorienting process of moving among facilities or alternating between several residences and institutions. For example, after struggling to recount years of different placements, 13-year-old Jackie sighed: "I haven't been home since, I don't— it's been a while . . . I guess it's for a long time now. I'm saying that I've been around and around and around. I went back and forth and back and forth."

### COMBINING METHODS

In this research, our semistructured interview schedule included both closed- and open-ended questions in order to develop a comprehensive picture of trauma in these girls' lives. We asked the respondents about their experiences with the 23 items listed on a Trauma Inventory. We also posed open-ended questions that enabled the girls to bring to the forefront aspects of their lives they deemed important to reveal. The narratives provide context and complexity and reveal additional experiences and the girls' appraisal of those events. As others have noted, inventories and open-ended methods each have particular strengths in the study of trauma and thus the use of both within a single study is particularly valuable (Duggal et al., 2000). The application of this dual approach to trauma measurement holds particular promise (and urgency) in the study of young female offenders. Recent studies that have used open-ended methods, including our own, have identified traumatic events that would have gone unnoticed if researchers were reliant on general-population trauma inventories. This has two important implications: (a) a population-specific inventory is needed to accurately capture the trauma experiences of incarcerated girls, and (b) further open-ended work is necessary to develop such an inventory. Besides the identification of traumatic events, open-ended data collection is invaluable in revealing the context of these events. Girls' narrative responses suggest that their trauma experiences are unique not only in type but also in perception, such as the apparent normalization of recurring events.

## DISCUSSION

The number of girls in trouble with the law is increasing, and as these young offenders enter detention and residential facilities they bring with them extensive and complex histories of trauma including loss and violence. Recent research indicates that even those who do not fully develop post-traumatic stress syndrome will suffer from the mental health effects of their untreated trauma histories. Given the dearth of overall mental health treatment within the juvenile justice system, and of trauma-related treatment specifically, it is likely that their troubled pasts will compound the probability of future difficulties. Given the substantial body of research linking trauma to a variety of subsequent problem behaviors including substance use, sexual risk-taking, and a predisposition to depression and additional trauma exposure, the need for intervention is particularly compelling. And yet, detailed information about girls' trauma histories are not routinely collected by juvenile justice agencies (Lewis, 2006; Simkins & Katz, 2002), and because mental health services are scarce in juvenile justice settings, institutions are ill-prepared to effectively intervene in this cycle.

The development of effective treatment programs to address trauma among adolescents is partially hampered by inconsistent or inadequate measures of trauma (Greenwald, 2000). Thus, as efforts to address trauma-related problems of girls while they are in the custody of the juvenile justice system are developed, an important initial consideration facing clinicians and researchers embarking on each new project is how to define and measure trauma.

Currently, the definition of and measurements for trauma among incarcerated girls are diverse. Growing evidence suggests that what is considered beyond the norm of life experiences for the general population (and thus likely to be considered traumatic) is very different for girls involved in the juvenile justice system. Research has begun to identify events specific to the population of primarily urban, poor minority juveniles and has, for example, begun to identify and ask about experiences such as finding or viewing a dead body (particularly in studies using the PTSD module of the DISC-IV), parental incarcerations (Smith, Leve, & Chamberlain, 2006), and girls' own committing offense (Cauffman, Feldman, Waterman, & Steiner, 1998) and incarceration (Ryder, 2003). The field is not yet at the stage, however, where researchers have a comprehensive understanding of the traumatic events experienced by this group. Given that the study of trauma is still a fledgling field, particularly as it pertains to girls in the justice system, we must be careful not to prematurely narrow applicable definitions, while we simultaneously work toward developing population-specific inventories.

The design and implementation of gender-specific policies and interventions for girls who have experienced and witnessed extensive trauma require definitions and measures that reflect and represent girls' experiences. To describe, understand, and explain social and psychological phenomena, social scientists need to be able to conceptualize them in meaningful ways. Theoretically the adequacy of a conceptualization is based on the extent to which a word or symbol used to represent a phenomenon is understood by all observers as having essentially the same meaning (Kaplan 1964; Lazarsfeld & Rosenberg, 1955). Moreover, in the realm of policy and programs where decisions and actions have an authentic and immediate impact on the lives of individuals, the conceptualization of trauma ought to be grounded in the experience of the people involved, that is, juvenile female offenders.

In this chapter we reviewed the varied ways that the nature and prevalence of trauma has been defined and measured among girls under custody of the juvenile justice system and suggest a classification of four approaches: studies that (a) use unstructured or semistructured interviews only, without a checklist of events; (b) use an inventory or checklist of events that is based on general population research; (c) assemble comprehensive and population-specific trauma inventories; and (d) combine a population-specific and relatively comprehensive inventory of events with open-ended questioning. It is our contention that future studies that use a combination of closed-ended inventories or "checklists" and semistructured, open-ended interviews are well situated to advance an inclusive definition (and thereby facilitate a comprehensive understanding) of the nature and scope of trauma as identified by incarcerated girls.

### Population-Specific Trauma Inventories

There is a general need for thorough and accurate assessment of trauma among adolescents in order to implement appropriate interventions (Strand, Sarmiento, & Pasquale, 2005). The research suggests that incarcerated girls routinely experience a unique but poorly defined set of traumas that are unlikely to be adequately addressed through general-population instruments. Studies that have focused on maltreatment, other specific traumatic events, or PTSD symptoms have each made significant contributions to the literature. Yet, on their own, each falls short of presenting a comprehensive profile of traumatic events in the lives of incarcerated girls. The criteria for PTSD, for example, draw heavily on aspects of terror, yet it is now recognized that "few traumatic events that cause long-lasting harm involve solely or even mostly terror" (Becker-Blease & Freyd, 2005, p. 405). Sexual abuse may involve no immediate fear for life, but the sense of betrayal and isolation may be as predictive of negative symptoms as the amount of terror (Herman, 1997). Other research suggests that even events considered "stressful," but not necessarily traumatic, can actually produce PTSD symptoms. In a general adult population sample, Mol and colleagues (2005) found that situations that they classified as life events (relational problems, problems with work, chronic illness) generated at least as many post-traumatic stress disorder (PTSD) symptoms as traumatic events when the life events were severe and chronic.

The review of approaches currently used in trauma-related studies and in our own work has helped to identify a number of areas for future research. For example, witnessing violence and victimizations are not always included on inventories, and yet focus group data and open-ended questioning with incarcerated girls consistently indicate extensive and extreme amounts of both. Furthermore, although many forms of victimization include loss (Becker-Blease & Freyd, 2005) few inventories specifically ask about or recognize such losses as traumatic (Carrion & Steiner, 2000). Girls' narratives, however, reveal that multiple forms of loss, victimization, and violence are closely linked in their lives.

Although a number of trauma-related instruments do include the death of a loved one, it is important to also specifically consider nonlethal losses of parents and other loved ones due to physical unavailability (e.g., incarceration) and psychological unavailability (e.g., mental health problems, drug and alcohol use) (Ryder, 2007; Smith, Leve, & Chamberlain, 2006). Parental absence may also result from divorce or legal separation, and instruments geared to this population should structure parental questions in such a way as to encompass the loss of parents who were never in a long-term committed relationship, the loss of relatives who may have served as primary caregivers, and multiple serial intimate partners of the girls' biological parents.

Other events that should be included in research specific to this population include losing homes in ways reflective of the chaos that characterizes many of these girls' lives, such as placement in foster care, detention, and other correctional facilities; family eviction; and being ordered to move out by a parent or other adult. Only a few inventories include loss of home, but narrative accounts indicate that this population commonly experiences out-of-home placements beyond foster care and juvenile justice commitments. Some of our respondents also referred to their experiences with serious and chronic illness, surgery, and disabilities—both their own and those of people close to them. The diminishment or loss of physical health should be addressed more directly in trauma inventories, such as in Cook et al.'s study (2005), which includes a life-threatening illness in the survey of adult female offenders.

Overall, most of our items specified the location of the event (home vs. community) but not all items were mutually exclusive. The porous boundaries between home and community violence may lessen the importance of the distinction, but it is best to err on the side of specificity and clarity while this area of research continues to develop. For example, an event such as "ever awakened by gunfire," which had a high frequency (61%) on our inventory and was discussed in the girls' narratives, typically is not addressed by other checklists, yet may be an important indicator of both home and community violence.

Our inventory was not specifically designed for girls, and we did not include items pertaining to reproductive issues (e.g., pregnancy, miscarriage, abortion) or risky sexual behaviors. Owen and Bloom (1997), however, found that 22% had entered a juvenile program or facility while pregnant. This was not examined as a traumatic event but, depending on the circumstances, pregnancy could be. Reproductive and sexual relations take on additional urgency in light of recent research on girls and young women sexually coerced and exploited by older men in group sex environments, placing them at risk for pregnancy and HIV/AIDS (Krauss et al., 2006, p. 59). Information about reproduction and sexually transmitted infections is important to collect systematically in future studies.

The young women's responses in our study also indicate the importance of wording in interview questions, particularly when referring to sensitive subjects such as sex and violence. When asking about experiences of "physical or sexual abuse," for example, one must be cautious about taking answers at face value; "abuse" has many different meanings. Furthermore, girls often have difficulty naming what has happened and may minimize events. They may not volunteer information unless asked directly and clearly and in terms that make sense to them developmentally, culturally, and socially (Prescott, 1998). As in any research, it is best to ask questions about specific acts that are operationalized (e.g., "hit/bit kicked" and "unwanted sexual touch" provide greater specificity than "physical abuse" and "sexual abuse") and mutually exclusive. Insensitive or vague questioning also may send the message that girls will be better off remaining silent. Conversely, narrative data can greatly augment our understanding of the nature and context of traumatic events and provide a space for girls to talk about their lives. We found that most of the young women wanted to talk—perhaps because few adults had demonstrated an interest in really listening to them. The research questions should always drive a particular study, and depending on the purpose, narrative data may or may not be appropriate. However, during this early stage of trauma studies, data derived from open-ended questions are critical to our understanding of girls' lives and help to build appropriate population-specific inventories.

The mental health needs of incarcerated girls are extensive and present unique challenges for the juvenile justice system. There is a particular need for programming to address the multiple and long-lasting effects of trauma as experienced by this population, which has been shown to be highly vulnerable. The creation of effective interventions, however, depends on empirical data that is population-specific. As the study of trauma among the general population of children continues to advance, it is important that instruments and measurements are refined to encompass the experiences of the growing number of justice-involved girls. Our research suggests that the field will be well served by studies that include both checklists that reflect a wide range of experiences and multiple forms of victimization and loss, as well as open-ended questioning that enables new information to emerge from girls' own testimony. The resultant data are essential to building comprehensive and population-specific trauma measures, working in service to girls' programmatic needs.

## References

Abram, K., Teplin, L., Charles, D., Longworth, S., McClelland, G., & Dulcan, M. (2004). Posttraumatic stress disorder & trauma in youth in juvenile detention. *Archives of General Psychiatry, 61*(4), 403–410.

Abrantes, A., Hoffmann, N., & Anton, R. (2005). Prevalence of co-occurring disorders among juveniles committed to detention centers. *International Journal of Offender Therapy and Comparative Criminology, 49*(2), 179–193.

Acoca, L. (1998). Outside/inside: The violation of American girls at home, on the streets, and in the juvenile justice system. *Crime & Delinquency, 44*(4), 561–589.

Alemagno, S., Shaffer-King, E., & Hammel, R. (2006). Juveniles in detention. How do girls differ from boys? *Journal of Correctional Health Care, 12*(1), 45–53.

American Psychiatric Association. (1994). *Diagnostic and statistical manual of mental disorders* (4th ed.). Washington, DC: Author.

Arnold, R. (1990). Processes of victimization and criminalization of Black women. *Social Justice, 17*(3), 153–166.

Battle, C., Zlotnick, C., Najavits, L., Guittierrez, M., & Winsor, C. (2003). Posttraumatic stress disorder and substance use disorder among incarcerated women. In P. C. Ouimette & P. J. Brown (Eds.), *Trauma and substance abuse: Causes, consequences and treatment of comorbid disorders* (pp. 209–225). Washington, DC: American Psychological Association.

Becker-Blease, K., & Freyd, J. (2005). Beyond PTSD. An evolving relationship between trauma theory and family violence research. *Journal of Interpersonal Violence, 20*(4), 403–411.

Belknap, J., Holsinger, K., & Dunn, M. (1997). Understanding incarcerated girls: The results of a focus group study. *The Prison Journal, 77*(4), 381–404.

Blackburn, A., Mullings, J., Marquart, J., & Trulson, C. (2007). The next generation of prisoners: Toward an understanding of violent institutionalized delinquents. *Youth Violence and Juvenile Justice, 5*(1), 35–56.

Bloom, B. (Ed.). (2003). *Gendered justice. Addressing female offenders*. Durham, NC: Carolina Academic Press.

Breslau, N., Chilcoat, H., Kessler, R., & Davis, G. (1999). Previous exposure to trauma and PTSD effects of subsequent trauma: Results from the Detroit Area Survey of Trauma. *American Journal of Psychiatry, 156*(6), 902–907.

Breslau, N., Davis, G., Andreski, P., & Peterson, E. (1991). Traumatic events and posttraumatic stress disorder in an urban population of young adults. *Archives of General Psychiatry, 48,* 216–222.

Briere, J. (1992). Methodological issues in the study of sexual abuse effects. *Journal of Consulting and Clinical Psychology, 60*(2), 196–203.

Brosky, B., & Lally, S. (2004). Prevalence of trauma, PTSD, and dissociation in court-referred adolescents. *Journal of Interpersonal Violence, 19*(7), 801–814.

Browne, A., & Finkelhor, D. (1986). Impact of child sexual abuse: A review of the research. *Psychological Bulletin, 99*(1), 66–77.

Carr, A. (2005). Contributions to the study of violence and trauma. Multisystemic therapy, exposure therapy, attachment styles, and therapy process research. *Journal of Interpersonal Violence, 20*(4), 426–435.

Carrion, V., & Steiner, H. (2000). Trauma and dissociation in delinquent adolescents. *Journal of the American Academy of Child & Adolescent Psychiatry, 39*(3), 353–359.

Cauffman, E., Feldman, S., Waterman, J., & Steiner, H. (1998). *Posttraumatic stress disorder among female juvenile offenders. Journal of the American Academy of Child and Adolescent Psychiatry, 37*(11), 1209–1216.

Clausen, A., & Crittenden, P. (1991). Physical and psychological maltreatment: Relations among types of maltreatment. *Child Abuse & Neglect, 15*(1/2), 5–18.

Cohen, L., Kessler, R., & Gordon, L. (1995). *Measuring stress*. New York: Oxford University Press.

Cook, S., Smith, S., Tusher, C., & Raiford, J. (2005). Self-reports of traumatic events in a random sample of incarcerated women. *Women & Criminal Justice, 16*(1/2), 107–126.

Crimmins, S., Brownstein, H., Spunt, B., Ryder, J., & Warley, R. (1998). *Learning about violence and drugs among adolescents. Final report to the National Institute on Drug Abuse*. Grant No. R01 DA08679. Washington, DC: National Institutes of Health.

Crimmins, S., Cleary, S., Brownstein, H., Spunt, B., & Warley, R. (2000). Trauma, drugs and violence among juvenile offenders. *Journal of Psychoactive Drugs, 32*(1), 43–54.

Crimmins, S., Langley, S., Brownstein, H. & Spunt, B. (1997). Convicted women who have killed children. A self-psychology perspective. *Journal of Interpersonal Violence, 12*(1), 49–69.

Cronon, W. (1992). A place for stories: Nature, history, and narrative. *The Journal of American History, 78*(4), 1347–1376.

Dembo, R., Schmeidler, J., Guida, J., & Rahman, A. (1998). A further study of gender differences in service needs among youths entering a juvenile assessment center. *Journal of Child and Adolescent Substance Abuse, 7*(4), 49–77.

Dembo, R., Williams, L., Lavoie, L., & Berry, E. (1989). Physical abuse, sexual victimization, and illicit drug use. *Violence and Victims, 4*(2), 121–138.

Dise-Lewis, J. (1988). The Life Events and Coping Inventory: An assessment of stress in children. *Psychosomatic Medicine, 50,* 484–499.

Dixon, A., Howie, P., & Starling, J. (2004). Psychopathology in female juvenile offenders. *Journal of Child Psychology and Psychiatry, 45*(6), 1150–1158.

Dixon, A., Howie, P., & Starling, J. (2005). Trauma exposure, posttraumatic stress, and psychiatric comorbidity in female juvenile offenders. *Journal of the American Academy of Child & Adolescent Psychiatry, 44*(8), 798–806.

Duggal, S., Malkoff-Schwartz, S., Birmaher, B., Anderson, B., Matty, M., Houck, P., et al., (2000). Assessment of life stress in adolescents: Self-report versus interview methods. *Journal of the American Academy of Child and Adolescent Psychiatry, 39,* 445–451.

English, D., Widom, C., & Brandford, C. (2001). *Childhood victimization and delinquency, adult criminality, and violent criminal behavior: A replication and extension.* Washington, DC: U.S. National Institute of Justice.

Finkelhor, D. (1995). The victimization of children: A developmental perspective. *American Journal of Orthopsychiatry, 65*(2), 177–193.

Finkelhor, D., Ormrod, R., & Turner, H. (2007). Poly-victimization: A neglected component in child victimization. *Child Abuse & Neglect, 3*(1), 7–26.

Gaarder, E., & Belknap, J. (2002). Tenuous borders: Girls transferred to adult court. *Criminology, 40*(3), 481–517.

Garland, A., Hough, R., McCabe, K., Yeh, M., Wood, P., & Aarons, G. (2001). Prevalence of psychiatric disorders in youths across sectors of care. *Journal of the American Academy of Child & Adolescent Psychiatry, 40*(4), 409–418.

Gavazzi, S., Yarcheck, C., & Chesney-Lind, M. (2006). Global risk indicators and the role of gender in a juvenile detention sample. *Criminal Justice and Behavior, 33*(5), 597–612.

Giaconia, R., Reinherz, H., Silverman, A., Pakiz, B., Frost, A., & Cohen, E. (1995). Traumas and posttraumatic stress disorder in a community population of older adolescents. *Journal of the American Academy of Child and Adolescent Psychiatry, 34*(10), 1369–1380.

Gilfus, M. (1992). From victims to survivors to offenders: Women's routes of entry and immersion in street crime. *Women and Criminal Justice, 4*(1), 63–89.

Gold, S. (2000). *Not trauma alone: Therapy for child abuse survivors in family and social context.* New York: Brunner/Mazel.

Golzari, M., Hunt, S., & Anoshiravani, A. (2006). The health status of youth in juvenile detention facilities. *Journal of Adolescent Health, 38*(6), 776–782.

Goodkind, S., Ng, I., & Sarri, R. (2006). The impact of sexual abuse in the lives of young women involved or at-risk of involvement with the juvenile justice system. *Violence Against Women, 12*(5), 456–477.

Gover, A., & MacKenzie, D. (2003). Child maltreatment and adjustment to juvenile correctional institutions. *Criminal Justice and Behavior, 30*(3), 374–396.

Grant, K., Compas, B., Stuhlmacher, A., Thurm, A., McMahon, S., & Halpert, J. (2003). Stressors and child and adolescent psychopathology: Moving from markers to mechanisms of risk. *Psychological Bulletin, 128*(3), 447–466.

Green, B., Miranda, J., Daroowalla, A., & Siddique, J. (2005). Trauma exposure, mental health functioning, and program needs of women in jail. *Crime & Delinquency, 51*(1), 133–151.

Greenwald, R. (2000). A trauma-focused individual therapy approach for adolescents with conduct disorder. *International Journal of Offender Therapy and Comparative Criminology, 44*(2), 146–163.

Harlow, C. (1999). *Prior abuse reported by inmates and probationers. Bureau of Justice Statistics Selected Findings.* Washington, DC: Office of Justice Programs. NCJ 172879.

Herman, J. (1997). *Trauma and recovery.* New York: Basic Books Inc.

Horowitz, K., Wiene, S., & Jekel, J. (1995). PTSD symptoms in urban adolescent girls: Compounded community trauma. *Journal of American Academy of Adolescent Psychiatry, 34*(10), 1353–1361.

Horwitz, A., Widom, C., & White, H. (2001). The impact of childhood abuse and neglect on adult mental health: A prospective study. *Journal of Health and Social Behavior, 4*(2), 184–210.

Hoyt, S., & Scherer, D. (1998). Female juvenile delinquency: Misunderstood by the juvenile justice system, neglected by social science. *Law and Human Behavior, 22*(1), 81–107.

Jackson, A., Veneziano, C., & Ice, W. (2005). *Violence and trauma. The past 20 and next 10 years. Journal of International Violence, 20*(4), 470–478.

Janoff-Bulman, R. (1992). *Shattered assumptions. Toward a new psychology of trauma.* New York: The Free Press.

Johnston, D. (1995) Effects of parental incarceration. In K. Gabel & D. Johnston (Eds.), *Children of incarcerated parents* (pp. 59–88). New York: Lexington Books.

Kaplan, A. (1964). *The conduct of inquiry: Methodology for behavioral science.* San Francisco: Chandler.

Kataoka, S., Zima, B., Dupre, D., Moreno, K., Yang, X., & McCracken, J. (2001). Mental health problems and service use among female juvenile offenders: Their relationship to criminal history. *Journal of the American Academy of Child and Adolescent Psychiatry, 40*(5), 549–555.

Kaufman, J., & Widom, C. (1999). Childhood victimization, running away and delinquency. *Journal of Research in Crime and Delinquency, 36*(4), 347–370.

Krauss, B., O'Day, J., Godfrey, C., Rente, K., Freidin, E., Bratt, E., et al., (2006). Who wins in the status games? Violence, sexual violence, and an emerging single standard among adolescent women. *Annals of the New York Academy of Sciences, 1087,* 56–73.

Lazarsfeld, P. F., & Rosenberg, M. (1955). *The language of social research: A reader in the methodology of social research.* New York: Free Press.

Lazarus, R., & Folkman, S. (1984). *Stress, appraisal and coping.* New York: Springer.

Lederman, C., Dakof, G., Larrea, M., & Li, H. (2004). Characteristics of adolescent females in juvenile detention. *International Journal of Law and Psychiatry, 27*(4), 321–337.

Lerner, F. (1996). Searching the traumatic stress literature. In E. Carlson (Ed.), *Trauma Research Methodology.* Lutherville, MD: The Sidran Press.

Lewis, M. (2006). *Custody and control: Conditions of confinement in New York's juvenile prisons for girls.* New York: Human Rights Watch/American Civil Liberties Association.

Luthar, S., & Zigler, E. (1991). Vulnerability and competence: A review of research on resilience in childhood. *American Journal of Orthopsychiatry, 61*(1), 6–22.

Maas-Robinson, S., & Thompson, P. (2006). Mood disorders in incarcerated women. In R. Braithwaite, K. Arriola, & C. Newkirk (Eds.), *Health issues among incarcerated women* (pp. 91–111). New Brunswick, NJ: Rutgers University Press.

Marsteller, F., Brogan, D., Smith, I., Ash, P., Daniels, D., Rolka, D., et al., (1997). *The prevalence of substance use disorders among juveniles admitted to regional youth detention centers operated by the Georgia Department of Children and Youth Services.* Center for Substance Abuse Treatment Final Report. Available at http://www.behav.com/projects/CSATFinalReport.html

McClellan, D., Farabee, D., & Crouch, B. (1997). Early victimization, drug use, and criminality. A comparison of male and female prisoners. *Criminal Justice and Behavior, 24*(4), 455–476.

McLeod, J., & Kessler, R. (1990). Socioeconomic status differences in vulnerability to undesirable life events. *Journal of Health and Social Behavior, 31,* 162–172.

Mitchell, K., & Finkelhor, D. (2001). Risk of crime victimization among youth exposed to domestic violence. *Journal of Interpersonal Violence, 16*(9), 944–964.

Mol, S., Arntz, A., Metsemaker, J., Dinant, G., Vilters-van Montfort, P., & Knottnerus, J. (2005). Symptoms of post-traumatic stress disorder after non-traumatic events: Evidence from an open population study. *British Journal of Psychiatry, 186,* 494–499.

National Association of State Mental Health Program Directors. (2001). *Position statement on mental health services in a juvenile justice population.* Alexandria, VA: Author. Available at http://www.nasmhpd.org/general_files/position_statement/JuvenileJustice.pdf

National Mental Health Association. (2004). *Mental health treatment for youth in the juvenile justice system. A compendium of promising practices.* Alexandria, VA: Author.

Newman, E. (2002) Assessment of PTSD and trauma exposure in adolescents. *Journal of Aggression, Maltreatment, and Trauma, 6*(1), 59–78.

Odgers, C., Reppucci, N., & Moretti, M. (2005). Nipping psychopathy in the bud: An examination of the convergent, predictive, and the theoretical utility of the PCL-YV among adolescent girls. *Behavioral Sciences and the Law, 23*(6), 743–763.

Owen, B., & Bloom, B. (1997). *Profiling the needs of young female offenders: A protocol and pilot study, final report.* NCJ 179988, Washington, DC: U.S. Department of Justice, National Institute of Justice.

Prescott, L. (1998). *Improving policy and practice for adolescent girls with co-occurring disorders in the juvenile justice system.* Delmar, New York: The GAINS Center.

Rivera, B., & Widom, C. (1990). Childhood victimization and violent offending. *Violence and Victims, 5*(1), 19–35.

Robertson, A., & Husain, J. (2001). *Prevalence of mental illness and substance abuse disorders among incarcerated juvenile offenders.* Mississippi State, MS: Mississippi Department of Public Safety, and the Mississippi Department of Mental Health, Division of Children and Youth Services.

Robinson, R. (2007). "It's not easy to know who I am": Gender salience and cultural place in the treatment of a "delinquent" adolescent mother. *Feminist Criminology, 2*(1), 31–56.

Ruchkin, V., Schwab-Stone, M., Koposov, R., Vermeiren, R., & Steiner, H. (2002). Violence exposure, posttraumatic stress, & personality in juvenile delinquents. *Journal of the American Academy of Child & Adolescent Psychiatry, 41*(3), 322–329.

Ryder, J. (2003). *Antecedents of violent behavior. Early childhood trauma in the lives of adolescent female offenders.* Unpublished doctoral dissertation, City University of New York.

Ryder, J. (2007). "I wasn't really bonded with my family": Attachment, loss and violence among adolescent female offenders. *Critical Criminology, 15*(1), 19–40.

Silverthorn, P., & Frick, P. (1999). Developmental pathways to antisocial behavior: The delayed-onset pathway in girls. *Development and Psychopathology, 11*(1), 101–126.

Simkins, S., & Katz, S. (2002). Criminalizing abused girls. *Violence Against Women, 8*(12), 1474–1499.

Smith, C., & Thornberry, T. (1995). The relationship between childhood maltreatment and adolescent involvement in delinquency. *Criminology, 33*, 451–477.

Smith, D., Leve, L., & Chamberlain, P. (2006). Adolescent girls' offending and health-risking sexual behavior: The predictive role of trauma. *Child Maltreatment, 11*(4), 346–353.

Snyder, H., & Sickmund, M. (2006). *Juvenile Offenders and Victims: 2006 National Report.* Washington, DC: U.S. Department of Justice, Office of Justice Programs, Office of Juvenile Justice and Delinquency Prevention.

Soloman, E., & Heide, K. (1999). Type III trauma: Toward a more effective conceptualization of psychological trauma. *International Journal of Offender Therapy and Comparative Criminology, 43*(2), 202–210.

Steiner, H., Garcia, I. G., & Matthews, Z. (1997). Posttraumatic stress disorder in incarcerated juvenile delinquents. *Journal of the American Academy of Child & Adolescent Psychiatry, 36*(3), 357–65.

Strand, V., Sarmiento, T., & Pasquale, L. (2005). Assessment and screening tools for trauma in children and adolescents. A review. *Trauma, Violence & Abuse, 6*(1), 55–78.

Teplin, L., Abram, K., McClelland, G., Dulcan, M., & Mericle, A. (2002). Psychiatric disorders in youth in juvenile detention. *Archives of General Psychiatry, 59*(12), 1133–1143.

Terr, L. (1990). *Too scared to cry.* New York: Harper Collins.

Thomas, J., Gourley, G., & Mele, N. (2005). The availability of behavioral health services for youth in the juvenile justice system. *Journal of the American Psychiatric Nurses Association, 11*(3), 156–163.

U.S. House of Representatives, Committee on Government Reform. (2004). *Incarceration of youth who are waiting for community mental health services in the United States.* Washington, DC: Author.

Valentine, P. (2000). Traumatic Incident Reduction I: Traumatized women inmates: Particulars of practice and research. *Journal of Offender Rehabilitation, 31*(3/4), 1–15.

Vincent, G., & Grisso, T. (2005). A developmental perspective on adolescent personality, psychopathology, and delinquency. In T. Grisso, G. Vincent, & D. Seagrave (Eds.), *Mental health screening and assessment in juvenile justice* (pp. 22–43). New York: The Guildford Press.

Wasserman, G., Ko, S., & McReynolds, L. (August 2004). Assessing the mental health needs of youth in juvenile justice settings. *Juvenile Justice Bulletin.* Washington, DC: Office of Juvenile Justice and Delinquency Prevention.

Whitbeck, L., & Simons, R. (1993). Life on the streets. The victimization of runaway and homeless adolescents. *Youth & Society, 2*(1), 108–125.

Widom, C. (1989). The cycle of violence. *Science, 244*(4901), 160–166.

Widom, C., Ireland, T., & Glynn, P. J. (1995). Alcohol abuse in abused and neglected children followed-up: Are they at increased risk? *Journal of Studies on Alcohol, 56*(2), 207–217.

Wood, J., Foy, D., Goguen, C., Pynoos, R., & James, C. (2002). Violence exposure and PTSD among delinquent girls. *Journal of Aggression, Maltreatment & Trauma, 6*(1), 109–126.

Zahn, M. (2006). The girls study group: Its creation and achievements. *The Criminologist, 31*(5), 1, 3–6.

Zlotnick, C. (1997). Posttraumatic stress syndrome (PTSD), PTSD comorbidity, and childhood abuse among incarcerated women. *Journal of Nervous and Mental Disease, 185*(12), 761–763.

# CHAPTER 4

# THE CHALLENGES OF POLICING THE MENTALLY ILL:

## An Exploration of Gendered and Ungendered Perspectives

**Mary Dodge**

**Terri Schreiber**

### ABSTRACT

In the 1960s, approaches to policing the mentally ill changed dramatically as the criminal justice system became overwhelmingly responsible for dealing with a displaced population. The movement toward deinstitution-alization created numerous complexities, as the "criminalization of the mentally ill" became the standard for dealing with disturbed individuals engaged in misdemeanor and felony offenses. A seemingly unrelated development in policing also altered law enforcement as a substantial number of female officers were assigned to patrol. The historical perspective that women entered the realm of policing based primarily on the notion of "helping others" in a social work role has become debatable. Recent research on policewomen suggests that crime fighting and excitement represent much of the appeal for all officers—male and female. Other researchers, however, have found that women in policing are more likely, compared to male counterparts, to approach arrest situations in a caring, compassionate manner, which may result in better communication and de-escalation of potentially violent encounters. This article presents exploratory research based on qualitative data that examines differences in gendered interactions between police officers and the mentally ill.

Two major trends in the 1960s had a significant impact on mentally ill individuals and law enforcement. First, the movement toward deinstitutionalization created a host of complexities as the "criminalization of the mentally ill" became the standard for dealing with disturbed individuals engaged in misdemeanor and felony offenses (Abramson, 1972). Law enforcement agencies became the primary responders with expectations that police officers could act as social workers or "street corner psychiatrists" as calls for service involving the mentally ill significantly increased (Teplin & Pruett, 1992). Second, there was a seemingly unrelated development as police departments experienced a substantial increase in the number of female officers assigned to patrol. Many scholars and practitioners expected that women in policing would result in a "gentler and kinder" approach that employed increased empathy and better communication in daily interactions with community members and suspects with special needs. Today, policing the mentally ill remains problematic, however, as researchers and practitioners attempt to identify commonalities among approaches and attitudes linked to officers that impact encounters and outcomes with the mentally ill. This study gives voice to the concerns, frustrations, and reality of policing the mentally ill based on the perspectives of male and female officers who relate the means and methods of dealing with the constant challenges they face in the field.

## THE IMPACT OF DEINSTITUTIONALIZATION ON POLICING

Many of the changes in public policy related to the mentally ill resulted from a social outcry that the conditions within state mental hospitals were deplorable, a belief that mentally ill persons were entitled to basic freedoms, and the introduction of new psychoactive drugs as treatment alternatives that alleviated the need for incapacitation (*Deinstitutionalization of the Homeless Mentally Ill*, 2006). The unanticipated consequences were, according to the *Deinstitutionalization* report, the lack of placement options and a surge in the homeless population as the mentally ill left their rooming houses, family homes, and other temporary shelters and began to "drift" from place to place without "goals, direction, or ties" (p. 4). The drift through life for the mentally ill population is motivated, in part, by desires to engage in alcohol or drug use, to shirk labels of being "ill," or to avoid monitoring by the mental health system. This has resulted in more homelessness and greater involvement in the criminal justice system. Police officers are commonly described as "primary gatekeepers" who have the authority and discretion to determine whether or not individuals with acute psychiatric disorders are routed to mental health facilities or through the criminal justice system (Lamb & Weinberger, 1998). Consequently, the role of the police officer on patrol continues to evolve as law enforcement agencies struggle to find solutions on how to manage this often untreated and, at times, "bizarre or disruptive" class of suspects and victims.

Police officers face limited options in cases involving the mentally ill: no action, informal resolutions, arrest, or commitment. Civil commitment laws were designed to create the legal basis for hospitalizing severely mentally ill persons if they exhibited behaviors that demonstrated that they were a danger to themselves, a danger to others, or gravely disabled. Over time, involuntary commitment became more difficult because of statutory requirements and the lack of bed space in the treatment facilities, which resulted in increased community presence of the mentally ill, and attempts by the police to find alternatives to resolve problematic situations (Cooper, McLearen, & Zapf, 2004; Laberge & Morin, 1995; Stefan, 1996; Teplin, 1984a). Numerous research studies have documented the difficulties and frustrations police face while processing mentally ill suspects at most hospitals, including, for example, long waits in emergency rooms, complicated admission procedures, refusals to admit, and quick releases (Fennell, 1991; Green, 1997; Laberge & Morin, 1995; Lamb & Grant, 1982; Teplin, 1984b). In most jurisdictions, the mentally ill offender may actually receive higher levels of care in jail, although overcrowding and underfunding limit the amount of treatment (Lamb & Weinberger, 1998).

Police departments continue to develop and test best practices in dealing with the challenges presented by the mentally ill. A 1996 survey of 194 police departments in the United States found that 96% of the departments, which served populations of 100,000, had few specialized response approaches for dealing with mentally ill persons, although 75% of the respondents rated agency personnel as being moderately or very effective when dealing with the population (Deane, Steadman, Borum, Veysey, & Morrissey, 1999). In most cases, officers are confident about their abilities to identify the mentally ill, although many express frustration over the lack of coordination with mental health professionals (Cooper et al., 2004; Green, 1997). Cooper et al., however, noted that their findings show that 3 out of 10 officers in the study were unaware that the department had a mental health liaison to assist with dispositions. Green's research in Honolulu identified two promising programs designed to assist officers: Project Outreach includes specialized personnel who can respond to crisis intervention, aid in assessment, and provide referrals to social service agencies; the Crisis Response System Program works with law enforcement in crisis intervention and runs a 12-bed shelter for the mentally ill, although additional evaluation research that examines the effectiveness of collaborative approaches is still needed to more fully understand what work works best.

Stereotypes held by the public and police are common, and perceptions of a high level of dangerousness often are attached to the mentally ill, although extensive studies show no greater proclivity toward violence by the mentally ill compared to the general population (Steadman et al., 1998; Watson, Corrigan, & Ottati, 2004). Research in England, for example, discovered that police officers were likely to stigmatize and discriminate against the mentally ill offender (Pinfold et al., 2003). Overall, previous research studies suggest that law enforcement agents view the mentally ill as extremely dangerous, particularly younger, less experienced officers (e.g., Kaminski, DiGiovanni, & Downs, 2004; Ruiz & Miller, 2004). Perceptions of dangerousness of the individual with mental illness can lead to self-fulfilling prophecies that result in violent rather than peaceful outcomes and may heighten the risk in an encounter merely from an officer's body language or tone of voice (Cooper et al., 2004; Ruiz & Miller, 2004). A survey of 164 police departments by Ruiz and Miller in Pennsylvania found that 43% of respondents agreed or strongly agreed that persons with mental illness are dangerous, and 49% said they felt "uneasy," worried," or "threatened" in the presence of the mentally ill. Watson et al. (2004), based on vignettes presented to 382 police officers, also found that a significant percentage believed that "schizophrenics" were less responsible for their situations, although more dangerous compared to suspects without a mental illness label.

Several research studies have explored police perceptions of the mentally ill and the decision-making process on whether to arrest or refer to mental health agencies (Cooper et al., 2004; Green, 1977; Ruiz & Miller, 2004). Green found that police officers with the greatest experience were less likely to take action if the suspect appeared to be suffering from a psychological disorder. The results also suggest that leniency in encounters with the mentally ill is tied to the strict requirements for an involuntary commitment. Green noted the unspoken expectations: "There is a significant amount of institutional pressure from the police department and the emergency room personnel for the police officers to solve the problems associated with the mentally ill on an informal basis" (p. 482). Research by Patch and Arrigo (1999) found that disposition depends on the personal beliefs, biases, and perceptions of the officer and that most agencies lack guidelines and policies.

## ARE WOMEN OFFICERS THE SAME OR DIFFERENT?

The historical perspective that women entered into the realm of policing based on the notion of "helping others" primarily in a social work role has become rather passé. In the 1960s, as an increasing number of women were assigned to patrol, stereotypical attributes of femininity that defined approaches to policing became less and less applicable. In fact, recent research on policewomen suggests that crime fighting and excitement represent the most appealing aspect of law enforcement for all officers—male and female (Parsons & Jesilow, 2001; Schulz, 1995).

Research on the differences between male and female officers is ambiguous at best, and results vary widely. The problem with many of the previous studies, according to Heidensohn (1992), has been the focus on "how women cope with police*men* rather than polic*ing*" (p. 84, emphasis in the original). Early research studies that evaluated job performance (measured by arrest rates, levels of patrol activity, and supervisory evaluations) found that policewomen performed comparable to their male counterparts in patrol duties (Bartol, Bergen, Volckens, & Knoras, 1992; Bloch & Anderson, 1974; see also Scarborough & Collins, 2002 for a detailed review of the literature).

Some studies have shown that women in policing are more likely, compared to male peers, to approach arrest situations in a caring, compassionate manner that results in better communication and de-escalation of potentially violent encounters. Belknap and Shelly (1995) argue that women are more communicative, less aggressive, and show more respect toward community members. Lersch (1998) discovered that male officers receive a higher number of citizen complaints and are more willing to use guns compared to women. Lonsway (2000) also found that women are less likely to use force in their routine duties and rely more heavily on communication compared to male officers. In contrast, earlier research by Grennan (1987) discovered no differences in the use of force by male and female officers. Few efforts, however, have been made to examine individual officer characteristics, particularly those associated with gender, and attitudes toward the mentally ill.

## POLICE OFFICERS RELATE THEIR PERSPECTIVES

The concerns and attitudes of police officers related to the mentally ill were explored through the use of qualitative interviews with representatives from three large metropolitan law enforcement agencies who discussed their attitudes, experiences, and training. Qualitative data were gathered from male and female officers, who were asked about their feelings, contacts, and interactions with the mentally ill. A convenience sample of 20 officers participated in in-depth, semi-structured interviews, and responses were categorized into major themes and compared by gender. The participants included 11 male officers, with a mean age of 39, who had an average of 14 years on the job experience. The female officers had a mean age of 44 and an average of 18 years of policing experience. The majority of officers worked patrol, although 5 of the interviewees were command staff and detectives.

All the officers agreed that the daily demands of dealing with the mentally ill are ubiquitous, and that police responses to the population are viewed as more of a challenge rather than a problem. Law enforcement, according to the officers, represents the "first line of defense" for the community. Many of the officers noted that they are required to constantly confront the issues surrounding mentally ill offenders whether they are engaging in proactive or reactive policing. Law enforcement, as noted by many of the respondents, must possess a large repertoire of skills in order to be effective with the mentally ill population. One officer commented: "They offer a different challenge. I believe with the emergence of mentally ill people being placed in society more now and the trend we have seen with that, obviously, we are dealing with them more and more. It is not a problem it is just a challenge."

Many of the officers noted that the prospect of dealing with a mentally ill person is "just part of the job," although sometimes "dangerous and distasteful." Police contacts, as noted by the respondents, generally involve "people suffering from major disorders" and, as one officer explained, the job requires that beyond the view that they are mentally ill, is the need to "view them as a crime victim or suspect as the situation warrants." Many officers noted the need for special attention, although the limited options for placement are a constant source of aggravation. A female commander stated: "I believe that it is very much a challenge but one that we must work with. Now we are receiving additional training to adequately address the issues in this community."

## ENCOUNTERS AND CONTACTS

Police officers agree that dealing with the mentally ill constitutes a large percent of what they do on patrol and the demographics of the population they encounter include a wide variety of ages, ethnic groups, and socioeconomic groups. As noted by one respondent: "Unfortunately, it's a very large part of our job. I have come to realize that mental illness is rampant in our city, and many of them require our help in one form or another." A detective with 17 years of experience noted:

> I have no problem dealing with the mentally ill. I deal with mentally ill people, not just every day, but a big chunk of my day. I work 10-hour shifts and I guarantee you that 4 to 4 1/2 hours of that shift is dealing with someone who has some sort of condition of mental illness.

The majority of incidents with the mentally ill that require police intervention are with the homeless who have psychological disorders or persons labeled as "retreatists," who have opted out of the mainstream. A former patrol officer noted that after 14 years on the streets, he experienced encounters with the homeless suffering from mental illness in large numbers:

> I would deal with a lot of homeless people. I think virtually all homeless people that I have dealt with could easily be diagnosed as having some sort of

mental handicap or illness. A few of them are what I like to call "self-selected" out of society, that is, there is not necessarily something diagnosable about them, except they do not like to deal with other people. They would rather live under a bridge than get a job. Those types are outnumbered by the homeless people who are mentally ill.

Many of the officers noted that encounters with the mentally ill, particularly the homeless population, are handled informally, and arrests are made according to the same standards as those made for any criminal suspect without regard to psychological disorders. An officer explained that an actual arrest after a call for service is rare and that most cases involving the mentally ill homeless can be settled with little intervention:

> There are a lot of people, especially homeless people, that will get off with just a warning because the victimization is a relatively minor thing, like trespassing or panhandling. When we show up to deal with the problem we need the individual to sign a complaint and be prepared to testify. Often, right from the very start, they will say, "Hey listen, I am really glad you are here, you know you have got to deal with this guy. I do not want him charged. I don't want to go to court. I don't want him to get into any trouble." They just can't have him panhandling in front of the store and scaring the customers. They just want him to leave.

Initiating an arrest in a minor or noncriminal situation involving the mentally ill is viewed by most officers as an ineffective method for dealing with the population. Arrest, noted one officer, is an option that should be used only as a "last resort." The difficulties of disposition and limited options present the same problems documented in previous research:

> You put them in the jail and now they are the jail's problem, as far as treating them or whatever. If you send them back out on the street—what is going to happen? You will be back out there with them. So, my opinion is put them where they can get some help, take them to a mental health clinic, which is *very* hard to get people in.

### HIGHER LEVELS OF SOPHISTICATION

The majority of respondents believe that police attitudes toward the mentally ill have changed and that the new generation of officers is better informed and more empathetic to their plight. One officer explained the transformation of views:

> The old attitudes have really phased out and probably existed in the retired folks. People have sought out training and have never had that approach to the mentally ill—the making fun, being abusive verbally or otherwise, those people aren't working the street anymore. I suspect they are not working at all.

Many of the officers mentioned recent efforts by their departments to provide better training on situations involving the mentally ill, particularly after critical, well-publicized incidents that have alienated community members.

Tragedy often spurs reform in the criminal justice system, and use-of-force incidents involving the mentally ill have heightened levels of awareness. Often, media and community pressure will help promote positive movements that result in increased specialized training. In many cities, use-of-force incidents have challenged and changed departmental policy and procedures related to how calls are handled. In one department, after a use-of-force incident that resulted in the death of a mentally disturbed and developmentally disabled young man, Crisis Invention Training was implemented to help heighten awareness and provide additional skills for officers on scene. An officer explained the push for training after the media frenzy:

> Our department faced a very critical incident several years ago in which an officer shot and killed a young person with mental issues who was armed with a knife. From that came a real push from the department and the citizens to give officers more tools to recognize and deal with those with mental issues. The big change to policy and practice was that on any call with a potential mental health issue the dispatcher is required to try to send a crisis-intervention trained officer.

### IDENTIFYING THE MENTALLY ILL

High arrest rates appear to be common for the mentally ill population. Teplin (2000) found that arrest rates were 67% greater for mentally ill suspects compared to those who were not mentally ill. She argued that the high number of mentally ill persons arrested reflected, in part, a lack of knowledge and failure by officers to recognize symptoms. For the police officers in this study communication represented the key element in identifying and dealing with the mentally ill. Generally, officers immediately recognize differences in speech and thought patterns. An officer explained: "When you walk up to them, they do not communicate the same ways that people who aren't mentally ill talk." The initial contact, however, may not reflect what eventually transpires in the encounter:

> There are indicators within the communication that you will pick up, but sometimes it takes a while and you will not know they are mentally handicapped or ill. Their story starts out okay, but then they get further into it and it gets more bizarre.

The officer shared the following experience on a call for help that seemed normal at first glance but deteriorated as further interaction with the alleged victim occurred:

> I had a guy call and I showed up at his house and he said that a lady was harassing him. I asked him what had occurred and at first it was perfectly normal. He said that he went to work this morning on a bus and saw this lady on the bus who started mocking him. I asked him, "Well, how do you know she was mocking you?" He responded that she was talking to other passengers on the bus and would start laughing and covering her mouth and looking at him. When he got off the bus, she started following him and was standing across the street from his house. I asked, "Did anyone else see her?" and he said, "No." He stated that this had been happening for several days and wanted help. I finally asked him if he was on any medication and he said, "Yes, I'm seeing a doctor for paranoid schizophrenia" but that his prescription had run out. I called him by his name and asked him if he thought this could have anything to with his problem.

He looked at me, and he was really serious, and asked: "Do you really think she is not really there . . . is this part of my problem?" I told him that it could be, but he should give us a call if any more problems occurred.

The officers identified the following as indications or cues that the contact person may be mentally ill: talking to one's self, disorderly appearance, agitated, fixated, erratic or delusional behavior, thoughts of persecution or paranoia, and overly anxious. An officer compassionately noted:

I believe that, for the most part, the mentally ill are easily recognizable. They may be acting out prior to our arrival, which may have forced the person to call the police. Many times they may speak in a nonsensible fashion for us, but they are speaking from their heart and believe they are making perfect sense. Most officers recognize the mentally ill.

### UNGENDERED PERSPECTIVES: COPS ARE COPS

Most interviewees, regardless of gender, believe that few differences exist between male and female officers when dealing with the mentally ill. Previous research studies also have discovered that policewomen view their job responsibilities and community encounters from the same perspective as male officers (Worden, 1993). The majority of male officers noted the similarities in approaches. One commented, for example, that "female officers who I have dealt with handled situations in much the same way that a male officer would handle the same situation." A female officer with 19 years of experience emphasized that the differences are based on individual people skills:

I think everyone is different. Some people have the skills that work, some people are enforcers, and some people are better at talking to people. It's just like any other job, but I don't think it is specific to gender at all.

She went on to note:

I honestly believe that in 19 years of having done this job that there really is not a difference between male and female officers, it is just a typical difference between people that you would find in any profession, but it's not specific to gender, in my opinion.

Responses to the mentally ill offender, as noted by most officers, may differ, but the communication styles and interactions are more likely a reflection of past experiences. A female lieutenant explained this perspective:

Female officers respond the way they are trained or with the experience they have at that particular point in time. I think all approaches are equal and not necessarily based on gender. Males, for example, who have had experience with mentally ill parties in their own families, respond differently than a female with no experience in that area.

Any differences that may emerge on how a call is handled are more likely to arise from suspect or victim perceptions, as noted by an officer, who commented:

The difference is not in how the officer perceives their role, but in how the victim or the patient perceives the officer. There are some situations where a man, who is going through some sort of crisis in his life, will not talk to a woman. I have had situations where female officers have come in or I would say that I am not getting anywhere with this guy and a female officer would start talking and build a rapport. I have had it the other way.

## ACKNOWLEDGING DIFFERENCES IN COMMUNICATION STYLES

Approximately one-third of the officers did mention differences between men and women on the job and believed, despite the emphasis on sameness, that communication and physical presence influence how male and female officers respond to a call and how gender influences public perceptions and reactions. A male lieutenant with 23 years of experience candidly commented: "Women are different because they are not men. Unless you are stuck on the politically correct beyond hope, men and women think and act differently. Also, the party contacted usually acts differently toward a female versus a male officer."

The mere presence of an officer responding to a call changes the event dynamics and may provoke either de-escalation or use-of-force incidents. In many cases, suspects may become more agitated or disoriented with the appearance of threatening authority figures, particularly male officers. Several male officers believed that "female officers appear less threatening and, therefore, may be able to have better dialogue with the mentally handicapped." A 46-year-old male lieutenant stated:

> Most female officers are less imposing in regards to physical stature, which by its very nature would create a more calming effect. Also, many female officers use communication skills rather than physical skills on a more frequent basis. However, this is a generalization that may not always be a factor in each case.

A few officers pointed to communication styles as the distinguishing feature between male and female officers. A male officer noted that his female colleagues tended to show more tolerance of the mentally disturbed and said that "it appears that the female officers are more patient with this class of offender." Likewise, a woman detective commented that policewomen encounters tend to be more positive because, in general, "females deal with our 'clients' different than males." Similarly, another woman officer pointed to enhanced interpersonal skills: "Every officer is different, but women generally are better at communication and have patience, which in turn creates better interactions with the mentally ill." A male officer commented: "Most female officers are able to establish rapport with the individual more quickly, but when the decision needs to be made to go hands on, they are similar to males. Some may believe that they can talk it out, which obviously creates an officer safety issue."

## CONCLUSION

Increased awareness of the plight of the mentally ill and more effective methods of policing have failed to entirely eradicate stereotypical fears and perceptions, despite significant attitudinal changes in law enforcement. In 2000, the shooting death of Ryan Schorr, a bipolar, prompted an in-depth study on how the police departments in

Pennsylvania view the mentally ill (Ruiz & Miller, 2004). The authors note the still-cautious and sometimes deadly interplay between police and the mentally ill:

> Police officers quite often fear persons with mental illness because they believe that most are unpredictable and dangerous. On the other hand, persons with mental illness have reason to fear the police because the police have the power to take them from their homes to a place that most do not want to go. Neither has an understanding of the other, and this can set the stage for a physical confrontation. When the scene becomes volatile, it is more likely that they can have the same result as that of the Schorr case. (Ruiz & Miller, 2004, p. 360)

Unarguably, the specifics of the case that prompted the Ruiz and Miller study are somewhat common, and similar events have occurred in many cities across the United States. Schorr had received treatment for his bipolar illness for many years prior to his death. Based on information from his roommate and input from Schorr's mother, an involuntary commitment procedure was put in place and executed by the police department. After being admitted to the hospital, Schorr was "placed in seclusion, where he became agitated and threatening" (*Schorr v. Borough of Lemoyne*, 2003, p. 2). Schorr managed to escape the facility after a crisis intervention worker entered his seclusion room, and he returned home without incident. The police were notified of the escape by the hospital and mother. When officers arrived at the home "a violent struggle ensued, during which Schorr shot at the police officer's left ring finger and ran outside. Schorr returned to his bedroom wielding pots and pans and was shot and killed by the police. Clearly, the sequence of events in the case that resulted in the use of lethal force mirrors other incidents involving the mentally ill.

The civil litigation brought by Ryan Schorr's family raised several issues that surround the treatment of the mentally ill by law enforcement. A primary question was whether or not the police response was a function of a failure to train the officers properly and, if by not providing adequate training, whether Schorr's constitutional rights had been violated. Ultimately, this case resulted in the use of lethal force to contain an individual that threatened the police with pots and pans, although the presence of the suspect's weapon mitigated the use of deadly force. More generally, the case raised questions about perceptions or stereotypes that may have contributed to the ultimate outcome and emphasized the need for specialized training.

The Ruiz and Miller (2004) study discovered several significant areas, both contextual and transitory, that illuminate the problems with policing the mentally ill. First, many law enforcement agencies fail to provide guidelines for handling the mentally ill. Second, police officers feel fear when executing a civil commitment order in the same way they would when executing an arrest warrant. Third, the perceived dangerousness of situations involving the mentally ill often results in a higher number of officers being dispatched to the call. Fourth, it is the "exception rather than the rule" to use physical force when handling the mentally ill. Finally, perceptions of the dangerousness of the individual with mental illness can lead to self-fulfilling prophecies that result in violent rather than peaceful outcomes.

Policing the mentally ill continues to be problematic for officers, despite more enlightened attitudes. Law enforcement agents believe that they have become more sophisticated in their attitudes and approaches over time, although training and collaboration among community agencies remains scarce. Perkins, Cordner, and

Scarborough (1999) noted five items that would assist in alleviating the tension among the police, persons with mental illness, and the mental health community:

1. Change stereotyped perceptions about people with mental illness.
2. Implement adequate training for police officers.
3. Develop clear agency policies and procedures.
4. Encourage constant communication among law enforcement, the medical community, and social service providers.
5. Simplify the process for involuntary commitment.

The perspectives of police officers in this study indicate the existence of an endemic and constant battle that is being fought with scarce resources. The mentally ill represent a vulnerable, yet, in some cases, dangerous population who challenge the skills and resources of law enforcement and the community. Officers experience a high level of frustration over the lack of alternative resolutions and the constant cycling of people through the mental health and criminal justice systems, but accept the reality that this population has nowhere to go. The problem is particularly acute in small cities that have no mental health facilities, and often, officers are forced to rely on jail as a solution with few hopes that treatment or long-term placement will occur. Steve Wright, a police commander and graduate of the FBI National Academy with 21 years of experience, candidly noted that officers are "scared to death" of the mentally ill and that their fear is grounded in previous dangerous situations that always remain salient and influence future encounters. These societal and occupational issues are unlikely to undergo rapid transformation in the near future.

Law enforcement has, by default, become the street corner social worker, and viewpoints that female officers may be better equipped to handle certain types of incidents and individuals are equivocal, and, often, ignore the realities of police work. When mentally ill persons were deinstitutionalized, they were afforded greater freedom, although most were released to an unknown future. Unexpectedly, part of their reintegration into the community and the responsibility for their safety became a law enforcement challenge. Almost simultaneously, an increasing number of women were joining police agencies and expanding their roles in law enforcement. The idea of females entering a primarily male-dominated career prompted perceptions, and in some instances the actual occurrence, of a kinder, gentler approach to policing. Overall, research and practice shows that in most instances "cops are cops" and the gender issue becomes less relevant than previously imagined. Female officers may present a more empathetic or compassionate side to policing, but during a crisis moment, the communication skills and patience associated with attributes typically ascribed to women are replaced by law enforcement skills and approaches that demand more authoritative behavior and decisive action. Overall, women officers are unlikely to approach policing in the nurturing manner that was originally anticipated.

# References

Abramson, M. F. (1972). The criminalization of mentally disordered behavior: Possible side-effect of a new mental health law. *Hospital and Community Psychiatry, 23,* 101–105.

Bartol, C. R., Bergen, G. T., Volckens, J. S., & Knoras, K. M. (1992). Women in small-town policing: job performance and Stress. *Criminal Justice and Behavior, 19*(3), 240–259.

Belknap, J., & Shelley, J. K. (1991). The new lone ranger: Policewomen on patrol. *American Journal of Police, 12,* 47–75.

Bloch, P., & Anderson, D. (1974). *Policewomen on patrol: Final report.* Washington, DC: Urban Institute.

Cooper, V. G., McLearen, A. M., & Zapf, P. A. (2004). Dispositional decisions with the mentally ill: Police perceptions and characteristics. *Police Quarterly, 7*(3), 295–310.

Deane, M. W., Steadman, H. J., Borum, R., Veysey, B. M., & Morrissey, J. P. (1999). Emerging partnerships between mental health and law enforcement. *Psychiatric Services, 50*(1), 99–101.

*Deinstitutionalization and the homeless mentally ill.* (2006). Retrieved October 2, 2006, from http://www.interactivist.net/housing/deinstitutionalization_2.html

Fennell, P. (1991, May). Diversion of mentally disordered offenders from custody. *Criminal Law Review,* 333–347.

Green, T. M. (1997). Police as frontline mental health workers, the decision to arrest or refer to mental health agencies. *International Journal of Law and Psychiatry, 20*(4), 469–486.

Grennan, S. (1987). Findings on the role of officer gender in violent encounters with citizens. *Journal of Police Science and Administration, 15*(1), 78–85.

Heidensohn, F. (1992). *Women in control? The role of women in law enforcement.* Oxford: Oxford University Press.

Kaminski, R, J., DiGiovanni, C., & Downs, R. (2004). The use of force between police and persons with impaired judgment. *Police Quarterly, 7*(3), 311–338.

Laberge, D., & Morin, D. (1995). The overuse of criminal justice dispositions: Failure of diversionary policies in the management of mental health problems. *International Journal of Law and Psychiatry, 18*(4), 389–414.

Lamb, H. R., & Grant, R. W. (1982). The mentally ill in an urban county jail. *Archives of General Psychiatry, 39,* 17–22.

Lamb, H. R., & Wienberger, L. E. (1998). Persons with severe mental illness in jails and prisons: A review. *Psychiatric Services, 49,* 483–492.

Lersch, K. M. (1998). Exploring gender differences in citizen allegations of misconduct: An analysis of a municipal police department. *Women & Criminal Justice, 9*(4), 69–79.

Lonsway, K. A. (2000). Hiring and retaining more women: The advantages to law enforcement agencies. *National Center for Women and Policing.* Retrieved January 9, 2007, from http://www.womenandpolicing.org/PDF/HiringAdvantage.pdf

Parsons, D., & Jesilow, P. (2001). *In the same voice: Women and men in law enforcement.* Santa Ana, CA: Seven Locks Press.

Patch, P. C., & Arrigo, B. A. (1999). Police officer attitudes and use of discretion in situations involving the mentally ill. *International Journal of Law and Psychiatry, 22*(1), 23–35.

Perkins, E., Cordner, G., & Scarborough, K. (1999). Policing handling of people with mental illness. In L. Gaines & G. Cordner (Eds.), *Policing perspectives: An anthology* (pp. 289–297). Los Angeles: Roxbury Publishing.

Pinfold, V., Huxley, P., Thornicroft, G., Farmer, P., Toulmin, H., & Graham, T. (2003). Reducing psychiatric stigma and discrimination: Evaluating an educational intervention with the police force in England. *Social Psychiatry and Psychiatric Epidemiology, 38*(6), 337–334.

Ruiz, J., & Miller, C. (2004). An exploratory study of Pennsylvania police officers' perceptions of dangerousness and their ability to manage persons with mental illness. *Police Quarterly, 7*(3), 359–371.

Scarborough, K. D., & Collins, P. A. (2002). *Women in public and private law enforcement.* Boston: Butterworth-Heinemann.

*Schorr v. Borough of Lemoyne,* No. 1: CV-010930, U.S. Dist. (Pa. May 30, 2003).

Schulz, D. M. (1995). *From social worker to crime fighter: Women in United States municipal policing.* Westport, CT: Praeger.

Steadman, H. J., Mulvey, E. P., Monahan, J., Robbins, P. C., Appelbaum, P. S., Grisso, T., et al. (1998). Violence by people discharged from acute psychiatric inpatient facilities and by others in the same neighborhoods. *Archives of General Psychiatry, 55*, 393–401.

Stefan, S. (1996). Issues relating to women and ethnic minorities in mental health treatment and law. In B. D. Sales & D. W. Shuman (Eds.), *Law, mental health, and mental disorder* (pp. 240–278). Pacific Grove, CA: Brooks/Cole.

Teplin, L. A. (1984a). Criminalizing mental disorder: The comparative arrest rate of the mentally ill. *American Psychologist, 39,* 794–803.

Teplin, L. A. (1984b). Managing disorder: Police handling of the mentally ill. In L. A. Teplin (Ed.), *Mental health and criminal justice* (pp. 157–175). Beverly Hills, CA: Sage.

Teplin, L. A. (2000, July). Keeping the peace: Police discretion and mentally ill persons. *National Institute of Justice Journal*, pp. 8–15.

Teplin, L. A., & Pruett, Pruett, N.S. (1992). Police as streetcorner psychiatrists: Managing the mentally ill. *International Journal of Law and Psychiatry, 15*, 139–156.

Watson, A. C., Corrigan, P. W., & Ottati, V. (2004). Police officers' attitudes toward and decisions about persons with mental illness. *Psychiatric Services, 55*(1), 49–53.

Worden, A. P. (1993). The attitudes of women and men in policing: Testing conventional and contemporary wisdom. *Criminology, 31,* 203–242.

## Acknowledgments

The authors would like to recognize and thank Kimberly Boyd, Laura Ketteler, and Brandi Thomas for their research efforts and applaud their exceptional interview skills. We also would like to express our appreciation for the officers who shared their experiences and invested their time in helping expand our understanding of the many complex issues involved in policing the mentally ill.

# CHAPTER 5
# IMPROVING POLICE INTERACTIONS WITH THE MENTALLY ILL:
## Crisis Intervention Team (CIT) Training

ও

**Laura Ketteler**
**Mary Dodge**

## ABSTRACT

Crisis Intervention Training (CIT) has emerged as the program of choice for progressive police departments that grapple with the challenges of dealing with mentally ill suspects. In Colorado, the need for specialized training was highlighted in the shooting of 15-year-old Paul Childs by a Denver police officer. Efforts by legislatures and government officials after the incident focused on training program implementation to help avoid the embarrassment and liability that resulted from intense media coverage on the use of force against a mentally disabled, special needs child. This chapter focuses on the structure of the CIT program with the Childs case as a backdrop for how and why the training may prevent the use of deadly force in police encounters with the mentally ill. In addition, qualitative data from female command officers offers insight into the effectiveness of CIT and delineates differences in gendered policing approaches by giving voice to women in law enforcement.

Traditionally, police officers have dealt with the mentally ill with little or no training, and primarily relied on past experiences as they assume the role of law enforcers, social workers, and psychologists to problem solve the unique and varied needs of a difficult population. Police officers provide up to one-third of all emergency mental health referrals and interact with more emotionally disturbed persons than any other occupational group outside the mental health field (Borum, Deane, Steadman, & Morrissey, 1998). Police encounters that involve emotionally disturbed persons are estimated to comprise 7% to 10% of all law enforcement contacts in large cities

(Cordner, 2006; Hails & Borum, 2003). Borum and colleagues (1998), based on the results of a survey of law enforcement personnel in three cities, found that 92% of patrol officers reported one encounter with a mentally ill person in crisis during the previous month and 84% reported more than one incident with an average of 6 per month. In one year, the New York Police Department estimated that officers responded to 36,000 emotionally disturbed person calls, averaging about 100 per day (Amnesty International, 1999).

Law enforcement is a unique profession that places a host of conflicting demands and duties on officers, and the overriding public expectation is that police personnel are adequately trained to bring all types of incidents to a safe conclusion. Policing the mentally ill is a sensitive subject and officers readily acknowledge the delicacies, complications, and perceived dangers involved in atypical encounters. Cordner (2006) notes that law enforcement personnel may encounter mentally ill persons under a variety of circumstances, including as offenders, disorderly persons, missing persons, complainants, victims, or persons in need of care. Police, according to Cordner, tend to rate calls involving the threat of suicide as the most difficult cases to handle (Thompson, Reuland, & Souweine, 2003). The uncertainty of behavior and wide array of situations that may involve the mentally ill complicate calls for officers who are trained in law enforcement tactics, but expected to act as mental health care providers. A female lieutenant with 20 years of experience identified the major challenges from a patrol officer's perspective as a "lack of knowledge about the person, chaotic behavior, unexplained mood swings, and family members with expectations that the police are psychologists" (personal communication, 2006).

In most cases, encounters between law enforcement and the mentally ill that involve noncriminal or misdemeanor offenses are easily resolved, though a relatively minor incident may demand a significant amount of patrol time. Additionally, complainants' expectations of what an officer should do to resolve a problematic or criminal situation are often unrealistic and the overriding public sentiment is that the mentally ill are a law enforcement problem. Police Chief Gary Margolis (2002), who testified before a senate judiciary committee, commented on the perception that the typical call for service involves community expectations that officers will rectify troublesome and sometimes rather routine situations:

> Many police encounters involve a person who is acting in a disorderly or disturbing manner—whether or not a crime has been committed. This may include a man muttering to himself in front of a store, or urinating on a street corner yelling obscenities at people passing by. Or a person standing in the middle of Main Street attempting to direct traffic. Or a person apparently homeless, passed out in the park. Many times concerned citizens place these calls requesting police assistance, though in some cases, business owners or others simply want to take the person from the area. (p. 2)

Police calls for services, however, are rarely mundane, and the unpredictability of the encounters with mentally ill or emotionally disturbed persons is well documented in the media and research literature. The Colorado Division of Criminal Justice lists the following calls from a major police department as examples of the wide variety of incidents that occur on any given day and notes that officers may respond with understanding, force, and/or fear (Passini-Hill & English, 2006, p. 1):

- A person who has been awake for 4 days and wants to commit suicide by cop.
- Someone who believes she is being stalked and microwaved by "them."
- A person who lives in a camper with 30 rats.
- A person writing in blood in a journal.
- A tenant who hears voices telling him to hurt his landlord.
- A woman who sees white bugs crawling all over her body.
- A person found in a bathtub full of water, clothed, with a knife.

The most important ingredients for success in handling calls involving the mentally ill in crisis are patrol officers' wide variety of tools and communication skills that can be used, especially during crisis situations.

## PERCEPTIONS OF DANGEROUSNESS AND USE OF FORCE

Widespread views among the public and law enforcement personnel are that mentally ill suspects are inherently more dangerous compared to other types of offenders, with the exception of intimate partner violence (Link, Phelan, Bresnahan, Stueve, & Pescosolido, 1999; Phelan & Link, 2004; Ruiz & Miller, 2004; Steadman, 1981). Consequently, encounters with the mentally ill that prompt emotions of fear in police officers are more likely to result in the escalation of force when circumstances involve a "strange-acting" person. Watson, Corrigan, and Ottati (2004) note that if a "heightened sense of risk causes officers to approach persons with mental illness more aggressively, they can escalate the situation and may evoke unnecessary violence" (p. 52). Departmental rules and policies on use of force are strict and clearly defined, but the de-escalation of dangerous situations often depends on individual good judgment, training, and, ultimately, the overriding goal of personal and public safety.

Only a small proportion of police interactions involve the use of force, and the majority of incidents involve lower levels of physical restraint (Adams, 1999; Fyfe, 1995; Garafolo & Bayley, 1989; Garner & Maxwell, 1996; MacDonald, Manz, Alpert, & Dunham, 2002; Terrill, 2003). Confrontations with impaired suspects that result in higher levels of force generally vary across situational contexts and are highly influenced by levels of compliance, officer experience, and training (Dodge, 2003; Garner, Schade, Hepburn, & Buchanan, 1995). An analysis of 2,592 use-of-force incidents in the Denver Police Department from 1996 through year-end 2002 showed that officers reported alcohol impairment in the majority of the cases (Dodge, 2003). Mental illness was indicated as the source of impairment in only 5% of the cases. Overall, the data suggest that encounters involving the use of force with the mentally ill are relatively low, although incidents and assumptions about the suspects' psychological status were reported from the officers' perspective. The results of the study, although inconclusive, may support interpretations that officers failed to recognize suspects who were suffering from a psychiatric disorder or that intoxication represented the overriding concern, and any other impairment was secondary in the arrest attempt. Other researchers also have found that officers' perception that a suspect is mentally impaired is unlikely to increase the use of force (Kaminski, Digiovanni, & Downs, 2004; Terrill & Mastrofski, 2002).

Unfortunately, specialized training for law enforcement on dealing with the mentally ill often is implemented only after a lethal force incident that creates a hue and cry among community members. In 1987, for example, Memphis police officers killed an African-American man with a long history of mental illness. The man was cutting himself when confronted by the police and was still holding the knife when he ran at the officers who opened fire (Vickers, 2000). Case examples involving the use of lethal force by police against the mentally ill generally represent the turning point for police departments that have neglected to implement comprehensive training.

> *Los Angeles, California.* In May 1999, a 54-year-old African-American home-less, schizophrenic woman, Margaret Laverne Mitchell, encountered the police while pushing her shopping cart down the street. She was shot and killed by one officer after brandishing a 13-inch screwdriver.

> *Philadelphia, Pennsylvania.* A series of fatal shootings have plagued the department in the past few years. Charles Love Kelly, who suffered from mental illness, was fatally shot by Amtrack police. Julio Morais was shot during a struggle with police and social workers who were attempting to initiate commitment. A woman, recently released from a psychiatric facil-ity, was shot after she ignored officers' orders to put down a knife. In another incident, a mentally ill woman, who had been seen running naked in the streets, was shot twice when she approached officers armed with a knife.

> *San Diego, California.* In April 2001, Gabindo Benjamin Flores, a 60-year-old mentally ill man, was shot and killed after he refused an order by police to drop a pair of household scissors. Flores had been released from a psychiatric ward the day before the incident. Attempts by the officers to use less-than-lethal force failed, and Flores was shot when he stabbed one of the officers. The year before, police use of force enraged the community when William Anthon Miller, a homeless man, was fatally shot as he rushed toward officers using a 3-foot tree branch as a weapon.

> *Portland, Oregon.* In September 2006, police officers were accused of using excessive force against James Philip Chasse, a schizophrenic, during an arrest. Chasse, who reportedly had no weapon and posed no threat to the officers, was subject to harsh arrest-control tactics that resulted in extensive injuries. Chasse suffered from broken ribs and a punctured lung and, despite his com-plaints, was ignored by officers and jail personnel. He died while being trans-ported to the hospital.

Calls for service that involve the mentally ill instantly become more challenging and demanding for law enforcement after an incident receives critical media coverage. When officers resort to lethal force to control situations involving mentally ill suspects or developmentally disabled offenders, communities often react with anger and dis-may—demanding reform. Officers readily acknowledge that departmental policy and procedural changes "are politically motivated from incidents which receive press or attention" (personal communications, 2006). Colorado's Crisis Intervention Training program, for example, became an essential aspect of police training after a lethal force encounter involving an African-American youth.

## THE PAUL CHILDS CASE

On July 5, 2003, Denver police officer James Turney shot and killed 15-year-old Paul Childs after receiving a radio call that the boy was chasing his mother with a knife. Childs, a few days earlier, was discharged from an adolescent psychiatric unit. At 1:10 p.m. a 911 call, made by his sister Ashley Childs, requested police assistance because her brother was upset with her mother and would not put down a knife. She told the dispatcher: "I said my brother has a knife and he is trying to stab my mother with it. He's like followin' her around an' when she turns her back, he'll try to stab her an' then she'll hurry up an' turn around. And' now he' followin' her with the knife" (Ritter, 2003). The family asserted that the only reason that they called the police was to come and calm Paul down.

At the time of the initial call, the dispatcher informed officers that the address had an extensive domestic and family violence history. When police arrived at the scene, family members were removed from the house and officers ordered Childs to drop the knife. Childs, who had epilepsy seizures and mental retardation, was shot by Turney when he failed to follow police instructions to drop the kitchen knife that he was clutching to his chest. Childs was 5 to 7 feet away from the officer holding a 13-inch knife. An officer who had completed Crisis Intervention Team training arrived and covered the other responding officers with a Taser drawn, but the situation had escalated to a deadly force encounter because of the proximity of Turney to the armed suspect. After the shooting, the CIT officer described his perceptions of Childs: "To me the kid looked like . . . I'll be honest with you, he looked almost high to me. It . . . like he was in a, he was in another world or somethin'. Uh, he wasn't listening to commands. Um, he wasn't there. I mean it, it was like he was talkin' to, to someone that, you know, a brick wall almost. Why he didn't listen to us, I don't know" (Ritter, 2003).

The incident enraged the community, and citizens viewed the use of force as an extreme response to the situation that further exacerbated racial tensions in the city. Critics also focused on a deadly force incident that occurred a year before the death of Childs. In that case, Turney and another officer shot and killed an 18-year-old African-American man with a hearing impairment who was wielding a pocket knife (DenverChannel.com, 2003). Ultimately, Denver's District Attorney concluded that Officer Turney had not committed a crime in the Childs' case and declined to press charges. The city's manager of safety, however, recommended that Turney be suspended for 10 months without pay for violating department rules related to safety by forcing the confrontation and elevating the risk of harm (Couch, 2004).

Helen Childs, Paul's mother, advocated for legislation that would be titled "Paul's Law." The law, which was introduced to the state house in January 2004, would require that all law enforcement officers and dispatchers in Colorado go through crisis-intervention training and receive special instruction on how to deal with people who have a mental illness or developmental disabilities (Reynolds, 2003). "I want this to be like the Amber Alert," Paul's mother stated. "I want this to be national" (Reynolds, 2003). Thus far, her efforts have been unsuccessful.

In January of 2004, the Denver Police Department announced a major reform, and the mayor unveiled a plan that called for an array of training programs and increased use of less-than-lethal equipment. This proposal was aimed at calming the rising anger about the department's use of force in the aftermath of the Childs' case (Couch, 2004). Four months after announcing this reform of the police department, city officials faced political delays, bureaucratic constraints, and a budget crunch that stalled efforts to provide additional training (Couch, 2004). The expansion of the department's Crisis Intervention Team training was delayed while the chief of police searched for the funding. Another major obstacle was the need to cover patrol duties while officers attended the training. The CIT course required overtime for 5 days for officers who would work extra hours, and the cost was estimated at about $300,000 dollars.

## THE NEED FOR TRAINING

Many of the mentally ill who are disturbing the peace or exhibiting bizarre behavior wind up in the criminal justice system, primarily because of the lack of placement options. The criminalization of the mentally ill has risen tremendously, and approximately 40% of the mentally ill have been arrested at some point in their lives (Hartwell, 2004). The Treatment Advocacy Center, established by the National Alliance for the Mentally Ill, estimates an average of 3.5 million Americans are suffering from some form of a severe mental illness, particularly after the deinstitutionalization movement in 1969, which placed more than 93% of the mentally ill population on the streets (Hartwell, 2004). Some research suggests that arrest rates for emotionally disturbed people exceed those without mental illness, although their offenses are comparable (Link, Monahan, Stueve, & Cullen, 1999; Teplin, 1984).

The association among criminality, substance abuse, and mental illness also represents a significant area of concern for patrol officers. Previous research shows that violent behavior in the mentally ill, although representing a small portion of the total population, is often associated with substance abuse or noncompliance with medication schedules (Cordner, 2006). People with mental illness and who have substance abuse problems are likely to become involved in police encounters. For the mentally ill, illegal medication or lack of prescription medication decreases rational decision making and increases the danger to themselves and others around them, especially police officers (Hartwell, 2004). Specially trained officers are better equipped to understand "odd" behaviors and identifying possible impairments.

Most rookie patrol officers encounter the mentally ill after receiving 8 to 10 hours of specialized instruction during academy training. A study conducted in California found that the average number of mental health training hours during an academy was 6.3, and only 83 out of 158 agencies provided any specialized mental health training (Vermette, Pinals, & Appelbaum, 2005). An increasing number of jurisdictions, however, have developed intervention models that include a cadre of officers who are specially trained in mental health issues.

## CRISIS INTERVENTION TEAMS

Crisis Intervention Team (CIT) training has emerged as the program of choice for progressive police departments that grapple with the challenges of dealing with mentally ill suspects. CIT, created by the Memphis, Tennessee, Police Department in 1988, was designed to provide officers with the skills and tools needed to assist in an array of experiences related to the mentally ill. The program was grounded in a community policing approach that included collaboration and education. The major goals of CIT training in Memphis included four basic ideals (Vickers, 2000):

1. Provide immediate response and management in crisis situations with the mentally ill.
2. Prevent, reduce, or eliminate injury to all parties involved.

**3.** Assist in finding appropriate care for the mentally ill.
**4.** Establish treatment programs that reduce recidivism.

The Memphis police department recognized that the achievement of positive out-comes depended on community alliances and teamed with the local chapter of the Alliance for the Mentally Ill, the University of Memphis, and mental health providers. Approximately 10% to 20% of the 1,800 officers in the department are trained, and CIT personnel respond to about 7,000 calls per year (Cochran, Deane, & Borum, 2000; Price, 2005).

CIT training varies across jurisdictions, but most programs include instructions on recognizing symptoms of mental illness, psychotropic medications, crisis de-escalation, defense weapon training, and role-playing exercises (Vickers, 2000). CIT programs are designed to raise an officer's level of awareness of mental illness, developmental dis-abilities, anxiety disorders and phobias, homelessness, and issues unique to the elderly. Trainees also are instructed in dealing with suicide, suicide by cop, legal issues, civil commitment, tactical consideration, and mental health community resources. CIT has been adopted by at least 24 major cities and includes 40 to 45 hours of training that focuses on crisis intervention and de-escalation. By September 2006, Colorado's CIT program had trained nearly 1,800 officers using the framework developed by the Memphis Police Department (Passini-Hill & English, 2006). The statewide program includes 14 counties and 63 police and sheriffs departments (Passini-Hill, Sinclair, & Reynolds, 2006).

Officers in Colorado who have undergone the training or completed the course are vocal supporters: "The CIT training is very thorough, very good and I would like to see every officer go through the program" (personal communication, 2006). An officer commented on the advantages of the training:

> We have a nationally recognized CIT program. We provide 45 hours of intense training both classroom and scenario for the officers. I think that this mixture of class and play-acting is very good. We have people with mental issues come in and serve as some of the instructors and, also, as the actors [in role-playing exercises]. (personal communication, 2006)

An increasing number of officers in Colorado are becoming trained, though many still remain uncertified. One officer noted the change:

> Approximately 5 years ago, the police department began to train officers to deal with the mentally disabled suspects. The training involves the cues in identifying mentally disabled suspects or victims and how to handle them if you believe you have encountered one. Role-playing works best for training. (personal communication, 2006)

### THE POWER OF ROLE-PLAYING EXERCISES

Training can inform and enhance officer performance when they are presented with the difficulties of confronting suspects or victims with psychological maladies. One officer explained that a primary challenge is the inability to "relate to the issues that they [men-tally ill] are dealing with." CIT training provides real-life situations, and role reversal exercises strengthen an officers' base of knowledge in a manner that encourages a more empathetic response. From the officer's perspective, role-playing, which is the most dreaded part of the training, has the greatest and longest lasting impact on the officers. Role-playing provides hands-on experience and makes a deep impression on trainees. A CIT-trained officer commented on his experience:

> We had a scenario where a woman was suffering from a severe schizophrenic disorder. She was actually really good at acting and she played a person who was suffering from a paranoid schizophrenic disorder, who believed there were people who were being swallowed. She was literally running around screaming at the top of her lungs. I was sent in to deal with her and it took me ten minutes to talk her down, but eventually, I did. We had scenarios like that all week long. In other cases, we had suicidal persons or a person suffering from narcotic withdrawal who doused herself with [fake] gasoline. She was doing crack and coming down and freaking out from the withdrawals. They sent one of us guys in to deal with her and to get her to give up the lighter. (personal communication, 2006)

Another CIT-trained officer explained the effectiveness of role-playing:

> We used situations where we talk for half the day about mentally disordered individuals and then the other half of the day we run scenarios with an acting troop. They bring in actors who have a case study, and, for instance, how a person with a paranoid disorder would act under certain circumstances. You walk into a room and there is a girl or guy sitting on a chair with a bottle of whisky between their legs and a knife to their throat—an honest to God real knife—and you would have to talk them down. The point is to recognize what sort of mental illness they are suffering from and provide them with options and alternatives. (personal communication, 2006)

Role-playing exercises make an impact in training, but the danger of portraying and perpetuating stereotypes is a concern for many CIT trainers. An officer described the following training scenario:

> Mine was an individual who was found with his car parked out in the middle of a field with the engine running and he was a very happy person, but he was wearing aluminum foil on his head and he had his radio station turned on static. He had a TV set up on top of the car, and he was trying to "pick up some waves."

Expert trainers note that "canned," stereotypical incidents or overacting can diminish effectiveness (Sinclair, personal communication, 2007).

"Voices" is another powerful training exercise in which the officers are surrounded by people who are whispering messages, including hate, violence, and self-destruction. During the whispering the officers are asked to complete a task that is given to them by the instructor, who is standing beside them. Completing the simple task is difficult because of the "voice" interference. The main point of the exercise is to show the officers how it would feel to be schizophrenic and help them to better understand someone who is in a crisis and who really hears the "voices."

CIT training also involves site visits to the local mental health facilities. This helps the officers better understand the mentally ill by facilitating conversations between the officers and the agency's clientele. Communication enhances empathy and helps in developing better relationships between officers and the citizens they encounter (Passini-Hill & English, 2006). Additionally, officers who have previous personal interactions, particularly involving family members or friends, are more sympathetic and compassionate toward the mentally ill offender.

Specialized training combined with street experience represents the most crucial aspects of how officers will respond to the mentally ill. The ability to handle mentally ill suspects often results from years of experience. An officer explained that the high number of response calls involving the mentally ill provide a great deal of on-the-job training:

> A lot of knowledge is learned. Values, ideas and concerns about people who are mentally ill and who we deal with on a regular basis are transmitted through the police department. If you go to a call and you are with a more experienced officer, you might ask: "Have you ever been here before?" And he or she might respond: "This is Linda's house. Don't worry about Linda; she just thinks that aliens are landing on her roof. She thinks that they are all digging a trench in her backyard. You know, she is just nuts." (personal communication, 2006)

## OUTCOME EVALUATIONS

The Memphis CIT program, according to Vickers (2000, p. 10), offered numerous benefits to the department and the criminal justice system in general, including:

- Reduced stigma and perception of danger attached to mental illness.
- Decreased use of deadly force.
- Reduced use of restraints.
- Fewer injuries to officers and citizens.
- Lower arrest rates.
- Fewer mentally ill sent to jail.

Overall, research evaluations suggest that CIT programs reduce the use of force, increase officer safety, and divert higher numbers of the mentally ill from jail by providing referrals to the health care system (Cochran et al., 2000; Dupont & Cochran, 2000; Steadman, Deane, Borum, & Morrissey, 2000; Strauss et al., 2005). Survey research in Georgia that focused on officer's knowledge and attitudes associated with the stigma attached to schizophrenics found that CIT-trained officers were more understanding, better educated, and reported less social distance (Compton, Esterberg, McGee, Kotwicki, & Oliva, 2006). In Colorado, survey research showed that the majority of CIT officers rated the program as beneficial. Responses from 363 officers revealed that 93% reported the training as being helpful in dealing with crisis situations, 83% reported that the skills were beneficial in maintaining safety for themselves and others, and 76% supported the addition of refresher courses (Passini-Hill & English, 2006).

Borum and colleagues (1998) evaluated the effectiveness of three models of police response to the mentally ill in Birmingham, Alabama; Knoxville, Tennessee; and Memphis, Tennessee. The Memphis CIT training was compared to one agency that relied on assistance from a mobile mental health crisis team and another that employed a team of in-house social workers to assist in calls. CIT officers reported higher levels of confidence in being prepared to deal with the mentally ill compared to their non-CIT counterparts. The CIT officers also reported a higher level of effectiveness in the program's ability to meet the needs of the mentally ill during a crisis, keeping them out of jail, and maintaining community safety. CIT-trained officers also recognized the importance of cross-agency collaboration, and respondents rated the helpfulness of the mental health system and emergency room higher compared to officers in the Birmingham and Knoxville departments. Officers in Memphis spent less than 30 minutes processing a subject for evaluation because of the streamlined referral process developed by the psychiatric emergency service and the department.

## GENDERED INTERACTIONS

The gender of both the officers and the mentally ill may play an important role in interactions and outcomes, although few empirical studies have explored the relationships and dynamics. Based on their experiences, police officers believe that the majority of incidents involve male mentally ill suspects, although many acknowledge that gender may vary with disorder. One officer explained:

> We generally deal with more male suspects, but it depends on the kind of mental disorder. I would say the schizophrenic subjects are half and half. The individuals who have issues with severe depression tend to be more female than male. The issues where people are just kind of out of touch with reality, who suffer from mental illnesses that are put into a situation where they are basically out of touch are typically males. (personal communication, 2006)

A female officer when asked about dealing with male versus female mentally ill suspects offered the following explanation for why she believes that more males are involved in incidents:

> I am not sure this is a statistically provable answer, but it has been my experiences to deal with more males. It seems like females would be more apt to take their meds, especially for bipolar personalities. I run into a lot of women who are schizophrenic, but they just think that everyone else is crazy. (personal communication, 2006)

Analysis of police incidents, however, suggest an almost even split between men and women with mental illness who need law enforcement assistance. Data from 3,402 calls for service in Colorado related to the mentally ill show that 53% involved incidents with men compared to 47% with females (Passini-Hill et al., 2006). A study of 1,422 police calls for service related to suicidal behavior in Toronto, Canada, during a 5-year period revealed that 56% of the calls involved females who were more likely to use chemical rather than physical methods (Matheson et al., 2005).

Every police incident is unique. Approaches and outcomes depend on the attitudes and dynamics between officers and the suspects. In some cases, male mentally ill suspects will react better to female officers and vice versa, although situational context plays an important role. Common misperceptions tend to underestimate violence by women. Robbins, Monahan, and Silver (2003) discovered that rates of violence over a 1-year period, overall, were similar for male and female patients discharged from psychiatric care facilities. The results of their study show that men were more likely to be drinking or taking street drugs and less likely to be taking prescribed psychotropic medication prior to a violent incident compared to women. Additionally, violent acts committed by men were more likely to result in serious injury, and their arrest rates were higher compared to women. In contrast, women were more likely to target family members and conduct violent acts in the home.

In the absence of training, interactions between police officers and the mentally ill are much more likely to depend on life experiences rather than gender. Leigh Sinclair, CIT Program Administrator for the Denver Police Department, explained that officers, regardless of gender, who have had family or friends with mental illnesses are more likely to embrace the CIT training (personal communication, 2007). Similarly, Compton et al. (2006) note that officers who volunteer for CIT programs are relatively well informed and self-report a higher exposure to individuals with mental illnesses.

The socialization of women as police officers often relies on their ability to blend with the boys, and masculine approaches to law enforcement continue to dominate the profession. In fact, a certain expectation exists that femininity is trained out as women enter training academies and seek to prove they are capable and competent officers. Anecdotal evidence suggests only that female officers are more resistant to CIT in group settings compared to attitudes they display individually (personal communication, 2007).

## CONCLUSION

Crisis Intervention Team training translates into thousands of citizens and officers becoming safer on the streets. Officers, who usually self-select to participate, report that the training is excellent and has been instrumental in enhanced community safety. Also, significant indicators show that CIT is a success. As the development and positive evaluations of CIT continue to grow, in-depth training is likely to become departmentalized and established as a fundamental part of police educational opportunities. The growth of CIT offers hope that understanding of the mentally ill will result in safer outcomes when de-escalation efforts help circumvent the use of lethal force.

The rapid evolution and adoption of CIT and crisis training offers numerous benefits to police departments, although programs lack a best practices model and seldom address gender-specific issues. The future success will depend on institutionalization of programs that become embedded in the police culture. Sinclair (personal communication, 2007) notes that the goals of CIT may depend on adopting a model that includes a non-sworn, in-house director as opposed to relying on a liaison from a mental health center. The future success of CIT programs, according to Sinclair, depends on expansion and flexibility and may include, for example:

- More emphasis on post-traumatic stress disorder.
- Training at all levels, including dispatchers.
- A focus on medical and developmental disorders.
- Increased treatment options.
- Building solid community collaboration.

Additionally, a continuum of training that includes all members of the community will further promote safety and treatment. The mentally ill, according to Sinclair, can be educated to better understand police actions and public reactions to their behavior. In fact, Cordner (2006) argues that encounters with the police are more dangerous for people with mental illness and notes that people with severe mental illness are four times more likely to be killed by police. Future efforts to further improve law enforcement approaches and education of the mentally ill using CIT training and community policing will reduce the number of critical incidents. A patrol officer noted the trend toward increased attention by departments, although she remains concerned about the lack of positive media and public support:

> During my 10 years as a police officer, I have observed more training being directed to the mentally ill. The training has provided me and other officers with tools in dealing with the mentally ill. Recently, the media has focused on the negative situation, which resulted in officers using deadly force. However, there are numerous situations which are positive, but they are rarely reported.

## References

Adams, K. (1999, October). What we know about police use of force. *Report to the National Institute of Justice*, "Use of force by police: Overview of national and local data" (NCJ 176330). Washington, DC: U.S. Department of Justice.

Amnesty International. (1999). *Mentally ill or homeless: Vulnerable to police abuse.* Retrieved March 4, 2007, from http://web.amnesty.org/library/index/.

Borum, R., Deane, M. W., Steadman, H. J., & Morrissey, J. (1998). Police perspectives on responding to mentally ill people in crisis: Perceptions of program effectiveness. *Behavioral Sciences and the Law*, *16*, 393–405.

Cochran, S., Deane, M. W., & Borum, R. (2000). Improving police response to mentally ill people. *Psychiatric Services*, *51*(10), 1315.

Compton, M. T., Esterberg, M. L., McGee, R., Kotwicki, R. J., & Oliva, J. A. (2006). Crisis intervention team training: Changes in knowledge, attitudes, and stigma related to schizophrenia. *Psychiatric Services*, *57*(8), 1199–1202.

Cordner, G. (2006, May). *People with mental illness*. Problem-Oriented Guides For Police Problem-Specific Guides Series #40. Office of Community Oriented Policing Services, U.S. Department of Justice.

Couch, M. P. (2004, April 28). Red tape, ink slows cop reform: Bureaucracy, budget issues stall mayor's police department changes. *Denver Post*, p. B1.

DenverChannel.com. (October 2003). Denver police officer James Turney shoots Childs four times. Retrieved October 3, 2006, from http://www.thedenverchannel.com

Dodge, M. (2003). *Use of force analysis 1996–2002*. Unpublished report prepared for the Denver Police Department, Denver, CO.

Dupont, R., & Cochran, S. (2000). Police response to mental health emergencies: Barriers to change. *The Journal of the American Academy of Psychiatry and the Law*, *28*(3), 338–344.

Fyfe, J. (1995). Training to reduce police-citizen violence. In W. Geller & H. Toch (Eds.), *And justice for all: Understanding and controlling police abuse of force*. Washington, DC: Police Executive Research Forum.

Garafolo, J., & Bayley, D. H. (1989). The management of violence by police patrol officers. *Criminology*, *27*, 1–27.

Garner, J. H., & Maxwell, C. D. (1996). Measuring the amount of force used by and against the police in six jurisdictions. Report to the National Institute of Justice, "*Use of force by police.*" (NCJ 176330). Washington, DC: U.S. Department of Justice.

Garner, J. H., Schade, T, Hepburn, J., & Buchanan, J. (1995). Measuring the continuum of force used by and against the police. *Criminal Justice Review*, *20*, 146–168.

Hails, J., & Borum, R. (2003). Police training and specialized approaches to respond to people with mental illness. *Crime & Delinquency, 49*(1), 52–61.

Hartwell, S. (2004). Triple stigma: Persons with mental illness and substance abuse problems in the criminal justice system. Retrieved February 5, 2007, from http://cjp.sagepub.com/cgi/content/abstract/15/1/84

Kaminski, R. J., Digiovanni, C., & Downs, R. (2004). The use of force between the police and persons with impaired judgment. *Police Quarterly, 7*(3), 311–338.

Link, B. G., Monahan, J., Stueve, A., & Cullen, F. T. (1999). Real in their consequences: A sociological approach to understanding the association between psychotic symptoms and violence. *American Sociological Review, 64*, 316–332.

Link, B. G., Phelan, J. C., Bresnahan, M., Stueve, A., & Pescosolido, B. A. (1999). Public conceptions of mental illness: Labels, causes, dangerousness, and social distance. *American Journal of Public Health, 89*, 1328–1333.

MacDonald, J. M., Manz, P. W., Alpert, G., & Dunham, R. G. (2002). Police use of force: Examining the relationship between calls for service and the balance of police force and suspect resistance. *Journal of Criminal Justice, 31*, 119–27.

Margolis, G. (July 2002). Criminal justice system and the mentally ill. FDCH Congressional Testimony, Senate Judiciary.

Matheson, F. I., Creatore, M. I., Gozdyra, P., Mosineddin, R., Rourke, S. B., & Glazier, R. H. (December 2005). Assessment of police calls for suicidal behavior in a concentrated urban setting. *Psychiatric Services, 56*(12), 1606–1609.

Passini-Hill, D., & English, K. (September 2006). Crisis intervention teams: A community-based initiative. *Elements of Change, 10*(2), pp. 1–8. Division of Criminal Justice, Colorado Department of Public Safety.

Passini-Hill, D., Sinclair, L., & Reynolds, S. (September 2006). *Statewide evaluation of crisis intervention teams (CIT) and service system response.* Paper presentation at the National CIT Conference.

Phelan, J. C., & Link, B. G. (2004). Fear of people with mental illnesses: The role of personal and impersonal contact and exposure to threat or harm. *Journal of Health and Social Behavior, 45*, 68–80.

Price, M. (2005). Commentary: The challenge of training police officers. *Journal of the American Academy of Psychiatry and the Law, 33*, 50–54.

Reynolds, D. (2003). *Teen's death prompts "Paul's Law."* Retrieved January 1, 2007, from http://www.inclusiondaily.com/archives/03/08/13.htm

Ritter, B. (October 16, 2003). *Investigation of the shooting death of Paul Nash Childs.* State of Colorado, Office of the District Attorney, Denver, CO.

Robbins, P. C., Monahan, J., & Silver, E. (2003). Mental disorder, violence, and gender. *Law and Human Behavior, 27*(6), 561–571.

Ruiz, J., & Miller, C. (2004). An exploratory study of Pennsylvania police officers' perceptions of dangerousness and their ability to manage persons with mental illness. *Police Quarterly, 7*(3), 359–371.

Steadman, H. J. (1981). Critically reassessing the accuracy of public perceptions of the dangerousness of the mentally ill. *Journal of Health and Social Behavior, 22*, 310–316.

Steadman, H. J., Deane, M. W., Borum, R., & Morrissey, J. (2000). Comparing outcomes of major models of police responses to mental health emergencies. *Psychiatric Services, 51*(5), 645–649.

Strauss, G., Glenn, M., Reddi, P., Afaq, I., Podolskaya, A., Rybakova, T., et al. (2005). Psychiatric disposition of patients brought in by crisis intervention teams police officers. *Community Mental Health Journal, 41*(2), 223–228.

Teplin, L. (1984). Criminalizing mental disorder: The comparative arrest rate of the mentally ill. *American Psychologist, 39*, 794–803.

Terrill, W. (2003). Police use of force and suspect resistance: The micro process of the police-suspect encounter. *Police Quarterly, 6*(1), 51–83.

Terrill, W., & Mastrofski, S. D. (2002). Situational and officer-based determinants of police coercion. *Justice Quarterly, 19*, 215–248.

Thompson, M. D., Reuland, M., & Souweine, D. (2003). Criminal justice/mental health consensus: Improving responses to people with mental illness. *Crime & Delinquency, 49*(1), 30–51.

Vickers, B. (2000, July). Memphis, Tennessee, police department's crisis intervention team. *Bulletin From the Field: Practitioner Perspectives.* U.S. Department of Justice.

Vermette, H. S., Pinals, D. A., & Appelbaum, P. S. (2005). Mental health training for law enforcement professionals. *Journal of the American Academy of Psychiatry and the Law, 33*, 42–46.

Watson, A. C., Corrigan, P. W., & Ottati, V. (2004, January). Police officers' attitudes toward and decisions about persons with mental illness. *Psychiatric Services, 55*(1), 49–53.

## Acknowledgments

The authors would like to thank Leigh Sinclair and all the police officers who were willing to share their insights and experiences. Also, thanks to Melissa Cooney and Jere Stahl for their comments and suggestions.

# CHAPTER 6
# WOMEN IN MENTAL HEALTH COURTS:

## A Femicentric-Integrated Approach of Service Delivery for Women with Multiple Disorders in Mental Health Courts

## Janice Joseph

### ABSTRACT

Mental health court programs have grown rapidly, from 1 in 1997 to 125 in 2006. However, research on these specialty courts has not kept pace with their growth. Using the limited information on female offenders in mental health courts, this chapter examines the extent to which female offenders use mental health courts and assesses the effectiveness of these courts to serve female offenders. First, the chapter provides an overview of these courts by discussing their purpose, characteristics, and process. The chapter also introduces the femicentric approach, as an analytical tool, which examines the heterogeneous and diverse populations of women served by mental health courts. In addition, an integrated model of service delivery for women with multiple disorders referred to mental health courts is presented. Finally, the chapter identifies policy implications and issues for future research.

In the past 20 years, the criminal justice system in the United States has been overwhelmed with individuals with serious mental illness. As a result, various forms of diversion programs have proliferated in an attempt to attenuate the tide. One such program is the mental health court system, and the number of these courts has increased rapidly over the past few years. Despite the rapid expansion of mental health courts, little empirical information about their operations or outcomes is available. One specific area where data are particularly lacking concerns the processing of women in these specialty courts. This chapter presents an overview of the mental health court system and then proposes an integrated model of service delivery for women with multiple disorders referred to mental health courts. Recommendations are also included.

# OVERVIEW OF MENTAL HEALTH COURTS

Since the opening of the Broward County court in 1997, the number of mental health courts has increased drastically with the passage of the America's Law Enforcement and Mental Health Project Act (P.L. 106-515), a federal law authorizing support for additional mental health court programs. In 2000, Congress passed and President Clinton signed into law S. 1865, a bill authorizing grants to communities to establish demonstration mental health courts. This legislation has increased interest in the creation of mental health courts. In 2002, the Bureau of Justice Assistance announced its first round of funding for mental health courts by providing grants of approximately $150,000 each to 24 local mental health courts in 2002 and 14 courts in 2003 (Bureau of Justice Assistance, 2004). These federal grant programs received further credibility from the President's New Freedom Commission on Mental Health report (2003), which recommended "widely adopting adult criminal justice and juvenile justice diversion and re-entry strategies to avoid the unnecessary criminalization and extended incarceration of nonviolent adult and juvenile offenders with mental illness" (Steadman & Redlich, 2006, pp. 43–44). In 2004, The Mentally Ill Offender Treatment and Crime Reduction Act was enacted, authorizing grants to states and localities to develop collaborative mental health and criminal justice responses, including jail diversion programs, for people with mental illness in the criminal justice system. In 2006, the U.S. Department of Justice also sent out a call for concept papers on the mental health courts program. In 1997, only four mental health courts existed in the country; by January 2004, 70 courts were in operation, and as of June 2005, there were approximately 125 operational courts in 36 states (Consensus Project, 2006).

## CHARACTERISTICS OF MENTAL HEALTH COURTS

To be eligible for participation in mental health courts, the defendant must meet several criteria including specific types of mental illness, specific types of offenses, and voluntariness of participation.

Some mental health courts serve only persons with serious and persistent mental illness (Severe Mental Illness/Persistent Mental Illness and Axis I disorders). Others accept clients with developmental disabilities, whereas others have less stringent criteria or restrictions and require only demonstrable mental health problems (Consensus Project, 2006)

Mental health courts generally handle misdemeanant and felony cases involving mentally ill defendants (Berstein & Selzer, 2004). The first-generation mental health courts (which include Broward County, Florida; King County, Washington; Clark County, Washington; Seattle, Washington; San Bernardino, California; Santa Barbara, California; Anchorage, Alaska; and Marion County, Indiana), which began in the mid- to late-1990s, initially accepted defendants with only misdemeanor charges (Goldkamp & Irons-Guynn, 2000; Griffin, Steadman, & Petrila, 2002). On the other hand, the second-generation mental health courts (Santa Clara County, California; Orange County, North Carolina; Allegheny County, Pennsylvania; Washoe County, Nevada; Brooklyn, New York; Bonneville County, Idaho; and Orange County, California) accept persons charged with felonies as well as misdemeanors (Steadman & Redlich, 2006). However, most second-generation courts place restrictions on the type of violent charges and criminal histories and are willing to apply a "totality of the circumstances" approach and examine the circumstances surrounding the crime, person, and overall situation before making a decision to accept or reject felons (Steadman & Redlich, 2006). Berstein and Selzer (2004) reported in their analysis of 20 mental health courts that 80% were willing to consider persons charged with violent acts. A survey conducted by the Council of State Governments (CSG) of mental health courts in 30 states in 2005 indicated that 34% of the courts deal with misdemeanors, 10% with felony cases, and 56% accept offenders who have committed misdemeanors and felonies (Consensus Project, 2006).

A requirement across all mental health courts is that participation should be voluntary. Defendants are invited to participate in the mental health court following a specialized screening and assessment. Defendants must affirmatively "opt-in" to receive treatment or decline participation in the court proceedings. The defendant has to agree to participate in treatment, generally through a contract with the judge. Voluntariness is crucial for participation in the mental health courts because the singling out of defendants with mental illnesses for different treatment by the courts could violate the equal protection guarantee of the 14th Amendment. Little knowledge is available on how (or if) the courts ensure that decision making is indeed voluntary (Berstein & Selzer, 2004).

## MENTAL HEALTH COURT PROCESS

Mental health courts have separate dockets, exclusively, with a judge, prosecutors, and defense attorneys who all have training in dealing with defendants with mental illnesses. The judge may preside over a mental health court held once or twice a week or as often as necessary. The mental health courts also have pretrial-services personnel, who are responsible for developing treatment plans, and probation officers who monitor defendants' compliance with the plans once incorporated into court orders. The professionals in these courts are familiar with existing service resources, and they work together with defendants and service providers to get the proper services for each defendant (Berstein & Selzer, 2004; Goldkamp & Irons-Guynn, 2000).

In terms of adjudication, there is no single "model" used by the mental health courts. Each court operates independently with its own rules and procedures and has its own way of addressing service issues (Berstein & Selzer, 2004). However, a guilty or no contest plea is required as a condition of participation. Griffin, Steadman, and Petrila (2002) identified three models: pre-adjudication, post plea-based, and probation-based. Under the pre-adjudication approach, the prosecutor can defer, suspend, or hold the charges in abeyance while the defendant participates in the agreed-upon treatment. The post-plea adjudication approach involves the adjudication of the offender but the disposition is deferred. Under the probation-based model, the defendant is convicted and sentenced to probation. The sentence may also include suspended or deferred jail time, and treatment is a condition of probation (Berstein & Selzer, 2004). It is clear that under the post-plea adjudication and the probation-based models, the defendant is referred to the mental health courts at a later stage of the criminal justice process than under the pre-adjudication plea. Consequently, it sometimes takes up to 28 days from referral to first appearance in court for post-plea defendants (Steadman, Redlich, Griffin, Petrila, & Monahan, 2005). This can imply that some defendants who are referred to mental health courts after a guilty plea are spending more time in jail as compared to earlier mental health courts. Forty percent of courts surveyed in 2005 revealed that they require a participant to enter a guilty plea (Consensus Project, 2006).

The mental health courts follow different models of supervision. One approach to supervision is for the courts to delegate the supervision of mental health court participants to community treatment providers who have to report back to the court on a regular basis and/or when difficulties arise. A second approach requires supervision to be provided by court staff or probation/parole officers. In this approach, the court staff or probation officer usually has a specific caseload and works exclusively with mental health court participants. The third approach necessitates that mental health staff and probation officers work together (Griffin, Steadman, & Petrila, 2002). First-generation mental health courts follow the three models, and although second-generation courts tend to fit one of these three models, the majority of them rely on supervision by personnel directly linked to the court. In general, the types of supervision employed by the first- and second-generation courts are similar, but the frequency with which they are used differs (Steadman & Redlich, 2006).

Some mental health courts apply a series of graduated sanctions and rewards to help improve compliance with treatment mandates. Mental health courts will impose sanctions on participants who fail to comply with the court-ordered conditions, ranging from reprimands from a judge, changes in treatment plans, community service, and jail incarceration (Griffin, Steadman, & Petrila, 2002). In their report on 20 mental health courts, Berstein and Selzer (2004) found that 64% of mental health courts were willing to place people in jail for noncompliance with the conditions. However, Steadman and Redlich (2006) reported that the second-generation courts were more willing to place people in jail than first-generation courts.

## CRITICISMS OF THE MENTAL HEALTH COURTS

One of the most positive aspects of mental health courts is that they serve a specific group of offenders. They also provide an alternative to incarceration that can exacerbate psychiatric symptoms, because mentally ill inmates are likely to be victimized while incarcerated. As an alternative to incarceration, mental health courts provide access to an array of community treatment and support services. These specialized courts can adapt to meet the needs of the participants and the communities in which the courts are located and the type of populations that they serve (Watson, Hanrahan, Luchins, & Lurigio, 2001).

There are, however, some problems with mental health courts. Mental health courts can serve only a limited number of people with mental illness. Although the number of courts has rapidly increased in recent years, many jurisdictions still do not offer them. In 2005, more than 40% of the mental health courts were located in California, Ohio, Florida, and Washington. In fact, only 15% and 11% were found in the Midwest and Northeast, respectively (Consensus Project, 2006). This limitation may be the result of a lack of funding and resistance to specialized courts on the part of some judges and prosecutors (Tashiro, Cashman, & Mahoney, 2000).

Another significant problem is the lack of ongoing resources to operate mental health courts and a shortage of mental health treatment services to support them (Goldkamp & Irons-Guynn, 2000). Existing services typically do not include an adequate range of services, and access can be difficult. In addition, these services can be costly. Steadman and colleagues (2001) concluded that without access to a range of mental health and supportive services, mental health courts have a limited impact on the people most in need of help.

Some critics believe that mental health courts further stigmatize and criminalize the mentally ill (Watson et al., 2000). Those who hold this view believe that stigma is increased when criminal courts are involved in the mental health system. They fear that, if services associated with mental health courts are adequately funded, more charges may be filed against people with mental illness to get them services, further criminalizing them (Lamb, Weinberger, & Reston-Parham, 1996).

A final concern is the quality of mental health courts outcome studies. A review of the few studies (by this author) that exist on mental health courts indicates that very few of these courts have been effectively evaluated. Few longitudinal studies were conducted to determine the overall impact and efficacy of the courts in reducing criminal behavior. In addition, the review revealed that the courts had no systematic and uniform way of collecting information on their clients. For example, some courts collected data on their clients by race and gender, whereas others did not. Others kept data on recidivism and sanctions, whereas others did not. It is clear that there is no consensus on what, how, and when the data should be collected. Without data collection, there can be no outcome evaluations.

## WOMEN IN MENTAL HEALTH COURTS

On any given day, tens of thousands of inmates with serious medical or mental health conditions are housed in federal, state, and local correctional facilities around the nation. Prevalence rates for certain mental illnesses such as schizophrenia and bipolar disorder are estimated to be significantly higher among prison and jail inmates than among the population at large (Conly, 2005).

Data regarding the number of women referred to and served by mental health courts are scant. However, the results of a survey of 113 mental health courts in which the gender of the client was identified are shown in Table 6.1. The data show that the number of women who are referred to the mental health court varies by jurisdiction.

**TABLE 6.1**  Number of Women in Mental Health Courts

| City/County | Year Started | Percentage/Number of Women |
|---|---|---|
| Superior Court of California, Orange County, Santa Ana, California | 2002 | 48% |
| Dougherty Superior Court, Mental Health/Substance Abuse Division, Albany, Georgia | 2002 | 50% |
| Orleans Parish Criminal District Court Mental Health Court, Louisiana | 2003 | 11 African-American women |
| McCurtain County Mental Health Court, Idabel, Oklahoma | 2004 | 80% |
| Dallas County Mental Health Jail Diversion Program, Dallas, Texas. | 2004 | 50% |
| Seattle Municipal Court, Seattle, Washington, started March, 1999 | 1999 | 25% |

*Data Source:* Consensus Project. (2005, December). Survey of Mental Health Courts.

The mental health court in Brooklyn reported that 23% of those referred to the court between March 2002 and 2004 were women (O'Keefe, 2006). A review of two of the largest mental health courts found that approximately 25% were women (Goldkamp & Irons-Guynn, 2000). A survey of seven second-generation mental health courts revealed that women were much more likely than men to be referred to mental health courts. The researchers also found that older, White women were more likely to be referred to the courts, which is similar to the practices of other types of diversion programs (Steadman & Redlich, 2006).

## GENDER-SENSITIVE SERVICES FOR MENTALLY ILL WOMEN

Women served by the mental health courts will have different mental health problems than men, and operationally the courts should adjust their practices that have been established for male offenders. Therefore, when mental health court personnel address the unique needs of women, it is important to take into consideration the complex and female-specific issues that they present. Although there are no comprehensive data regarding the multiple disorders evident in women in mental health courts, research on women with mental illness has unequivocally indicated that women with mental illness are at significantly greater risk for multiple psychosocial problems. Likewise, research on women in the criminal justice system suggests also that the majority of women are likely to suffer from co-occurring disorders and trauma due to violence.

Using the femicentric approach,[1] this section provides an analysis of the specific needs of women who will be served by the mental health courts. Many of these mentally ill women are likely to have multiple disorders.

### FEMICENTRIC APPROACH

The femicentric approach is a female-centered approach that integrates a female-based perspective and a female-based analysis into understanding the problems of women in society. It focuses on the perspectives of the female including her vulnerability as a female and her unique experiences, and on female-based services. This approach also examines females' roles and responsibilities, access to and control over resources, and her social position in society. Central to this approach is an understanding of the concept of femininity that makes women and girls vulnerable in our society. It implies that special attention be given to females and that strategies should be adopted to ensure the elimination of their disadvantage and vulnerability in society.

As an analytical tool, the femicentric approach is rooted in a systematic process and challenges the assumption that everyone is affected by policies, programs, and legislation in the same way regardless of gender. It, therefore, assesses the implications for females in any planned action, including legislation, policies, or programs, and provides guidelines for the integration of the female perspective into the decision-making process. Femicentric analysis offers a systematic, analytic tool that can be used to examine diversity within and between populations and subgroups (according to age, culture, socioeconomic status, sexual orientation, race, ethnicity, education, location, etc.). In other words, this perspective examines the multifaceted experiences of females and the social context that defines and controls them.

In practice, the femicentric approach focuses on the development of female-sensitive policies and practices that address the practical and strategic needs of females. It seeks to give guidance to programmers and practitioners on how to devise programs that will benefit women and girls. This approach also requires that interventions be redesigned using frameworks that protect and promote the rights of females. An essential feature of the femicentric approach is a focus on strategies for the empowerment of women and girls, thereby helping clients to take control of their own destinies.

In general, this approach represents a paradigmatic shift from the mainstream-centric or male-focused approach of understanding social phenomenon to a reframing of the issue with the female as the central focus. Thus, this paradigmatic shift is a critical step in integrating females' needs and rights at all levels of society.

The feminicentric approach is necessary for understanding females with multiple disorders served by the mental health courts. This approach will provide a better understanding of the relationship between these multiple disorders and how they impact women's lives. This approach legitimizes and officially recognizes the experiences of women with mental illness and other disorders. This will help to transform their experiences from mere "individual" and "isolated" experiences to experiences of an important segment of society that needs specific attention. Consequently, policy makers and practitioners in the mental health courts can use the femicentric approach to adopt female-related services for these offenders.

## FEMALE-SENSITIVE NEEDS OF MENTALLY ILL WOMEN

Many diversion programs and specialty courts are female insensitive because they often use a male-oriented approach. Very few diversion programs recognize that women have substantially different health and mental health needs from men. Consequently, most diversion programs in specialty courts do not provide appropriate treatment modalities and referrals to appropriate community-based services for women (Hills, 2004). However, substance abuse treatment with gender-specific programs improve retention and outcomes for women in substance abuse treatment (Zerger, 2002). For example, a Los Angeles study that examined women treated in publicly funded residential drug treatment programs found that participants in women-only programs were twice as likely to complete treatment compared to women in mixed-gender programs (Grella, 1999).

In order to best serve women, mental health courts have to provide policies, procedures, and programs that are female-specific, taking into account the specific needs of women relative to men. There are, however, very few specialized programs in mental health courts for women defendants. One such program in Florida, called OPTIONS, started in January 2000 as part of the Broward County Mental Health Court. It was funded by the Edward Byrne Memorial State and Local Law Enforcement Assistance Program, Bureau of Justice Assistance, U.S. Department of Justice. As a demonstration project, it was designed to: (a) divert mentally ill adult women from the criminal justice system; (b) provide innovative mental health treatment designed especially for this community through careful evaluation, and arrange for medical treatment including psychopharmacological evaluation for women; (c) conduct research, outcome evaluation, and cost-benefit analysis, and (d) disseminate program information to other communities. Although designed for referrals primarily from the mental health court, the OPTIONS program received requests from a variety of other programs in the court and mental health community. Probation officers, for example, referred clients needing similar treatment who had other contact with the criminal justice system; parole officers referred clients being discharged from prison; and mental health workers referred clients being discharged from the psychiatric hospitals including the "Cottages," a program designed for those within the mental health court system needing immediate hospitalization (Levant & Walker, 2002).

During the first year of its operation, the program served 64 women even though the program was designed for 40 women. It provided comprehensive psychological, psychiatric, and neuropsychological evaluation, and integrated treatment including outpatient therapy, psychopharmacology, rehabilitation, and integration into the community for its clients. The program also worked with the local chapter of the National Alliance for the Mentally Ill (NAMI), families of the clients, and the other agencies in the community. Evaluation of the program indicated that very few of the women were rearrested after they began attending the program. Despite its apparent success, unfortunately the funding was discontinued for FY 2001 (Levant & Walker, 2002).

## WOMEN WITH CO-OCCURRING DISORDERS

The term "co-occurring disorders" is used to indicate the simultaneous diagnosis of a substance use disorder and a serious mental illness (Office of Applied Studies, 2004a). People with substance abuse disorders are more likely to develop mental illness and people with mental illness are more likely to develop a substance abuse disorder. Many people with mental illnesses also may "self-medicate" with alcohol or drugs and need chemical dependency treatment. Likewise, persons with substance abuse disorders are likely to have a mental illness. Women represent 48% of adults with co-occurring disorders (Office of Applied Studies, 2004b). Rach-Beisel, Scott, and Dixon (1999) found in their study that, although the estimates of the prevalence of substance use disorders vary by population, there was a higher prevalence among persons with severe mental illness. They also reported that severe mental illness is negatively affected by a substance use disorder, and they suggested that an integrated approach to the treatment of both disorders would be the most promising treatment strategy. It is clear that having a mental illness tends to increase the probability of having a substance abuse disorder.

Compared to others in the criminal justice system, individuals with mental illnesses are more likely to be using drugs or alcohol when they commit a crime, to have been homeless in the prior 12 months, and to have been in jail or prison or on probation prior to their current sentence (Ditton, 1999). Prevalence of substance use disorders among those with severe mental disorders in local jails is extremely high (National GAINS Center, 2004). Research by Alemagno and associates (2004) found that females in jails were significantly more likely than males to be at risk for co-occuring disorders. A review of two of the largest mental health courts found that between 25% and 45% both had a major mental illness and a substance abuse disorder (Goldkamp & Irons-Guynn, 2000). The regular use of drugs and alcohol by inmates in jails and prisons contributes to or exacerbates their health and mental health conditions (Conly, 2005). It is clear that mental illness and substance abuse often have a symbiotic relationship and that many of the offenders referred to mental health courts are likely to have co-occurring disorders: mental illness and substance abuse problems.

Given the pervasiveness of substance abuse among women offenders in the criminal justice system, mental health courts will have to serve women with substance abuse problems. Although co-occurring disorders affect both men and women, women with co-occurring disorders are likely to have distinct problems, patterns of engagement, and treatment needs (Alexander, 1996; DiNitto, Webb, & Rubin, 2002; Mallouh, 1996). Consequently, these women with co-occurring disorders will present unique challenges to diversion programs, especially if these experiences contributed to their involvement in criminal activity (Hills, 2004). Unfortunately, women who are mentally ill and have substance abuse problems often have to acquire service from two different agencies because many women with co-occurring disorders do not attend treatment services designed to treat both mental health and substance abuse problems (Center for Substance Abuse Treatment, 2005; Epstein, Vorburger, & Murtha, 2004; Office of Applied Studies, 2004b). According to the results of Substance Abuse and Mental Health Services Administration's (SAMHSA) National Survey on Drug Use and Health, 48% of adults in the United States with co-occurring health and substance use disorders sought either mental health or substance abuse treatment, whereas only 12% of this group received both types of services (Epstein et al., 2004).

Very few mental health court services incorporate mental illness and substance abuse treatment for women. Ohio is one of the few states that provides coordinated services through the court system for women with co-occurring disorders. In March 2001, the Alternative Interventions for Women (AIW) program started in Cincinnati, Ohio, as an innovative program of identification, early intervention, and treatment for female offenders with co-occurring mental health and substance abuse disorders to help support criminal justice and sentencing sanctions. The program provides an array of assessment and treatment services for women with co-occurring mental health and substance abuse disorders including (a) screening and early identification, in-depth assessment and referral, and (b) treatment. This program, led by the Court Clinic, is a collaborative effort across the criminal justice, mental health, and substance abuse systems. This program is funded through a partnership with The Health Foundation of Greater Cincinnati, the Hamilton County Probation Department, the Hamilton County Department of Pretrial Services, the Hamilton County Community Mental Health Board, and the Hamilton County TASC. Women referred by the Court receive an in-depth clinical assessment performed by Court Clinic assessment specialists and licensed clinical psychologists. The clinical assessment determines whether the woman meets criteria for co-occurring mental health and substance abuse disorders and is appropriate for referral to the Alternative Interventions for Women treatment program. Services are gender-specific and address not only women's pathways to crime, but also the importance of relationships, self-efficacy, and self-esteem for recovery. The program employs an all-female staff and offers a safe environment for the clients. During its first two years of operation (March, 2001–March, 2003), the Alternative Interventions for Women program screened more than 4,500 women at Pretrial Services, completed in-depth assessments and made treatment recommendations for more than 400 women, and initiated treatment with 90 women with co-occurring mental health and substance abuse disorders. Sixteen of these women graduated successfully from the treatment program and were connected with community resources as needed. The average length of stay for these graduates was one year. The Alternative Interventions for Women program is unique in that each of the systems agreed to come together collaboratively, pool resources, and commit to providing a continuum of services to treat this underserved population (Grace & Melton, 2003).

## MENTALLY ILL WOMEN WITH TRAUMA

Violence in the lives of women and children is so widespread it is sometimes described as an "epidemic" in American society. Women receiving mental health care are rarely asked about a history of sexual or physical abuse (Levin & Blanch, 1998). According to Markham (2003), mental illnesses such as depression, post-traumatic stress disorder, and substance abuse occur in 60% to 90% of battered women. Research shows that the overwhelming majority of women defendants in the criminal justice system have extensive histories of childhood and adult abuse that may result in homelessness, substance abuse, and economic marginality that force them into survival by illegal means. Therefore, given the prevalence of sexual and physical abuse of women in society, mental health courts are likely to be serving trauma survivors.

The effects of violence and the resulting trauma can substantially affect the mental, physical, emotional, and economic well-being of the victim. Women who experience physical abuse as children are at increased risk for mental illness (Moses, Reed, Mazelis, & D'Ambrosio, 2003). Sexual or physical abuse has been associated with post-traumatic stress disorder, anxiety, depression, psychotic symptoms, personality disorders, as well as suicidal tendencies, risky sex and drug practices, and substance abuse (Goodman et al., 1997).

Appropriate treatment for the mentally ill woman who has experienced violence must be trauma-specific. Trauma-specific services are those designed to directly address the effects of trauma, with the main goals of healing and recovery. Trauma-specific services take into account the special needs of women in relation to their gender and experiences of trauma. These services incorporate procedures and strategies that are designed for traumatized women and administered in a trauma-sensitive environment. This approach uses techniques and programs that are noncoercive, nonthreatening, and will not retraumatize the clients (Moses, Reed, Mazelis, & D'Ambrosio, 2003). Mental health providers need to be aware of the impact of trauma in women's lives, and the need to address this in trauma-sensitive treatment approaches. Mental health courts should, therefore, attempt to provide trauma-sensitive services for women and provide or refer women to programs that incorporate an awareness of trauma and abuse into all aspects of treatment (Hills, 2004).

## SOCIAL CONTEXT OF MENTAL ILLNESS: ISSUES OF CULTURE, PARENTING, AND POVERTY

The femicentric approach recognizes that women of differing ages, socioeconomic status, geographic locations, ethno-cultural backgrounds, abilities, and sexual orientations have different concerns and needs, all of which should be addressed by the mental health courts. Race, ethnicity, gender, and culture are associated with variations in prevalence, diagnoses, and treatment of substance abuse and mental disorders and must be considered in treating co-occurring disorders.

The 2001 report of then Surgeon General David Satcher, *Mental Health: Culture, Race, and Ethnicity*, found that the health needs of certain racial and ethnic minorities are unmet, and thus these groups suffer a greater loss to their overall health. He suggested that racial and ethnic minorities should be better represented among health and mental health care providers and that all providers offer culturally competent services (U.S. Department of Health and Human Services, 2001).

Cultural background determines how individuals describe symptoms and assign meanings to them, how they cope with personal difficulties, whether they are willing or reluctant to seek treatment, and how they confront the stigma associated with both substance abuse and mental disorders (U.S. Department of Health and Human Services, 2001). Because different cultural groups view mental illness differently, the mental health courts should offer services that take into account the cultural backgrounds of the clients. Likewise, diagnoses should be as free as possible of cultural biases. One of the fundamental requirements of culturally appropriate services is that mental health providers identify and then work in conjunction with natural support systems within the racial and ethnic minority communities they serve (Greenbaum, 1998). Culturally relevant and culturally appropriate services for women in mental health courts should incorporate an understanding of traditions and beliefs of the diverse cultural backgrounds and focus on the strengths of their cultures, especially minority cultures, which focus on collectivity rather than individuality. Culturally competent services should also be consumer-driven, community-based, and accessible to the clients and their families. In other words, the mental health courts should use ethno-specific approaches and meaningful services for women in mental health courts.

Many women in the mental health courts will be parents who value their roles as mothers. However, historically, most treatment philosophies and services for these women have neither considered the importance of women's roles as mothers nor included their children. Very often mentally ill mothers are expected to fit into the male-oriented treatment paradigms of nonparents. The system does not treat them as parents and often ignores this aspect of their lives and personhood (Cogan, 1998). Although a number of these women do not have custody of their children, motherhood is a major source of identity and self-worth, as well as a source of shame and guilt (Ackerson, 2003). Mentally ill mothers need support and assistance in dealing not only with their illnesses, but also with life stressors, especially those of parenting. Services for mentally ill mothers should, therefore, include counseling on parenting and joint programs for mothers and children, if possible. In general, mental health courts should include parenting needs in their assessments of women with mental illness.

For decades, one question has been: Does poverty breed mental illness, or does mental illness result in poverty? The two problems are clearly related and tend to go together, because socioeconomic status is a very important dimension of mental illness and mental illness can affect one's economic status.

Draine and associates (2002) argued that poverty plays a pivotal role in mental illness. They suggest that "poverty moderates the relationship between serious mental illness and social problems" (p. 565). A study based on a database of 34,000 patients with two or more psychiatric hospitalizations in Massachusetts during 1994–2000 revealed that unemployment, poverty, and housing unaffordability were correlated with the risk of mental illness. The results of this study imply that socioeconomic status impacts the development of mental illness directly, as well as indirectly through its association with adverse economic stressful conditions among lower-income groups (Hudson, 2005).

This class disparity is quite evident in the criminal justice system because the majority of persons enmeshed in the system are poor. Because research has indicated that the majority of persons who are mentally ill are poor, one can assume that the majority of defendants in mental health courts are poor. Low-income people with mental disorders are at increased risk of unemployment and homelessness. However, the specific needs of mothers with children, especially those who are homeless, often are not met in existing treatment programs. Lack of childcare is a significant barrier for many homeless women with substance abuse who are seeking treatment (Zerger, 2002). Mental illness services, treatment, and intervention strategies used by mental health courts should pay special attention to the impact of unemployment, economic displacement, and housing dislocation (including homelessness). These individuals require comprehensive services that address both the addiction and poverty-related problems that affect treatment outcome.

## AN INTEGRATED APPROACH TO SERVICE DELIVERY

The mental health courts should address not only the psychological and physical needs of the women they serve, they should do this in an integrated way. Integrated treatment services that treat multiple problems have been found to be more effective than nonintegrated services (Drake et al., 2001).

It is clear that women served by the mental health courts are likely to have a multiplicity of disorders, including drug abuse/addiction and trauma. There is a complex and multifaceted relationship between mental illness, drug abuse, and trauma. For women, mental illness, substance abuse, and violence are interrelated. Experiences of abuse may increase the risk of substance abuse or mental health problems, whereas substance abuse problems may put women at a greater danger of being sexually and physically abused, leading to trauma. Women who suffer from trauma as a result of violence may develop mental health problems. Women who have experienced any form of sexual abuse as children are also three times more likely than other women to report drug dependence as adults (Zickler, 2002). Likewise, individuals with post-traumatic stress disorder may be more likely those without post-traumatic stress disorder to abuse substances (Jacobsen et al., 2001), and the combination of trauma and co-occurring disorders makes an individual all the more vulnerable to victimization (Calhoun et al., 2000). Physical and/or sexual abuse may also lead to the development of mental health symptoms, substance abuse, and a wide range of physical health problems. Regardless of which pathology leads to the other (the time-ordering of these pathologies), the relationship between them is profound (see Figure 6.1). Women with a history of mental illness, substance abuse, and trauma have multiple service needs that are best met through integrated and coordinated systems of care, and a holistic approach to treatment. Recovery can be achieved only through attention to the interconnectedness of these issues that face women, and through the creation of multidisciplinary, interconnected, and comprehensive services system delivery models.

Despite the relationship between mental illness and other disorders, mental health, substance abuse, and trauma issues are usually addressed by separate service systems in a compartmentalized and disconnected way. Currently, service delivery systems are woefully inadequate in identifying and meeting the needs of women affected by trauma, psychiatric disorders, and substance abuse.

There are three approaches to service delivery for individuals with multiple disorders. First, there is the sequential approach in which the individual receives one type of treatment for one disorder (either mental health or substance abuse) followed by treatment for the other disorder, with treatment provided by two different agencies (Ries, 1993). This was the approach that the OPTIONS program (discussed above) used because those women who were still using alcohol and drugs were sent to a community detoxification center before they began the OPTIONS program (Levant & Walker, 2002). Second, there is also the parallel approach in which different agencies offer mental health services and treatment for other disorders simultaneously. However, these services are rarely coordinated. Finally, there is the integrated services approach in which the individual participates in concurrent and coordinated clinical treatment of both mental illnesses and other disorders provided by the same clinician or treatment team, often in a single agency (Ries, 1993). It is clear that both the sequential and parallel approaches use separate service systems with different treatment philosophies, eligibility criteria, and operating procedures that work in isolation from each other. For the best results, services and treatment for mentally ill clients with multiple disorders should be concurrent and carefully coordinated (Minkoff, 1989; Osher & Kofoed, 1989; Ridgely et al., 1987), particularly because women with multiple disorders may have difficulty navigating multiple treatment systems. For many women with multiple disorders in mental health courts, successful treatment would require addressing multiple aspects of their lives. Consequently, an integrated service delivery approach that would offer a continuum of services for women should be used in the mental health courts.

## INTEGRATED SERVICES DELIVERY APPROACH

The term "services integration" is a construct that has been applied to efforts to develop service delivery systems that are responsive to the multiple needs of persons at risk (Stevens & Rielly, 2000, p. 4). An integrated service delivery approach can be viewed as the use of coordinated multiple services delivered by the same clinician or teams of clinicians for a single client. It refers to the organization of activities between or among different agencies or entire service systems designed toward improving the coordination of services between agencies or systems. It consists of the same health professionals who provide interventions that are bundled together, so that the clients receive consistent treatment, with no division between mental health disorders or other types of disorders (Drake et al., 2001; Rach-Beisel et al., 1999; Substance Abuse and Mental Health Services Administration, 2002). This approach eliminates the need for the clients to consult with separate teams and programs for treatment. In addition, "services integration strategies for this population must not only develop networks of care, but must also address the structural characteristics within those systems of care that fragment, retraumatize, and fail to address the needs that women themselves express" (Stevens & Rielly, 2000, p. 3). Integrated service delivery approaches should use comprehensive and coordinated community-based services including wraparound services, multisystemic therapy, and multidimensional therapeutic care, and be delivered by a multidisciplinary treatment team that includes a diverse team of professionals.

Through the collaboration of services, the mental health courts can provide women with a safe environment to begin the process of recovery from mental illness, substance use disorders, and histories of trauma and abuse. By incorporating a vast array of services under an integrated conceptual framework, women with mental health problems can be treated taking into account their individual level and scope of dysfunction. Moreover, the development of an integrated service delivery model

**FIGURE 6.1**    Integrated Model and Relationship between the Disorders

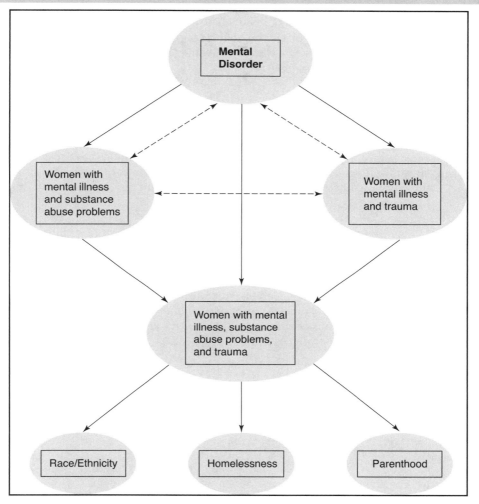

utilizes the most effective treatment technologies used for treating addiction, trauma, and mental illness. Providing appropriate, integrated services for these clients will not only allow for their recovery and improved overall health, but can also ameliorate the effects their disorders have on their family, friends, and society at large. The integrated model is shown in Figure 6.1.

## RECOMMENDATIONS

Research, policy, and program initiatives have traditionally ignored the multiple needs of women with mental illness. At this early point in the development of mental health courts, there is a paucity of information on the effectiveness of mental health courts in the lives of the clients, especially women. Valid assessment, for example, is critical for the evaluation of mental health courts. Uniform standardized instruments have not been developed, and more work needs to be done to validate the assessment tools that measure the effectiveness of mental health courts. The following are some recommendations for the improvement of the effectiveness of service to mentally ill women who are served by mental health courts.

### POLICY-RELATED

- The services for females should be "female-centered." Services in mental health courts for women must reflect the diversity of women in American society, and they must develop innovative approaches to address the multiple vulnerabilities of these women. Policy or program initiatives that fail to take the whole woman into account are doomed to be less effective and, most likely, more costly.
- Information about best practices and evaluations of mental health services in the United States and internationally would be a highly useful resource for professionals, front-line workers, and policy makers in the development of comprehensive programs for the heterogeneous and diverse populations served by mental health courts.
- Standardized service plans and treatment protocols should be used by all the mental health courts in an attempt to eliminate inconsistency. Successful well-developed programs could serve as models for replication. The development of new intervention strategies must be explored as well.

### DATA COLLECTION

Mental health courts need to collect comprehensive data on the following:

- The number of women they serve, their characteristics, and criminal histories.
- The type of services available to women, how often they receive services, and how they received these services.
- Criminal justice outcomes, such as the number of arrests during and subsequent to program participation, type of charge, number and types of violations, and number of admissions to jail or prison during program participation.
- Mental health outcomes, such as the effects of the services on participants' mental health symptoms and overall functioning, changes in symptoms, changes in quality of life, number of inpatient hospitalizations, and number of emergency room admissions.
- Court processes such as how many defendants are referred to the courts, how many are accepted, and the reasons for nonacceptance.

### PREVENTION

Studying and treating the end stages of mental illness is considerably more difficult than understanding and intervening early in the course of the illness. The number of women who enter the mental health courts could be prevented if states provide short-term, intensive, community support services for the mentally ill immediately after discharge from hospitals or shelters. In other words, states need to develop their community-based mental health services. In addition, states need to reduce the barriers to treatment, which include fragmentation of treatment services, lack of adequate mental health-care coverage, lack of adequate financial support, lack of prerelease planning, homelessness, and laws regarding involuntary commitment to mental institutions. States need to create more effective and comprehensive community-based services for women with mental illness. These services should be available and accessible to mentally ill women, and these services are essential to prevent their involvement in the criminal justice system. States need to continue to develop community-based intervention strategies and support services among severely mentally ill adults, thereby diverting them away from the criminal justice system.

### FUTURE RESEARCH

A number of research foci can be identified for further research. Longitudinal data is needed to understand when and how the services provided by mental health courts have prevented and reversed the effects of mental illness and other types of related disorders. Women with multiple disorders and risk factors, such as homelessness and unemployment, should be followed over a long period of time to determine their patterns of adjustment and the quality of life after being served by the mental health courts.

Mental health courts need to collect comprehensive information on program services, operational components, and service delivery. The use of experimental designs to test program impacts can be useful to evaluate mental health courts. These evaluations should be specific about how and when the data were collected.

Mental health courts also need to conduct multiyear studies to determine the long-term impacts of mental health courts on clients, primarily women. Such data will be necessary to give a more accurate picture about their operations and effect on recidivism. In addition, mental health courts should collect information on other postprogram outcomes such as employment, health, family problems, parent-child relationships, and drug use.

Mental health courts also need to study whether the costs of operating these programs are lower than the economic benefits of incarceration. Consequently, these courts should collect cost data, and the methods used to analyze this dimension of mental health courts should be consistent throughout the nation so that valid comparisons can be made.

## CONCLUSION

The number of mentally ill persons entering into the criminal justice system has increased dramatically over the past several decades. This has been the result of the failure of mental health institutions, the process of deinstitutionalization, and the inadequacy of community-based mental health services. Mental health courts can help female offenders obtain access to services, and they can divert them from further involvement in the criminal justice system if these services are carefully designed and implemented. However, without an understanding of the scope of the problem, practitioners in mental health courts cannot adequately develop comprehensive, supportive, and accessible services for women with mental illness, and so intervention programs are likely to fail.

The growing body of interdisciplinary research shows that mental health courts will deal with a heterogeneous and diverse population of women. These women will be from various cultural backgrounds, ages, and religions and will have multiple disorders. Recovery for women served by the mental health courts may be achievable only through the creation of a multidisciplinary and comprehensive service system that will address attention to the interconnectedness of the problems that mentally ill women face. If such an integrated approach is not taken, these women will recycle through the mental health system, the drug treatment system, and criminal justice systems again and again. However, providing appropriate, integrated services for these women will not only allow for their recovery and improved overall health, but also reduce costs and ameliorate the effects that their disorders have on their family, friends, and society at large. The challenge, therefore, is for mental health courts to provide multidisciplinary and integrated services that are female-centered and female-friendly for women who are referred to the mental health courts.

## References

Ackerson, B. J. (2003). Parents with serious and persistent mental illness: Issues in assessment and services. *Social Work, 48*(2), 187–194.

Alemagno, S., Shaffer-King, E., Tonkin, P., & Hammel, R. (2004). *Characteristics of arrestees at risk for co-existing substance abuse and mental disorder.* Washington, DC: U.S. Department of Justice.

Alexander, M. J. (1996). Women with co-occurring addictive and mental disorders: An emerging profile of vulnerability. *American Journal of Orthopsychiatry, 66*(1), 61–70.

Berstein, R., & Selzer, T. (2004). *The role of mental health courts in system reform.* Washington, DC: Bazelon Center for Mental Health Law.

Bureau of Justice Assistance. (2004). *Programs: Mental health courts.* Retrieved August 27, 2004, from http://www.ojp.usdoj.gov/BJA/grant/mentalhealth.html

Calhoun, P. S., Sampson, W. S., Bosworth, H. B., Feldman, M. E., Kirby, A. C., Hertzberg, M. A., Wampler, T. P., Tate-Williams, F., Moore, S. D., & Beckham, J. C. (2000). Drug use and validity of substance use self-reports in veterans seeking help for posttraumatic stress disorder. *Journal of Consulting and Clinical Psychology, 68*(5), 923–927.

Center for Substance Abuse Treatment. (2005). *Substance abuse treatment for persons with co-occurring disorders.* Treatment Improvement Protocol (TIP) Series, Number 42. DHHS Publication No. (SMA) 05-3992. Rockville, MD: Substance Abuse and Mental Health Services Administration.

Cogan, J. C. (1998). The consumer as expert: Women with severe mental illness and their relationship based needs. *Psychiatric Rehabilitation Journal, 22*(2), 142–154

Conly, E. (2005). *Helping inmates obtain federal disability benefits: Serious medical and mental illness, incarceration, and Federal Disability Entitlement Programs.* Washington, DC: U.S. Department of Justice.

Consensus Project. (2006). *Mental heath courts: A national snapshot.* Retrieved December 21, 2006, from http://consensusproject.org/mhcp/national-snapshot.pdf

DiNitto, D. M., Webb, D. K., & Rubin, A. (2002). Gender differences in dually-diagnosed clients receiving chemical dependency treatment. *Journal of Psychoactive Drugs, 34*(1), 105–117.

Ditton, P. M. (1999, July). *Mental health and treatment of inmates and probationers* (NCJ 174463). Washington, DC: U.S. Department of Justice, Office of Justice Programs, Bureau of Justice Statistics.

Drake, R. E., Essock, S. M., Shaner, A., Carey, K. B., Minkoff, K., Kola, L., Lynde, D., Osher, F. C., Clark, R. E., & Rickards, L. (2001). Implementing dual diagnosis services for clients with severe mental illness. *Psychiatric Services, 52*, 469–476.

Epstein, J., Barker, P., Vorburger, M., & Murtha, C. (2004). *Serious mental illness and its co-occurrence with substance use disorders, 2002* (DHHS Publication No. SMA 04-3905, Analytic Series A-24). Rockville, MD: Substance Abuse and Mental Health Services Administration.

Goldkamp, J. S., & Irons-Guynn, C. (2000). *Emerging judicial strategies for the mentally ill in the criminal caseload: Mental health courts in Fort Lauderdale, Seattle, San Bernardino, and Anchorage* (NCJ 182504). Washington, DC: U.S. Bureau of Justice Assistance.

Goodman, L. A., Rosenberg, S., Mueser, K., & Drake, R. (1997). Physical and sexual assault history in women with serious mental illness: Prevalence, correlates, treatment and future research directions. *Schizophrenia Bulletin, 23,* 685–697.

Grace, M., & Melton, M. C. (2003). *Alternative interventions for women.* Retrieved October 24, 2006, from http://www.sconet.state.oh.us/ACMIC/resources/alternative.pdf

Greenbaum, S. D. (1998). The role of ethnography in creating linkages with communities: Identifying and assessing neighborhoods' needs and strengths. In M. Hernandez & M. R. Isaacs (Eds.), *Promoting cultural competence in children's mental health services* (pp. 119–132). Baltimore: Paul H. Brookes.

Grella, C. E. (1999). Women in residential drug treatment: Differences by program type and pregnancy. *Journal of Health Care for the Poor and Underserved 10*(2), 216–229.

Griffin, P. A., Steadman, H. J., & Petrila, J. (2002). The use of criminal sanctions in mental health courts. *Psychiatric Services, 53*(10), 1285–1289.

Hills, H. (2004). *The special needs of women with co-occurring disorders diverted from the criminal justice system.* Delmar, NY: The National GAINS Center.

Hudson, C. (2005). Socioeconomic status and mental illness: Tests of the social causation and selection hypotheses. *American Journal of Orthopsychiatry, 75*(1), 3–18.

Jacobsen, L. K., Southwick, S. M., & Kosten, T. R. (2001). Substance abuse disorders in patients with posttraumatic stress disorders: A review of the literature. *The American Journal of Psychiatry, 158*(8), 1184–1190.

Lamb, H. R., Weinberger, L. E., & Reston-Parham, C. (1996). Court intervention to address the mental health needs of mentally ill offenders. *Psychiatric Services, 47*(3), 275–281.

Levant, R. F., & Walker, L. (2002). *Treatment for mental health court clients.* Retrieved September 21, 2006, from http://www.drronaldlevant.com/smi.html

Levin, B. L., & Blanch, A. K. (1998). *Women's mental health services: A public health perspective.* Thousand Oaks, CA: Sage.

Mallouh, C. M. (1996). The effects of dual diagnosis on pregnancy and parenting. *The Journal of Psychoactive Drugs, 28*(4), 367–380.

Markham, D. W. (2003). Mental illness and domestic violence: Implications for family law litigation. *Clearinghouse Review Journal of Poverty Law and Policy, 37,* 1–2, 3–35.

Minkoff, K. (1989). An integrated treatment model for dual diagnosis of psychosis and addiction. *Hospital and Community Psychiatry, 40,* 1031–1036.

Moses, J. D., Reed, B. G., Mazelis, R., & D'Ambrosio, B. (2003). *Creating trauma services for women with co-occurring disorders.* Delmar, NY: Policy Research Associates.

National GAINS Center. (2004). *The prevalence of co-occurring mental illness and substance use disorders in jails.* Retrieved October 18, 2006, from http://www.gainscenter.samhsa.gov/text/disorders/PrevalenceCo-OccurringMentalIllness_Winter_2004.asp.

O'Keefe, K. (2006). *The Brooklyn Mental Health Court evaluation planning, implementation, courtroom dynamics, and participant outcomes.* Retrieved December 22, 2006, from http://www.courtinnovation.org/_uploads/documents/BMHCevaluation.pdf

Office of Applied Studies. (2004a). *The DASIS report: Admissions with co-occurring disorders.* Rockville, MD: Substance Abuse and Mental Health Services Administration. Retrieved September 12, 2006, from http://www.oas.samhsa.gov/2k4/dualTX/dualTX.pdf

Office of Applied Studies. (2004b). *The NSDUH report: Women with co-occurring serious mental illness and a substance use disorder.* Rockville, MD: Substance Abuse and Mental Health

Services Administration. Retrieved September 12, 2006, from http://www.oas.samhsa.gov/2k4/femDual/femDual.pdf

Osher, F. C., & Kofoed, L. L. (1989). Treatment of patients with psychiatric and psychoactive substance abuse disorders. *Hospital and Community Psychiatry, 40,* 1025–1030.

Ridgely, M. S., Osher, F. C., & Talbott, J. A. (1987). *Chronic mentally ill young adults with substance abuse problems: Treatment and training issues.* Rockville, MD: Alcohol, Drug Abuse and Mental Health Administration.

Ries, B. F. (1993). Clinical treatment matching models for dually diagnosed patients. *Recent Advances in Addictive Disorders, 16*(1), 167–175.

Steadman, H. J., Davidson, S., & Brown, C. (2001). Mental health courts: Their promise and unanswered questions. *Psychiatric Services, 52*(4), 457–458.

Steadman, H. J., & Redlich, A. D. (2006). *An evaluation of the Bureau of Justice Assistance mental health court initiative.* Delmar, NY: Policy Research Associates.

Steadman, H. J., Redlich, A. D., Griffin, P., Petrila, J., & Monahan, J. (2005). From referral to disposition: case processing in seven mental health courts *Behavioral Sciences and the Law, 23,* 215–226.

Substance Abuse and Mental Health Services Administration. (2002). Report to Congress on the prevention and treatment of co-occurring substance abuse disorders and mental disorders. U.S. Department of Health and Human Services. Retrieved January 10, 2007, from www.samhsa.gov/reports/congress2002/index.html

Tashiro, S., Cashman, V., & Mahoney, B. (2000). *Institutionalizing drug courts: A focus group meeting report.* U.S. Department of Justice, Drug Courts Program Office, Office of Justice Programs. Retrieved December 22, 2006, from http://www.ncjrs.gov/html/bja/idc/intro.html

U.S. Department of Health and Human Services. (2001). *Mental health: Culture, race, and ethnicity. A supplement to mental health: A report of the surgeon general.* Washington, DC: Author.

Watson, A., Hanrahan, P., Luchins, D., & Lurigio, A. (2001). Mental health courts and the complex issue of mentally ill offenders. *Psychiatric Services, 52*(4), 477–481.

Zerger, S. (2002). *Substance abuse treatment: What works for homeless people?: A review of the literature.* Nashville, TN: National Health Care for the Homeless Council.

Zickler, P. (2002). Childhood sex abuse increases risk for drug dependence. *NIDA Notes 17*(1).

# CHAPTER 7
# WOMEN IN JAIL:
## Mental Health Care Needs and Service Deficiencies

❧

**Phyllis Harrison Ross**
**James E. Lawrence**

## ABSTRACT

The number of women offenders confined in U.S. jails continues to grow at a rate significantly exceeding that of men, creating over the past 20 years a special-needs population of unprecedented size. Jails have been notorious for neglect of health care for women, in particular their mental health care. Women continue to have a profound impact on correctional systems in terms of increasing and intensified demand for mental health services hitherto not delivered on a large scale in jails. The result of high rates of incarceration of women as a social sanction of choice and increased involvement of poor and minority women in behaviors regarded as criminal has been to concentrate unprecedented numbers of women with serious mental health problems in jails. The mental health problems of urban women of color who most often find themselves incarcerated are usually more severe and intractable than those of their male counterparts. Often, these needs have been ignored by these women or given low priority in the community setting in favor of meeting the needs of male domestic partners and children. The result is that women prisoners with mental disorders are disproportionately represented in the nation's jails.

This chapter examines the changing demographics of women offenders, the scope and prevalence of women's mental health problems, and three critically problematic outcomes illustrative of impediments to adequate mental health care for women. A recommended model for case finding, mental health assessment, crisis intervention, and continuity of care, fine-tuned to address the special needs of women, is discussed.

## INTRODUCTION

In response to the past 20 years' unprecedented increase in the number of incarcerated women, particularly poor and minority women, this chapter addresses the specific mental health care needs of women in U.S. jails. These local community institutions have become the repositories and service providers of last resort for women with multiple psychosocial needs, including mental health service needs. Unlike large prison systems, local jails are imbedded in urban and suburban communities and regularly cycle the local criminal clientele to and from these communities. Nevertheless, most local jails have been notorious for their neglect of women and their health care needs. Their mental health care needs, in particular, are driven in part by attitudes toward "bad" women with comorbid psychiatric and substance abuse disorders and a collateral failure to plan adequately for delivery of jail-based mental health services. The influx of a new, poorly understood clientele at risk directly from the community, compounded by the lack of planning for adequate services, has been graphically illustrated by breakdowns in mental health care and, in some cases, associated catastrophic outcomes.

Beginning in the 1980s, the population of incarcerated women underwent profound change as did the impact of women on jail systems. Some of this is related to the fact that U.S. jail populations became the world's largest during the previous decade (Butterfield, 1992). However, the real change in focus on women is associated with the impact on correctional systems of increasing and intensified demand for specialized health care services hitherto not delivered on a large scale in jails. The combined effects of high rates of incarceration used as the social sanction of choice and the increased involvement of poor and minority women in behaviors regarded as criminal has been to concentrate unprecedented numbers of women with serious mental disorders in local correctional institutions. The forces driving this change are unlikely to abate as this new century progresses, particularly as the population becomes increasingly culturally diverse.

As differentiated from prisons and prison systems that provide very stable long-term incarceration long after arrest and initial detention, jails and local penitentiaries are used for the detention of persons awaiting trial on criminal charges or detained as material witnesses or contempt, and for persons serving short determinate sentences for low-level crimes. Except in the largest cities that operate large jail complexes, most U.S. states have a jail in every county, typically located in the county seat, and occasionally a second freestanding institution for short sentence servers. Nearly all of these facilities are under the jurisdiction of elected county sheriffs, with a small minority operated by their state correctional authorities or local departments of correction not reporting to the county sheriff. Jails are therefore largely autonomous, virtually unique institutions, with policies, resources, and services provided on a mostly *ad hoc* basis.

Even the largest jail systems, such as those urban institutions in California, New York, Texas, and Florida, have not traditionally been called upon to respond to the specialized health care needs of large populations of women or even to provide basic parity of quality and availability of the care afforded men. Jail health systems have been largely defined and operated by men for a nearly exclusive male clientele (Alemagno, 2001). In New York, for example, eight county jails (14%) had no services for women in 2005; in fact, they were unable even to detain many of the women committed into custody. Women committed in these counties were boarded out to the relatively few facilities that would accept them, leaving incarcerated women far from home, children, family supports, and legal counsel (New York State Commission of Correction, 2004). The closed and punitive nature of life in jail amplifies impediments to health care access widely experienced by poor women in the community at large, as does the episodic, discontinuous approach to health care encounters within jail settings.

The mental health problems of urban women of color are usually more severe and intractable than those of their male counterparts. Often, their treatment needs have been deferred or ignored in favor of meeting the needs of domestic partners and children. A study of women as they left jail upon transfer to prison found high rates of major depression, dysthymia, anxiety disorder, and panic disorder, often comorbid with alcohol and drug abuse and dependency (Jordan, Schlenger, et al., 1996). A California study found that more than 40% of incarcerated women met the criteria for a DSM-III-R (IV) diagnosed mental disorder. Anxiety disorders predominated among incarcerated mothers and grew proportionately as time passed. A high prevalence of depression was found (Fogel & Martin, 1992). Moreover, even when compelling mental health care needs are identified, incarcerated women remained profoundly misdiagnosed and underserved, according to mental health professionals who have studied this clientele. Less that one-quarter of female inmates in Chicago who had severe mental disorders and needed services received them while in jail. Half of the women detainees diagnosed with schizophrenia or florid bipolar disorder received services, but only 15% of women detainees with depression received services. Men and women were found to be managed differently in this setting. This was attributed in the Chicago study to disparities in resources applied to the needs of women offenders, particularly where their numbers in terms of their proportion of the overall jail population were low, raising the per capita cost of treating women (Teplin, Abram, & McClelland, 1997). More recent work in this field suggests that other impediments to adequate services include gender-specific negative attitudes and beliefs about the problems of women in a male-dominated setting, and the need for gender-specific approaches to women patients aggravated by a failure to recognize the differential potency of the jail setting as a stressor precipitating higher levels of mental distress, somatization, anxiety, and depression in confined women (Lewis, 2006; Lindquist & Lindquist, 1997).

As both the volume and intensity of demand for mental health services rise in coming years, jail administrators will be required to critically examine traditional male-centered mental health care delivery models and refocus on the needs of women. An emphasis on screening and early case finding, timely referral for services, a differential approach to women patients with consequent improved mental health assessment, supervision, maintenance of family connections and ongoing supportive care, as well as a revision of attitudes and beliefs antithetical to quality care must eventuate as women offenders become an ever larger segment of the criminal justice clientele.

In this chapter we examine women offenders as they change the demographic of jail populations, the scope and prevalence of mental health problems among women jail inmates, and their mental health service needs. Some breakdowns in access to and quality of mental health care with fatal consequences are presented in case studies from New York, the nation's fourth largest jail system, along with some recommendations for improved service.

**FIGURE 7.1** Women In U.S. Jails: 1994–2004 (Thousands)

Women in U.S. Jails: 1994–2004 (Thousands)

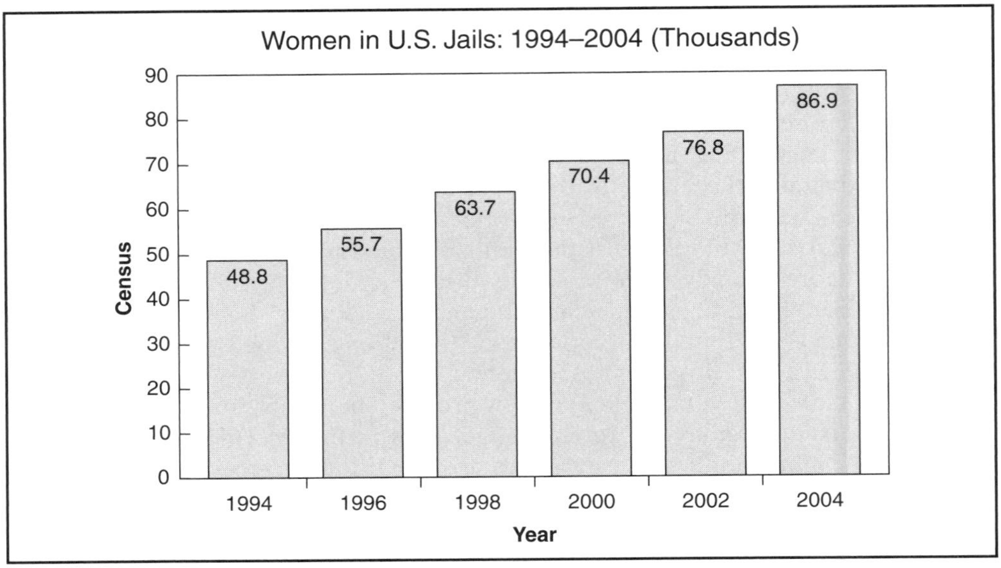

*Source:* U.S. Department of Justice 1998, 2005

## WOMEN IN CUSTODY

The last half of the 1980s saw a dramatic increase in the number of women committed to local jails. Nationally, the census of women in jail increased 6.2% annually between 1994 and 2004, a rate two-thirds greater than that of men over the same period (see Figure 7.1).

## HEALTH CARE NEEDS OF WOMEN OFFENDERS

The social histories of women prisoners are instructive in exploring their mental health problems as a group. The vast majority of women prisoners are poor people of color with substandard housing, legitimate incomes of just over $600 a month, and dependent children (Dixon, 2005). Nationally, 37% of women jail inmates reported being sexually abused before age 18, with 48% reporting abuse histories overall. Half of abused women inmates admitted they were hurt by spouses or boyfriends. Increasingly, family abuse is described. These women have limited access to the community-based mental health care system and limited experience in negotiating its complexities. To an increasing extent, women as a group are immersed in the illicit drug culture as alcoholics, addicts, or the domestic partners of alcoholics and addicts. Because they have been disproportionately victimized and often left solely responsible for dependent children, they are more likely to have been without medical insurance and medical care and more likely to have developed mental health problems (Harrison Ross & Lawrence, 2002).

A study of women jail inmates in Ohio jails in 2004 described the typical female inmate as aged 25–29 and unmarried with a least one child. She is likely to have been the victim of sexual abuse as a child and of physical abuse as an adult. She is also likely to have an alcohol and/or drug abuse problem with age of onset as early as 15 years. She has dropped out of high school, is on public assistance, has few skills, and holds mainly low-wage jobs (Alemagno & Dickie, 2005).

As the population of women in jail has burgeoned, it has become increasingly clear to practitioners and researchers that the array of psychosocial issues these women have correlates to mental disorder and mental health treatment needs. Substance abuse, family fragmentation, economic instability, and social isolation have particular relevance to the mental health treatment needs of this population (Singer, 1995). Incarcerated women have been in the past and are increasingly reported to have extensive and overlapping experience with the criminal justice and mental health service systems (Lamb & Grant, 1983).

## MENTAL DISORDERS AMONG WOMEN IN JAIL

Wherever women jail inmates have been available in numbers sufficient for reliable study, their mental health service needs have been shown to exceed those of men. Human Rights Watch reports that as many as one in five inmates in jail are seriously and persistently mentally ill and that figures for women in jail are higher, as high as 29% of all women prisoners (Butterfield, 2003). Anxiety and depression are the most prevalent mental health problems among women prisoners, with some evidence that many women suffer from post-traumatic stress disorder while in jail. Mothers and those without children typically show similarly high levels of depression. The mean depression level shown by a sample of incarcerated women assessed with The Center for Epidemiologic Studies' Perceived Depression Scale was more than twice that found in general population samples of women using the same instrument. Moreover, these patterns did not abate over the period of incarceration, as might be expected if they were purely situational (Forney, Inciardi, & Lockwood, 1991). There is also suspicion that bipolar disorder in women is misdiagnosed and underdiagnosed in jail and prison (Good, 1978), as it is in the general population among women of color.

Linda Teplin's landmark study of 1,272 pretrial women jail inmates in 1996 revealed that more than 80% of the sample met the criteria for one or more lifetime psychiatric disorders. Seventy percent of the sample were symptomatic within 6 months of being interviewed for the study. The most common disorders were drug dependence, post-traumatic stress disorder (PTSD), and major depressive disorder. Clearly, a pool of substantial psychiatric morbidity is found among female jail detainees (Teplin, Abram, & McClelland, 1996). This was particularly problematic in view of deeper study of the data from this sample (Teplin et al., 1997), which revealed that only 15% of these detainees with depression received mental health services in jail and that only 25% of all of those with severe mental disorder received any mental health services. Haywood et al. found that, although the American Correctional Association standards for detention facilities describe essential mental health treatment components, research into actual delivery and efficacy of these services is scarce (2000).

Other researchers have obtained results remarkably similar to Teplin's. A sample of women leaving North Carolina jails upon their entry into state prison exhibited somewhat higher rates of antisocial personality disorder as might be expected of convicted felons, but similar rates of borderline personality disorder and PTSD (Jordan et al.,

1996). Catharine Lewis found that one-third of women inmates had been physically abused, and a further third sexually abused before their first incarceration. Her study of 136 female felons yielded a rate of major depressive disorder of 36% and of post-traumatic stress disorder of 41% (Lewis, 2006) Reported rates of PTSD in women are particularly troubling in jail, where being locked up in a small space by intimidating male authority figures can be a potent stressor. A woman's first symptoms of PTSD may be encountered in jail, something not considered for either sex until recently. Women victims of abuse may become floridly ill when subjected to confinement, separation from children, strip searches, and other stressors reminiscent of abuse (Dvoskin, 1990).

It is also increasingly apparent that deinstitutionalization masquerades as *trans-institutionalization* (i.e., a shift in institutional venue to jail rather than the intended community placement) and has begun to show its effects among women, effects long seen only among men. The prevalence of mental disorder among women in jail can only mean that women who, before trans-institutionalization, should have been hospitalized, then enrolled in intensive outpatient programs, now find themselves in jail. Studies done in California have shown that there has been a nearly universal diversion of women from community mental health care to jail through a failure to address problems such as homelessness, prostitution, violent acting-out behaviors, inability to care for children, and impediments to access to mental health insurance and services (Bachrach, 1984; Lamb & Grant, 1983). More recent studies indicate that mental health policies diverting ever-increasing numbers of persons with serious mental illness (an ever-larger fraction of which are women) to the street combined with diminished tolerance of disruptive public behaviors, unfit parenting, and self-medication with illicit drugs have resulted in the greatest increase of the use of jails as surrogate mental institutions in the United States since Colonial times, when lunatics were seen as a public safety problem, and women lunatics were viewed as even more shockingly dangerous (Lurigio, Fallon, & Dincin, 2000).

## BREAKDOWNS IN WOMEN'S MENTAL HEALTH CARE IN JAIL: THREE CASE STUDIES

Over the past two decades, a consensus has emerged between correctional practitioners and mental health professionals as to the essential elements of an adequate and appropriate mental health service delivery system in local correctional facilities: (a) intake screening at booking, including suicide prevention screening; (b) evaluation with crisis intervention of newly admitted inmates screened as positive for mental health services need; (c) assessment of competency to stand trial and assist in one's own defense; (d) use of psychoactive medications to treat inmates with mental disorders; (e) substance abuse counseling; (f) therapeutic follow-up and supportive care and maintenance of family connections; (g) external hospitalization to stabilize acute mental disorder; and (h) case management with a discharge planning component. A 1997 survey of 3,300 U.S. jails of all sizes revealed wide variation in the provision of essential service components, which in many cases contributes to service gaps, lapses in continuity of care, and catastrophic breakdowns in services. Most U.S. jails reported a screening component for newly received inmates that incorporated suicide prevention. But only half of the jails surveyed had a formal crisis intervention protocol, the lack of this feature being most prevalent in small and very small jails. Only half of all jails reported use of psychiatric medications, less than 30% of small jails. Twenty percent of jails had a discharge-planning component (Steadman & Veysey, 1997).

A much different picture emerged from the same study in New York, which surpasses most states in affording jail-based mental health services. All services are provided by 100% of New York City-based jails. Virtually all upstate New York urban, suburban, and rural jails provide screening with suicide prevention, verbal therapy, medication, crisis intervention, supportive follow-up care, and case management (Steadman & Veysey, 1997).

It should be noted that the authors were at pains to point out that neither the New York nor the national jail service data indicated the extent or effectiveness of services, rather, that the service is self-reported as provided. For example, it is axiomatic that effective mental health evaluation with crisis intervention and use of psychoactive medications presupposes the availability of a physician psychiatrist. In fact, in 22 of 57 New York counties (39%), the jail mental health program was without the regular services of a psychiatrist at the jail. Many similar lapses and unmet needs remain hidden in systems self-reported as adequate. Moreover, little attention is paid to the female inmate population. As Singer notes, women have too often been seen as "expendable," bad girls," and "difficult to treat." Their mental health problems arise from the psychosocial issues previously discussed, which are complex, not always responsive to medication, often regarded as not legitimate, and in any event poorly understood for lack of adequate clinical and research investigation (1995). In an environment replete with service gaps, ignorance of, and prevailing attitudes and beliefs about women and their problems, mental health service breakdowns are inevitable (Hilliman, 2006).

In New York, state law provides for a governor-appointed Correction Medical Review Board, comprised of physicians and attorneys, which is mandated to investigate and report on the cause and circumstances of the death of any prison or jail inmate. The board makes public findings along with recommendations to prevent recurrence, where warranted.

# LORECIA C.[1]

Lorecia C. was a 39-year-old Native American woman who had been a New York State court officer for 12 years until she became mentally disabled and went on extended sick leave for the 2 years prior to her arrest. In 2000, Lorecia allegedly entered an auto dealership where she wrote a check for a $64,000 luxury car, a criminal act clearly relevant to her history of mental disorder. Lorecia was arrested in her home, whereupon she reported a history of psychiatric treatment and to be currently taking psychoactive medications. The police took her to the hospital emergency department where she was diagnosed with depressive disorder, not otherwise specified, and was ordered to take her reported current medications, Wellbutrin, Neurotonin, and Trazodone. However, the physician, who observed Lorecia's judgment to be impaired, determined that she was "psychiatrically

---
[1]All case study surnames are pseudonyms.

fit for confinement," a term that has no clinical definition or significance. She was arraigned and sent to the largest county jail facility in New York State, without transmittal to the jail of any of the history and current presentation elicited at the emergency department.

Notwithstanding this lapse, Lorecia was administered a suicide-prevention screening upon admission to jail, which she promptly failed. Her psychiatric history was again elicited, as was concern for her law enforcement affiliation and obvious signs of depression. Lorecia was not placed in housing under suicide prevention precautions, or any enhanced observation, and a "routine" referral for mental health evaluation was made. Lorecia was medically screened on the same day by a physician in the jail medical department. Her psychiatric medications were noted. The physician later reported that he thought Lorecia "looked fine," noted "anxiety vs.

manipulation," and ordered a single dose of anti-anxiety medication but none of her other medications. Lorecia was placed in the protective custody housing area because of her law enforcement background, but no mental health observation or suicide prevention precautions were undertaken. On the day following Lorecia's placement in protective custody, the "routine" mental health evaluation referral, made based upon the completed high-risk screening, was processed by the mental health unit secretary, who although she had no professional training or experience, noted that the referral was nonemergent. No qualified mental health treatment staff member ever saw Lorecia's high-risk screening instrument.

On the day following her arrest, shortly after having been refused her initial telephone call due to interference with mealtime, Lorecia C. fatally hanged herself in her cell.

# PENELOPE S.

Penelope S. was a 57-year-old public school teacher retired with mental disability. She had a questionable history of head injury and both alcoholism and psychiatric treatment. Her mother committed suicide by hanging when Penelope was age 26. Penelope was hospitalized in 1985, with a diagnosis of bipolar affective disorder. She was hospitalized in 1986 after a suicide attempt. She took 20 mg of buspirone daily. Penelope was arrested for aggravated harassment and violation of probation in October 1998, and committed to the second largest county jail in New York State. At the time of her commitment, she was taking desipramine and Navane. She was immediately seen in jail for evaluation by a psychologist and diagnosed as adjustment disorder with mixed emotional features, with bipolar disorder ruled out.

Penelope was referred to a psychiatrist. The psychiatrist made no diagnosis but rather discontinued Penelope's medications, giving no reason other than he saw "no acute need" at the time. Five days after admission to jail, Penelope told her housing area correction officer that she "wished she was dead" and was thinking of "ways

to hurt myself." Her cell assignment was relocated to the "mental health housing area" for better observation and a referral was made to the facility mental health unit.

Penelope was seen by a social worker the day following her suicidal speech. The clinician found Penelope depressed and anxious with suicidal ideation. A "suicide watch" consisting of correction officer checks at 15-minute intervals was ordered. No other action or referral for services occurred. Penelope was found fatally hanged in her cell one day later, while on " suicide watch."

Three days after Penelope's death, the psychiatrist who saw her 2 weeks before her death prepared an incident report in which he wrote an expanded clinical note detailing Penelope's previous hospitalizations, suicide gesture, medications taken, results of the psychiatrist's purported mental status examination, and his reasons for discontinuing her antidepressant and antipsychotic medications (her age and history of alcoholism). The psychiatrist claimed to have explained everything to Penelope and promised the patient he would see her again—in 2 weeks.

# NANCY B.

Nancy B. was a 17-year-old Latino girl who was sent to the third largest jail in New York State for allegedly threatening her mother with a knife. The presiding judge at Nancy's arraignment ordered a jail-based psychiatric competency examination, that she be placed under suicide prevention precautions, indicated that she was prescribed psychoactive medications, and listed the names and telephone numbers of the two private mental health clinicians who were treating her at the time of her arrest. At the time of her admission to jail, Nancy was screened for suicide risk and reported a psychiatric treatment history and a history of suicide attempt. Nancy was placed in the mental observation housing area. Her examination by a psychiatric nurse elicited two recent psychiatric hospitalizations and an antidepressant medication regimen. Later on the day of her admission to jail, a psychiatric social worker removed Nancy from suicide prevention precautions because her history featured "no real suicide attempts." That same evening, Nancy received her court-ordered psychiatric examination, which by state law was to be limited to her competency to stand trial. The examining psychiatrist found Nancy competent, but inexplicably discontinued her antidepressant medication.

Two days following her admission to jail, Nancy was seen by a clinical psychologist who documented Nancy's report of "countless" previous suicide gestures and his observation that Nancy's insight and judgment were poor. He characterized Nancy as suffering from chronic depression but as "manipulative." He recommended that Nancy be moved out of mental health housing, a recommendation not followed by the uninformed corrections staff.

Nancy remained in jail without her antidepressant medication for two weeks. She was seen again by the psychologist who was convinced Nancy was "manipulating" her parents. Nancy had problems with other inmates, and was in and out of protective custody and mental observation. Nancy spoke to her mother, who thought she sounded depressed. She had multiple nosebleeds and often appeared distressed. Nancy spoke by telephone with her private psychologist. She remained without antidepressant medication. Precisely 2 weeks after admission to jail, Nancy B. was found fatally hanged from the control crank of her cell window.

## JAIL MENTAL HEALTH CARE: QUALITY AND EFFECTIVENESS

The three foregoing case studies illustrate remarkable similarities in breakdowns in jail mental health services for women. All three cases occurred in the largest facilities in the state, each with a highly developed, well-financed mental health service delivery system. All three facilities staffed qualified, well-credentialed providers. Yet, each failed to provide adequate care at a critical juncture with catastrophic results. Clearly, in these cases, outcomes for these women were unrelated to the sophistication of mental health services available.

All three of the women studied were screened at intake by the same objective risk assessment instrument. All scored as high risks for suicide attempt. All were referred for mental health evaluation. Each gave a history of psychiatric treatment with hospitalization. All three women carried a current DSM-IV diagnosis of psychiatric morbidity. Each of the three women were taking prescribed psychotropic medications, and all had their therapeutic regimens summarily terminated without rationale by licensed, credentialed clinicians who, in turn, missed or ignored hallmarks of mental health crisis. The mental health clinicians involved viewed all three women detainees as "manipulative," and therefore malingering and unworthy of professional attention despite abundant evidence to the contrary.

Postmodern local correctional facility experience has shown that there is little mystery regarding the operational components required for establishing a credible, comprehensive mental health care service for women. Poor correctional mental health care for women is not a function of staff or equipment, but rather a manifestation of pervasive and insidious attitudes, behaviors, and beliefs that influence government policy and clinical practice. Women offenders need to develop living and coping skills that raise confidence and self-esteem necessary to avoid high-risk behaviors, to negotiate the complexities of the mental health and substance abuse treatment system, and to adopt mental well-being as a primary personal value. Mental health care providers should be required to demonstrate satisfactory skills for delivery of respectful and considerate care in a sexually and culturally diverse population while in postgraduate training and on a mandatory continuing medical education basis (Harrison Ross & Lawrence, 2002).

Catharine Lewis notes that clinicians must learn to recognize and accept gender differences. Equal services do not necessarily deliver parity. The same service may not be effective across gender lines because women have vastly different pathways into jail, patterns of mental disorder, family responsibilities, and trauma and abuse histories versus males. Comorbidity with substance abuse where women are concerned should not be dismissed in jail. Histories of victimization, fears of victimization while incarcerated, actual abuse in jail including sexual involvement with staff, and the post-traumatic stress disorder overlay among women patients has a profound impact on the level of risk in jail and on response to treatment (Lewis, 2006). Of paramount importance when assessing and treating women in jail is the recognition of the individual as differentiated from other inmates in an environment where treating every inmate "the same" is a pre-eminent correctional value. Particular attention to multidisciplinary case management models of care will work to avoid lapses and breakdowns seen in the case studies presented here. Use of a therapeutic community in a case-managed setting will form attachments, provide containment, facilitate the communication and involvement so important to women, and facilitate empowerment (Lewis, 2006). Teleconferencing in its various forms, which is rapidly becoming web-based and quite inexpensive, can serve as a potent resource multiplier, is useful in maintaining family ties, and thus is now an essential adjunct to quality mental health care in jail.

Mental health care for women in jail should not seek to guard the access gate to the mental health care system, but rather to find clients and draw them into the promotion and maintenance of mental health as part of the community continuum of services in which the jail is so manifestly imbedded. This demands that mental health service providers not trouble themselves over whether women in jail are worthy of receiving services, but rather to implement vigorous protocols for the identification of, and intervention in, mental health service needs; emphasize wellness; promote continuity; eradicate abuse; and place a premium on care that is respectful and considerate. The present demand-for-service, episodic style of outpatient mental health care in jail treats each encounter as unprecedented, each complaint as isolated. It is the single greatest impediment to quality of care. Hope springs eternal that reduction in unnecessary incarceration will reduce demand for scarce specialized services, but jails are already serving as the social net of last resort in the United States, trending toward the growth of women jail populations, not diversion (Harrison Ross & Lawrence, 2002). For the increasing numbers of women for whom jail provides neither punishment nor deterrence, but rather a measure of respite from hopelessly untenable life situations and access to health and other human services unavailable in the outside community (Butterfield, 1992), quality mental health services that meet their differential needs, planned referrals to post-incarceration services, Medicaid enrollment, family planning, drug abuse treatment, and coordination of health maintenance between mothers and their children should be the norm. The jail, for better or worse, has become integral to the community and will increasingly be called upon to function like the community service institution it has truly become.

## References

Alemagno, S. (2001). Women in jail: Is substance abuse counseling enough? *American Journal of Public Health*, *91*(5), 798–800.

Alemagno, S., & Dickie, J. (2005). Employment issues of women in jail. *Journal of Employment Counseling*, *42*, 67–74.

Bachrach, L. L. (1984). Deinstitutionalization and women: Assessing the consequences of public policy. *American Psychologist*, *39*(10),1171–1177.

Butterfield, F. (1992, July 19). Are American jails becoming shelters from the storm? *The New York Times*, A9.

Butterfield, F. (2003, October 22). Study finds hundreds of thousands of inmates mentally ill. *The New York Times*, A14.

Dvoskin, J. A. (1990). Jail-Based Mental Health Services. In H. J. Steadman (Ed.), *Jail diversion for the mentally ill: Breaking down the barriers.* Boulder, CO: National Institute of Corrections.

Fogel, C. I., & Martin, S. L. (1992). The mental health of incarcerated women. *Western Journal of Nursing Research*, *14*(1), 30–47.

Forney, M. A., Inciardi, J. A., & Lockwood, D. (1991). Exchanging sex for crack cocaine: A comparison of women from rural and urban communities. *Journal of Community Health*, *17*(2), 73–85.

Good, M. I. (1978). Primary affective disorder, aggression and criminality: A review and clinical study. *Archives of General Psychiatry*, *35*(8), 954–960.

Harrison Ross, P., & Lawrence, J. E. (2002). Health Care for Women Offenders: Challenge for the New Century. In R. Gido and T. Alleman (Eds.), *Turnstile justice: Issues in American corrections*. Upper Saddle River, NJ: Prentice Hall.

Haywood, T. W. (2000). Characteristics of women in jail and treatment orientations. *Behavior Modification*, *24*(3), 307–324.

Hilliman, C. (2006). Assessing the impact of virtual visitation on familial communication and institutional adjustment for women in prison. Dissertation, ProQuest Information and Learning Company. Ann Arbor, MI. UMI Number: 3213134.

Jordan, B. K., Schlenger, W. E., et al. (1996). Prevalence of psychiatric disorders among incarcerated women. *Archives of General Psychiatry*, 53, 513–519.

Lamb, H. R., & Grant, R. W. (1983). Mentally ill women in a county jail. *Archives of General Psychiatry*, *40*, 363–368.

Lewis, C. (2006). Treating incarcerated women: Gender matters. *Psychiatric Clinics of North America*, *29*, 773–789.

Lindquist, C. H., & Lindquist, C. A. (1997). Gender differences in distress: Mental health consequences of environmental stress among jail inmates. *Behavioral Sciences and the Law*, 15, 503–523.

Lurigio, A. J., Fallon, J. R., & Dincin, J. (2000). Helping the mentally ill in jails adjust to community life: A description of a postrelease ACT program and its clients. *International Journal of Offender Therapy and Comparative Criminology*, *44*(5), 532–548.

New York State Commission of Correction. (1997). *In the matter of the death of Nancy B\** (96-M-191). Albany: NY. Author.

New York State Commission of Correction. (2000a). *In the matter of the death of Penelope S\** (98-M-247). Albany, NY: Author.

New York State Commission of Correction. (2000b). *In the matter of the death of Lorecia C\** (00-M-007). Albany, NY: Author.

New York State Commission of Correction. (2004). *Statewide data compilation from sheriffs' annual reports: 2004.* Albany, NY: Author.

Singer, M. I. (1995). The psychosocial issues of women serving time in jail. *Social Work, 40*(1), 103–113.

Steadman, H., & Veysey, B. (1997). *Providing services for jail inmates with mental disorders.* Washington, DC: National Institute of Justice, Research in Brief.

Teplin, L. A., Abram, K. M., & McClelland, G. M. (1997). Mentally disordered women in jail: Who receives services? *American Journal of Public Health, 87,* 604–609.

Tonkin, P., Dickie, J., Alemagno, S., et al. (2004). Women in jail: "Soft skills" and barriers to employment. *Journal of Offender Rehabilitation, 38*(40), 51–72.

U.S. Department of Justice, Bureau of Justice Statistics. (1999). *Prior abuse reported by inmates and probationers.* Washington, DC: Author.

U.S. Department of Justice, Bureau of Justice Statistics. (1998). *Correctional populations in the United States, 1997.* Washington, DC: Author.

U.S. Department of Justice, Bureau of Justice Statistics. (2006). *Prison and jail inmates at midyear 2005.* Washington, DC: Author.

Weiskopf, G., & Josil, R. (1999). *Forensic mental health: Final report presented to the New York State Conference of Local Mental Hygiene Directors.* Clifton Park, NY: Weiskopf Consulting Services.

# CHAPTER 8

# THE CONTRIBUTION OF CHILDHOOD TRAUMA TO ADULT PSYCHOPATHOLOGY IN DUALLY DIAGNOSED DETAINEES

## Implications for Gender-Based Jail and Reentry on Trauma-Informed Services[1]

**Nahama Broner**

**Sarah Kopelovich**

**Damon W. Mayrl**

**David P. Bernstein**

## ABSTRACT

Little attention has focused on the impact of childhood trauma on adult psychiatric, substance use, and criminal justice status among jail detainees with co-occurring mental and addictive disorders. Of 212 participants, 59% of women and 34% of men experienced one or more of the five types of childhood trauma, retrospectively, assessed. Women were twice as likely as men to experience sexual and emotional abuse and neglect, and to have experienced these subtypes of trauma, along with physical neglect in more severe degrees. However, there were no differences in prevalence or severity between men and women on childhood experience of emotional and physical abuse. Subtypes of abuse by

*(continued)*

[1]This study was partially funded by the U.S. Department of Health and Human Services Substance Abuse and Mental Health Administration, Centers for Mental Health Services and Substance Abuse Treatment, Grant Number SM97-006. The first author's work was also supported by a National Institute for Mental Health postdoctoral mental health services research fellowship, Grant Number MH16242-20, through the Institute on Health, Health Care Policy and Aging Research, Rutgers University. The opinions expressed in this manuscript are those of the authors and do not necessarily reflect the views of the funding institutions. Correspondence should be directed to the first author at 121 West 27th Street, Suite 1001, New York, NY 10001 or nbroner@rti.org

gender differentially contributed to the variables assessed. Childhood trauma accounted for 6% to 20% of the variance in psychiatric symptoms, with gender and its interactions controlled. Sexual abuse independently predicted historical factors associated with risk for violent recidivism and drug abuse, and emotional abuse independently predicted psychopathy, borderline personality symptoms, risk for violence, and general life satisfaction. Being female and abused significantly contributed to clinical risk for violent recidivism. The study's results support the need to integrate trauma screening, risk assessment, and treatment into interventions to affect psychiatric and public safety outcomes.

## INTRODUCTION

Research indicates that estimates of prevalence of childhood trauma in the community vary widely, dependent upon the definition of abuse, composition of sample, method of data collection, and depth of questioning (Berliner & Elliot, 2002; Goodman, Rosenberg, Mueser, & Drake, 1997; Holmes & Slap, 1998). According to the National Child Abuse and Neglect Data System (NCANDS), of the 872,000 reported incidents of child maltreatment in 2004 (a rate of 11.9 per 1,000 children), 62% experienced neglect, 18% experienced physical abuse, 10% were sexually abused, 7% were emotionally abused, 2% were medically neglected, and an additional 15% experienced other types of maltreatment, such as abandonment and explicit threats of harm (U.S. Department of Health and Human Services [DHHS], 2006). Although these rates are considered underestimations of actual prevalence in the United States (DHHS, 2005; Prevent Child Abuse America, 2003), and particularly underestimate sexual abuse rates for which males are estimated at 17% and females at 28% (Finkelhor, Hotaling, Lewis, & Smith, 1990; Rind, Tromovitch, & Bauserman, 1998), they nevertheless roughly correspond to most undifferentiated estimates of child maltreatment found in the literature, which usually fall below 5% (Emery & Laumann-Billings, 1998; Finkelhor & Dzuiba-Leatherman, 1994). As described below, when assessing criminal and clinical subpopulations, higher prevalence rates of childhood maltreatment are found compared to those reported in national community samples (e.g., Bernstein, 2000; Goodman et al., 2001; James & Glaze, 2006).

Research suggests that childhood trauma plays a contributory role in a wide range of psychopathology and dysregulated behavior; relevant to the current study is the relationship established in prior studies between childhood trauma and addiction, mental disorders and symptoms, and violence and criminal behavior. The current study tests these previously reported associations by assessing the effect of childhood victimization as a distal factor on proximal psychopathology and criminal behavior in an adult dually diagnosed mental and addictive disordered detainee population.

# CHILDHOOD TRAUMA AND ADULT VIOLENCE AND CRIMINALITY

Research into the relationship between childhood trauma and adult violence has been ongoing since Curtis (1963) first proposed the idea that violence might breed violence in a brief clinical note. Research has since provided strong evidence that childhood abuse and neglect has a significant association with adult violence and hostility and across populations and using various methodologies (Cloitre, Tardiff, Marzuk, Leon, & Portera, 2001; Curtis, Leung, Sullivan, Eschbach, & Stinson, 2001; Fagan, 2005; Fehon, Grilo, & Lipschitz, 2001; Finkelhor & Dziuba-Leatherman, 1994; Haapasalo & Pokela, 1999; Lipschitz, Kaplan, Sorkenn, Chorney, & Asnis, 1996; Malinosky-Rummell & Hansen, 1993; Ornduff, Kelsey, & O'Leary, 2001; Roy, 1999; Roy, 2001a; Widom, 1989a; Widom, 1989b; Widom & Ames, 1994). The association between previous victimization and subsequent delinquency is commonly referred to as the *cycle of violence theory* and posits that maltreated children are at an increased risk for engaging in violent criminal offenses (Fagan, 2005). In a series of studies using a prospective cohort of subjects with official records of abuse and neglect ($n = 908$) and a matched comparison group ($n = 667$), childhood victimization increased overall risk for violent offending and arrest, particularly for males and African-Americans (Rivera & Widom, 1990; Widom, 1989a; Widom, 1989b). In their retrospective review of 604 incarcerated males using record review and interviews, Dutton and Hart (1992) found that men with a history of being abused as a child were three times more likely to perpetrate violent acts than their nonabused counterparts. Similarly, in the MacArthur Risk Assessment Study (Monahan, 2000), there was a positive association between experienced deviant parental behaviors and post-hospital discharge violence among psychiatric patients, as well as between childhood physical abuse and post-discharge violence.

Consistent with the association between childhood trauma and adult violence, studies indicate a relationship between childhood maltreatment and an increased risk for legal involvement (whether for a violent offense or not) and incarceration (Ouimette, Kimerling, Shaw, & Moos, 2000; Widom, 1989a; Widom & Ames, 1994). In a community survey of 3,362 adults throughout the United States, having been sexually touched before puberty was associated with a 10% increase in likelihood of incarceration (Curtis et al., 2001). Abused and neglected children have a greater number of arrests on average, offend earlier, and offend more frequently than nonabused and nonneglected controls (Widom, 1989b). Sexually abused males are twice as likely to have legal problems as nonabused peers (Holmes & Slap, 1998), and childhood sexual abuse in substance-abusing female offenders is related to adult criminal behavior, although this relationship may be mediated by adolescent substance abuse (Grella, Stein, & Greenwell, 2005). In a sample of 830 men and women receiving detoxification services, victims of childhood abuse reported more lifetime arrests, arrests related to substance use, and arrests related to mental health symptoms (Brems, Johnson, & Neal, 2004).

# CHILDHOOD TRAUMA AND SUBSTANCE USE

Community studies indicate that abused individuals have higher rates of legal and illegal drug abuse and risky drug practices (Duncan, Saunders, Kilpatrick, Hanson, & Resnick, 1996; Goodman et al., 1997; Mullen, Martin, Anderson, Roman, & Herbison,

1993). Although estimates vary, studies of substance users indicate rates of childhood abuse of at least 59% for women and 28% for men (Bernstein, 2000; Deykin & Buka, 1997; Gil-Rivas, Fiorentine, Anglin, & Taylor, 1997; Ouimette et al., 2000; Windle, Windle, Scheidt, & Miller, 1995). A study of psychiatric inpatients found that patients reporting either physical or physical and sexual abuse were more likely to have histories of drug abuse than nonabused patients (Brown & Anderson, 1991). Women who experienced childhood maltreatment may be particularly susceptible to adult substance problems; those with child abuse histories are at three times the risk for substance use disorders as women who did not experience childhood victimization (Berley & Bebout, 2004). A prospective study examining a community sample of young adults ($n = 375$) found that drug abuse varied by gender and type of abuse reported. Physically abused males were more likely to receive a DSM-III-R diagnosis of drug abuse/dependence than nonabused controls (40% vs. 8%), whereas sexually abused females were more than five times as likely to meet the criteria for drug abuse or dependence than nonabused female controls (43.5% vs. 7.9%; Silverman, Reinherz, & Giaconia, 1996).

The results of empirical studies on childhood trauma and alcoholism have proven insufficient in establishing an etiological relationship between childhood maltreatment and adult alcohol abuse (Langeland & Hartgers, 1998). Although some studies have found no relationship between alcohol abuse and childhood trauma (e.g., Mullen et al., 1993), others have found a limited positive correlation. Although victims of childhood abuse in one study were not more likely to abuse alcohol than nonabused controls, Duncan et al. (1996) did find that they began drinking an average of three years earlier than their nonabused peers and drank more days in the previous year. Several studies have found that a relationship between child maltreatment and alcohol abuse existed only among women (Horwitz, Widom, McLaughlin, & White, 2001; Miller, Downs, & Testa, 1993; Schuck & Widom, 2001; Wexler, Lyons, Lyons, & Mazure, 1997; Widom, Ireland, & Glynn, 1995; Widom & White, 1997), whereas other studies have found a relationship for both men and women but primarily with sexual abuse (Galaif, Stein, Newcomb, & Bernstein, 2001; Langeland & Hartgers, 1998; Windle et al., 1995)

## CHILDHOOD TRAUMA AND PSYCHOPATHOLOGY

The prevalence of childhood trauma is elevated in psychiatric populations. Goodman and colleagues (2001) found that approximately two-thirds of severely mentally ill inpatients had a history of physical or sexual assault. A study of psychiatric outpatients found the rate of childhood physical abuse at 34% and the rate of childhood sexual abuse at 44% (Lipschitz et al., 1996). Studies of males with psychiatric disorders have put the rate of childhood abuse anywhere from 6% to 37% (Cloitre et al., 2001; Holmes & Slap, 1998), and studies of severely mentally ill women have found rates of physical abuse from 34% to 87% and of sexual abuse from 26% to 65% (reviewed in Goodman et al., 1997). According to James and Glaze (2006), past physical and sexual abuse is three times as high among jail, state, and federal inmates with mental health problems as among those without mental health problems (17% to 24% vs. 6% to 8%). To a great extent, this three-to-one ratio of past abuse among inmates with and without mental illness is consistent regardless of whether it is past physical abuse or past sexual abuse. The real difference is found in comparing abuse across gender where 2½ times as many women with mental illness experience physical and sexual abuse as do men (68% vs. 24%) and 5½ times as many women without mental illness experience physical and sexual abuse as do men without mental illness.

A 1993 review of 45 studies found that sexual abuse accounted for approximately 15% to 45% of variance in the development of psychological symptoms (Kendall-Tackett, Williams, & Finkelhor, 1993). Other reviews and discrete studies of men and women also indicate a relationship between various types of childhood maltreatment and subsequent development of symptoms, as well as an association with a broad range of disorders (e.g., affective, anxiety, dissociative, psychotic, eating, and personality; Goodman et al., 1997; Holmes & Slap, 1998). However, research most consistently has demonstrated a relationship between childhood trauma and post-traumatic stress disorder (PTSD), depression, and Cluster B personality disorders along with symptoms.

Both retrospective and prospective studies have demonstrated a link between childhood trauma and PTSD (Epstein, Saunders, & Kilpatrick, 1997; Widom, 1999). In a nationwide telephone survey, Duncan et al. (1996) found that victims of childhood physical abuse were five times more likely to have a lifetime history of PTSD and 10 times more likely to have PTSD at the time of the interview. A retrospective study of chemically dependent adolescents found that the overall risk of developing PTSD among those suffering abuse was 41.6% (33% of males and 57% of females), with females 1.7 times more likely to develop PTSD than males (Deykin & Buka, 1997). Widom's prospective study offers slightly lower estimates, finding 37.5% of sexual abuse, 32.7% of physical abuse, and 30.6% of neglect victims developing adult PTSD (Widom, 1999).

Similarly, research findings consistently demonstrate a positive relationship between childhood trauma and adult depression (Duncan et al., 1996; Gil-Rivas, Fiorentine, Anglin, & Taylor, 1997; Roy, 1999; Wexler et al., 1997). A recent literature review (Hill, 2006) reported relative homogeneity in study findings regarding the association between childhood maltreatment and adult depression over the past 15 years. Yet many studies fail to account for the distinction between endogenous depression—characterized by a distinct set of symptoms, a presumed biogenic etiology, and an absence of precipitating stressors—versus nonendogenous depression—conceptualized as a reaction to environmental stimuli—in outcome studies of childhood trauma (Harkness & Monroe, 2002).

In contrast to the established relationship between childhood maltreatment and depressive and trauma disorders, there is a lack of empirical consistency directly relating childhood trauma and other major mental disorders. However, consistent findings indicate that psychotic symptoms rather than psychotic diagnoses are a corollary of childhood trauma, particularly when severity and frequency of abuse is accounted for. One recent study using a large community sample ($n = 4,045$) found that childhood trauma increased the risk for positive psychotic symptoms, and that the risk for developing psychotic symptoms increased with frequency of abuse (Janssen et al., 2004). A review of recent research also found a causal, dose-effect relationship between childhood trauma and psychotic symptoms (Read, van Os, Morrison, & Ross, 2005). The studies included in this review—and consequently the ability to infer a causal relationship based on their findings—have been criticized, however, on the basis that many concerned the prevalence of childhood abuse in inpatient psychiatric samples, and few included a healthy control group or controlled for potential confounders (Morgan, Fisher, & Fearon, 2006).

A substantial body of research has established a relationship between childhood trauma and the subsequent development of personality disorders (Brown & Anderson, 1991; Cloitre et al., 2001; Goodman et al., 1997; Horwitz et al., 2001; Luntz & Widom, 1994; Windle et al., 1995). In a prospective study of 639 youths through early adulthood, participants with documented reports of childhood abuse or neglect were more than four times as likely to be diagnosed with a personality disorder in early adulthood (Johnson, Cohen, Brown, Smailes, & Bernstein, 1999). The study found that, in addition to antisocial personality disorder, evidence of childhood maltreatment was associated with an increased risk for the development of any personality disorder. In a retrospective study, however, Cluster B personality disorders occurred more commonly among abused psychiatric outpatients than among nonabused outpatients (Wexler et al., 1997). Of the Cluster B disorders, the most consistent findings have been for antisocial and borderline personality disorders. Among a sample of 99 male and female psychiatric inpatients, those with borderline personality disorder were significantly more likely to self-report multiple types of childhood trauma than patients without borderline personality disorder (Sansone, Songer, & Miller, 2005). This study complements a number of other studies linking childhood trauma and borderline personality disorder (e.g., Helgeland & Torgersen, 2004; Sabo, 1997; Sansone, Sansone, & Gaither, 2004; Zanarini, Gunderson, & Marino, 1989).

In terms of antisocial personality, and consistent with findings linking childhood abuse and neglect with adult criminality and violence, a number of studies have found an association between childhood trauma and an increased risk for developing antisocial personality disorder. Because antisocial acts are a diagnostic feature of antisocial personality disorder, some studies have attempted to control for criminal history to minimize the possibility of such acts mediating diagnosis. One such prospective study of abused and nonabused children in a Midwestern metropolitan area found that childhood victimization significantly predicted both diagnosis and symptoms of antisocial personality disorder controlling for demographic characteristics and arrest history (Luntz & Widom, 1994). Another prospective study of 639 children followed into young adulthood found that the risk of developing antisocial personality disorder was positively associated with physical abuse and neglect, but not sexual abuse, which was more strongly associated with an increased risk for borderline personality disorder (Johnson et al., 1999). A study among alcoholics in inpatient treatment found that individuals who had been both sexually and physically abused as children had the highest rates of antisocial personality disorder, regardless of gender (Windle et al., 1995).

Although a relationship between childhood maltreatment and antisocial behaviors is well supported, empirical assessments of the link between childhood trauma and adult psychopathy are limited. Weiler and Widom (1996) found significantly higher Psychopathy Checklist-Revised (PCL-R) scores among victims of childhood abuse and/or neglect than the matched control group, controlling for demographic characteristics and criminal history, although few participants met the PCL-R cutoff score for psychopathy. The authors suggest that the relationship between childhood victimization and adult violence may be mediated by psychopathic characteristics. Similarly,

Koivisto and Haapasalo (1996) found some evidence of an association between childhood maltreatment and adult psychopathy as measured by the PCL-R in a sample of Finnish violent offenders even though PCL-R scores were obtained using only limited file information.

## ABSENCE OF RESEARCH ON DUALLY DIAGNOSED POPULATIONS

Despite the strong relationships between childhood trauma and substance use and mental illness, very few studies have examined the rates and correlates of childhood abuse and neglect among known dually diagnosed community treatment or criminal justice samples. Most studies that have involved individuals with co-occurring mental and addictive disorders have identified them only through results analysis rather than as a specifically defined sample. These studies look at the rates of mental disorders among abused substance-using populations (Bernstein, Stein, & Handelsman, 1998; Deykin & Buka, 1997; Gil-Rivas et al., 1997; Grella et al., 2005; Haller & Miles, 2004; Knisely, Barker, Ingersoll, & Dawson, 2000; Langeland, Draijer, & van den Brink, 2004; Roy, 2001a; Windle et al., 1995) or at rates of substance use, abuse, or dependence among abused mentally ill populations (Brown & Anderson, 1991; Goodman et al., 1997; Goodman & Fallot, 1998; Goodman et al., 2001; Heffernan, Cloitre, Tardiff, Marzuk, Portera, & Leon, 2000).

The need for study of the potential long-term effects of childhood trauma in a dually diagnosed sample is particularly relevant to the criminal justice population where rates of co-morbid addictive and mental disorders among those self-reporting or assessed with such problems are high for both men and women compared to community and nonincarcerated clinical populations, and even higher for incarcerated women compared to men (Abram & Teplin, 1991; Abram, Teplin, & McClelland, 2003; Alemangno, Shaffer-King, Tonkin, & Hammel, 2004; Broner, Lamon, Mayrl, & Karopkin, 2003; James & Glaze, 2006; Teplin, Abram, & McClelland, 1996). As noted, rates of childhood physical and sexual abuse and neglect are also elevated among those incarcerated compared to community samples, and particularly among inmates with mental health and co-occurring substance use problems and for women (Adams, 2002; Battle, Zlotnick, Najavits, Gutierrez, & Winsor, 2003; Fickenscher, Lapidus, Silk-Walker, & Becker, 2001; James & Glaze, 2006).

The literature reviewed generally suggests that childhood trauma is associated with the onset and increased severity of substance use and behavioral dysregulation (e.g., violence, criminal justice involvement, Cluster B personality disorders), general psychiatric symptoms, and increased risk for the development of PTSD and depression. However, few studies have tested whether or not such a distal variable as childhood trauma significantly explains the current symptomatic, diagnostic, and behavioral risk presentation of a dually diagnosed incarcerated population when all of these variables are allowed to compete for explanation. Further, few studies have had the opportunity to simultaneously compare the contribution of five subtypes of childhood abuse and neglect—emotional abuse, physical abuse, sexual abuse, emotional neglect, and physical neglect—to a comprehensive set of psychiatric variables, and comparatively for men and women within the same sample, to better determine the utility of including childhood trauma in screening and risk assessment and management, as well as how treatment type selection can be better informed by the differential effects of trauma subtype and by gender. The purpose of the present study is to test previous research findings in a dually diagnosed incarcerated male and female sample through performing intercorrelations of these factors by gender and with gender controlled, using reliable and standard measures, assessing a broad range of childhood trauma, and evaluating a broad range of psychopathology including psychopathy, major mental disorders, borderline and antisocial personality disorders, drug and alcohol use, violence, and criminal behavior.

## METHODS

### SAMPLE

The sample of 212 adult detainees is described by gender in the Results section and in Tables 8.1 through 8.3. Participants were on average 35 years old, with 10½ years of education and by majority male (56%), single (60%), minority (60% black/African-American, 26% Hispanic/Latino(a), 14% white/other), and unemployed (82% at arrest, 31% never employed). The majority of the sample had a history of homelessness (61% homeless within 12 months prior to arrest; 24% homeless at arrest with an additional 31% of those housed without a regular place to sleep), medical problems (61% overall with 4% tuberculosis, 7% Hepatitis B, 9% AIDS, and 18% HIV representing infectious disorders at baseline), and mental health and substance abuse treatment (94%). Although all participants had one of four eligible mental disorders per psychiatric records, standardized Diagnostic Interview Schedule (DIS-IV; Robins, Cottler, Bucholz, & Compton, 1998) disorders are reported: 48% major depression, 27% schizophrenia, and 22% bipolar. The remaining 3% were diagnosed with primary PTSD. Overall combining primary and co-occurring trauma, 37% reached DIS-IV criteria for PTSD, and 20% had an Axis II antisocial personality disorder. All participants reached the criteria for an alcohol or drug disorder per standardized measures and per chart diagnoses; primary chart diagnoses included polysubstance abuse/dependence (54%), cocaine (19%), alcohol (9%), opioids (9%), cannabis (7%), and other hallucinogens or stimulants (3%).

Almost half of the sample self-reported engaging in violent behavior (43% within 90 days of arrest and 45% self-reported being charged with a violent offense in the past) and the majority (95%) had previous criminal justice involvement, generally beginning in early adulthood (mean = 20.63). At the time of study enrollment, 52% were charged with a top charge of drug possession or sale, 13% with an offense categorized as violence against a person, 4% with a nonviolent offense against a person, 13% each with property and procedural (parole or probation) violation offenses, and 6% with a minor offense.

### PROCEDURE

Eligibility included participants meeting the New York City Department of Mental, Health, Retardation and Alcoholism Services funded NYC-LINK diversion program criteria: presentenced legal status, charge of a B felony or lower (e.g., rape, drug possession or sale, assault, robbery, burglary, possession of a weapon, and other lower charges), and psychiatric status (Severely and Persistently Mentally Ill, SPMI, per New York State Office of Mental Health criteria requiring an Axis I disorder, low functioning, and past hospitalization), as well as research study criteria (current chart diagnosis of major depression, bipolar disorder, schizophrenia or schizoaffective disorder, and a substance abuse or dependence disorder). Potential participants under age 18 with mental retardation, florid psychosis, or not meeting the program and research criteria were excluded from the study. Participants in this study were part of a baseline sample of adult jail detainees accepted for diversion (intervention) and like comparison detainees from the New York City site of a longitudinal multisite police and jail diversion study (Broner, Lattimore, Cowell, & Schlenger, 2004; Broner, Mayrl, & Landsberg, 2005; Lattimore, Broner, Sherman, Frisman, & Shafer, 2003), and who had completed childhood trauma questionnaires. As described elsewhere, the study sample was significantly more likely to be female, less likely to have a violent charge, more likely to have a bipolar or depressive disorder, and less likely to have a nonstudy disorder in concert with study inclusion criteria than those excluded or not consenting to participate (Broner et al., 2005).

At the time of the baseline assessment, all participants were receiving jail mental health treatment. Interviews were administered in English or Spanish in the jail facility in which the participant was housed. Participants were not provided incentives for the baseline assessment, but were informed of incentives for follow-up interviews. The study received a Certificate of Confidentiality along with Internal Review Board approval with prisoner representation, from New York University, New York City Department of Health, and RTI International.

Interviewers either held or were working toward their Masters' degree or Ph.D. in psychology or social work. Interviewer training consisted of conducting three mock interviews, scoring five interviews to 98% proficiency, participating in specialized instrument training for the DIS-IV, HCR-20 (Webster, Douglas, Eaves, & Hart, 1997), Brief Psychiatric Rating Scale (BPRS; Overall & Gorham, 1988), and Psychopathy Check List-Screening Version (PCL-SV, Hart, Cox, & Hare, 1995), and intermittent observation and scoring checks once in the field.

## MEASURES

As part of a federal cross-site evaluation, a protocol was developed that included demographic, psychosocial, criminal justice, and health and services questions in addition to the inclusion of standardized measures. The protocol was back-translated into Spanish for nonstandardized questionnaires, with Spanish versions of standardized instruments incorporated. Standardized measures included in the battery and their psychometric properties have been described in detail in the longitudinal multisite and single site outcome publications of this baseline sample (Broner et al., 2004/2005) and thus are only listed here. Childhood trauma was measured through the Childhood Trauma Questionnaire-Short Form (CTQ; Bernstein et al., 2003), a retrospective self-report instrument screening five categories of childhood trauma (emotional abuse, physical abuse, sexual abuse, emotional neglect, and physical neglect), yielding a continuous trauma score and severity scores for subscales.

Six measures were used for mental health domains: (a) the DIS-IV (Robins et al., 1998) depression (with dysthymia and generalized anxiety for rule-out purposes), mania, psychosis, post-traumatic stress, and antisocial personality (with conduct disorder administered to distinguish adult-only conduct from personality disorder criterion) modules; (b) the Borderline subscale of the Personality Diagnostic Questionnaire-4+ (PDQ-4; Hyler, 1994) administered to provide a measure of lability and externalizing symptoms; (c) the Colorado Symptom Index (CSI; Shern et al., 1994) to assess psychotic and affective symptoms, (d) the SF-12 (Ware, Kosinski, & Keller 1996) to provide a brief global measure of mental (mental health component score, MCS) and physical (physical health component score, PCS) health; (e) the BPRS (Overall & Gorham, 1988), an objective assessment of current symptom presentation; and the Post-Traumatic Checklist-Civilian Version (PCL-CV; Weathers, Litz, Huska, & Keane, 1994).

Two instruments were incorporated to measure psychopathy and risk for violent recidivism: the PCL-SV (Hart et al., 1995) and the HCR-20 (Webster et al., 1997), a 3-factor scale that includes the PCL score as part of its historical risk factors. Two instruments were used to estimate alcohol and drug abuse/dependence, using a 5-point cut-score: the Michigan Alcohol Screening Test (MAST; Zung, 1979) and the Drug Abuse Screening Test (DAST; Skinner, 1982). Finally, to measure participants' perceived quality of life, the Lehman Quality of Life Interview (QOLI; Lehman, 1988) was administered; the life satisfaction subscale (GLS) is reported.

### STATISTICAL METHODS

Bivariate analyses were conducted for comparative gender analyses on demographic, psychosocial, criminal justice, and diagnostic characteristics. A correlational matrix was developed of the relationship between childhood trauma and its subtypes measured through the CTQ and the variables of interest (violence and recidivism risk, psychopathology, substance use, health, quality of life) and by gender. A hierarchical linear model for continuous variables with logistical regression analyses for dichotomous variables was developed through backwards step-wise deletion of significant bivariate analyses and with variables found consistently significant in prior research, controlling for gender to describe the overall contribution of trauma and its subtypes to the variables of interest.

### RESULTS

#### GENDER DIFFERENCES

Although homelessness, medical co-morbidity, unemployment, poverty, prior criminal justice involvement, and violence were prevalent problems for both men and women, there were a number of differences by gender for baseline sample characteristics (Tables 8.1 through 8.3). As described in Table 8.1, women were more likely to be living with a partner or spouse at arrest (33% vs. 20%) and to have a child under the age of 12 (62% vs. 39%), less likely to have as much education (10 years vs. 11 years) or a GED (13% vs. 38%), less likely to have ever been employed (57% vs. 78%), to have been unemployed in the year preceding the arrest (20% vs. 39%) or in the 30 days prior to their arrest (13% vs. 23%), and more likely to have been diagnosed with HIV (28% vs. 10%), although equally likely to be diagnosed with AIDS.

**TABLE 8.1** Demographic Characteristics by Gender

| Variable | Total Sample (n = 212) | | | Men (n = 119) | | | Women (n = 93) | | |
|---|---|---|---|---|---|---|---|---|---|
| | mean | sd | range | mean | sd | range | mean | sd | range |
| Age | 35.17 | 8.23 | 18–65 | 35.79 | 8.77 | 19–65 | 34.39 | 7.46 | 18–56 |
| Education level[1] | 10.52 | 2.49 | 1–17 | 10.95 | 2.59 | 3–17 | 9.97 | 2.25 | 1–17 |
| Income | 1855.20 | 3726.20 | 0–30688 | 1674.44 | 2669.21 | 0–15000 | 2077.22 | 4718.76 | 0–30688 |

| Variable | | Total Sample % | n | Men % | Women % |
|---|---|---|---|---|---|
| Gender | Male | 56.1 | 119 | 100.0 | – |
| | Female | 43.9 | 93 | – | 100.0 |
| Race/ethnicity[2] | African-American | 60.2 | 127 | 54.2 | 67.7 |
| | Hispanic/Latino | 25.6 | 54 | 26.3 | 24.7 |
| | White/Other | 14.2 | 30 | 19.5 | 7.5 |
| Education[3] | High School diploma | 17.5 | 37 | 18.5 | 16.1 |
| | GED | 26.9 | 57 | 37.8 | 12.9 |
| | Neither | 55.7 | 118 | 43.7 | 71.0 |
| Homelessness | Within year | 61.3 | 130 | 63.0 | 59.1 |
| | Within month | 24.1 | 51 | 20.2 | 29.0 |
| Unemployment history | Never employed[4] | 31.1 | 66 | 21.8 | 43.0 |
| | Unemployed past year[5] | 69.3 | 147 | 61.3 | 79.6 |
| | Unemployed, month prior to arrest[6] | 78.8 | 167 | 72.3 | 87.1 |
| | Unemployed at arrest | 81.6 | 173 | 77.3 | 87.1 |
| Health problems | Any serious health problem | 61.3 | 130 | 57.1 | 66.7 |
| | HIV+[7] | 17.7 | 37 | 10.2 | 27.5 |
| Family situation | Living with spouse or partner at arrest[8] | 25.9 | 55 | 20.2 | 33.3 |
| | Legally married at time of arrest | 14.2 | 30 | 12.6 | 16.3 |
| | Has child under age 12[9] | 49.0 | 103 | 39.0 | 62.0 |
| Treatment history | Any service use history | 93.8 | 198 | 94.1 | 93.5 |
| | Mental health treatment | 90.6 | 192 | 91.6 | 89.2 |
| | Drug/alcohol treatment | 61.1 | 129 | 57.6 | 65.6 |

[1] $t = 2.895$, df $= 210$, $p = .004$

[2] $\chi^2 = 6.861$, df $= 2$, $p = .032$ (Of Blacks and Whites, women are more likely to be Black.)

[3] $\chi^2 = 19.191$, df $= 2$, $p = .000$ (Of those without a high school diploma, men are more likely to have a GED.)

[4] $\chi^2 = 10.904$, df $= 1$, $p = .001$

[5] $\chi^2 = 8.156$, df $= 1$, $p = .004$

[6] $\chi^2 = 6.864$, df $= 1$, $p = .009$

[7] $\chi^2 = 10.558$, df $= 1$, $p = .001$

[8] $\chi^2 = 4.709$, df $= 1$, $p = .030$

[9] $\chi^2 = 10.917$, df $= 1$, $p = .001$

**TABLE 8.2** Mental and Addictive Baseline Diagnoses

| Variable | | Total Sample % | n | Men % | Women % |
|---|---|---|---|---|---|
| Mental disorders | Schizophrenias[1] | 26.6 | 53 | 33.9 | 17.8 |
| | Bipolar disorders[2] | 22.1 | 44 | 32.1 | 10.0 |
| | Major depressive disorders[3] | 48.2 | 95 | 36.1 | 62.9 |
| | PTSD | 37.2 | 74 | 31.8 | 43.8 |
| | Antisocial PD[4] | 19.8 | 40 | 14.4 | 26.4 |
| Addictive disorders | Alcohol use[5] | 9.0 | 19 | 13.4 | 3.2 |
| | Cannabis use | 7.1 | 15 | 9.2 | 4.3 |
| | Opioid use | 9.0 | 19 | 6.7 | 11.8 |
| | Cocaine use | 19.3 | 41 | 16.8 | 22.6 |
| | Polysubstance use | 54.2 | 115 | 51.3 | 58.1 |
| | Other substance use | 1.4 | 3 | 2.5 | 0.0 |

[1]$\chi^2 = 6.594$, df = 1, $p = .010$
[2]$\chi^2 = 13.933$, df = 1, $p = .000$
[3]$\chi^2 = 14.046$, df = 1, $p = .000$
[4]$\chi^2 = 4.503$, df = 1, $p = .034$
[5]$\chi^2 = 6.682$, df = 1, $p = .010$

**TABLE 8.3** Criminal Justice Information

| Measure | Total sample (n = 212) mean | sd | range | Men (n = 119) mean | sd | range | Women (n = 93) mean | sd | range |
|---|---|---|---|---|---|---|---|---|---|
| Age at first arrest | 20.63 | 7.31 | 6–51 | 19.82 | 7.52 | 6–51 | 21.72 | 6.90 | 9–40 |
| Total arrests, previous year | 2.31 | 3.24 | 1–32 | 2.16 | 1.90 | 1–12 | 2.51 | 4.40 | 1–32 |

| Measure | | Total Sample % | n | Men % | Women % |
|---|---|---|---|---|---|
| Primary arrest charge | Violent offense against person | 12.7 | 27 | 16.0 | 8.6 |
| | Nonviolent offense against person | 3.8 | 8 | 5.0 | 2.2 |
| | Drug offense, sale, or possession[1] | 52.4 | 111 | 38.7 | 69.9 |
| | Property crime[2] | 12.7 | 27 | 17.6 | 6.5 |
| | Procedural violation | 12.7 | 27 | 16.0 | 8.6 |
| | Minor offense | 5.7 | 12 | 6.7 | 4.3 |
| Previously arrested | | 96.2 | 204 | 96.6 | 95.7 |
| Previously convicted | | 82.9 | 178 | 83.2 | 82.6 |
| Arrested for violent act within 12 months prior to arrest | | 17.0 | 36 | 18.5 | 15.1 |
| Committed act of violence within 90 days prior to arrest | | 42.7 | 90 | 42.0 | 43.5 |

[1]$\chi^2 = 20.420$, $p = .000$
[2]$\chi^2 = 5.887$, $p = .015$

There were no significant differences between men and women in terms of age; income; race or ethnicity; whether the participant was living with a child under the age of 18 at the time of arrest; homelessness, shelter living, or instability of living arrangement; employment status at arrest; health problems (with the exception of HIV); and treatment service use history. However, on a subjective measure of health (see Table 8.4), the SF-12 Physical Health scale, male detainees received slightly, but significantly, higher scores than female detainees. Consistent with the few differences in living circumstances and demographic characteristics, there was no difference between male and female appraisal on the QOLI of General Life Satisfaction (Table 8.4).

There were significant differences between men and women on the major diagnoses assessed through the DIS-IV. Table 8.2 depicts the diagnoses and Table 8.4 displays the measures, some of which are relevant to the discussion of diagnostic and accompanying symptom differences between men and women. Men were more likely to reach the criteria for a diagnosis of schizophrenia (34% vs. 18%) or bipolar disorder (32% vs. 10%) than women participants. This was consistent with the BPRS, on which male detainees received significantly higher total scores than female detainees (52.39 vs. 43.72), indicating greater overall levels of objectively rated psychopathology in males (see Table 8.4). Women were significantly more likely to reach the criteria for major depression (63% vs. 36%) and for the full criteria of antisocial personality disorder (26% vs. 14%; see Table 8.2). Although a higher proportion of female than male detainees was given a diagnosis of PTSD (32% for men vs. 44% for women, Table 8.2), this difference was also not statistically significant, and there were no differences between men and women on the PCL-CV, a measure of PTSD symptoms (see Table 8.4). There were also no differences between men and women on the borderline personality disorder scale of the PDQ-4 or on a more global self-report measure of mental health symptoms as measured by the SF-12 mental health component score (see Table 8.4).

With regard to primary substance use disorders, collected from clinical charts, the only significant gender difference was for alcohol, for which men were significantly more likely than women to be diagnosed with an abuse or dependence disorder (13% vs. 3%); however, the sample size for alcohol as a primary diagnosis was only 19 participants (see Table 8.2). When alcohol problems were specifically assessed regardless of primary diagnosis, as shown in Table 8.4, male detainees were significantly more likely than female detainees to receive MAST alcohol problem scores that fell in the symptomatic range (males = 85.6%, $n = 113$; females = 67.7%, $n = 67$; $\chi^2(1) = 10.57$, $p < .001$), indicative of primary alcohol dependence and supporting chart diagnoses. On the other hand, male and female detainees obtained comparable scores on the DAST, a measure of the severity of their drug problems. A very high proportion of both male and female detainees received DAST scores that fell in the symptomatic range (males = 87.1%, $n = 115$; females = 91.9%, $n = 91$; $\chi^2(1) = 1.35$, n.s.) and consistent with primary substance use diagnoses.

In terms of criminal justice involvement and violence (Table 8.3), there were no differences between men and women with regard to the age of first arrest, number of arrests during the previous year, whether that arrest was violent, nights incarcerated in the year prior to arrest (women: M = 47.08, s.d. = 86.42, range = 0–365 vs. men: M = 70.15, s.d. = 101.97, range = 0–357), if ever arrested or convicted, or whether a violent

**TABLE 8.4** Gender Differences in Measures of Childhood Trauma and Psychiatric Symptoms and Problems

| Instrument | Men (n = 113) | | | Women (n = 93) | | | Total Sample (n = 212) | | |
|---|---|---|---|---|---|---|---|---|---|
| **Childhood trauma questionnaire** | mean | sd | range | mean | sd | range | mean | sd | range |
| Emotional abuse score | 12.60 | 5.83 | 5–25 | 13.22 | 6.47 | 5–25 | 12.87 | 6.11 | 5–25 |
| Physical abuse score | 11.84 | 5.39 | 5–25 | 11.99 | 6.71 | 5–25 | 11.91 | 5.99 | 5–25 |
| Sexual abuse score[1] | 8.58 | 6.22 | 2–25 | 13.15 | 8.27 | 5–25 | 10.58 | 7.53 | 2–25 |
| Emotional neglect score[2] | 12.28 | 5.08 | 4–25 | 14.72 | 6.08 | 5–25 | 13.35 | 5.66 | 4–25 |
| Physical neglect score[3] | 9.15 | 4.15 | 4–24 | 10.68 | 5.02 | 5–24 | 9.82 | 4.61 | 4–24 |
| Minimization/denial score | 0.35 | 0.72 | 0–3 | 0.25 | 0.69 | 0–3 | 0.31 | 0.71 | 0–3 |
| Hare psychopathy checklist | | | | | | | | | |
| Part 1 adjusted score[4] | 5.94 | 2.92 | 0–12 | 4.45 | 2.81 | 0–11 | 5.26 | 2.96 | 0–12 |
| Part 2 adjusted score | 8.91 | 2.32 | 1–12 | 8.27 | 2.43 | 1–12 | 8.62 | 2.37 | 1–12 |
| Total adjusted score[5] | 14.85 | 4.42 | 4–24 | 12.71 | 4.34 | 1–23 | 13.88 | 4.51 | 1–24 |
| HCR-20 risk assessment | | | | | | | | | |
| Historical items total[6] | 14.56 | 3.27 | 7–20 | 12.96 | 3.45 | 6–20 | 13.84 | 3.44 | 6–20 |
| Clinical items total | 5.98 | 1.90 | 1–10 | 5.77 | 2.02 | 0–10 | 5.89 | 1.95 | 0–10 |
| Risk management total | 6.30 | 1.88 | 1–10 | 6.65 | 1.91 | 3–10 | 6.05 | 1.90 | 1–10 |
| Total score | 26.87 | 5.31 | 12–40 | 25.37 | 6.17 | 12–39 | 26.19 | 5.75 | 12–40 |
| Brief psychiatric rating scale[7] | 52.39 | 12.24 | 32–95 | 43.72 | 8.17 | 28–63 | 48.55 | 11.45 | 28–95 |
| Colorado symptom inventory | 44.96 | 12.41 | 20–75 | 43.57 | 10.64 | 15–69 | 44.32 | 11.62 | 15–75 |
| PDQ-4 borderline personality | 5.43 | 2.16 | 0–9 | 5.60 | 2.08 | 0–9 | 5.51 | 2.12 | 0–9 |
| Post-traumatic checklist | 45.44 | 17.07 | 17–83 | 42.76 | 17.67 | 15–85 | 44.22 | 17.35 | 15–85 |
| Michigan alcoholism screening test | 30.84 | 99.89 | 0–1082 | 15.10 | 17.35 | 0–86 | 23.90 | 75.84 | 0–1082 |
| Drug abuse screening test | 11.27 | 5.62 | 0–20 | 12.40 | 4.71 | 0–19 | 11.77 | 5.26 | 0–20 |
| SF-12 | | | | | | | | | |
| Mental health | 34.27 | 13.74 | 9.10–67.39 | 31.782 | 11.24 | 7.43–58.29 | 33.16 | 12.71 | 7.43–67.49 |
| Physical health[8] | 51.81 | 10.11 | 24.70–68.93 | 48.10 | 10.86 | 23.35–66.52 | 50.15 | 10.59 | 23.35–68.93 |
| Quality of life general satisfaction | 3.16 | 1.45 | 1.00–7.00 | 3.00 | 1.43 | 1.00–6.50 | 3.09 | 1.44 | 1.00–7.00 |

[1]$t(166.076) = -4.438, p = .000$ [F = 35.412]

[2]$t(210) = -3.187, p = .002$

[3]$t(177.215) = -2.366, p = .019$ [F = 7.288]

[4]$t(200) = 3.679, p = .000$

[5]$t(200) = 3.466, p = .001$

[6]$t(200) = 3.376, p = .001$

[7]$t(195.350) = 6.028, p = .000$ [F = 9.445]

[8]$t(187) = 2.436, p = .016$

act was committed in the 90 days prior to arrest. However, the current arrest for women was more likely to have been a drug offense (70% vs. 39%) and significantly less likely to have been for a property offense (7% vs. 18%). There were no other gender differences for other current charge offense categories. When lifetime types of charges were assessed, again differences for drug and property offenses were consistent with current charges (e.g., 82% lifetime drug offenses for women vs. 66% for men, $\chi^2 (1) = 4.934, p < .05; 27\%$ for women vs. 50% for men for lifetime property crimes, $\chi^2 (1) = 15.356, p < 001$); however, men were also more likely to have been arrested for a violent offense (54% vs., 32%, $\chi^2(1) = 12.753, p < .001$), a nonviolent crime against a person (23% vs. 11%, $\chi^2(1) = 5.229, p < .05$), procedural offense (64% vs. 43%, $\chi^2(1) = 11.827, p < .001$), or a minor offense (54% vs. 46%, $\chi^2(1) = 5.230, p < .05$) during their lifetime.

As shown in Table 8.4, male detainees received significantly higher total psychopathy scores on the PCL-SV compared to female detainees. Twenty-nine percent ($n = 33$) of male detainees obtained psychopathy scores in the probable psychopathy range, compared to 17.9% ($n = 17$) of female detainees ($\chi^2(1) = 3.90, p < .05$). Another 42.3% ($n = 47$) of male detainees obtained psychopathy scores in the intermediate range, compared to 33.7% ($n = 32$) of female detainees ($\chi^2(1) = 1.62$, n.s.). Males also received significantly higher scores on the core interpersonal and affective symptoms of psychopathy (PCL-SV Part I items), but not on antisocial behavior items (PCL-SV Part II items). More male detainees (47.6%, $n = 30$) than female detainees (31%, $n = 22$) were also judged to be at high risk of violent recidivism based on the HCR-20's overall risk assessment score ($\chi^2(1) = 3.89, p < .05$). Male detainees also received significantly higher scores than female detainees on the HCR-20's Historical items. However, there were no differences between male and female detainees on the HCR-20's Clinical or Risk Management items.

In terms of childhood trauma scales, female detainees scored significantly higher than males on the CTQ's Sexual Abuse and Emotional Neglect scales, but not on the Emotional Abuse, Physical Abuse, or Physical Neglect scales. Fifty-nine percent of women ($n = 55$) reported having been sexually abused while growing up, compared to 33.6% of men ($\chi^2(1) = 13.75, p < .001$). Women were also more than twice as likely to report severe sexual abuse in childhood (46.2%), compared to male detainees (20.2%; $\chi^2(1) = 16.41, p < .001$). Childhood emotional neglect and physical neglect were also more prevalent experiences for women than for men. Seventy-seven percent ($n = 72$) of women reported having been emotionally neglected in childhood, compared to 64.7% ($n = 77$) of men ($\chi^2(1) = 4.04, p < .05$). Women were twice as likely as men to report severe emotional neglect in childhood (females = 32.3%, $n = 30$; males = 16%, $n = 19$; $\chi^2(1) = 7.80; p < .01$). Sixty-four percent ($n = 60$) of women reported childhood physical neglect, compared to 60.5% ($n = 72$) for men, a difference that was not statistically significant ($\chi^2(1) = .36$, n.s.). However, women were almost twice as likely as men to report severe physical neglect (females = 32.3%, $n = 30$; males = 17.6%, $n = 21$; $\chi^2(1) = 6.10; p < .01$). There were no significant gender differences in the prevalence of childhood emotional abuse (females = 68.8%, $n = 64$; males = 68.9%, $n = 82$; $\chi^2(1) = 0$; n.s.) or physical abuse (females = 64.5%, $n = 60$; males = 74.8%, $n = 89$; $\chi^2(1) = 2.64; p < .1$), or in the prevalence of severe emotional abuse (females = 36.6%, $n = 34$; males = 32.8%, $n = 39$; $\chi^2(1) = 0.33$; n.s.) or physical abuse (females = 36.6%, $n = 34$; males = 41.2%, $n = 49$; $\chi^2(1) = 0.47$; n.s.).

## CORRELATES OF CHILDHOOD TRAUMA IN MALE AND FEMALE DETAINEES

Childhood trauma, as measured retrospectively by the CTQ, was associated with a variety of adult psychiatric symptoms and problems in female and male detainees, as described in Table 8.5. Childhood trauma was related to the degree of psychopathy, assessed by the PCL-SV, in both male and female detainees. In male detainees, higher scores on the CTQ's Emotional Abuse, Physical Abuse, and Sexual Abuse scales were associated with significantly higher overall levels of psychopathy, as indicated by PCL-SV total scores, and with higher levels of antisocial behavior, as indicated by the scores on PCL-SV Part II items. In contrast, Physical Abuse was the only type of childhood trauma that was significantly associated with the interpersonal and affective symptoms of psychopathy (PCL-SV Part I items) in men. Female detainees showed a more limited pattern of relationships between childhood trauma and psychopathy. In females the CTQ's Emotional Abuse scale was significantly related to the PCL-SV total psychopathy scores, Part I scores and Part II scores. No other type of childhood trauma was associated with psychopathology in women.

Childhood trauma was also associated with risk of violent recidivism, as assessed by the HCR-20. In male detainees, higher scores on the CTQ's Emotional Abuse, Physical Abuse, and Sexual Abuse scales were associated with higher levels of overall risk, as indicated by the HCR-20's Total Risk score, and with higher levels of risk based on the HCR-20's Historical Risk items. The identical pattern of relationships was found in women: Emotional, Physical, and Sexual Abuse scores were significantly correlated with HCR-20 Total Risk and Historical Risk scores. In addition, in female detainees only, Emotional Abuse and Physical Abuse were significantly correlated with Clinical Risk scores, and Emotional Abuse with Risk Management scores.

When childhood trauma was examined in relationship to DSM-IV mental disorders, as assessed by the DIS-IV, no significant associations were found for diagnoses of schizophrenia, bipolar, or major depression, in either males or females, with the exception of schizophrenia for men only and only for the Physical Neglect scale. Childhood trauma was significantly associated with a diagnosis of PTSD on the DIS-IV and with scores on the PCL-CV, a measure of PTSD symptoms. In male detainees, Emotional Abuse, Physical Abuse, and Sexual Abuse were significantly associated with PTSD diagnoses on the DIS-IV, and with PCL-CV total trauma symptom scores. In female detainees only, sexual abuse scores were significantly correlated with a DIS-IV diagnosis of PTSD. However, in women all five types of childhood trauma measured with the CTQ were significantly associated with PCL-CV trauma symptom total scores. A relationship, although gender and type of abuse specific, was also found for the two personality disorders assessed. Childhood trauma and antisocial personality disorder were correlated for women, but not for men and specifically associated with emotional abuse and physical abuse. Childhood trauma also showed significant relationships with symptoms of borderline personality disorder as measured on the PDQ-4. In both male and female detainees, higher emotional abuse, physical abuse, and sexual abuse scores were associated with more severe borderline personality disorder symptomatology.

In terms of symptoms, rather than diagnoses, similarly, no significant relationships were found between types of childhood trauma and total scores on the BPRS (Table 8.5). However, childhood trauma was associated with self-report levels of general psychiatric distress on the CSI, but in male detainees only. In males, higher emotional

**TABLE 8.5** Correlations of Childhood Trauma with Alcohol, Drugs, Mental and Physical Health, Violent Recidivism Risk, and Quality of Life Measures

| Measure | Emotional Abuse | | Physical Abuse | | Sexual Abuse | | Emotional Neglect | | Physical Neglect | |
|---|---|---|---|---|---|---|---|---|---|---|
| | *men* | *women* | *men* | *women* | *men* | *women* | *men* | *women* | *men* | *women* |
| **Hare psychopathy checklist** | | | | | | | | | | |
| Part 1 adjusted score | .093 (n = 110) | .240* (n = 92) | .233* (n = 110) | .084 (n = 92) | .112 (n = 110) | .071 (n = 92) | -.038 (n = 110) | .060 (n = 92) | .139 (n = 110) | .136 (n = 92) |
| Part II adjusted score | .268** (n = 110) | .270** (n = 92) | .203* (n = 110) | .191 (n = 92) | .261** (n = 110) | .156 (n = 92) | .075 (n = 110) | -.023 (n = 92) | .032 (n = 110) | .004 (n = 92) |
| Total adjusted score | .205* (n = 110) | .305** (n = 92) | .262** (n = 110) | .157 (n = 92) | .209* (n = 110) | .130 (n = 92) | .013 (n = 110) | .019 (n = 92) | .112 (n = 110) | .091 (n = 92) |
| **HCR-20 risk assessment** | | | | | | | | | | |
| Historical | .405*** (n = 111) | .338*** (n = 91) | .299** (n = 111) | .294** (n = 91) | .383*** (n = 111) | .302** (n = 91) | .140 (n = 111) | .112 (n = 91) | .061 (n = 111) | .043 (n = 91) |
| Clinical | -.004 (n = 110) | .376*** (n = 91) | .111 (n = 110) | .279** (n = 91) | .103 (n = 110) | .162 (n = 91) | .013 (n = 110) | .189 (n = 91) | .181 (n = 110) | .174 (n = 91) |
| Risk management | .064 (n = 110) | .234* (n = 91) | .109 (n = 110) | .128 (n = 91) | .041 (n = 110) | .192 (n = 91) | .122 (n = 110) | .071 (n = 91) | .097 (n = 110) | .154 (n = 91) |
| Total | .276** (n = 110) | .385*** (n = 91) | .257** (n = 110) | .295** (n = 91) | .286** (n = 110) | .281** (n = 91) | .144 (n = 110) | .146 (n = 91) | .135 (n = 110) | .129 (n = 91) |
| **Diagnostic interview schedule** | | | | | | | | | | |
| Schizophrenia | .143 (n = 109) | -.108 (n = 90) | .055 (n = 109) | .073 (n = 90) | .153 (n = 109) | -.020 (n = 90) | .061 (n = 109) | -.141 (n = 90) | .205* (n = 109) | -.136 (n = 90) |
| Bipolar disorder | .186 (n = 109) | .130 (n = 90) | .101 (n = 109) | .068 (n = 90) | .130 (n = 109) | -.018 (n = 90) | .045 (n = 109) | .050 (n = 90) | .001 (n = 109) | -.199 (n = 90) |
| Major depression | -.009 (n = 108) | .076 (n = 89) | .041 (n = 108) | .099 (n = 89) | -.011 (n = 108) | .138 (n = 89) | .147 (n = 108) | .068 (n = 89) | .114 (n = 108) | .092 (n = 89) |
| PTSD | .291** (n = 110) | .181 (n = 89) | .282** (n = 110) | .119 (n = 89) | .265** (n = 110) | .255* (n = 89) | .113 (n = 110) | .120 (n = 89) | .118 (n = 110) | .016 (n = 89) |
| Antisocial PD | .100 (n = 111) | .278** (n = 91) | .151 (n = 111) | .239* (n = 91) | .148 (n = 111) | .141 (n = 91) | .010 (n = 111) | .081 (n = 91) | -.025 (n = 111) | .059 (n = 91) |
| Brief psychiatric rating scale total | .042 (n = 113) | .155 (n = 90) | .153 (n = 113) | .197 (n = 90) | .167 (n = 113) | .136 (n = 90) | .059 (n = 113) | .137 (n = 90) | .063 (n = 113) | .206 (n = 90) |
| Colorado symptom inventory | -.271** (n = 109) | -.102 (n = 93) | -.156 (n = 109) | -.185 (n = 93) | -.305*** (n = 109) | -.124 (n = 93) | -.116 (n = 109) | -.125 (n = 93) | -.043 (n = 109) | -.130 (n = 93) |
| PDQ-4 borderline personality disorder | .310*** (n = 109) | .215* (n = 88) | .203* (n = 109) | .215* (n = 88) | .275** (n = 109) | .205 (n = 88) | .128 (n = 109) | .050 (n = 88) | .029 (n = 109) | .100 (n = 88) |
| PTSD checklist | .395*** (n = 95) | .365*** (n = 79) | .353*** (n = 95) | .380*** (n = 79) | .328*** (n = 95) | .338* (n = 79) | .184 (n = 95) | .373*** (n = 79) | .085 (n = 95) | .306** (n = 79) |
| Michigan alcoholism screening test | .155 (n = 118) | -.112 (n = 93) | .191* (n = 118) | -.118 (n = 93) | .211* (n = 118) | -.122 (n = 93) | -.110 (n = 118) | -.224* (n = 93) | -.062 (n = 118) | -.065 (n = 93) |
| Drug abuse screening test | .215* (n = 118) | .285** (n = 92) | .215* (n = 118) | .296** (n = 92) | .274** (n = 118) | .316** (n = 92) | .119 (n = 118) | .093 (n = 92) | .160 (n = 118) | .263* (n = 92) |
| **SF-12** | | | | | | | | | | |
| Mental health | -.241* (n = 105) | -.274* (n = 84) | -.211 (n = 105) | -.196 (n = 84) | -.238* (n = 105) | -.301** (n = 84) | -.171 (n = 105) | -.271* (n = 84) | -.128 (n = 105) | -.241* (n = 84) |
| Physical health | .023 (n = 105) | .009 (n = 84) | .119 (n = 105) | -.058 (n = 84) | .141 (n = 105) | -.023 (n = 84) | .002 (n = 105) | .016 (n = 84) | -.055 (n = 105) | .047 (n = 84) |
| Quality of life general satisfaction | -.241** (n = 119) | -.264* (n = 93) | -.192* (n = 119) | -.122 (n = 93) | -.176 (n = 119) | -.185 (n = 93) | -.269** (n = 119) | -.206* (n = 93) | -.007 (n = 119) | -.228* (n = 93) |

$* p < .05 ** p < .01 *** p < .001$

abuse, physical abuse, and sexual abuse scores were associated with greater distress on the CSI. No such relationships were found in female detainees. On a third measure of mental health, a briefer and more general distress index, the SF-12, childhood trauma, was associated with overall mental health scores. In male detainees, higher emotional abuse, physical abuse, and sexual abuse scores were associated with significantly poorer mental health on the SF-12. In female detainees, higher emotional abuse, sexual abuse, emotional neglect, and physical neglect scores were associated with poorer overall mental health, with Physical Abuse scores also approaching statistical significance. Childhood trauma was not associated with overall physical health scores on the SF-12. Finally, childhood trauma was related to general life satisfaction on the QOLI for both men and women. In male detainees, higher levels of emotional neglect were associated with less general life satisfaction. In women, higher levels of emotional abuse, emotional neglect, and physical neglect were associated with less general life satisfaction.

Also as described in Table 8.5, childhood trauma was related to the severity of drug and alcohol problems, as measured by the DAST and MAST, respectively. In both male and female detainees, higher emotional abuse, physical abuse, and sexual abuse scores were associated with significantly more severe drug problems on the DAST. The relationship between childhood trauma and severity of alcohol problems was less consistent. In male detainees, physical abuse and sexual abuse scores were significantly correlated with the severity of alcohol problems, whereas in female detainees emotional neglect showed an unexpected inverse relationship with alcohol problems and no other significant associations were found.

### EFFECTS OF CHILDHOOD TRAUMA, CONTROLLING FOR GENDER

To further examine the effects of gender and childhood trauma, we conducted a series of hierarchical regression analyses, using the various psychiatric symptom and problem variables that we examined in the correlational analyses as the dependent variables. In these analyses, gender was entered at the first step, the five types of childhood trauma at the second step, and the five interactions between gender and types of childhood trauma at the third step. In this way the "main effects" of childhood trauma on psychiatric symptoms and problems were evaluated after the effects of gender were statistically controlled, and the interaction of gender and childhood trauma could be tested for statistical significance. When continuous variables were used as the dependent measures, hierarchical linear regression was used. When dichotomous diagnostic variables were the dependent measures, logistical regression analysis was performed.

With only one exception, the HCR-20's Clinical Risk score, none of the interactions between gender and childhood trauma were found to be statistically significant. Thus, with this one exception—female gender predicts clinical risk for violent recidivism in interaction with childhood trauma—the relationships between childhood trauma and the psychiatric symptom and problem variables were not significantly different for male and female detainees, after the "main effects" of gender and childhood trauma were statistically controlled.

At the second step of the model, the set of five childhood trauma variables accounted for a significant amount of variance in most of the psychiatric variables we examined, including the PCL-SV Total Psychopathy Part I and II scores, HCR-20 Total Risk risk and Historical Risk risk scores, PCL-CV Total score, PDQ-4 Borderline scale,

DAST, MAST, SF-12 Mental Health score, and QOLI General Llife Satisfaction score. Thus, childhood trauma as a whole remained a significant predictor of each of these psychiatric variables, even after the effects of gender had been accounted at the previous step in the model. In these analyses, the set of childhood trauma variables accounted for 5.5% (PCL-SV Part I scores) to 19.6% (HCR-20 Historical item scores) of the variance in psychiatric symptoms and problems, after the effects of gender had been statistically removed.

When the set of childhood trauma variables was found to be significant, we examined the independent effect of each type of trauma by testing the significance of its beta-weight. Thus, at the second step in the model, the significance of the beta-weight for each trauma variable showed its unique contribution to predicting psychiatric symptoms and problems, when all of the other types of trauma had been simultaneously controlled.

In several of the regression analyses, the CTQ's Sexual Abuse scale emerged as an independent predictor of variance in the dependent measures, whereas in several other analyses, the CTQ's Emotional Abuse scale was an independent predictor of variance. Sexual Abuse emerged as a significant independent predictor of the HCR-20's Historical items and the DAST, while nearly reaching significance for the PCL-CV and the SF-12 Mental Health scale. Thus, Sexual Abuse was the only type of childhood trauma that explained any unique variance in these psychiatric variables, when all forms of childhood trauma were allowed to "compete" with each other for variance in the same model. For several other dependent variables, the CTQ's Emotional Abuse scale was the only trauma variable that made a unique positive contribution to the regression model, including the PCL-SV Total Psychopathy and Part II scores, the HCR-20 Total risk score, the Borderline scale of the PDQ-4, and the General Life Satisfaction Scale of the QOLI. In addition, the Emotional Neglect scale made a significant negative contribution to the regression model for a few of the dependent variables (the PCL-SV Total Psychopathy and Part I scores, MAST, and QOLI's General Life Satisfaction scale), a finding that appears to represent a suppressor effect, which may be attributable to the high degree of intercorrelation between the CTQ's Emotional Abuse and Emotional Neglect scales. Physical Neglect showed similar suppressor effects for the HCR-20's Historical items scale.

## SUMMARY AND DISCUSSION

The study was purposely limited to a multiple-problem, seriously mentally ill, substance-using jail detainee population. Thus, comparisons of childhood abuse and neglect prevalence, and correlations between these events and adult pathology and behavior with other studies of different clinical subpopulations or community samples, are limited. Further, although a broader set of problem areas was assessed than usually tested within one study (e.g., mental and addictive disorders, symptoms, violence, criminal justice, and life satisfaction), several other major areas of research regarding the positive association between childhood trauma and negative adult behavior and events were not studied, such as: revictimization (e.g., Irwin, 1999; Messman & Long, 1996; Messman-Moore & Brown, 2004; Messman-Moore, Long, & Siegfried, 2000; Ornduff et al., 2001), suicide (e.g., Blaauw, Arensman, Kraaij, Winkel, & Bout, 2002; Brown, Cohen, Johnson, & Smailes, 1999; Dube, Anda, Felitti, Chapman, Williamson, & Giles,

2001; Goodman et al., 1997; Roy, 2001b; Richie & Johnsen, 1996), and a broader range of medical problems and health risk behaviors (e.g., Bensley, Van Eenwyk, & Simmons, 2000; Goodman & Fallot, 1998; Kendall-Tackett, 2002; Messina & Grella, 2006; Paul, Catania, Pollack, & Stall, 2001).

The primary limitations, however, of this study are the lack of collateral confirmation of abuse histories (although official records tend to underreport; Widom, Weiler & Cottler, 1999) and the limits of adult retrospection on childhood events when used to identify the current effects of those events (Goldman, Juliette, & Padavachi, 2000; Widom et al., 1994; Widom et al., 1999), as well as the limits of this design to infer etiology that is more accurately assessed via a prospective design (Widom, Raphael, & DuMont, 2004). Nonetheless, the study afforded the opportunity to compare male and female detainees with serious mental disorders and co-occurring substance use on a number of variables. This was in addition to the primary focus of assessing gender-specific effects and overall contribution of childhood trauma to adult psychopathology and dysfunctional behavior to guide screening, assessment, and integration of interventions during incarceration and community reintegration post-release.

More than half (59%) of the sample self-reported one or more of the five childhood trauma experiences assessed, comparable to rates found among incarcerated substance abusers and psychiatric populations in other studies (e.g., Goodman et al., 1997; McClellan et al., 1997), but higher for overall and subtype prevalence than reported in a Bureau of Justice Statistics (BJS) survey of jail and prison inmates (James & Glaze, 2006). The differences in rates with BJS may be due to a number of factors including that: almost half of our sample were female in contrast to rates found in correctional settings, the surveys from which the BJS data were derived assessed only physical and sexual childhood abuse, a standardized instrument was not used to assess childhood trauma, and mental illness was defined solely through self-reported psychiatric symptoms or hospitalization rather than research diagnosis.

Male and female study participants were equally likely to experience high rates of homelessness, medical comorbidity, unemployment, poverty, prior criminal justice involvement (number of arrests, convictions, or days incarcerated), to have engaged in violent behavior, to self-report psychiatric symptoms, to be drug using, to be diagnosed with post-traumatic stress disorder or borderline personality disorder, and to have been physically (65% female vs. 75% male) or emotionally abused (69%) and physically neglected (64% women vs. 61% men).

Overall, women in this sample were less likely than men to have a disabling pathology of schizophrenia, bipolar disorder, objectively assessed psychiatric symptoms that correspond with these diagnoses, primary alcohol dependence (although in contrast to the literature reviewed, is in concert with McClellan, Farabee, & Crouch, 1997, for an incarcerated female and male population), psychopathy (with rates for women and men comparable to other forensic populations; Hart, Hare, & Harpur, 1997), risk for violent recidivism, and a broad range of lifetime criminal justice involvement. Women were also less likely to have as many years of education, to have a GED, or to have been employed. Women were more likely to be diagnosed with depression or antisocial personality disorder, be HIV positive, have more lifetime arrests and convictions for drug-related charges, to live with a partner or spouse and to have young children under their care, to have been sexually abused (59% vs. 34%) and emotionally neglected

(77% vs. 65%), and to have experienced as a child twice the severity of sexual abuse, and physical and emotional neglect as men. Although childhood rates for men were very high and associated with deleterious outcomes apparent in adulthood, women in this sample experienced more traumatic events in childhood, and those traumatic events were more severe than were those among men, a finding that complements previous studies (Cutler & Nolen-Hoeksema, 1991; James & Glaze, 2006).

Women require linkage to and ongoing support for education, employment, child care, and development of relationship and parenting skills, and likely require longer and more comprehensive services involvement than men to achieve reintegration goals and affect recidivism (e.g., Alemagno et al., 2004; Green, Miranda, Daroowalla, & Siddique, 2005; Hartwell, 2001; Hartwell, 2004). Most interventions today advocate a wraparound approach that encourages self-sufficiency, provides housing, and offers integrated mental health and substance abuse treatment. In part, this need for increased involvement of service agencies is based on the range of psychosocial issues that require intervention for self-sufficiency and in part because this population is also more vulnerable to additional co-morbidity, including medical problems (particularly HIV infection) that further complicate service delivery, receipt, and adherence. Other studies have demonstrated that childhood sexual abuse is associated with HIV risk behaviors (e.g., Bensley et al., 2000) and that childhood abuse in general is associated for women with an increased risk for developing a compendium of other complex and chronic medical problems (Messina & Grella, 2006).

The evidence of these needs and the inherent difficulty of addressing them while struggling with mental illness, addiction, criminal behavior, family issues, housing, stigma, and poverty lends further support to the concept of coordinated treatment and provision of psychosocial services with primary and specialized medical care. Incarceration can provide initial access to needed services, their continuation, or cause the disruption of those services that were being received in the community prior to arrest (Blitz, Wolff, & Paap, 2006). A coordinated comprehensive care approach is particularly important during incarceration to identify, assess, treat, and plan for the service needs of clients and for successful community integration (Dlugacz et al., 2007).

Women and men shared several important similarities and a few significant differences in how early maltreatment may be expressed through pathology during adulthood. Being female and abused significantly contributed to clinical risk for violent recidivism. In particular, emotional, physical, and sexual abuse were each associated with criminality and dysregulation, with an increased risk for violent recidivism and psychopathy. Additionally for women, physical and emotional abuse increased the odds for developing antisocial personality, a finding that differs from Zlotnick's (1999) study of 85 incarcerated women, which did not find an association between psychopathy or antisocial personality and childhood trauma, but did not specifically assess emotional abuse or compare men and women. Further, the contribution of childhood trauma to adult violence, arrest, and incarceration across gender is well established as described in the literature reviewed and replicated in an outcome study of this sample that indicates childhood trauma, although distal, is not only contributory, but a predictor of re-arrest and incarceration (Broner et al., 2005) for both men and women. Further, for substance abuse treatment of offenders, the additional recommended emphasis on addressing criminal thinking and behavior

(Fletcher & Chandler, 2006) should be applied with this dually diagnosed criminal justice population and augmented with anger management and other violence prevention strategies, particularly among those who have experienced emotional, physical, and sexual abuse.

For men and women, emotional, physical, and sexual abuse and additionally emotional neglect for women, contributed to drug use and diagnosis. The relationship was more limited for alcohol. Only emotional neglect correlated with women's alcohol use and diagnosis, whereas physical and sexual abuse were the primary contributors for men's alcohol use. The differential effects of subtypes of trauma mediated by gender on alcohol use may help explain the mixed findings in the literature regarding the relationship between alcohol and trauma.

As consistently established, trauma was associated with PTSD and its symptoms. For men, emotional, physical, and sexual abuse each contributed to diagnosis and current trauma symptoms. Emotional, physical, and sexual abuse, as well as emotional neglect, were associated with current trauma symptoms for women, although only sexual abuse contributed to a diagnosis of PTSD. Tailored treatment and services, as well as harm reduction, has been regularly recommended for those incarcerated, because previously traumatized adults are particularly prone to retraumatization by the jail or prison experience (Kupers, 1996). In other studies of the seriously mentally ill noncriminal justice population, PTSD, whether related to childhood or adult events, has been shown to contribute to substance use, medical problems, other co-occurring psychiatric illnesses, and the type and frequency of service use (Mueser et al., 2004). Thus, untreated trauma and its sequelae directly and indirectly influence recidivism, incarceration, revictimization, and a host of other factors that increase the risk of criminal justice involvement, further providing evidence for the central role of addressing trauma in correctional, community supervision and reentry programming.

As compared to women, depending on the type of childhood abuse and neglect experienced, men were additionally affected in terms of internal organization, thinking, and affect regulation. In addition to childhood trauma's association with adult substance use, trauma diagnosis, and symptoms and quality of life, for men these experiences during childhood were also associated with psychotic diagnosis (through physical neglect), affective and psychotic symptoms (through emotional and sexual abuse), and affective lability (e.g., borderline personality symptoms, through emotional, physical and sexual abuse).

When gender effects were removed, childhood trauma contributed to adult PTSD and trauma symptoms, borderline personality symptoms, psychopathy, risk for violent recidivism, drug and alcohol dependence, affective global symptoms (although not affective diagnoses), and diminished general life satisfaction. These findings are in concert with the research literature reviewed at the beginning of this chapter. Childhood trauma explained 6% to 20% of the variance of psychopathology and criminogenic behavior, similar to several of the studies reviewed by Kendall-Tackett et al. (1993), although these studies were focused on sexual abuse. Of the subtypes of childhood trauma, sexual abuse independently predicted the risk of violent recidivism and substance abuse and dependence, and emotional abuse predicted psychopathy, risk for violent recidivism, borderline personality symptoms, and general life satisfaction. In terms of the interaction between gender and childhood trauma, the only significant interaction was for women who had an increased clinical risk for violent recidivism.

Thus, findings indicate the utility of including emotional abuse into screening (in addition to sexual and physical abuse that are more commonly included) and risk assessment for similar criminal justice populations, considering the unique symptomatic and behavioral expression of trauma experience for men and women and by subtype, and making routine gender-specific trauma treatment.

## CONCLUSION

Although brief screens have been developed for mental and addictive disorders for use by jail and prison staff (e.g., Dlugacz, Broner, & Lamon, 2007), trauma is neither systematically included or assessed for this population as part of a formal correctional screening process or risk-management assessment. In part, this is because childhood trauma's utility as a predictor of negative outcomes for this population has not been well established and in part because brief screening instruments are a recent development (e.g., Bernstein et al., 2003; Thombs, Bernstein, Ziegelstein, Bennett, & Walker, 2007). A second issue is training and professional support. Nonmental health professionals may be uncomfortable asking explicit questions and potentially lack guidance from clinical staff and follow-up support for clients who may be become flooded during questioning. Although childhood abuse is often noted in the clinical records of inmates who have received mental health treatment, clinical forensic staff seldom receive the trauma training needed on how to incorporate the implications of childhood abuse into the services they provide (Adams, 2002).

In spite of the clear evidence that treatment needs of women differ from those of men, few programs to date tailor treatment services for dually diagnosed female offenders (Huntington, Moses, & Veysey, 2005; Peugh & Belenko, 1999). In recent years, however, there has been an increase in the number of programs for incarcerated or community-based criminal-justice-involved adults that integrate victimization experiences and recognize the association between early trauma and subsequent behavior and within a holistic approach (Welle, Falkin, & Jainchill, 1997). However, the majority of programs were designed for males and fail to address previous victimization experiences or female-specific issues (Henderson, Schaeffer, & Brown, 1998). Further, most of these programs were originally designed for male sex offenders with sexual abuse histories—a distinctly different population and with very different treatment needs.

A female-specific approach is one that accounts for the unique life experiences and physical and emotional needs of women and that subsequently facilitates treatment efficacy (National GAINS Center, n.d.). Further, a trauma-sensitive approach promotes therapeutic and institutional practices that minimize retraumatization and directly addresses abuse histories. An evidence-base for gender- and trauma-sensitive treatments within jails and prisons is emerging (Clark, 2002). One source of emerging programming is from the substance abuse field, where evidence-based model programs that integrate trauma and substance abuse treatment through a gender-specific informed framework are being tested with co-occurring populations (e.g., Najavits, in press). Another evidence-based program that has emerged from the mental health/co-occurring field was designed to serve women with co-occurring mental and addictive disorders and trauma histories and emphasizes the need for an integrated, trauma-informed, consumer-involved, and comprehensive approach (Huntington et al., 2005). However, generally these programs primarily target sexual abuse and adult violence.

The differential as well as cumulative effect of abuse types could further guide the development of curriculum that helps in the understanding of triggers and strategies to address them.

If childhood trauma increases the risk for violence and recidivism, contributes to self-injurious behavior, and increases general psychiatric symptoms—all indicators of dysregulation and potential impulsivity—then programs whose mission is to stabilize, reintegrate, and reduce public safety risk will have a mixed effect without targeted intervention. In fact, a multisite study of diversion programs in which childhood trauma was not generally assessed or targeted indicated little effect on mental health symptoms, although this was also likely due to the lack of integrated mental health sub-stance abuse treatment in several sites (Broner et al., 2004). Further, without monitor-ing or other structured intervention to regulate client behavior, little effect was found for general diversion on violence risk and criminal justice recidivism (Broner et al., 2004; Broner et al., 2005). Simply targeting treatment access through diversion and the provision of generic services will not affect some of the serious psychiatric symptoms that are a consequence of trauma experiences. Likewise, without specific focus on anger management, affect regulation, and criminal thinking, also in part a consequence of early trauma, antisocial, violent, or recidivist behavior—public safety risks—will likely not be affected. Given the prevalence of childhood trauma and the complexity of the appropriate treatment, a trauma specialist should be included in correctional and community-based criminal justice programs.

Individual interventions that address trauma, substance use, depression, medica-tion management, risk behavior, employment, dysregulation, and criminal thinking are ample, but empirical study of their combined effect, sequence of interventions, and dosing are not. Further, to add to the complexity of designing correctional and community-based interventions is the brief length of stay in jail versus prison, the lack of evidenced-based services actually implemented, the availability of trauma special-ists and who are cross-trained in the other needed clinical interventions, and resources allocated for screening and treatment. Although the screening of trauma subtype may have particular utility for risk assessment, targeting the specific early experience versus its adult presentation through treating specific symptoms and disorders is unclear and requires study.

## References

Abram, K. M., & Teplin, L. A. (1991). Co-occurring disorders among mentally ill jail detainees: Implications for public policy. *American Psychologist, 46*, 1036–1045.

Abram, K. M., Teplin, L. A., & McClelland, G. M. (2003). Comorbidity of severe psychiatric dis-orders and substance use disorders among women in jail. *American Journal of Psychiatry, 160*(5), 1007–1010.

Adams, J. (2002). Child abuse: The fundamental issue in forensic clinical practice. *International Journal of Offender Therapy and Comparative Criminology, 46*(6), 729–733.

Alemagno, S. A., Shaffer-King, E., Tonkin, P., & Hammel, R. (2004). *Characteristics of arrestees at risk for co-existing substance abuse and mental disorder*. Retrieved May 25, 2005, from http://www.ncjrs.org/pdffiles1/nij/grants/207142.pdf

Battle, C. L., Zlotnick, C., Najavits, L. M., Gutierrez, M., & Winsor, C. (2003). Posttraumatic stress disorder and substance use disorder among incarcerated women. In P. Ouimette & P. J. Brown (Eds.), *Trauma and substance abuse: Causes, consequences, and treatment of comorbid disorders* (pp. 209–225). Washington, DC: American Psychological Association.

Bensley, L. S., Van Eenwyk, J., & Simmons, K. W. (2000). Self-reported childhood sexual and physical abuse and adult HIV-risk behaviors and heavy drinking. *American Journal of Preventive Medicine, 19*(2), 151–158.

Berliner, L., & Elliott, D. M. (2002). Sexual abuse of children. In J. E. B. Myers, L. Berliner, J. Briere, C. T. Hendrix, C. Jenny, & T. A. Reid (Eds.), *The APSAC handbook on child maltreatment,* 2nd ed., (pp. 55–78). Thousand Oaks, CA: Sage.

Bernstein, D. P. (2000). Childhood trauma and drug addiction: Assessment, diagnosis, and treatment. *Alcoholism Treatment Quarterly, 18,* 19–30.

Bernstein, D. P., Stein, J. A., & Handelsman, L. (1998). Predicting personality pathology among adult patients with substance use disorders: Effects of childhood maltreatment. *Addictive Behaviors, 23*(6), 855–868.

Bernstein, D. P., Stein, J. A., Newcomb, M. D., Walker, E., Pogge, D., Ahluvalia, T., Stokes, J., Handelsman, L., Medrano, M., Desmond, D., & Zule, W. (2003). Development and validation of a brief screening version of the Childhood Trauma Questionnaire. *Child Abuse and Neglect, 27,* 169–190.

Blaauw, E., Arensman, E., Kraaij, V., Winkel, F. W., & Bout, R. (2002). Traumatic life events and suicide risk among jail inmates: The influence of types of events, time period and significant others. *Journal of Traumatic Stress, 15*(1), 9–16.

Blitz, C. L., Wolff, N., & Paap, K. (2006). Availability of behavioral health treatment for women in prison. *Psychiatric Services,* 57, 356–360.

Brems, C., Johnson, M. E., & Neal, D. (2004). Childhood abuse history and substance use among men and women receiving detoxification services. *American Journal of Drug and Alcohol Abuse, 30*(4), 799–821.

Broner, N., Lattimore, P. K., Cowell, A. J., & Schlenger, W. E. (2004). Effects of diversion on adults with co-occurring mental illness and substance use: Outcomes from a national multi-site study. *Behavioral Sciences and the Law, 22,* 519–541.

Broner, N., Lamon, S. S., Mayrl, D. W., & Karopkin, M. G. (2003). Arrested adults awaiting arraignment: Mental health, substance abuse, and criminal justice characteristics and needs. *Fordham Urban Law Journal, 30*(2), 663–721.

Broner, N., Mayrl, D. W., & Landsberg, G. (2005). Outcomes of mandated and nonmandated New York City jail diversion for offenders with alcohol, drug, and mental disorders. *The Prison Journal, 85*(1), 18–49.

Brown, G. R., & Anderson, B. (1991). Psychiatric morbidity in adult inpatients with childhood histories of sexual and physical abuse. *American Journal of Psychiatry, 148,* 55–61.

Brown, J., Cohen, P., Johnson, J. G., Smailes, E. M. (1999). Childhood abuse and neglect: Specificity and effects on adolescent and young adult depression and suicidality. *Journal of the American Academy of Child & Adolescent Psychiatry, 38*(12), 1490–1496.

Cloitre, M., Tardiff, K., Marzuk, P. M., Leon, A. C., & Portera, L. (2001). Consequences of childhood abuse among male psychiatric inpatients: Dual roles as victims and perpetrators. *Journal of Traumatic Stress, 14,* 47–61.

Cohen, P., Brown, J., & Smailes, E. (2001). Child abuse and neglect and the development of mental disorders in the general population. *Development and Psychopathology, 13*(4), 981–999.

Curtis, G. C. (1963). Violence breeds violence–perhaps? *American Journal of Psychiatry, 120,* 386–387.

Curtis, Jr., R. L., Leung, P., Sullivan, E., Eschbach, K., & Stinson, M. (2001). Outcomes of child sexual contacts: Patterns of incarceration from a national sample. *Child Abuse and Neglect, 25,* 719–736.

Cutler, S. E., & Nolen-Hoeksema, S. (1991). Accounting for sex differences in depression through female victimization: Childhood sexual abuse. *Sex Roles, 24*(7–8), 425–438.

Deykin, E. Y., & Buka, S. L. (1997). Prevalence and risk factors for posttraumatic stress disorder among chemically dependent adolescents. *American Journal of Psychiatry, 154,* 752–757.

Dlugacz, H. A., Broner, N., & Lamon, S. S. (2007). Implementing reentry—Establishing a continuum of care for adult jail and prison releases with mental illness. In M. Piasecki & O. Thienhaus (Eds.), *Correctional psychiatry*. Kingston, New Jersey: Civic Research Institute, Inc.

Dube, S. R., Anda, R. F., Felitti, V. J., Chapman, D. P., Williamson, D. F., & Giles, W. H. (2001). Childhood abuse, household dysfunction, and the risk of attempted suicide throughout the life span: Findings from the adverse childhood experiences study. *JAMA: Journal of the American Medical Association, 286*(24), 3089–3096.

Duncan, R. D., Saunders, B. E., Kilpatrick, D. G., Hanson, R. F., & Resnick, H. S. (1996). Childhood physical assault as a risk factor for PTSD, depression, and substance abuse: Findings from a national survey. *American Journal of Orthopsychiatry, 66*, 437–448.

Dutton, D. G., & Hart, S. D. (1992). Evidence for long-term, specific effects of childhood abuse and neglect on criminal behavior in men. *International Journal of Offender Therapy and Comparative Criminology, 36*(2), 129–137.

Emery, R., & Laumann-Billings, L. (1998). An overview of the nature, causes, and consequences of abusive family relationships: Toward differentiating maltreatment and violence. *American Psychologist, 53*, 121–135.

Epstein, J. N., Saunders, B. E., & Kilpatrick, D. G. (1997). Predicting PTSD in women with a history of childhood rape. *Journal of Traumatic Stress, 10*(4), 573–588.

Fagan, A. A. (2005). The relationship between adolescent physical abuse and criminal offending: Support for an enduring and generalized cycle of violence. *Journal of Family Violence, 20*(5), 279–290.

Fehon, D. C., Grilo, C. M., & Lipschitz, D. S. (2001). Gender differences in violence exposure and violence risk among adolescent inpatients. *Journal of Nervous and Mental Disease, 189*, 532–540.

Fickenscher, A., Lapidus, J., Silk-Walker, P., & Becker, T. (2001). Women behind bars: Health needs of inmates in a county jail. *Public Health Reports, 116*(3), 191–196.

Finkelhor, D., & Dziuba-Leatherman, J. (1994). Victimization of children. *American Psychologist, 49*, 173–183.

Finkelhor, D., Hotaling, G., Lewis, I. A., & Smith, C. (1990). Sexual abuse in a national survey of adult men and women: Prevalence, characteristics, and risk factors. *Child Abuse and Neglect, 14*, 19–28.

Fletcher, B., & Chandler, R. K. (2006). *Principles of drug abuse treatment for criminal justice populations: A research-based guide.* Bethesda, MD: U.S. Department of Health and Human Services, National Institutes of Health, National Institute on Drug Abuse.

Galaif, E. R., Stein, J. A., Newcomb, M. D., & Bernstein, D. P. (2001). Gender differences in the prediction of problem alcohol use in adulthood: Exploring the influence of family factors and childhood maltreatment. *Journal of Studies on Alcohol, 62*, 486–493.

Gil-Rivas, V., Fiorentine, R., Anglin, M. D., & Taylor, E. (1997). Sexual and physical abuse: Do they compromise drug treatment outcomes? *Journal of Substance Abuse Treatment, 14*, 351–358.

Goldman, L. A., Juliette, D. G., & Padayachi, U. K. (2000). Some methodological problems in estimating incidence and prevalence in child sexual abuse research. *The Journal of Sex Research, 37*(4), 305–314.

Goodman, L. A., & Fallot, R. D. (1998). HIV risk-behavior in poor urban women with serious mental disorders: Association with childhood physical and sexual abuse. *American Journal of Orthopsychiatry, 68*(1), 73–83.

Goodman, L. A., Rosenberg, S. D., Mueser, K. T., & Drake, R. (1997). Physical and sexual assault history in women with serious mental illness: Prevalence, correlates, treatment, and future research directions. *Schizophrenia Bulletin, 23*, 685–696.

Goodman, L. A., Salyers, M. P., Mueser, K. T., Rosenberg, S. D., Swartz, M., Essock, S. M., Osher, F. C., Butterfield, M. I., & Swanson, J. (2001). Recent victimization in women and men with severe mental illness: Prevalence and correlates. *Journal of Traumatic Stress, 14*, 615–632.

Grella, C. E., Stein, J. A., & Greenwell, L. (2005). Associations among childhood trauma, adolescent problem behaviors, and adverse adult outcomes in substance-abusing women offenders. *Psychology of Addictive Behaviors, 19*(1), 43–53.

Green, B. L., Miranda, J., Daroowalla, A., & Siddique, J. (2005). Trauma exposure, mental health functioning, and program needs of women in jail. *Crime Delinquency, 51*(1), 133–151.

Haapasalo, J., & Pokela, E. (1999). Child-rearing and child abuse antecedents of criminality. *Aggression and Violent Behavior, 4*(1), 107–127.

Haller, D. L., & Miles, D. R. (2004). Personality disturbances in drug-dependent women: Relationship to childhood abuse. *American Journal of Drug and Alcohol Abuse, 30*(2), 269–286.

Harkness, K. L., & Monroe, S. M. (2002). Childhood adversity and endogenous versus nonendogenous distinction in women with major depression. *American Journal of Psychiatry, 159*, 387–393.

Hart, S. D., Cox, D. N., & Hare, R. D. (1995). *The HARE PCL:SV: Psychopathy Checklist Screening Version*. Niagara Falls, NY: Multi-Health Systems Inc.

Hart, S. D., Hare, R. D., & Harpur, T. (1997). The Revised Psychopathy Checklist (PCL-R): An overview for researchers and clinicians. In P. McReynolds & J. Rosen (Eds.), *Advances in psychological assessment, 8*. New York: Plenum.

Hartwell, S. (2001). Female mentally ill offenders and their community reintegration needs: An initial examination. *International Journal of Law and Psychiatry, 24*, 1–11.

Hartwell, S. (2004). Triple stigma: Persons with mental illness and substance abuse problems in the criminal justice system. *Criminal Justice Policy Review, 15*(1), 84–99.

Heffernan, K., Cloitre, M., Tardiff, K., Marzuk, P. M., Portera, L., & Leon, A. C. (2000). Childhood trauma as a correlate of lifetime opiate use in psychiatric patients. *Addictive Behaviors, 25*, 797–803.

Helgeland, M. I., & Torgersen, S. (2004). Developmental antecedents of borderline personality disorder. *Comprehensive Psychiatry, 45*(2), 138–147.

Henderson, D., Schaeffer, J., & Brown, L. C. (1998). Gender-appropriate mental health services for incarcerated women: Issues and challenges. *Family and Community Health, 21*(3), 42–53.

Hill, J. (2006). Child maltreatment and depression in adults: Implications for prevention. *Clinical Neuropsychiatry: Journal of Treatment Evaluation, 3*(1), 23–28.

Holmes, W. C., & Slap, G. B. (1998). Sexual abuse of boys: Definition, prevalence, correlates, sequelae, and management. *Journal of the American Medical Association, 280*, 1855–1862.

Horwitz, A. V., Widom, C. S., McLaughlin, J., & White, H. R. (2001). The impact of childhood abuse and neglect on adult mental health: A prospective study. *Journal of Health and Social Behavior, 42*, 184–201.

Huntington, N., Moses, D. J., & Veysey, B. (2005). Developing and implementing a comprehensive approach to serving women with co-occurring disorders and histories of trauma. *Journal of Community Psychology, 33*(4), 395–410.

Hyler, S. E. (1994). *PDQ-4+: Personality Diagnostic Questionnaire-4+*. New York: New York State Psychiatric Institute.

Ireland, T., & Widom, C. S. (1994). Childhood victimization and risk for alcohol and drug arrests. *International Journal of the Addictions, 29*(2), 235–274.

Irwin, H. J. (1999). Violent and nonviolent revictimization of women abused in childhood. *Journal of Interpersonal Violence, 14*(10), 1095–1110.

James, D. J., & Glaze, L. E. (2006). Mental health problems of prison and jail inmates. Washington, DC: U.S. Department of Justice, Office of Justice Programs, Bureau of Justice Statistics, NCJ 213600

Janssen, I., Krabbendam, L., Bak, M., Hanssen, M., Vollebergh, W., de Graaf, R., & van Os, J. (2004). Childhood abuse as a risk factor for psychotic experiences. *Acta Psychiatrica Scandinavica, 109*(1), 38–45.

Johnson, J. G., Cohen, P., Brown, J., Smailes, E. M., & Bernstein, D. P. (1999). Childhood maltreatment increases risk for personality disorders during early adulthood. *Archives of General Psychiatry, 56*, 600–606.

Kendall-Tackett, K. A. (2002). The health effects of childhood abuse: Four pathways by which abuse can influence health. *Child Abuse and Neglect, 6/7*, 715–730.

Kendall-Tackett, K. A., Williams, L. M., & Finkelhor, D. (1993). Impact of sexual abuse on children: A review and synthesis of recent empirical studies. *Psychological Bulletin, 113*, 164–180.

Knisely, J. S., Barker, S. B., Ingersoll, K. S., & Dawson, K. S. (2000). Psychopathology in substance abusing women reporting childhood sexual abuse. *Journal of Addictive Diseases, 19*, 31–44.

Koivisto, H., & Haapasalo, J. (1996). Childhood maltreatment and adulthood psychopathy in light of file-based assessments among mental state examinees. *Studies on Crime and Crime Prevention, 5*(1), 91–104.

Kupers, T. A. (1996). Trauma and its sequelae in male prisoners: Effects of confinement, overcrowding, and diminished services. *American Journal of Orthopsychiatry, 66*(2), 189–196.

Langeland, W., Draijer, N., van den Brink, W. (2004). Psychiatric comorbidity in treatment-seeking alcoholics: The role of childhood trauma and perceived parental dysfunction. *Alcoholism: Clinical and Experimental Research, 28*(3), 441–447.

Langeland, W., & Hartgers, C. (1998). Child sexual and physical abuse and alcoholism: A review. *Journal on Studies of Alcohol, 59*(3), 336–348.

Lattimore, P. K., Broner, N., Sherman, R., Frisman, L., & Shafer, M. (2003). Comparing pre-booking and post-booking diversion programs and baseline characteristics of mentally ill substance using individuals with justice involvement: A multi-site study. *Journal of Contemporary Criminal Justice, 19*(1), 30–64.

Lehman, A. F. (1988). A quality of life interview for the chronically mentally ill. *Evaluation and Program Planning, 11*, 51–62.

Lipschitz, D. S., Kaplan, M. L., Sorkenn, G. L., Chorney, P., & Asnis, G. M. (1996). Prevalence and characteristics of physical and sexual abuse among psychiatric outpatients. *Psychiatric Services, 47*, 189–191.

Luntz, B. K., & Widom, C. S. (1994). Antisocial personality disorder in abused and neglected children grown up. *American Journal of Psychiatry, 151*, 670–674.

Malinosky-Rummell, R., & Hansen, D. J. (1993). Long-term consequences of childhood physical abuse. *Psychological Bulletin, 114*(1), 68–79

McClellan, D. S., Farabee, D., & Crouch, B. M. (1997). Early victimization, drug use, and criminality: A comparison of male and female prisoners. *Criminal Justice and Behavior, 24*(4), 455–476.

Messina, N., & Grella, C. (2006). Childhood trauma and women's health outcomes in a California prison population. *American Journal of Public Health, 96*(10), 1842–1848.

Messman, T. L., & Long, P. J. (1996). Child sexual abuse and its relationship to revictimization in adult women: A review. *Clinical Psychology Review, 16*(5), 397–420.

Messman-Moore, T. L., & Brown, A. L. (2004). Child maltreatment and perceived family environment as risk factors for adult rape: Is child sexual abuse the most salient experience? *Child Abuse and Neglect: The International Journal, 28*(10), 1019–1034.

Messman-Moore, T. L., Long, P. J., & Siegfried, N. J. (2000). The revictimization of child sexual abuse survivors: An examination of the adjustment of college women with child sexual abuse, adult sexual assault, and adult physical abuse. *Child Maltreatment: Journal of the American Professional Society on the Abuse of Children, 5*(1), 18–27.

Miller, B. A., Downs, W. R., & Testa, M. (1993). Interrelationships between victimization experiences and women's alcohol use. *Journal of Studies on Alcohol, Supplement No. 11*, 109–117.

Monahan, J. (2002). The MacArthur studies of violence risk. *Criminal Behaviour and Mental Health, 12*, S67–S72.

Morgan, C., Fisher, H., & Fearon, P. (2006). Child abuse and psychosis: Comment. *Acta Psychiatrica Scandinavica, 113*(3), 238.

Mueser, K., Salyers, M. P, Rosenberg, S. D., Goodman, L. A., Essock, S. M., Osher, F. C., Swartz, M. S., Butterfield, M. I., & 5 Site Health and Risk Study Research Committee (2004). Interpersonal trauma and posttraumatic stress disorder in patients with severe mental illness: Demographic, clinical, and health correlates. *Schizophrenia Bulletin, 30*(1), 45–57.

Mullen, P. E., Martin, J. L., Anderson, J. C., Romans, S. E., & Herbison, G. P. (1993). Childhood sexual abuse and mental health in adult life. *British Journal of Psychiatry, 163*, 721–732.

Najavits, L. M. (in press). Seeking safety: An evidence-based model for trauma/PTSD and substance use disorder. In K. Witkiewitz & G. A. Marlatt (Eds.), *Evidence based relapse prevention.* Amsterdam: Elsevier.

National GAINS Center for People with Co-Occurring Disorders in the Justice System (n.d.). *Addressing the needs of women with co-occurring disorders in the criminal justice system.* Retrieved August 23, 2006, from http://www.gainscenter.samhsa.gov/pdfs/Women/Address_Specific_Needs.pdf

Ornduff, S. R., Kelsey, R. M., & O'Leary, K. D. (2001). Childhood physical abuse, personality, and adult relationship violence: A model of vulnerability to victimization. *American Journal of Orthopsychiatry, 71*, 322–331.

Ouimette, P. C., Kimerling, R., Shaw, J., & Moos, R. H. (2000). Physical and sexual abuse among women and men with substance use disorders. *Alcoholism Treatment Quarterly, 18*, 7–17.

Overall, J. E., & Gorham, D. R. (1988). The Brief Psychiatric Rating Scale (BPRS): Recent developments in ascertainment and scaling. *Psychopharmacology Bulletin, 24*, 97–99.

Paul, J. P., Catania, J., Pollack, L., & Stall, R. (2001). Understanding childhood sexual abuse as a predictor of sexual risk-taking among men who have sex with men: The Urban Men's Health Study. *Child Abuse & Neglect, 25*, 557–584.

Peugh, J., & Belenko, S. (1999). Substance-involved women inmates: Challenges to providing effective treatment. *Prison Journal, 79*(1), 23–44.

Prevent Child Abuse America. (2003). *What everyone can do to prevent child abuse: 2003 child abuse prevention community resource packet.* Chicago: Prevent Child Abuse America, Department of Health and Human Services, and National Clearinghouse on Child Abuse and Neglect Information.

Read, J., van Os, J., Morrison, A. P., & Ross, C. A. (2005). Childhood trauma, psychosis, and schizophrenia: A literature review with theoretical and clinical implications. *Acta Psychiatrica Scandinavica, 112*(5), 330–350.

Richie, B. E., & Johnsen, C. (1996). Abuse histories among newly incarcerated women in a New York City jail. *JAMWA, 51*, 111–114, 117.

Rind, B., Tromovitch, P., & Bauserman, R. (1998). A meta-analytic examination of assumed properties of child sexual abuse using college samples. *Psychological Bulletin, 124*, 22–53.

Rivera, B., & Widom, C. S. (1990). Childhood victimization and violent offending. *Violence and Victims, 5*(1), 19–35.

Robins, L., Cottler, L., Bucholz, K., & Compton, W. (1998). *Diagnostic Interview Schedule for DSM-IV (DIS-IV).* St. Louis, MO: Washington University School of Medicine, Department of Psychiatry.

Roy, A. (1999). Childhood trauma and depression in alcoholics: Relationship to hostility. *Journal of Affective Disorders, 56*, 215–218.

Roy, A. (2001a). Childhood trauma and hostility as an adult: Relevance to suicidal behavior. *Psychiatry Research, 102*, 97–101.

Roy, A. (2001b). Childhood trauma and suicidal behavior in male cocaine dependent patients. *Suicide and Life-Threatening Behavior, 31*, 194–196.

Sabo, A. N. (1997) Etiological significance of associations between childhood trauma and borderline personality disorder: Conceptual and clinical implications. *Journal of Personality Disorders, 11*(1), 50–70.

Sansone, R. A., Sansone, L. A., & Gaither, G. A. (2004). Multiple types of childhood trauma and borderline personality symptomatology among a sample of diabetic patients. *Traumatology, 10*(4), 257–266.

Sansone, R. A., Songer, D. A., & Miller, K. A. (2005). Childhood abuse, mental healthcare utilization, self-harm behavior, and multiple psychiatric diagnoses among inpatients with and without a borderline diagnosis. *Comprehensive Psychiatry, 46*(2), 117–120.

Schuck, A. M., & Widom, C. S. (2001). Childhood victimization and alcohol symptoms in females: Causal inferences and hypothesized mediators. *Child Abuse and Neglect, 25,* 1069–1092.

Shern, D. L., Wilson, N. Z., Cohen, A. S., Patrick, D. C., Foster, M., Bartsch, D. A., & Demmler, J. (1994). Client outcomes II: Longitudinal client data from the Colorado Treatment Outcome Study. *Milbank Quarterly, 72*(1), 123–143.

Silverman, A. B., Reinherz, H. Z., & Giaconia, R. M. (1996). The long-term sequelae of child and adolescent abuse: A longitudinal community study. *Child Abuse and Neglect, 20,* 709–723.

Skinner, H. A. (1982). Drug abuse screening test. *Addictive Behavior, 7,* 263–371.

Staley, D., & El Guebaly, N. (1990). Psychometric properties of the Drug Abuse Screening Test in a psychiatric patient population. *Addictive Behaviors, 15*(3), 257–264.

Teplin, L. A, Abram, K. M., & McClelland, G. M. (1996). Prevalence of psychiatric disorders among incarcerated women: I. Pretrial jail detainees. *Archives of General Psychiatry, 53*(6), 505–512.

Thombs, B. D., Bernstein, D. P., Ziegelstein, R. C., Bennett, W., & Walker, E. A. (2007). A brief two-item screener for detecting a history of physical or sexual abuse in childhood. *General Hospital Psychiatry, 29*(1), 8–13.

U.S. Department of Health and Human Services, Administration on Children, Youth, and Families. (2005). *Child maltreatment 2003* [online]. Washington, DC: U.S. Government Printing Office. Accessed July 3, 2006, from http://www.acf.hhs.gov/programs/cb/pubs/cm03/index.htm

U.S. Department of Health and Human Services, Administration on Children, Youth, and Families. (2006). *Child maltreatment 2004* [online]. Washington, DC: U.S. Government Printing Office. Accessed July 3, 2006, from http://www.acf.hhs.gov/programs/cb/pubs/cm04/insidecover.htm

Ware, J. E., Kosinski, M., & Keller, S. D. (1996). A 12-item short-form health survey: SF-12 construction and preliminary tests of reliability and validity. *Medical Care, 34,* 220–233.

Weathers, F. W., Litz, B. T., Huska, J. A., & Keane, T. M. (1994). *PCL Checklist-Civilian Version.* Boston: National Center for PTSD, Behavioral Science Division.

Webster, C., Douglas, K., Eaves, D., & Hart, S. (1997). *HCR-20: Assessing risk of violence.* Burnaby, British Columbia: Mental Health, Law, and Policy Institute of Simon Fraser University.

Weiler, B. L., & Widom, C. S. (1996). Psychopathy and violent behavior in abused and neglected young adults. *Criminal Behavior and Mental Health, 6*(3), 253–271.

Welle, D., Falkin, G. P., & Jainchill, N. (1997). Current approaches to drug treatment for women offenders: Project WORTH. *Journal of Substance Abuse Treatment, 15*(2), 151–163.

Wexler, B. E., Lyons, L., Lyons, H., & Mazure, C. M. (1997). Physical and sexual abuse during childhood and development of psychiatric illnesses during adulthood. *Journal of Nervous and Mental Disease, 185*(8), 522–524.

Widom, C. S. (1989a). Child abuse, neglect, and adult behavior: Research design and findings on criminality, violence, and child abuse. *American Journal of Orthopsychiatry, 59,* 355–367.

Widom, C. S. (1989b). The cycle of violence. *Science, 244,* 160–166.

Widom, C. S. (1999). Posttraumatic stress disorder in abused and neglected children grown up. *American Journal of Psychiatry, 156,* 1223–1229.

Widom, C. S., & Ames, M. A. (1994). Criminal consequences of childhood sexual victimization. *Child Abuse and Neglect, 18,* 303–318.

Widom, C. S., Ireland, T., & Glynn, P. J. (1995). Alcohol abuse in abused and neglected children followed-up: Are they at increased risk? *Journal of Studies on Alcohol, 56*, 207–217.

Widom, C. S., Raphael, K. G., & DuMont, K. A. (2004). The case for prospective longitudinal studies in child maltreatment research: Commentary on Dube, Williamson, Thompson, Felitti, & Anda. *Child Abuse and Neglect, 28*(7), 715–722.

Widom, C. S., Weiler, B. L., & Cottler, L. B. (1999). Childhood victimization and drug abuse: A comparison of prospective and retrospective findings. *Journal of Consulting and Clinical Psychology, 67*, 867–880.

Widom, C. S., & White, H. R. (1997). Problem behaviours in abused and neglected children grown up: Prevalence and co-occurrence of substance abuse, crime and violence. *Criminal Behaviour and Mental Health, 7*(4), 287–310.

Windle, M., Windle, R. C., Scheidt, D. M., & Miller, G. B. (1995). Physical and sexual abuse and associated mental disorders among alcoholic inpatients. *American Journal of Psychiatry, 152*, 1322–1328.

Zanarini, M. C., Gunderson, J. G., & Marino, M. F. (1989). Childhood experiences of borderline patients. *Comprehensive Psychiatry, 30*(1), 18–25.

Zlotnick, C. (1999). Antisocial personality disorder, affect dysregulation and childhood abuse among incarcerated women. *Journal of Personality Disorders, 13*(1), 90–95.

Zung, B. J. (1979). Psychometric properties of the MAST and two briefer versions. *Journal of Studies on Alcohol, 40*(9), 845–859.

# CHAPTER 9
# ADDRESSING THE MENTAL HEALTH NEEDS OF WOMEN OFFENDERS

ॐ

## Barbara E. Bloom
## Stephanie Covington

## ABSTRACT

There is a growing body of research documenting the mental health needs of women offenders. Bloom, Owen, and Covington (2003) addressed the relationship between substance abuse, trauma, and mental health and noted that these are three critical interrelated issues in the lives of women offenders. Although they are therapeutically linked, these issues historically have been treated separately. One of the most important developments in mental health care over the past several decades is the recognition that a substantial proportion of women offenders have experienced trauma and that these traumatic experiences play a vital and often unrecognized role in the evolution of a woman's physical and mental health problems. Gaps in health care provision exist in mental health, physical health, prevention, follow-up, and transitional services for women across the criminal justice spectrum. This chapter discusses the need to develop gender-responsive mental health services for women offenders and offers recommendations for program content.

*Women in American society have life experiences that differ from men's in important ways. Many of these—sexual assault, domestic violence, poverty, and discrimination—hurt women's mental and physical health.*

AMERICAN PSYCHOLOGICAL ASSOCIATION

## INTRODUCTION

The number of women in jail, in prison, on probation, or on parole in the United States has increased dramatically over the past several decades and now exceeds one million. Women entering the correctional system are at high risk for substance use disorders and mental health problems. According to the Bureau of Justice Statistics, 73% of the female prisoners in state institutions and 47% in federal institutions used drugs regularly prior to their incarceration (Mumola, 1999). Data from other studies suggest that as many as 80% of incarcerated women meet the criteria for at least one lifetime psychiatric disorder (Jordan, Schlenger, Fairbank, & Caddell, 1996; Teplin, Abram, & McClellan, 1996). Substance abuse or dependence, post-traumatic stress disorder (PTSD), and depression appear to be some of the most common mental health problems among female prisoners.

There is a growing body of research on the mental health needs of women offenders. One major finding from this research is that incarcerated women are more likely than their male counterparts to report extensive histories of physical, sexual, and emotional abuse (Messina, Burdon, Hagopian, & Prendergast, 2006). Surveys conducted among incarcerated women also have shown a strong link between childhood abuse and adult mental health problems, particularly depression, post-traumatic stress, panic, and eating disorders (Messina & Grella, 2006). In a 2006 study of the impact of traumatic childhood events on a sample of drug-dependent female offenders, Messina and Grella found that greater exposure to childhood adverse events was associated with behavioral problems in adolescence and adulthood as well as with physical and mental health problems.

Although they are therapeutically linked, substance abuse, post-traumatic stress, and mental health problems have been treated separately. One of the most important developments in mental health care over the past several decades is the recognition that a substantial proportion of women offenders have experienced trauma and that this plays a vital and often unrecognized role in the evolution of a woman's physical and mental health problems (Bloom, Owen, & Covington, 2003).

There are important mental health differences between incarcerated women and women in general. For example, 12% of females in the general population have symptoms of a mental disorder, compared to 73% of females in state prisons, 61% in federal prisons, and 75% in local jails (James & Glaze, 2006). Another study, comparing incarcerated women matched by age and ethnicity to those in the community, found that incarcerated women have a significantly higher incidence of mental health disorders, including schizophrenia, major depression, substance use disorders, psychosexual dysfunction, and antisocial personality disorder (Ross, Glaser, & Stiasny, 1988).

Women offenders characteristically are poor, women of color, unemployed, and the mothers of young children. They also have significant substance abuse issues and multiple physical and mental health problems (Bloom, Owen, & Covington, 2003). Incarcerated women typically have experienced some forms of abuse, including sexual assault, domestic violence, and other physical and psychological abuse. Although a history of abuse and family-related problems are common issues among female inmates, many correctional systems do not screen for childhood or adult abuse when determining possible therapeutic interventions (Morash, Bynum, & Koons, 1998).

According to the Bureau of Justice Statistics, at midyear 2005, female prison and jail inmates had many more mental health problems than did male prisoners.

Seventy-three percent of women in state prisons had mental health problems versus 55% of males, and 75% of women in local jails had mental health problems versus 63% of males. Twenty-three percent of females in state prisons and local jails said that they had been diagnosed with mental disorders by mental health professionals in the past year (James & Glaze, 2006). This is nearly three times the number of male inmates (8%) who had been told that they had mental disorders.

Three-quarters of the female inmates in state prisons who had mental health problems met the criteria for substance dependence or abuse. Thirty-four percent had used powdered or crystalline ("crack") cocaine, and 17% had used methamphetamines in the month prior to each of their arrests. Sixty-eight percent had experienced past physical or sexual abuse, 17% had been homeless in the year prior to their arrests, and 47% had a parent who abused alcohol or drugs (James & Glaze, 2006).

Teplin, Abram, and McClellan (1996) found that most incarcerated women who had psychiatric disorders did not receive treatment. The findings of a study of lifetime use of mental health and substance abuse treatment services by incarcerated women by Jordan et al. (2002) suggest that:

> There is a subgroup of troubled women whose impairments result not only in their receiving mental health and/or substance abuse treatment services, or both, but also in their being repeatedly incarcerated. (p. 324)

The authors also state that they do not know why, despite having been in treatment, the women continued to exhibit serious mental health problems and to engage in behaviors that led to incarceration. One hypothesis suggested by the high prevalence of exposure to trauma among the women inmates is that their disorders may be trauma related and that the previous treatments may not have addressed their traumatic experiences.

A study by Green, Miranda, Daroowalla, and Siddique (2005) that explored exposure to trauma, mental health functioning, and treatment-program needs of women in jails found high levels of exposure to trauma (98%)—especially interpersonal trauma (90%)—and domestic violence (71%) among incarcerated women, along with high rates of PTSD, substance abuse problems, and depression. Thirty-six percent of the women had mental disorders. These findings suggest that many incarcerated women are unlikely to achieve the goals of economic and social independence, family reunification, and reduced involvement in criminal activities without adequate attention to their PTSD and other mental health problems (p. 145). The authors emphasize that, unless traumatic victimization experiences, functional difficulties, and other mental health needs are taken into account in program development, incarcerated women are unlikely to benefit from in-custody and postrelease programs.

## UNDERSTANDING TRAUMA

The terms "violence," "trauma," "abuse," and "post-traumatic stress disorder" (PTSD) often are used interchangeably. One way to clarify these terms is to think of trauma as a response to violence or some other overwhelmingly negative experience. Trauma is both an event and a particular response to an event. *The Diagnostic and Statistical*

*Manual of Mental Disorders* (American Psychiatric Association, 1994) (also known as the *DSM-IV*), used by mental health providers, defines "trauma" as follows:

> . . . involving direct personal experience of an event that involves actual or threatened death or serious injury, or other threat to one's physical integrity; or a threat to the physical integrity of another person; or learning about unexpected or violent death, serious harm, or threat of death or injury experienced by a family member or other close associate. The person's response to the event must involve intense fear, helplessness or horror (or in children, the response must involve disorganized or agitated behavior. (p. 424)

PTSD is one type of disorder that results from trauma. The *DSM IV* lists the following symptoms of PTSD (pp. 427–429):

- Re-experience of the event through nightmares and flashbacks.
- Avoidance of stimuli associated with the event (e.g., if a woman was assaulted by a blonde man, she may fear and want to avoid men with blonde hair).
- Estrangement (the inability to be emotionally close to anyone).
- A numbing of general responsiveness (feeling nothing most of the time).
- Hypervigilance (constantly scanning one's environment for danger, whether physical or emotional).
- An exaggerated startle response (a tendency to jump at loud noises or unexpected touch).

There are two types of PTSD: simple and complex. A single traumatic incident in adulthood (such as a flood or accident) may result in simple PTSD. Complex PTSD usually results from multiple incidents of abuse and/or violence (such as childhood sexual abuse and domestic violence).

A review of studies that examined the combined effects of post-traumatic stress disorder and substance abuse found more co-occurring mental disorders, medical problems, psychological symptoms, in-patient admissions, interpersonal problems, lower levels of functioning, poor compliance with aftercare and motivation for treatment, and other significant life problems (such as homelessness, HIV, domestic violence, and loss of custody of children) in women with both disorders than in women with PTSD or substance abuse alone (Najavits, Weiss, & Shaw, 1997).

Although PTSD is a common diagnosis associated with abuse and trauma, the most common mental health problem for women who are survivors of trauma is depression.

When working in the criminal justice system, it is important to know that the vast majority of female offenders have been physically and/or sexually abused, both as children and as adults. Women often have their first encounters with the law as juveniles who have run away from home to escape violence and physical or sexual abuse. Prostitution, property crime, and drug use can then become ways of life.

There is a difference between women and men in terms of their risk for physical and sexual abuse. Both female and male children are at risk in childhood, from family members and other people known to them. However, there are significant gender differences over a life span. In adolescence, boys are at risk if they are gay, young men of color, or gang members. Their risk is from people who dislike or hate them. For a young woman, the risk is in her relationships from the person(s) to whom she is saying, "I love you." For an adult man, the risk for abuse comes from being in combat or being a victim of crime, and the perpetrator usually is a stranger. For an adult woman, the risk is again in her relationship with the person to whom she says, "I love you." Clinically, we think that this may account for the increase in mental health problems for women. It is more confusing and distressing to have the person who is supposed to love and care for you do harm to you than it is to be harmed by someone who dislikes you or is a stranger to you (Covington, 2007b).

Of course, different women have different responses to violence and abuse. Some may respond without trauma because they have coping skills that are effective for a specific event. Sometimes trauma occurs but is not recognized immediately, because the violent event is perceived as normal.

Many women who used to be considered "treatment failures" because they relapsed can now be understood to be trauma survivors who returned to alcohol or other drugs in order to medicate the pain of trauma. By integrating trauma treatment with addiction treatment, we reduce the risk of trauma-based relapse.

Although services designed for women that acknowledge their typical victimization experiences are becoming more widespread, and a variety of approaches targeting gender-based needs have been proposed (Bloom, Owen, & Covington, 2003; Covington, 1998, 1999, 2003, 2007b; Zlotnick, Najavits, Rohsenow, & Johnson, 2003), such specialized services tend to be the exceptions rather than the rule. Gaps in substance abuse treatment and in physical and mental health care exist during incarceration and on reentry into the community. While in the correctional system, women have little access to gender-responsive substance abuse and mental health services. After completing their prison sentences, they are released into their communities with little transitional support or integrated services that address their substance abuse, trauma, and mental health needs.

In conceptualizing treatment programs for women, it is essential that providers combine theory and practice from a multidisciplinary perspective. Increased sensitivity to women's specific needs is necessary in order to design effective programs.

## THEORETICAL PERSPECTIVES

In order to develop gender-responsive substance abuse and mental health services for women, it is essential to have a theoretical framework. This is the knowledge base that creates the foundation upon which programs are developed. Four fundamental theories for creating women's services include: pathways theory, theory of women's psychological development, trauma theory, and addiction theory.

### PATHWAYS THEORY

Research on women's pathways into crime indicates that gender matters. Steffensmeier and Allen (1998) note how the "profound differences" between the lives of women and men shape their patterns of criminal offense. Many women on the social and economic margins of society struggle to survive outside legitimate enterprises, which brings them into contact with the criminal justice system. As was previously mentioned, because of their gender, women are at greater risk for experiences such as sexual abuse, sexual assault, and domestic violence. The most common pathways to crime are based on survival (of abuse and poverty) and substance abuse. Pollock

(1998) asserts that female offenders have histories of sexual and/or physical abuse that appear to be the major roots of their subsequent delinquency, addiction, and criminality.

In summary, pathway research has identified such key issues in producing and sustaining female criminality as histories of personal abuse, mental illness tied to early life experiences, substance abuse and addiction, economic and social marginality, homelessness, and harmful relationships.

## THEORY OF WOMEN'S PSYCHOLOGICAL DEVELOPMENT

Theories that focus on female development, such as the relational model, posit that the primary motivation for women throughout life is the establishment of a strong sense of connection with others. Relational-Cultural Theory (RTC) developed from an increased understanding of gender differences and, specifically, of the different ways in which women and men develop psychologically (Miller, 1986, 1990). According to RCT, females develop a sense of self and self-worth when their actions arise out of, and lead back into, connections with others. Connection, not separation, is the guiding principle of growth for girls and women.

The importance of understanding Relational-Cultural Theory is reflected in the recurring themes of relationship and family seen in the lives of female offenders. Females are far more likely than males to be motivated by relational concerns.

Disconnection and violation rather than growth-fostering relationships characterize the childhood experiences of most women in the criminal justice system. For example, women offenders who cite drug abuse as self-medication often discuss personal relationships as the causes of their pain. The relational aspects of addiction are also evident in the research that indicates that women are more likely than men to turn to drugs in the context of relationships with drug-abusing partners in order to feel connected. A relational context is critical to successfully addressing the reasons that women commit crimes, the motivations behind their behaviors, the ways they can change their behaviors, and their reintegration into the community (Covington, 2007a).

## TRAUMA AND ADDICTION THEORIES

Trauma and addiction are interrelated issues in the lives of women offenders. Although they are therapeutically linked, historically these issues have been treated separately. Trauma and addiction theories provide critical elements in the integration of and foundation for gender-responsive services in the criminal justice system (Covington, 2007b).

### Trauma Theory

As the understanding of traumatic experiences has increased, mental health conceptualizations and practice have needed to be changed accordingly. It is now considered necessary for all service providers to become "trauma informed" if they want to be effective. Trauma-informed services are services that are provided for problems other than trauma but require knowledge concerning the impact of violence against women and other traumatic experiences. According to Harris and Fallot (2001), trauma-informed services:

- Take the trauma into account.
- Avoid triggering trauma reactions and/or retraumatizing the individual.

- Adjust the behavior of counselors, other staff members, and the organization to support the individual's coping capacity.
- Allow survivors to manage their trauma symptoms successfully so that they are able to access, retain, and benefit from these services.

Becoming trauma informed is particularly important for the criminal justice system. The standard operating practices (searches, seclusion, and restraint) may traumatize and/or retraumatize women. There also is an inherent cultural conflict in the criminal justice system: correction is based on a culture of control, whereas treatment is based on a culture of change. The high rates among incarcerated women of severe childhood maltreatment, as well as the high rates of physical and sexual abuse in their adolescent and adult lives, underscore the importance of understanding the process of trauma. This is a critical step in the rehabilitation of women (Covington, 2003).

Figure 9.1 helps to explain the process of trauma and its interrelationships with substance abuse and mental health disorders.

Trauma begins with an event or experience that overwhelms a woman's normal coping mechanisms. There are physical and psychological reactions in response to the

**FIGURE 9.1**

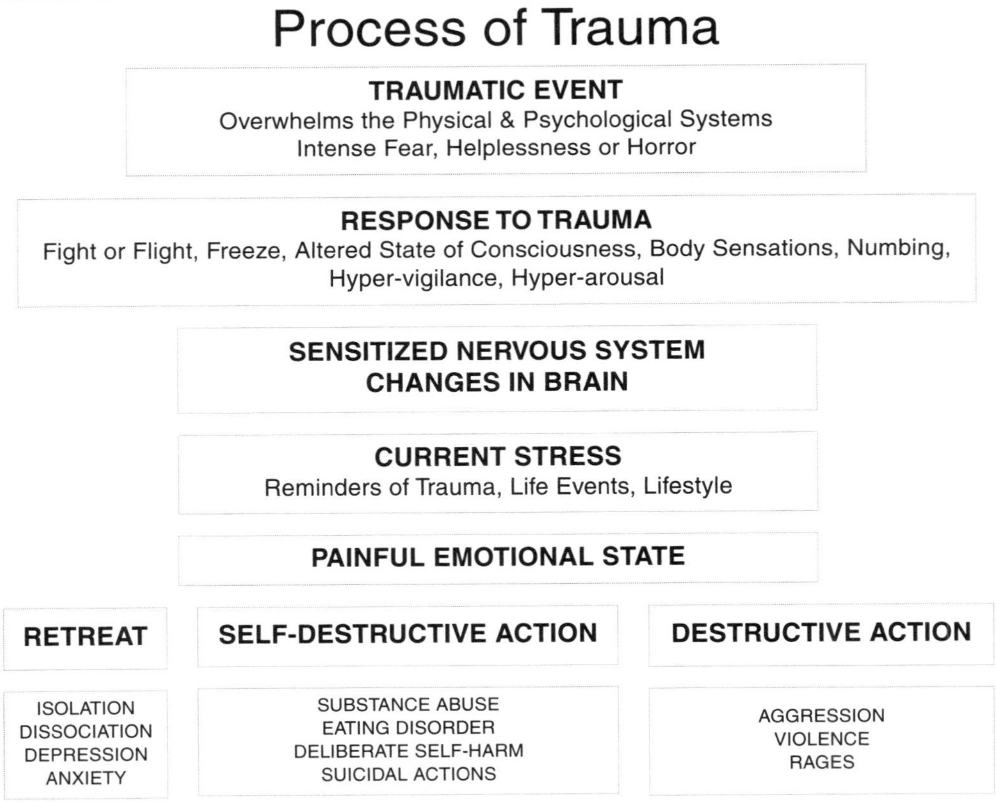

# Process of Trauma

**TRAUMATIC EVENT**
Overwhelms the Physical & Psychological Systems
Intense Fear, Helplessness or Horror

**RESPONSE TO TRAUMA**
Fight or Flight, Freeze, Altered State of Consciousness, Body Sensations, Numbing,
Hyper-vigilance, Hyper-arousal

**SENSITIZED NERVOUS SYSTEM
CHANGES IN BRAIN**

**CURRENT STRESS**
Reminders of Trauma, Life Events, Lifestyle

**PAINFUL EMOTIONAL STATE**

| **RETREAT** | **SELF-DESTRUCTIVE ACTION** | **DESTRUCTIVE ACTION** |
|---|---|---|
| ISOLATION DISSOCIATION DEPRESSION ANXIETY | SUBSTANCE ABUSE EATING DISORDER DELIBERATE SELF-HARM SUICIDAL ACTIONS | AGGRESSION VIOLENCE RAGES |

event: these are normal reactions to an abnormal or extreme situation. This creates a painful emotional state and subsequent behaviors. The behaviors can be placed into three categories: retreat, self-destructive action, and destructive action. Women are more likely to retreat or be self-destructive, whereas men are more likely to engage in destructive behavior (Covington, 2003).

### Addiction Theory

Historically, addiction research and treatment have been focused on men, even though women's addictions span a wide range, from alcohol and other types of drug dependence to smoking, gambling, sex, eating, and shopping (Straussner & Brown, 2002).

The holistic health model of addiction, with the inclusion of the environmental and sociopolitical aspects of disease, is the theoretical framework recommended for the development of women's services (Covington, 1999; 2007b). This is consistent with information from the National Institute on Drug Abuse (NIDA) and the Center for Substance Abuse Treatment (CSAT):

- The reality, based on 25 years of research, is that drug addiction is a brain disease, one that disrupts the mechanisms responsible for generating, modulating, and controlling cognitive, emotional, and social behavior (NIDA, 1998).
- Alcohol and drug use disorder, or addiction, is a progressive disease, with increasing severity of biological, psychological, and social problems over time (CSAT, 1994).

Although the field of addiction treatment considers addiction to be a "chronic, progressive disease," its treatment methods are more closely aligned to those of the emergency-medicine specialist than those of the chronic-disease specialist (White, Boyle, & Loveland, 2002). Recent articles assert that treating severe and chronic substance use disorders through screening, assessment, admission, and brief treatment, followed by discharge and minimal aftercare, is ineffective and results in shaming and punishing clients for failing to respond to an intervention design that is inherently flawed.

An alternative to the acute intervention model is behavioral health recovery management (BHRM). This concept grew out of and shares much in common with "disease-management" approaches to other chronic health problems, but BHRM focuses on quality-of-life outcomes, as defined by the individual and family. It also offers a broader range of services earlier and extends treatment well beyond the usual end of traditional treatment services. BHRM models extend the current continuum of care for addiction by including: (a) pretreatment (recovery-priming) services, (b) recovery mentoring through primary treatment, and (c) sustained post-treatment recovery-support services (White, Boyle, & Loveland, 2002).

This updated and expanded perspective of disease offers a more helpful approach to the treatment of addiction for women because it is comprehensive and multidimensional. The holistic health model allows service providers to treat the primary problem of addiction while simultaneously addressing the many issues that women bring to treatment, such as genetic predisposition, health consequences, shame, isolation, and a history of abuse, or a combination of these. For example, although some women may have a genetic predisposition to addiction, it is important to acknowledge that many have grown up in environments in which drug dealing, substance abuse, and addiction are ways of life. When addiction has been a core part of the multiple aspects of a woman's life, the treatment process requires a holistic, multidimensional approach.

## WOMAN-CENTERED TREATMENT

Specific elements are needed to create gender-responsive programs for women. For women, recovery is a process of transformational change. This type of profound change is not linear and simple, nor does it occur in isolation. The process of recovery and healing for women occurs in deep connection with themselves and others. In addition to the four theories discussed previously—pathways, women's psychological development, trauma, and addiction—as foundations on which to design mental health services, other important elements are: the clinical issues that create the content of the program, the therapeutic approaches, and the structure of the program, its context, and its environment (Covington, 2007b).

### PROGRAM CONTENT

The Center for Substance Abuse Treatment (CSAT) operates within the U.S. Public Health Service, an agency of the U.S. Department of Health and Human Services. CSAT funds ongoing studies of women's addiction and treatment, establishes minimum standards for treatment, and provides demonstration models for treatment in programs around the country. It recognizes the need for gender-responsive treatment for women that takes into account physical, psychological, emotional, spiritual, and sociopolitical issues. CSAT identifies the following clinical issues as essential to a comprehensive treatment program (1999):

- The process of addiction, especially gender-specific issues related to addiction (including the social, physiological, and psychological consequences of addiction and factors related to the onset of addiction).
- Low self-esteem.
- Race, ethnicity, and cultural issues.
- Gender discrimination and harassment.
- Disability-related issues, where relevant.
- Relationships with family members and significant others.
- Attachments to unhealthy interpersonal relationships.
- Interpersonal violence, including incest, rape, battering, and other abuse.
- Eating disorders.
- Sexuality, including sexual functioning and sexual orientation.
- Parenting, child care, and child custody.
- Grief related to the loss of alcohol or other drugs, children, family members, or partners.
- Employment.
- Appearance and overall health and hygiene.
- Isolation related to a lack of support systems (which may or may not include family members and/or partners) and other resources.
- Life-plan development.

This list indicates that therapeutic addiction and mental health programs for women need to assess all domains of a woman's life in order to obtain an accurate picture of her life. Many women's programs do not have the resources to address all the issues listed above, so providing referrals when they cannot provide services themselves is essential.

The following sections discuss in more depth some of the essential clinical issues to be addressed.

## TRAUMA

Judith Herman's work offers a three-stage model for providing trauma services (1997). *Safety* is the first stage of work with trauma survivors. Women in the criminal justice system often feel unsafe and unable to participate when services are provided. Trauma can skew a woman's relational experiences and hinder her psychological development. Because it can affect the way a woman relates to staff members, her peers, and the therapeutic environment, it is helpful to ask, "Is this person's behavior linked to her trauma history?" However, traditional addiction and mental health treatments often do not deal with trauma issues in early recovery, even though it is a primary trigger for relapse among women and may be underlying their mental health disorders. Many treatment providers lack the knowledge of what is needed in order to do this work.

Here are three important things that you can do in treatment:

1. Educate women as to what abuse and trauma are. Women often do not know that they have been abused, nor do they have an understanding of PTSD.
2. Validate their reactions. It is important that women learn that their responses are normal, given their experiences. The DSM has stated that trauma responses are normal reactions to abnormal situations.
3. Provide coping skills. There are grounding and self-soothing techniques (i.e., breathing exercises) that women can learn to help themselves cope with their traumatic experiences. (See Covington, 2003, for specific techniques to use in individual and group therapy.)

### Avoid Revictimization and Retraumatization

A woman who has experienced a traumatic event also has experienced increased vulnerability. She may have difficulty tolerating, expressing, and/or modulating her emotions. This results in what is called emotional dysregulation. An example of this is when she overresponds to neutral cues and underresponds to danger cues. Therefore, traumatized women are at increased risk of similar, repeated revictimization.

"Retraumatization" refers to the psychological and/or physiological experience of being "triggered." A single environmental cue related to the trauma—such as the time of year, a smell, or a sound—can trigger a full fight-or-flight response. Because women often are triggered in criminal justice settings, staff members in some jurisdictions are being trained through the use of a new curriculum designed to reduce seclusion and restraint (Center for Mental Health Services, 2005). The traditional belief is that seclusion and restraint need to be used in mental health settings for safety reasons. However, both patients and staff members are reporting an increased sense of safety and security when seclusion and restraint are reduced. Trauma survivors are used to having their boundaries ignored and their protests dismissed. A crucial element of successful treatment involves attention to these components of a woman's experience. Again, safety is critical for women who are trauma survivors.

## CO-OCCURRING DISORDERS

Co-occurring disorders (CODs) are complex, and the historic division in the mental health and substance abuse fields often has resulted in contradictory treatment. As mentioned earlier, one study revealed that 75% of the women in state prisons who had mental health disorders also had substance abuse problems (James & Glaze, 2006). It often is difficult to know whether a psychiatric disorder existed for a woman before she began to abuse alcohol or other drugs or whether the psychiatric problem emerged after the onset of substance abuse. Women in early recovery often show symptoms of mood disorders, but these can be temporary conditions associated with withdrawal from drugs. Also, women may be more likely to seek help from mental or physical health-care systems than from specialized addiction services. Therefore, their mental health problems may be identified sooner than their addictive disorders.

As noted earlier, one of the most important developments in health care since the 1980s is the recognition that serious traumatic experiences often play an unrecognized role in a woman's physical and mental health problems. For many women a co-occurring disorder is trauma related. The Adverse Childhood Experiences Study (Felitti, Anda, Nordenberg, Williamson, Spitz, Edwards, Koss, & Marks, 1998), which shows a strong link between childhood trauma and adult physical and mental health problems, was the model for a study with female offenders. Eight types of childhood traumatic events were assessed: emotional abuse and neglect, physical neglect, physical abuse, sexual abuse, family violence, parental separation/divorce, incarceration of a family member, and out-of-home placement. A score of 5 or more increased the risk of both mental and physical health problems in a person's adult life. For women who scored 7 or more, the risk of a mental health problem was increased by 980% (Messina & Grella, 2006).

Addicted women are more likely to experience the following co-occurring disorders: depression, dissociation, post-traumatic stress disorder, other anxiety disorders, eating disorders, and personality disorders. Mood disorders and anxiety disorders are the most common. Women are commonly diagnosed as having "borderline personality disorder" (BPD) more often than men. Many of the descriptors of BPD can be viewed differently when one considers a history of childhood and adult abuse. The American Psychiatric Association is considering adding the diagnosis of "complex PTSD" in the next edition of the DSM (Herman, 1997).

Research suggests that preexisting psychiatric disorders improve more slowly for recovering substance abusers and need to be addressed directly in treatment. However, the presence of a psychiatric disorder can adversely influence the course of addiction treatment, and vice versa. Problems often become magnified, and co-occurring mental disorders often result in poor psychosocial functioning, health problems, medication noncompliance, relapse, homelessness, and suicidal behavior (Drake, 2006).

In order to work with women with mental health and substance abuse issues, the treatment team needs to know the symptoms and diagnoses of mental illnesses, the roles of medications, the process and symptoms of addiction, and the needed credentials of mental health providers. The team also needs to have a treatment philosophy. All of these need to be filtered through the lens of trauma.

Integrated treatment for women with co-occurring disorders means concurrent, not sequential, treatment. Dual recovery strategies are needed that employ effective treatment strategies from both the mental health and substance abuse treatment fields.

## SOCIETAL REALITIES

A gender-responsive treatment program is based on an understanding of the role of socialization in women's lives. It acknowledges the social and political structures that support inequality, which leads to low self-esteem among women, lower pay for women, and high rates of violence against women.

Being able to acknowledge the impact of socialization and its implicit messages allows women to put their own individual issues into the larger social context. Many women understand their issues only as individual pathologies, rather than as the risks and consequences of being born female.

## THERAPEUTIC APPROACHES

A number of approaches and modalities have been found to be effective with women. Some are more research based than others because rigorous research studies on many women-specific treatment approaches are still lacking. In fact, the term "evidence based," which currently is considered a criterion for interventions to be used, has no universal definition. A 2005 Presidential Task Force of the American Psychological Association said, "Evidence-based practice (EBP) is defined as the integration of the best available research and clinical expertise within the context of patient characteristics, culture, values, and preferences" (Goodheart, Kazdin, & Sternberg, 2006, p 000). The research clearly indicates that, regardless of the therapeutic approach used, the central factors that influence whether or not a modality is effective appear to be related to the characteristics of the treatment *alliance*. The therapeutic alliance refers to the relationship between the clinician and the client. In order to fully address the needs of women, therapeutic programs must use a variety of interventions with behavioral, cognitive, affective/dynamic, and systems perspectives.

## STRUCTURE OF THE PROGRAM (CONTEXT AND ENVIRONMENT)

While the clinical issues create the program content, the structure creates the context and environment. How a program is designed and implemented impacts a woman's treatment experience. When the structural element is integrated with the theoretical foundation and the clinical issues, the framework for gender-responsive treatment is established. The following are the structural elements of gender-responsive programming (Covington & Bloom, 2007).

### INDIVIDUALIZED TREATMENT

Woman-centered treatment regards each client as unique, with individual life circumstances, goals, priorities, patterns of recovery, and treatment needs. Treatment needs to be individualized in order to be effective.

### WOMEN-ONLY GROUPS

Women tend to engage in group therapy more often than men. This phenomenon may be linked to gender norms that support the suppositions of the relational model. Groups encourage the development of a sense of belonging and connection to others, which helps to motivate women to stay in the process. However, most groups in correctional settings are not group therapy. Often they are just groups of people sitting in a circle doing individual work with the facilitators.

Many researchers and practitioners believe that the treatment needs of women with substance use and mental health disorders are best met in women-only groups (facilitated by women). Women's complex histories of sexual and physical abuse, the greater tendency toward social isolation, and the stronger stigma attached to women's substance abuse all call for treatment that could not take place in mixed-gender groups. Yet many community-based programs continue to provide only co-ed services. Experience shows that many women do not talk as freely when men are present. They may be uncomfortable discussing their addictions, mental health, sexual histories, relationships, childcare issues, and other personal topics when males are present. In addition, many women believe that only women can understand how they feel and react to things. This is especially true of women who have been dominated or abused by men. Experience also shows that men tend to dominate in mixed-gender groups.

Finally, women-only groups afford women the opportunity to compare their attitudes about parents, partners, and children, and their feelings about things that have happened to them. The group members can suggest new possibilities for feeling, perceiving, and behaving.

### THE PHYSICAL ENVIRONMENT

Women recover best in an atmosphere that is warm and welcoming for them and their children. The environment needs to reflect the diverse cultures of the staff members and clients. To emphasize women's strengths, female role models from many cultures can be highlighted. A connection to women's history and heroines can play an important role in bolstering self-esteem for women.

A child-friendly space dedicated to childcare and age-appropriate equipment and activities for children are essential when children are included in a community program or when they visit a jail or prison. There need to be games and other learning opportunities that engage children in developing communication skills, relationships, and healthy forms of expression.

## THE PSYCHOLOGICAL ENVIRONMENT

Any teaching and/or rehabilitation process would be unsuccessful if its environment were to mimic the dysfunctional systems that women already have experienced. Therefore, program and treatment strategies should be designed to undo some of the prior damage. This can be particularly challenging in criminal justice settings. Therapeutic community norms need to be consciously designed to be different: safety with oneself and with others is paramount.

Work with trauma survivors has shown that social support is critical for recovery and has encouraged practitioners to take a new look at the "therapeutic milieu." This refers to a carefully arranged environment designed to reverse the effects of exposure to interpersonal violence. A therapeutic culture contains the following five elements, all fundamental in both institutional settings and the community:

- *Attachment*: a culture of belonging.
- *Containment*: a culture of safety.
- *Communication*: a culture of openness.
- *Involvement*: a culture of participation and citizenship.
- *Agency*: a culture of empowerment (Haigh, 1999).

Women need both psychological-emotional and physical space. In both in-prison/jail programs and community programs, the physical layout needs to provide some sense of privacy and space in which women can be quiet and meditative. Some treatment programs are so focused on schedules that each day is totally activity driven. However, women need some unscheduled time for contemplation and reflection.

## STRENGTH-BASED TREATMENT

In a traditional treatment model, the clinician typically approaches assessment with a problem focus: "What is missing in the client?" "What is wrong with the client?" A woman who is entering mental health services probably is already struggling with a poor sense of self because of the stigma attached to her mental health issues, her addiction, her parenting history, her trauma, or her criminal record. It may be nontherapeutic to add another problem to the woman's list of perceived failures.

Strength-based (asset) treatment shifts the focus from targeting problems to identifying the multiple issues a woman must contend with and the strategies she has adopted to cope. This is referred to as assessing a woman's "level of burden" (Brown, Melchior, & Huba, 1999). Burdens are conditions such as psychological problems, homelessness, HIV/AIDS, other health issues, addiction, and physical and sexual abuse. The focus is on support, rather than on confrontation, to break down a woman's defenses.

In using a strength-based/asset model, a counselor helps a client to see the strengths and skills she already has that will help her to manage her symptoms and become sober and drug-free. The counselor looks for the seeds of health and strength, even in a woman's symptoms. For example, she may portray a client's relational difficulties as efforts to connect, rather than as failures to separate or disconnect.

## CHALLENGES

Providing quality mental health services for women in criminal justice settings involves confronting a variety of systemic barriers. First, the criminal justice system is based on "care, custody, and control." It was not designed for the provision of mental health services. Many of the standard practices traumatize and retraumatize women. This exacerbates their symptoms of mental distress.

The mental health field has its own set of challenges:

- *History of the DSM:* It is ironic that with the current insistence on the use of evidence-based practices, the DSM itself is not being discussed or challenged. When one reviews the history of the development of this manual, it becomes clear why Robert Spitzer, the veteran editor of the DSM, laments that unreliability in psychiatric diagnosis is "still a real problem, and it's not clear how to solve the problem" (Spiegel, 2005, p 000).
- *DSM and the Pharmaceutical Industry:* A recent article (Cosgrove, Krimsky, Vijayaraghavan, & Schneider, 2006) examines the degree and type of financial ties to the pharmaceutical industry of panel members responsible for revisions to the DSM. Of the 170 panel members, 95 (56%) had one or more financial associations with companies in the pharmaceutical industry. One hundred percent of the members of the panels on "Mood Disorders" and "Schizophrenia and Other Psychotic Disorders" had financial ties to drug companies. This can result in care that unduly emphasizes drug treatments while the adverse effects of drugs are downplayed (Moncrieff, Hopker, & Thomas, 2005).
- *Bias and the DSM:* Unfortunately, research on mental illness is exceedingly complicated, and little is known about its causes and cures. Virtually none of the standard diagnostic categories has been empirically validated (Caplan & Cosgrove, 2004). In addition, members of marginalized groups suffer when we base our conceptions of normalcy on the behaviors and worldviews of dominant social groups, and the consequences of sexism, racism, homophobia, and the "struggle with poverty are misinterpreted as evidence of individual psychopathology" (Bullock, 2004, p 000). For example, in 1987 the Women and Mental Health Committee of the Canadian Mental Health Association recommended dispensing with unvalidated diagnostic labels and, instead, naming many of the known causes of women's suffering, including poverty, violence, and lack of social and political power and resources.

## CONCLUSION

Addressing the mental health needs of women offenders involves a gender-responsive approach that includes comprehensive services that take into account the content and context of women's lives. Programs need to consider the fact that a woman cannot be treated successfully in isolation from her social support network. Coordinating systems that link a broad range of services promote a continuity-of-care model that integrates substance abuse, trauma, and mental health. As the fields of substance abuse and mental health begin to work with women offenders in a more integrated and comprehensive way and use the lens of trauma as a way to understand their lives, the criminalization of women's survival behaviors ultimately may be reduced.

# References

American Psychiatric Association. (1994). *Diagnostic and statistical manual of mental disorders* (4th ed.). Washington, DC: Author.

American Psychological Association. http://www.apa.org/

Bloom, B., Owen, B., & Covington, S. (2003). *Gender-responsive strategies: Research, practice, and guiding principles for women offenders*. Washington, DC: National Institute of Corrections.

Brown, V., Melchior, L., & Huba, G. (1999). Level of burden among women diagnosed with severe mental illness and substance abuse. *Journal of Psychoactive Drugs*, *31*(1), 31–41.

Bullock, H. (2004). Diagnosis of low-income women. In P. Caplan & L. Cosgrove (Eds.), *Bias in psychiatric diagnosis* (pp. 115–120). Latham, MD: Jason Aronson.

Caplan, P., & Cosgrove, L. (Eds.). (2004). *Bias in psychiatric diagnosis*. Latham, MD: Jason Aronson.

Center for Mental Health Services. (2005). *Roadmap to seclusion and restraint free mental health services* (DHHS Pub. No. (SMA) 05-4055). Rockville, MD: Department of Health and Human Services.

Center for Substance Abuse Treatment. (1994). *Practical approaches in the treatment of women who abuse alcohol and other drugs*. Rockville, MD: Department of Health and Human Services, Public Health Service.

Center for Substance Abuse Treatment. (1999). *Substance abuse treatment for women offenders: Guide to promising practices*. Rockville, MD: U.S. Department of Health and Human Services, Public Health Service, Substance Abuse and Mental Health Services Administration.

Cosgrove, L., Krimsky, S., Vijayaraghavan, M., & Schneider, L. (2006) . Financial ties between DSM-IV panel members and the pharmaceutical industry (DOI: 10.1159/000091772). *Psychotherapy and Psychosomatics*, *75*, 154–160.

Covington, S. (1998). Women in prison: Approaches in the treatment of our most invisible population, *Women and Therapy*, *21*, 141–155.

Covington, S. (1999). *Helping women recover: A program for treating substance abuse*. San Francisco: Jossey-Bass.

Covington, S. (2003). *Beyond trauma: A healing journey for women*. Center City, MN: Hazelden.

Covington, S. (2007a). The relational theory of women's psychological development: Implications for the criminal justice system. In R. Zaplin (Ed.), *Female offenders: Critical perspectives and effective interventions* (2nd ed.). Sudbury, MA: Jones and Bartlett.

Covington, S. (2007b). *Women and addiction: A gender-responsive approach* (The Clinical Innovators Series). Center City, MN: Hazelden.

Covington, S., & Bloom, B. (2007). Gender-responsive treatment and services in correctional settings. In E. Leeder (Ed.), *Inside and out: Women, prison, and therapy* (pp. 9–34). New York: Haworth Press.

Drake, R. (2006). *Treating co-occurring disorders* (The Clinical Innovators Series). Center City, MN: Hazelden.

Felitti, V. J., Anda, R. F., Nordenberg, D., Williamson, D. F., Spitz, A. M., Edwards, V., Koss, M. P., & Marks, J. S. (1998). The relationship of adult health status to childhood abuse and household dysfunction. *American Journal of Preventive Medicine*, *14*, 245–258.

Goodheart, C., Kazdin, A., & Sternberg, R. (Eds.). (2006). *Evidence-based psychotherapy: Where practice and research meet*. Washington, DC: American Psychological Association.

Green, B., Miranda, J., Daroowalla, A., & Siddique, J. (2005). Trauma, exposure, mental health functioning, and program needs of women in jail. *Crime & Delinquency*, *51*(1), 133–151.

Haigh, R. (1999). The quintessence of a therapeutic environment: Five universal qualities. In P. Campling, R. Haigh, & Netlibrary, Inc. (Eds.), *Therapeutic communities: Past, present, and future* (pp. 246–257). London: Jessica Kingsley Publishers.

Harris, M., & Fallot, R. D. (2001). *Using trauma theory to design service systems.* San Francisco: Jossey-Bass.

Herman, J. (1997). *Trauma and recovery* (Rev. ed.). New York: Basic Books.

James, D., & Glaze, L. (2006). *Mental health problems of prison and jail inmates* (NCJ 213600). Washington, DC: Bureau of Justice Statistics.

Jordan, B., Schlenger, W., Fairbank, J., & Caddell, J. (1996). Prevalence of psychiatric disorders among incarcerated women. *Archives of General Psychiatry, 53*(6), 1048–1060.

Jordan, B., Schlenger, W., Fairbank, J., & Caddell, J. (2002). Lifetime use of mental health and substance abuse treatment services by incarcerated women felons. *Psychiatric Services, 53*(3), 317–325.

Messina, N., Burdon, W., Hagopian, G., & Prendergast, M. (2006). Predictors of prison therapeutic communities treatment outcomes: A comparison of men and women participants. *American Journal of Drug and Alcohol Abuse, 31*(1), 7–28.

Messina, N., & Grella, C. (2006). Childhood trauma and women's health outcomes: A California prison population. *The American Journal of Public Health, 96*(10), 1842–1848.

Miller, J. B. (1986). *What do we mean by relationships?* (No. 22, Working Paper Series). Wellesley, MA: Stone Center.

Miller, J. B. (1990). *Connections, disconnections, and violations* (No. 33, Working Paper Series). Wellesley, MA: Stone Center.

Moncrieff, J., Hopker, S., & Thomas, P. (2005). Psychiatry and the pharmaceutical industry: Who pays the piper? *Psychiatric Bulletin, 29*, 84–85.

Morash, M., Bynam, T., & Koons, B. (1998). *Women offenders: Programming needs and promising approaches.* Washington, DC: National Institute of Justice.

Mumola, C. J. (1999). *Substance abuse and treatment: State and federal prisoners.* Washington, DC: Bureau of Justice Statistics.

Najavits, L., Weiss, R., & Shaw, S. (1997). The link between substance abuse and post-traumatic stress disorder in women: A research review. *American Journal of Addictions, 6*(4), 273–83.

National Institute on Drug Abuse. (1998). What we know: Drug addiction is a brain disease. In *Principles of addiction medicine* (2nd ed.). Chevy Chase, MD: American Society of Addiction Medicine.

Pollock, J. (1998). *Counseling women in prison.* Thousand Oaks, CA: Sage.

Ross, H., Glaser, F., & Stiasny, S. (1988). Sex differences in the prevalence of psychiatric disorders in patients with alcohol and drug problems. *British Journal of Addictions, 83*, 1179–1192.

Spiegel, A. (2005, January 3). The dictionary of disorder: How one man revolutionized psychiatry. *The New Yorker*, 2–11.

Steffensmeier, D., & Allen, E. (1998). The nature of female offending: Patterns and explanation. In R. Zaplin (Ed.), *Female offenders: Critical perspectives and effective interventions* (pp. 5–29). Gaithersburg, MD: Aspen.

Straussner, S., & Brown, S. (2002). *The handbook of addiction treatment for women: Theory and practice.* San Francisco: Jossey-Bass.

Teplin, L., Abram, K., & McClellan, G. (1996). Prevalence of psychiatric disorders among incarcerated women: 1. Pretrial detainees. *Archives of General Psychiatry, 53*(6), 505–512.

White, W., Boyle, M., & Loveland, D. (2002). Alcoholism/addiction as a chronic disease: From rhetoric to clinical reality. *Alcoholism Treatment Quarterly, 20*(3/4), 107–130.

Zlotnick, C., Najavits, L., Rohsenow, D., & Johnson, D. (2003). A cognitive-behavioral treatment for incarcerated women with substance abuse disorder and posttraumatic stress disorder: Findings from a pilot study. *Journal of Substance Treatment, 25*, 99–105.

# CHAPTER 10
# WOMEN DESTINED TO FAILURE:

## Policy Implications of the Lack of Proper Mental Health and Addiction Treatment for Female Offenders[1]

**Lanette P. Dalley**
**Vicki Michels**

### ABSTRACT

The number of incarcerated women nationally has increased dramatically in recent years, and North Dakota has experienced one of the largest increases. To gain a better understanding of the mental health and addiction treatment needs of this increasing population, the presented study was conducted. Standardized measures, review of records, and focus groups were completed. Significant mental health disorders and addictions were found among the majority of women. If these finding are representative of women prisoners nationally, significant mental health and addiction treatment programming in prison is necessary in order to enable the women to function in mainstream society. Treating women prisoners benefits not only the women but also their children and society.

## INTRODUCTION

The female prison population has dramatically increased during the past two decades. The Bureau of Justice Statistics (BJS) (2004) found that since 1995 the total number of female prisoners increased 53%, while the total number of male prisoners increased only 32% (Beck, 2004 p. 4).[2] The recent surge of female prisoners has added to the

---

[1]This research was funded by the North Dakota Department of Corrections, which also provided permission for distribution and publication of this study. The findings do not necessarily reflect the views or opinions of the North Dakota Department of Corrections.

[2]According to the BJS (2005), the female prison population increased from 68,468 to 104,848 between 1995 and 2004. The male prison population increased from 1,057,406 to 1,391,781between 1995 and 2004. Further, it should be noted that the increase in the sentencing of females to prison is not an isolated occurrence. (p. 4).

complexities of managing the prison population. More importantly, it has brought to light the fact that compared to male offenders, female offenders are more likely to have mental illnesses, addiction, and health problems (Alemagno & Dickie, 2002; Ditton, 1999; LeClair, 1990; Marquart, Brewer, Simon, & Morse, 2001) This is particularly so for mentally ill prisoners because the number of mentally ill prisoners far exceeds the mentally ill in the general population (Hodgins, 1995; Teplin, Abrams, & McClelland, 1996).

Several developments may account for the rise of mentally ill and addicted women in the criminal justice system (Emerging Judicial Strategies for the Mentally Ill, 2000). The deinstitutionalizing of the mentally ill within the mental health system during the 1960s and 1970s resulted in the diversion of large numbers of mentally ill individuals into community-based mental health systems (Whitmer, 1979). However, as many experts have asserted, community-based mental health systems did not effectively manage the mentally ill as was intended (Abram & Teplin, 1991; Torrey, Stieber, Ezekiel, Wolfe, Sharfstein, Noble, & Flynn, 1993). Instead, by default, the criminal justice system absorbed these individuals at various levels of the system, without the adequate resources to properly deal with them. Fostering the displacement of these individuals were mandatory sentencing policies developed in the 1980s that targeted drug offenders and substantially reduced judges' discretion in sentencing. Thus, women came to be more likely imprisoned for committing drug-related crimes and, inadvertently, the criminal justice system incarcerated many of these same women who were mentally ill as well. (Ditton, 1999; Emerging Judicial Strategies for the Mentally Ill, 2000).

Although there are studies focusing on female offender addiction problems, only recently have studies begun to emerge on their co-occurring disorders and the associated or aggravated health problems (Anderson, Rosay, & Saum, 2002; Henriques, 2002). Exacerbating these often chronic and complex problems is the fact that women are also more likely than men to be single parents, victims of sexual and physical abuse, have fewer job skills, and difficulty maintaining relationships with their children (Dalley, 2002; Enos, 2001; Gable & Johnston, 1996; Greenfeld & Snell, 1999; Pollock, 1998). Upon further examination, research has also found that female offenders are different from male offenders in other significant ways.

Recent studies, for example, have identified an intergenerational cycle of incarceration among female offenders (Dalley, 2002; Gable & Johnston, 1996; Mumola, 2000). Seventy percent of female inmates are mothers of minor children (Greenfeld & Snell, 1999). Inmate mothers also have substantial histories of family incarceration, parental addiction, abuse, and neglect (Mumola, 2000; Pollock, 1998). The data also suggest that children of imprisoned mothers have experienced similar traumatic childhood events and are more likely to be imprisoned, becoming the second and, in some cases, the third generation of inmates (Gable & Johnston, 1996).

The majority of inmate mothers will be reunited with their children. When the women are released from prison, unrealistic expectations are placed upon them. They are expected to find housing, employment, and day care, and to parent their children who often have severe behavioral problems. Adding to these expectations, women are also charged with maintaining their sobriety and coping with their mental illnesses. However, these women have been unable to meet these expectations prior to imprisonment, and without viable in-prison and postrelease programming to assist them, their failure is essentially guaranteed.

Unfortunately, female offender problems are not addressed adequately during their imprisonment and so continue after their release. Their high recidivism rates of 52% within 3 years of release demonstrate the failure of correctional programming and treatment to adequately address reentry and reintegration issues. Therefore, they continue to have great difficulties managing their lives without using drugs and copying positively with their mental illnesses after their release (Greenfeld & Snell, 1999; Holtfreter & Morash, 2003; Morash, Bynum & Koons, 1998).

## FOCUS OF STUDY

In recent years, like many states, North Dakota has experienced a tremendous surge in the number of female prisoners. Examining this further, the average increase of female prisoners in the United States was 4.7% between 1995 and 2004. However, 11 states far exceeded this average. Of the 11 states that had an average annual increase of more than 10% between 1995 and 2004, North Dakota (18.0%) led the way in the female incarceration rate, followed by Montana (17.4%) and West Virginia (15.1%) (Bureau of Justice Statistics, 2005, p. 5). Thus, the primary goals of this study at the North Dakota Women's Correctional Center were to: (a) gather data on this fairly new population of women prisoners, including inmate mothers and their children (i.e., demographics, family history, mental health, substance abuse, parenting, etc.); (b) gain permission to survey their children; and (c) present an assessment of female inmate needs to the North Dakota Corrections Department (i.e., mental health, addiction, and parenting). It is important to note that although the majority of the women provided written permission to interview their children, the majority of the caregivers refused to allow access to the children. Therefore, the study was unable to achieve one of its primary goals—obtaining the children's perceptions of their needs and concerns.

## RESEARCH METHODS/PROCESS

The study was conducted at the James River Correctional Facility using data from 63 women participants (total $n = 103$). To assess the women's needs, six interrelated methods were used. First, data were gathered administering a demographic survey to all 63 women who had children. The survey focused on two of each women's children (randomly chosen $n = 69$), their family, and social history. Next, secondary data from the Addiction Severity Index (ASI) were gathered and collected by the addiction treatment staff at the facility. These data came from 53 women who consented to give access to their ASI. Third, the women completed the Symptom Checklist 90 – R, which was used to assess their symptoms of mental illness ($n = 63$). Fourth, the women were administered the Child Behavioral Checklist pertaining to their children (the same children randomly selected in the demographic survey ($n = 69$). Fifth, seven focus group interviews were conducted with only inmate mothers, in order to enrich the quantitative survey data on their relationship with their children ($n = 45$). Finally, the women's correctional files were reviewed to provide more information on the women's legal and social histories (i.e., arrests, re-arrests, technical probation violations, child custody, mental illness).

Quantitative data analysis included descriptive statistics, *t*-tests, and analysis of variance. Qualitative data from the focus group interviews provided a more in-depth examination of the population.

## OVERVIEW

First, the sample findings are reported, including demographics and family, social, and legal histories. Next, identified problems and needs are addressed, focusing on addictions, medical conditions, mental health issues, and relationships with children. These findings are integrated with a discussion of postrelease issues. Essentially, the study presents a profile of female offenders who have complex problems, underscoring the critical need for preprison, prison, and postprison programming to address addiction and mental health disorders.

## CHARACTERISTICS OF FEMALE PRISONERS

### GENERAL DEMOGRAPHICS

Sixty-three out of 103 women participated in the study. However, not all information was available for all 63 women. Some of the women had not completed the Addiction Severity Index at the time this study was conducted, some of them were lacking prison records, and, in a few cases, the women refused to sign consent forms for participation in the study.

The majority of the women who participated were White (76%), 14% were Native American, and 10% "mixed race." The average age was 33 (range 19–59 years old). Forty-five of the 63 women had children (71.4%). Almost half of the women had a high school diploma (46%), 33% had no high school diploma, and the remaining 21% had some college. Sixty percent were involved in educational programs in prison (GED, vocational education, college, etc.). The majority of the women were employed prior to incarceration (either full time—57%, or part time—15%). This explains why the majority earned less than $10,000 a year in income (69%). Half of the women did not have a car, and 44% did not have a driver's license. It is not uncommon for many of these women to live in rural areas where direct access to transportation is essential, particularly for those who have children.

### FAMILY HISTORY

Forty percent of the women reported being raised by both parents. Another 32% come from single-family households, raised by their mothers. Almost one-fourth reported being placed in a foster home sometime during their childhood (24%). They also experienced transient childhoods. In fact, 35% moved 5 or more times, ranging from 5 to 20 times. The primary reasons were related to changes in parental employment, financial need, and foster care placement. When asked about their religion, half of the women reported that they were Protestant. The second most reported religion was Roman Catholic (35%). The remaining 15% claimed a different religion or did not claim a religion.

Evident in their childhood histories were parents who used legal and illegal substances that negatively influenced their upbringing. Specifically, a majority of the women's parents used alcohol (73%), and a smaller number of their parents used drugs (21%). In both situations, almost half of the women reported that their parents' drug use or alcohol use negatively affected their upbringing (46%). The most common type of negative impact was neglect. In addition to parental neglect, 32% indicated that they had been sexually abused. There was also a cycle of familial incarceration. Sixty-seven percent of the women had a family member in prison, either currently or in the past. Of the 67%, 46% had an immediate family member in prison, and 21% had an extended family member in prison.

## SOCIAL HISTORY

More than half of the women reported that they were married (54%), whereas the remaining 46% were unmarried—20% were divorced and 32% separated. The majority of the women (70%) also reported they had been involved in violent relationships with significant others. Coupled with the experience of domestic violence were reports of head injuries (44%). The mothers reported having 93 children under the age of 18, with the average age of the minor children being 8 years old.

## LEGAL/CRIMINAL HISTORY

Perhaps not surprising, 40% of the women had their first contact with the criminal justice system before their eighteenth birthday. In addition, 30% had been placed in juvenile detention ranging from one to seven times. Many of these same women continued their criminal behaviors into adulthood. Only 13% of the women had not been jailed previously. The rest noted being jailed from 1 to 20 times. In addition, 20% of the women had been imprisoned more than one time, ranging from two to four times. Perhaps more striking is the fact that 70% of the 63 women were on probation at the time of their current conviction.

## INTERPRETATION OF THE WOMEN'S CHARACTERISTICS RESULTS

The findings illustrate a history of family instability, with related significant problems early in life. Many were raised in single-parent homes (32%) with parents whose substance abuse negatively affected their parenting. Twenty-four percent of the women experienced foster care as children. In many of their families, having a member who experienced prison was not unusual (52%), and the women's first contact with the justice system began as juveniles (40%). These family backgrounds were related to the women's unstable adult lives. The majority of the women have children, but almost half (46%) of the women were single mothers. Seventy percent have experienced domestic violence. They have had frequent encounters with the legal system, and most were already on probation at the time of their current conviction. As one woman noted during a focus group interview:

> My mom was an alcoholic and my dad was an addict, he was an alcoholic and addict and neglect(ful), you know my mom just dropped us off with my uncle one day and that was it. He turned us over to welfare and I lived in a foster home all my life until I was older. I was like 17 almost 18 when I was seven months pregnant with my first one and that was when I finally got to go and

stay with her. You know, that or give up my little guy and I wasn't going to give up my kid. So, you know I chose to go live with this addicted, alcoholic mom. That lasted two months. I was out of there and on my own and that was it. . . . Oh yeah, I had all of that. Domestic abuse, my husband tried to kill me like three times. (inmate 08, group II)

## SPECIAL CONSIDERATIONS OF FEMALE OFFENDERS

As other studies have found, female offenders often have unique characteristics and needs. North Dakota female offenders are no exception. This section will outline the women's reported chronic addiction and mental health issues, as well as parenting concerns and problems with children.

### THE FEMALE OFFENDER'S ADDICTIONS

As noted above, the Addiction Severity Index (ASI) was used to assess the female offenders' addiction problems. The ASI is a commonly used assessment tool that has been found to have good reliability and validity (McLellan, Kushner, Metzger, Peters, Grissom, Pettinati, & Argeriou, 1992). Before presenting the findings on addictions, it is important to note that for each data section of the ASI, results will vary. For example, data were unavailable for prisoners who had just arrived at the JRCC. Further, for some long-term prisoners, there was not a compatible version of the ASI on file. Others refused access to the ASI. Below is the description of the range of possible scores.

### ADDICTION SEVERITY INDEX POSSIBLE SCORES

| | |
|---|---|
| 0–1 | No problem, treatment not necessary |
| 2–3 | Slight problem, treatment probably not necessary |
| 4–5 | Moderate problem, treatment probably necessary |
| 6–7 | Considerable problem, treatment necessary |
| 8–9 | Extreme problems, treatment absolutely necessary |

Tables 10.1 and 10.2 provide the severity scores for drugs and alcohol:

Figure 10.1 describes the relationship between the women's offenses and alcohol and drug use.

**TABLE 10.1** Severity Rating for Drugs

| Rating Offenders | Percent/Number of Female |
|---|---|
| 0–1 | 37.7% (20) |
| 2–3 | 7.5% (4) |
| 4–5 | 18.9% (10) |
| 6–7 | 32.1% (17) |
| 8–9 | 3.8% (2) |
| Total | 100% ($n$ = 53 women)* |

*Data not available for 10 women.

**TABLE 10.2** Severity Rating for Alcohol

| Rating Offenders | Percent/Number of Female |
|---|---|
| 0–1 | 54.7% (29) |
| 2–3 | 7.5% (4) |
| 4–5 | 26.4% (14) |
| 6–7 | 9.4% (5) |
| 8–9 | 2% (1) |
| Total | 100% ($n$ = 53 women)* |

*Data not available for 10 women.

## INTERPRETATION OF THE ASI SEVERITY RATINGS FOR DRUGS AND ALCOHOL

Drawing from Tables 10.1 and 10.2 and Figure 10.1, many of the women reported having significant problems with drugs or alcohol. This is also confirmed by the fact that half of the women had been in drug and alcohol treatment at least once before their imprisonment, some as many as five or more times. Others also had a juvenile history of in-patient drug and alcohol treatment (16%). Examining the data further, results reveal that more women reported having drug problems as compared to alcohol problems. Specifically, 55% of the 53 women needed treatment for drug addictions, with

**FIGURE 10.1** Alcohol and Drug Severity Rating by Offense

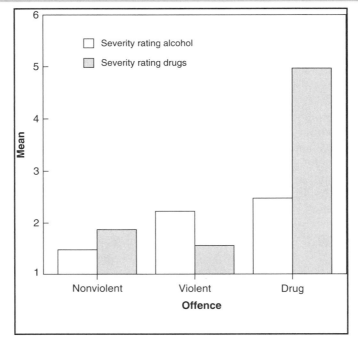

36% of the women who need treatment having considerable or extreme problems with drug addictions. Twenty-five percent also indicated that they were considerably or extremely bothered by drug problems (i.e., cravings, obsessive thoughts) in the 30 days prior to incarceration.

An analysis of variance (ANOVA) was used to compare the mean drug severity ratings and alcohol severity ratings of nonviolent offenders, violent offenders, and those who have drug-related offenses. Not surprisingly, the results of the ANOVA indicate that drug offenders had significantly higher drug severity ratings as compared to the nonviolent and violent offenders ($p < .01$). The three groups were not different between each other on the alcohol severity ratings.

## OTHER SIGNIFICANT ISSUES FOUND IN ASI DATA

### ALCOHOL: THE GATEWAY DRUG

It is important to examine at what age the women began using mood-altering substances. What substance was the "gateway" drug for these women? Alcohol appears to be the drug most women first started using. Seventy percent reported that alcohol was the first drug they used. Table 10.3 summarizes the age of first alcohol usage. Almost 38% of the women reported alcohol usage onset at the age of 13 or younger, with 8% starting between the ages of 3 to 9 years old. Thus, for these women, alcohol was clearly the "gateway" drug. In addition, 32% of the 60 women were treated for their alcohol addictions, with 53% who had previous treatment receiving multiple treatments, ranging from 2 to 13 times prior to their current imprisonment.

Later, many of the women became involved not only with drugs but with more serious IV drug usage. Specifically, 45% of the 60 women reported using a needle at least once in their lives, but more importantly, 40% considered themselves IV drug users. Finally, 20% of the women reported that they had overdosed, ranging from 1 to 8 times.

Another indication of the power of drugs in their prior preimprisonment lives was the 20% who reported spending more than $1,000 on drugs during the month before their imprisonment (ranging from $1,000–$9,000). In addition, 43% of the 60 women had drug treatment with the majority (61% of the 43%) having multiple treatments ranging from 2 to 14 times.

| TABLE 10.3   Age of Onset of Alcohol Usage | |
| --- | --- |
| 13 and under | 38% (23) |
| 14–18 | 55% (33) |
| 19 and above | 7% (4) |
| Total | 100% ($n = 60$ women)* |

*Data available for only 60 women.

## CHRONIC MEDICAL CONDITIONS

Until recently, the medical problems of prisoners were not a popular topic for research. However, during the past decade, U.S. correctional systems at all levels (federal, state, and local) have experienced a tremendous increase in the number and type of chronic medical conditions among inmates. Further, the increase in female prisoners has brought unique and often more complex health problems.

Of the 54 women who responded, more than half had chronic medical problems that would impact their lives (56%). Examples of some of the serious medical conditions include: hepatitis C, HIV, diabetes, asthma, arthritis, and migraines. Two women had also given birth in prison in the past, and one woman was pregnant at the time the study was conducted. Understandably, because of chronic medical problems, almost half of the women completing the ASI had experienced some type of associated medical problem in the past 30 days (46%). According to their correctional records, 31% of the women had been prescribed some type of medication.

## WOMEN'S MENTAL HEALTH ISSUES

The SCL-90-R (Symptoms Checklist-90-revised) was used to assess the symptoms in eight mental health categories. The SCL-90-R is a well-known assessment tool with good validity and reliability (Derogatis, 1994). What follows is a description of the SCL-90-R mental health categories, along with the reported percentages of women who scored in the "at risk range" for that particular scale (Derogatis, 1994 pp. 9–12).

1. *Somatization.*   Reflects distress arising from perceptions of bodily dysfunction. Complaints focus on cardiovascular, gastrointestinal, and respiratory. Pain and discomfort of the gross musculature functions and associated feelings of anxiety are common. Examples of common symptoms are: headaches, dizziness, pains in chest or back, nausea, and feeling weak. 44%
2. *Obsessive Compulsive.*   Reflects thoughts, impulses, and actions that are experienced as unremitting and irresistible. Behavior and experiences of more general cognitive performance deficits are also included. Examples of common symptoms are: repeated unpleasant thoughts that won't leave their minds, worried about sloppiness or carelessness, trouble concentrating, and having to repeat the same actions such as touching, counting, or washing. 52%
3. *Interpersonal Sensitivity.*   Reflects feelings of inadequacy and inferiority, particularly in comparison to other people. Common symptoms are self-deprecation and self-doubt, marked by discomfort during interpersonal interactions. Examples of common symptoms are: feelings of shyness, inferiority, and self-consciousness. 54%
4. *Depression.*   Reflects a withdrawal of interest in life, lack of motivation, and loss of vital energy. Feelings of hopelessness and thoughts of suicide are common. 70%
5. *Anxiety.*   Reflects feelings of nervousness, tension, and trembling that are often marked by panic attacks and feelings of terror, apprehension, and dread. 49%
6. *Hostility.*   Reflects thoughts and feelings, or actions, that are characteristic of the negative affect state of anger. Examples of common symptoms are: aggression, irritability, rage, and resentment. 46%

**TABLE 10.4** Number of Mental Health Problems

| Number of Problems | Percentage/Number of Women |
|---|---|
| 0 | 15.9% (10) |
| 1 | 7.9% (5) |
| 2 | 3.2% (2) |
| 3–4 | 9.5% (6) |
| 5–6 | 25.4% (16) |
| 7–8 | 20.6% (13) |
| 9 | 17.5% (11) |
| Total | 100% ($n$ = 63 women)* |

*Data available for only 61 women.

7. *Phobic Anxiety.* Reflects a persistent fear response that is irrational and disproportionate to the situation that leads to avoidance or escape behavior. Examples of common symptoms are: feeling afraid in open spaces, feeling that most people cannot be trusted, and feeling that others will take advantage of you if you let them. 29%

8. *Paranoid Ideation.* Reflects characteristics of hostility, suspiciousness, grandiosity, fear of loss of autonomy, and delusions as the primary symptoms of this disorder. 62%

9. *Psychoticism.* Reflects a withdrawn, isolated, and schizoid lifestyle, as well as experiencing hallucinations. This particular dimension examines the extent of the problem from mild interpersonal alienation to dramatic psychosis. Examples of common symptoms are: the idea that someone else can control their thoughts, hearing voices that others cannot hear, and having thoughts that are not their own. 64%

The findings indicate that, in many cases, the women have at least one area of mental health in which they are experiencing distress. Across categories, many of the women reporting mental health distress are experiencing symptoms in the "at risk range" in *more than one* of the categories. Table 10.4 illustrates that of the 63 women who completed the SCL-90-R, the majority had multiple mental health problems. In fact, 76% scored in a range high enough on two or more of the scales to be considered "at risk" or "positive for having mental health problems." Only 15.9% did not have any scores in the "at risk" range.

It is also interesting to note that those women who committed violent offenses (16%) have significantly higher phobic/anxiety $t$-scores ($p < .01$) as compared with individuals who committed drug offenses. Furthermore, nonviolent offenders had higher phobic/anxiety $t$-scores than drug offenders, but the difference did not quite reach the significance level ($p = .05$ not $p < .05$). No other significant differences were found between any other SCL-90-R scores and type of offense.

## INTERPRETATION OF THE MENTAL HEALTH RESULTS

The female offenders at the JRCC are clearly experiencing significant and disabling mental health conditions. This is also confirmed by the fact that 35% of the women had received inpatient mental health services, some as many as four or more times. Almost one-quarter of the women had also been in a juvenile psychiatric placement during adolescence (22%). In addition, 62% scored in the "at risk range" in terms of the number of symptoms, intensity, and the depth of their psychological distress. Given that many of the women had had psychiatric problems and presented symptoms prior to coming into prison, it is very unlikely that the symptoms reported on the SCL-90-R are explained only by the stress of the prison environment.

When comparing this population's scores to both general and outpatient psychiatric patients, they differ significantly from the general population, but not significantly from the psychiatric population, except on the paranoia scale. On the paranoia scale, the women prisoners' average score was significantly higher, meaning they experience more of these symptoms than the outpatient psychiatric group. The level of mental health problems obviously impacts their personal and social functioning, including their ability to parent. Perhaps more important to the prison environment, the types of behaviors that result from these types of mental illnesses will make the women more difficult to manage in the prison setting, particularly for those women who have symptoms of paranoia, depression, and psychosis.

The majority of the women (71%) are mothers, and most will be reunited with their children. Their significant addiction and mental health problems are likely to greatly impact their relationship with their children and their ability to parent. In particular, the basic premise of *the intergenerational cycle of incarceration* suggests that children who experience traumatic childhood events (abuse, neglect, parental addiction) in addition to parental incarceration are more likely than other children to be imprisoned (American Correctional Association, 1990; Earls & Reiss, 1994; Gable & Johnston, 1995; Widom, 1995). As the profile of these mothers suggests, many of their children have experienced most, if not all, of the factors predictive of an intergenerational cycle of incarceration, making them at risk for becoming the second or, in some cases, the third generation of incarcerated family members.

## CHILDREN OF FEMALE OFFENDERS

Children of imprisoned mothers are often referred to as the "silent" victims of enforced separation (Gable & Johnston, l995; Henriques, 1982). It is therefore important to focus on who these children are. Their profile will provide more insight into the parenting issues their mothers faced prior to imprisonment and, more importantly, what the children will face with the release of their mothers.

It is important to note here that the information on these children is based on each mother's perception of the child and may not accurately reflect the child's life. Some of the women have had little contact with their children since they have been in prison, with some having been away from their children prior to being incarcerated. It is common to find women prisoners lacking education about child development. This decreases their ability to identify children's problems. Because of disruptions in parent-child relationships and/or the lack of knowledge about child development, it is possible that these women simply cannot form judgments about the current functioning of their children.

### GENERAL DEMOGRAPHICS

As noted above, the profile here is based on a random sample of 69 children, 34 male and 35 female. Again, the average age of the children is 8 years old.

**TABLE 10.5** Types of Children's Problems

| | |
|---|---|
| Developmental Problems | 36  (25) |
| Abandonment | 30% (21) |
| Neglect | 29% (20) |
| Delinquency | 12% (8) |
| Teenage Pregnancy* | 25% (3) |
| Sexual Abuse | 6% (4) |
| Other Problems** | 65% (45) |
| Total | ($n = 126$) |

*This percentage is based on the 12 adolescent girls in the sample.

** Other problems include mental health, health, and behavior.

### CHILDREN'S PROBLEMS BEFORE AND DURING MATERNAL IMPRISONMENT

Overall, 62% of the children were experiencing some type of problem. In many cases, the children were experiencing multiple problems. Table 10.5 summarizes reported problems as identified by the mothers on the demographic survey.

The mothers each completed a Child Behavioral Checklist on their children ($n = 66$). For the 29 children between the ages of 1 1/2 to 5 years, only 1 child exhibited behavior that scored in the "clinically significant range" on the attention scale. No other scales were significant for this age group. The mothers reported more problems for the 37 children in the age range of 6 to 18 years. Again, some of the children were viewed as having more than one problem (see Table 10.6).

During the focus group interviews, the women were asked to reflect on their children's problems. Many of the women reported that their neglect of their children was often due to their addictions. Two women described the negative effect that drugs had on them emotionally as, "Drugs numb you. You're not as responsive, and as caring (inmate 01, group V) or as nurturing" (inmate 48, group V).

Other women discussed neglecting their children's physical needs. For example, one woman candidly admits to buying drugs in place of taking care of her children's physical needs:

**TABLE 10.6** Child Behavioral Checklist: Ages 6–18 Results

| | |
|---|---|
| Anxiety/depression | 11% (4) |
| Withdrawn/depression | 11% (4) |
| Somatic | 11% (4) |
| Social problems | 8% (3) |
| Thought disorders | 3% (1) |
| Attention | 5% (2) |
| Rule breaking | 8% (3) |
| Aggression | 5% (2) |
| Total | ($n = 37$) |

. . . . before I would go out and buy them anything like clothes or anything, I would go out and buy myself some weed or some dope or some alcohol, before I would think about my children. The reason I got the charges was because of what I did instead of paying my kid's rent. I went and took my money and I went and bought myself an eight ball and got evicted and got busted for drugs, you know, it was my own stupidity. I put myself before my kids. (inmate 08, group II)

Another problem that these children often endured was being separated from their mothers (longer than 24 hours) prior to their mother's current imprisonment.

## SEPARATION

Separation is an important issue for these children. As the psychological theory of attachment suggests, in order for children to become emotionally healthy adults, they must form a strong and *uninterrupted* attachment to a *consistent* and nurturing caregiver (Gaudin, 1985). The consequences of interrupting the attachment can seriously impact children long term. As Ainsworth and Bowlby (1991) suggest, "the quality of attachment indicates the character of a parent-child relationship and is a good predictor of a child's future behavior" (p. 307). This study also provides some insight into the quality of the mother-child relationship prior to their imprisonment.

The study found that the vast majority of the children were separated from their mothers at least one time (78%), and 26% were separated three or more times. The number of times these children were separated ranged from 1 to 50 times. The most frequently reported reasons for separation were jail, giving custody to someone else, and maternal hospitalizations. Possibly, underlying these reported reasons for separation are the women's significant addiction and mental health problems. For example, if a women is arrested for selling drugs and is sentenced to jail, she may have to give up custody of her child to someone else. Also, even if not arrested, the addiction, in some cases, resulted in the child being left with someone else while they went on a drug or alcohol binge. One woman discussed the impact the separations and her addictions have had on her children:

> I went to court, got put on probation, took off out of town, went and got myself all set back up and that lasted seven months. Same old routine, started up, sure enough my oldest one he seen it right away. Grandma, my mom is going to end up in jail and it is all going to start again . . . he was right, a week later there was my probation officer tapping me on the shoulder, and I was sitting in a bar, "Oh, Hi." All messed up I was . . . I just didn't care. My brother told me you know, we came to get you twice, no I'll be home at 10:30 I promise . . . you need to be home with your kids, but they are fine you guys are taking care of them. They're okay, just put them to bed I'll be home tonight and I never made it home. Nine months later I still haven't made it home. And my baby . . . he tells grandma my mommy not coming home from work and that was like three months after. (inmate 08, group II)

Essentially, the women's addictions were their first priority, resulting in their children's needs being placed "on the back burner." Furthermore, the women discussed how they attempted to hide their use of drugs/alcohol from their children by either hiring babysitters or taking them to a relative's home. One woman describes this candidly, stating: "I'd be on the run 3, 4 days at a time and my sister would go to my house and watch my kids for two packs of cigarettes, yeah! I've got it made!" (inmate 21, group II)

### VISITATION

Visitation between the women and their children is another problem. For example, 32% of the children have never visited their mothers while they were in prison, and only 2% saw their mothers once a week. The most common time interval for the children visiting their mothers was once a month (18%). The remainder of the children visited their mothers ranging from every 2 to 4 months, every 6 months, to once a year.

The two major reasons for the lack of visitation included: caregivers' refusal to allow the children to visit (22%), and the distance from the children's home to the prison being too great (19%). Coupled with the separation and visitation problems, the children also experienced changes in their caregivers, legal custody, and living situations.

### CUSTODY AND CHANGES IN CHILDREN'S LIFE

Twenty-five percent of the 69 children were in state custody and 11% were in foster care. Thirty-three percent were currently living with their natural fathers and the remainder with other family members. Since their mother's incarceration, 35% of the children experienced a custody change. Eleven percent of the mothers reported that the father of their children had also experienced jail.

In addition, one-quarter of the children had experienced one change in their daily caregiver, and an additional 11% had changed caregivers twice since their mothers were imprisoned. Coupled with experiencing a change in caregivers, 20% changed homes once, and 16% had changed homes twice.

### AGENCY INTERVENTION

One of the few positive findings of this study was that 68% of the children were receiving some kind of intervention from social or criminal justice agencies, including social services, school-based speech and occupational therapists, and/or therapy through a local mental health unit. Because the children had multiple problems, it was not uncommon for children to be receiving services from more than one agency. However, the remaining children (32%) were not receiving intervention. This clearly leaves unanswered questions regarding the welfare of these children.

## PARENTING

As the data have demonstrated thus far, the women have significant personal issues that have influenced their lives and those of their children. Most notably, prior to their current imprisonment, the women were often single mothers who were experiencing significant emotional and substance abuse problems, in addition to attempting to parent their often troubled children. In addition, it was not uncommon for these women to be involved in volatile relationships. All of these personal issues increase the likelihood of their neglecting their children and again being separated again from their children. As one woman stated in the focus group interview:

> The most important thing is the focus on your kids and for me I know as long as I have that urge for that addiction, I have that urge to do things that I was doing, I am never going to be able to take care of my children. You know it's not just having a house, it's not just having money, and food, it's having that mental ability and strength to know what to do (inmate 24, group III)

Another woman openly discussed her lack of parenting skills:

> I was a typical child having children . . . and now without my children I don't have them . . . because of my mistakes . . . not because I was a bad mother, I tried my hardest but I just didn't have the skills, I don't have the skills to be a parent right now and that's what landed me in here. (inmate 23, group IV)

## POSTRELEASE ISSUES

This study demonstrates that most of the female offenders and their children will be reunited with few (if any) new skills to maintain healthy relationships. As such, these female offenders need intensive addiction and mental health treatment, as well as program support, for learning life skills and developing healthy interpersonal relationships in order to reenter and reintegrate into their neighborhoods and communities.[3]

When the women are released, unrealistic expectations, based on their past and present functioning, are placed on them. They are expected to find housing, employment, and day care for their children, in addition to parenting their children who in most cases have serious emotional and behavioral problems. Compounding these problems are the dual problems of sobriety maintenance and mental health stability. In the past, most of these women have not been able to do so. Indeed, as the findings suggest, the women's daily lives before imprisonment were a struggle to survive, and they rarely experienced living drug-free, productive lives. In fact, the women expressed a great deal of fear regarding their reunions with their children, obtaining employment, and maintaining their sobriety. One woman described during a focus group interview her anxiety of being released and reunited with her son:

> They [correctional system] gave me work release, all of a sudden I came back from working and they said you're going home the next day. Not preparing my son, or family for any of this. My son was so emotional, it was hard for him to come to the bus stop even. They put me on a bus, they dropped me off at that little bus thing and just left me, just gave me money and left. I mean this is all between one night and the next morning. I had to go to my job and tell them that I couldn't be at work, when I had a full time job. I was working

---

[3]Other studies have found similar conclusions. See Carp, S., & Schade, L. (1992). Tailoring facility programming to suit female offenders' needs. *Corrections Today, 54* (6), 152–159; Pollock, J. (1998). *Counseling female offenders.* Thousand Oaks, CA: Brooks/Cole.

90 hours a week, not even preparing me for any of this. I walk off the bus and here is my son, mother and my dog. . . . I mean my son was devastated, he wasn't ready, he knew I was coming two months later, he wasn't ready for right then and there. I mean this was hard. He didn't want to come in the car. (inmate 54, group VII)

Another woman describes her experiences of being released from prison and failing to maintain her sobriety and live a productive, crime-free life:

I went back to my ex, the one that is my youngest children's father, the one that I ended up in here over. I stabbed him in the knee. We had been together for 6 years and we have nothing but a violent relationship throughout, and we have two children together and when I got out of prison the first time I went back to him, I didn't have nowhere to go and we thought we could start over and move to a different place and so we moved to a different county, across North Dakota, Fargo and we ended up living in cars and motels and churches and this and that it was just . . . I ended up relapsing and no matter what I tried to do, you know, I asked my probation officer for help, I asked her where I could go, what I could do, and she goes if you don't find a place for your kids soon they are going to get taken away from you. She was not of any service to me at all. (inmate 23, focus group IV)

## IMPLICATIONS AND RECOMMENDATIONS

### PREPRISON PROGRAMMING

The study indicates that probation by itself was not enough of a deterrent; 70% of the women were on probation prior to their incarceration. Given the mental health, medical, and addiction problems of these women, early intervention for the addiction and mental health is critical when a woman first comes in contact with the criminal justice system. This also will be a more cost-effective strategy than waiting until there are multiple contacts with the criminal justice system, and at a time when their symptoms have likely become more severe. Early treatment will not only decrease the likelihood of future incarcerations but also improve the mother-child relationship and improve the chances of breaking the destructive cycle

### PROGRAMMING

In order to better prepare these women to face life's daily challenges and reduce recidivism, it is recommended that correctional systems develop two types of programming: (a) prison programming that includes both intensive mental health and addiction treatment, and ongoing aftercare groups until they are released; and (b) comprehensive medical care. The findings suggest that female offenders have multiple chronic problems and behaviors that require a significant amount of treatment and practicing of new life skills to be able to successfully stabilize their lives. Programs that include relaxation training, depression management, and cognitive retraining (which may be particularly useful for those with paranoid, anxious, depressive, and aggressive thinking) should be considered because these symptoms were common among the women. Psychiatric, psychological, general mental health, and medical services should be used collaboratively with the addiction services. A multidisciplinary team approach will be very important, given the level and multitude of the women's symptoms.

Both staff and the women in this study report that little treatment is offered because of staffing shortages due to lack of funding. Offering structured programs that can be implemented on a consistent basis with adequate follow-up will save the states money in the long run. If these women's mental health and addiction disorders are stabilized before they are released, the likelihood of recidivism will be reduced and, hopefully, will reduce the intergenerational cycle of incarceration. Prison programs like Cornerstone in Oregon have been studied and have demonstrated a reduced recidivism rate among offenders (Field, 1989).[4]

Along with helping the women stabilize their addictions and mental health symptoms, a parenting program is strongly recommended. A parenting program would include education on parenting techniques, arranging for visitation and transportation for visitation, and having a liaison between the mothers and social services or current caregivers. A parenting coordinator would educate the women about the state and federal laws regarding custody, coordinate phone calls between the women and their legal representative for their custody issues, arrange for volunteers for the program, and apply for grants to fund aspects of the parenting program.

This type of programming might relieve a significant amount of the case managers' time and effort taken up by these custody matters. Case managers and corrections officers' time spent in managing behavioral problems may also be reduced. The women expressed anxiety regarding their lack of knowledge about their parental rights and their children's current living situation. This anxiety is likely manifested on the unit as behavioral problems. We observed a significant amount of demanding, needy, and uncooperative behavior when the women were worried about custody issues. Examples of these types of parenting programs can be found at the Shokapee Women's Prison in Minnesota and the Nebraska Women's Correctional Center.

Another observation that was made was that the women had access to very few jobs or had jobs that lasted only a few hours a week. Many of the women slept in until late in the day, which does not help them prepare for the structure of a productive life. If the women are to be prepared for applying for a job, keeping a work schedule, maintaining sobriety, managing their mental health problems, stabilizing their health, as well as taking care of their children and household, this should be reflected in the prison programming. These women are often unrealistic in their expectations about how they would support themselves and their children; for example, although 30% of the women were unemployed and even when employed, 57% were in unskilled jobs, 80% stated they were unconcerned about employment problems. Job-related programming should also be included in the prison programming. Having jobs while in prison may also help in decreasing behavioral problems, because the women will have jobs to occupy their time.

---

[4]See also Pollock, J. (1998). *Counseling female offenders.* Thousand Oaks, CA: Brooks/Cole, which provides an in-depth description of programs and treatments for imprisoned women.

### POSTRELEASE PROGRAMMING

A transitional postrelease program should be established to foster successful reunification. A successful postrelease program would include a variety of services to the women and their children with the idea of reuniting them slowly without the fear of the women losing their parental rights. Postrelease programs for inmate mothers and their children do exist in the United States, although they are few in number. Three facilities that have such postrelease programs for inmate mothers and their children are discussed below.

1. *The Jane Addams Women and Children's Center.* Located in Aurora, Illinois. The center houses 10 women on parole and their 10 infants. The average stay is 3 to 14 months (although exceptions are made to allow the women to stay up to 24 months). The facility only serves women who are pregnant during their imprisonment and after giving birth they are admitted into the program.
2. *The Phoenix House.* Located in Monrovia, California. The center has two facilities: one houses 31 women on parole and 6 children; the other houses 40 women on parole and 20 children. Both centers limit the children's age to 10 years old. The average length of stay is 6 to 15 months.
3. *The Huntington House.* Located in New York City, New York. The facility houses 19 single women (many of whom are women on parole) who have 1 to 4 children. This is a homeless shelter for single women and mothers who typically have children in foster care. The women must reside in the shelter for 6 months before providing them with an apartment to share with their children for an additional 6 months. The age limit for the children is under 15. The program provides aftercare (day reporting, home visits, and referrals). The average length of stay is 12 to 18 months.

## CONCLUSION

In conclusion, the data clearly show that the women need ongoing addiction and mental health treatment before, during, and after their imprisonment. "A window of programmatic opportunity exits, and if prisons are to stem the tide of recidivism, they must carefully and efficiently assign prisoners to treatment programs . . . that will prepare them to 'make it' in the free community" (Marquart et. al., 2001, p. 319). Although preprison, prison and postprison programming are all very expensive, in the long run it is more cost-effective particularly if we can prevent some of the women's children from becoming the second and third generation of inmates. An investment in these families while the women are in prison may reduce costs in the years to come by helping these families to break the generational pattern of legal, medical, mental health, and addiction problems.

## References

Abram, K., & Teplin, L. (1991). Co-occurring disorders among mentally ill jail detainees: Implications for public policy. *American Psychologist, 46*, 1036–45.

Alemagno, S., & Dixie, J. (2002) Screening of women in jail for health risks and needs. *Women and Criminal Justice, 13*(4), 97–108.

Anderson, T. L., Rosay, A. B., & Saum, C. (2002, March). The impact of drug use and crime involvement on health problems among female drug offenders. *The Prison Journal, 82*(1), 50–68.

Beck, A. J. (2005). *Prisoners in 2004* (Report number 210677). Washington, DC: Bureau of Justice Statistics, U.S. Department of Justice.

Carp, S., & Schade, L. (1992). Tailoring facility programming to suit female offenders' needs. *Corrections Today, 54*(6), 152–159.

Dalley, L. (2002). Policy implications relating to female offenders and their children: Will the past be prologue? *The Prison Journal, 82*(2), 234–268.

Derogatis, L. (1994). *Symptoms Checklist-90-Revised.* Upper Saddle River, NJ:Pearson.

Ditton, P. (1999) (Report number 174463). Washington, DC: Bureau of Justice Statistics, U.S. Department of Justice.

Emerging judicial strategies for the mentally ill. (April, 2000). Retrieved November 6, 2005, from http://www.ncjrs.org/html/bja/mentalhealth/intro.html

Enos, S. (2001). *Mothering from inside.* Albany: State University of New York Press.

Greensfeld, L. A., & Snell, T. L. (1999) *Women offenders* (Report number 175688). Washington, DC: Bureau of Justice Statistics, U.S. Department of Justice.

Hartwell, S. (2001). Female mentally ill offenders and their community reintegration needs: an initial examination. *International Journal of Law and Psychiatry, 24*(1), 1–11.

Henriques, Z. (2002). Diversion programming: Integrating treatment with criminal justice sanction for women with co-occurring disorders. In S. Davidson & H. Hill (Eds.), *Series on women with mental illness and co-occurring disorders, 2.* Delmar, NY: National Gains Center.

Hodgins, S. (1995). Assessing mental disorder in the criminal justice system: Feasibility versus clinical accuracy. *International Journal of Law and Psychiatry, 18*, 15–28.

Holtfreter, K., & Morash, M. (2003). The needs of women offenders: Implications for correctional programming. *Women & Criminal Justice, 14*(2/3), 137–160.

Leclair, D. (1990). *The incarcerated female offender—offender, victim, or villain?* Boston: Massachusetts Division of Corrections, Research Diversion.

Marguart, J. W., Brewer, V. E., Simon, P., & Morse, E. (2001). Lifestyle factors among female prisoners with histories of psychiatric treatment. *Journal of Criminal Justice, 29*, 319–328.

McLellan, T., Kushner, H., Metzger, D., Peters, R., Grissom, G., Pettinati, H., & Argeriou, M. (1992). *Addiction severity index—criminal justice questionnaire.* Ridgeland, MS: Accurate Assessments.

Morash, M., Bynum, T., & Koons, B. (1998). *Women offenders: Programming needs and promising approaches.* Washington DC: National Institute of Justice.

Mumola, C. (2000). *Incarcerated parents and their children* (Report number 182335). Washington, DC: Bureau of Justice Statistics, U.S. Department of Justice.

Pollock, J. (1998). *Counseling female offenders.* Thousand Oaks, CA: Brooks/Cole.

Strick, S. B. (1990, Fall). A demographic study of 100 admissions to a female forensic center: Incidences of multiple charges and multiple diagnoses. *Journal of Psychiatry and Law,* 435–448.

Teplin, L., Abram, K., & McClelland, G. (1996). Prevalence of psychiatric disorders among incarcerated women: Pretrial jail detainees. *Archives of General Psychiatry, 53*, 505–512.

Torrey, F. E., Stieber, J., Ezekiel, J., Wolfe, S., Sharfstein, J., Noble, J., & Flynn, L. (1992). *Criminalizing the seriously mentally ill: The abuse of jails as mental hospitals.* Arlington, VA: National Alliance for the Mentally Ill.

van Wormer, K. (2001). *Counseling female offenders and victims: A strength-restorative approach.* New York: Springer.

Whitmer, G. E. (1979). From hospitals to jails: The fate of California's deinstitutionalized mentally ill. *American Journal of Orthopsychiatry, 50*, 65–75.

# CHAPTER 11

# PRISON-BASED PROGRAMMING FOR WOMEN WITH SERIOUS MENTAL ILLNESS

#### ❧

**Andrew Harris**

**Arthur J. Lurigio**

## ABSTRACT

This chapter explores the elements of effective, gender-responsive mental health services for women inmates with serious mental illness, from admission to community reentry. First, the general policy context is presented, examining the role of the courts, accrediting bodies, and professional associations in defining the parameters of minimally adequate services in prison. Second, the essential practices associated with the planning and implementation of effective systems of care and intervention for mentally ill women inmates are described. Finally, the chapter addresses resources and summarizes policies for handling more effectively and humanely the problems of women offenders with serious mental illness.

## INTRODUCTION

Punitive crime-control policies caused state prison populations to increase steadily from the mid-1980s to the beginning of the 2000s (Mauer & Chesney-Lind, 2001). In 1990, for example, 684,554 adult inmates were incarcerated in state prisons. By the end of 2002, the number had grown to 1,209,640, a 77% increase (Harrison & Beck, 2003). Growth in state prison populations led to widespread prison overcrowding and an unprecedented flurry of new prison construction across the country (Harrison & Beck, 2002). Throughout the era of burgeoning prison expansion, women constituted approximately 5% to 6% of the country's annual inmate population. However, the rate of growth in the number of imprisoned women vastly exceeded that of men. Since 1990, for example, the number of men in prison increased 77%, whereas the increase among women was 108% (Beck & Harrison, 2001). At the end of 2001, some 76,200 women were incarcerated in state prisons, constituting 7% of the inmate population (Harrison & Beck, 2002).

During the past two decades, women have become one of the fastest-growing segments of the U.S. prison population. Between 1995 and 2005, the number of women in prison grew an average of 5% per year, compared with just a 3% annual increase of men during the same period. As of 2005, state and federal prisons held 107,518 women, up from 68,468 a decade earlier (Harrison & Beck, 2006).

Many studies have shown that the experience of being in prison is markedly different for women and men (e.g., Greer, 2000; Pollack, 2002; Sharp, 2003). As the population of women prisoners grew, prison staff began attending to women prisoners' specific problems. For example, correctional administrators' awareness of women inmates' needs led administrators to modify prison environments and programs to make them more gender sensitive (see, e.g., Pollock, 2002; Stinchcomb & Fox, 1999). Specifically, surveys consistently have found higher rates of mental health problems among female than male prison inmates (Beck & Maruschak, 2001). James and Glaze (2006), applying a fairly broad-based definition of mental health problems, estimated that 73% of women inmates exhibit such problems, compared with 55% of men.

Epidemiological surveys that used more restrictive, clinically based definitions of mental illness have found higher rates of mental disorders among women than men inmates in most major diagnostic categories. For example, compared with male prisoners, female prisoners manifested approximately ½ times the lifetime prevalence rates of major depression (22% vs. 13%), dysthymia (8% vs. 6%), and generalized anxiety disorders (29% vs. 20%); double the rate of post-traumatic stress disorder (10% vs. 5%); and roughly comparable rates of schizophrenia and bipolar disorder. Among all these categories, the rates of psychiatric disorders found among women inmates were dramatically higher than those found among women participants in community-based epidemiological surveys of psychiatric disorders (Veysey & Bichler-Robertson, 2002).

Apart from overall rates of disorders, women present a wide range of unique service challenges for correctional administrators and those charged directly with treating their multifaceted needs. The first challenge relates to the role of trauma in the lives of women prisoners. National surveys indicate that approximately 57% of women entering prison report histories of physical abuse (approximately four times the rate of men), 39% report histories of sexual abuse (approximately eight times the rate of men), and 37% report being victimized as children (approximately 2 1/2 times the rate of men) (Harlow, 1999). As we discuss in this chapter, a history of trauma figures prominently in both the delivery of effective clinical services and the formulation of correctional management strategies for women with mental disorders.

The second challenge relates to the psychological stressors associated with separation from children. An estimated 65% of women entering prison have minor children, and approximately 64% of the women lived with their children prior to incarceration (Mumola, 2000). Beyond the toll exacted on the children, women in such circumstances typically experience guilt and anxiety over the separation, significantly complicating their adjustment to the prison environment and increasing the risk of depression and other psychiatric conditions while incarcerated.

The third challenge relates to the complicating role of co-occurring substance use disorders among incarcerated women with mental illness. With an estimated 60% of women in prison meeting the criteria for substance abuse or dependence (Mumola, 2006), women entering prison are at higher risk than their male counterparts of experiencing co-occurring mental illness and substance use disorders. From clinical and public safety standpoints, the integrated prison-based treatment and case management of co-occurring disorders is a vital component of successful community reintegration for women returning from prison.

This confluence of issues—the disproportionate prevalence of serious mental disorders among women in prison, coupled with the complicating role of such factors as trauma, substance abuse, and separation from children—underscores the demand for an abundant spectrum of prison-based services. These interventions must not only attend to core clinical features but also structure services in a manner that recognizes the complex constellation of needs presented by women offenders with mental illness, and the critical importance of continuity of care postrelease.

This chapter explores the elements of effective, gender-responsive mental health services for women inmates with serious mental illness, from admission to community reentry. First, we briefly set the general policy context in which the topic is embedded and examine the role of the courts, accrediting bodies, and professional associations in defining the parameters of minimally adequate services in prison. Second, we describe the essential practices associated with the planning and implementation of effective systems of care and intervention for mentally ill women inmates. Finally, we consider the key issue of resources and summarize policies for handling more effectively and humanely the problems of women offenders with serious mental illness.

## POLICY CONTEXT

The principles of useful prison-based services for women with serious mental illness have been discussed recently in the context of three basic policy developments: expanded calls for cross-system collaboration between the public mental health and criminal justice systems, increasing attention to the programmatic implications of the growing number of women in the prison population, and the influx of former inmates in need of community-based systems of care for successful reentry.

Cross-system approaches that focus on the problem of mental illness in our nation's prisons have surged to the forefront of national discussions about the sizeable number of mentally ill persons in the criminal justice system at every step in the process, from arrest to postincarceration release. Showcasing innovations at the state and local levels, the Criminal Justice-Mental Health Consensus Project—a multiyear initiative spearheaded by the Council of State Governments—has highlighted best practices and underscored the demand for coordinated efforts between the criminal justice and mental health systems in handling the problems and treatment needs of persons with mental illness in the criminal justice system.

At the federal level, the President's New Freedom Commission, building on the landmark 1999 report by the U.S. Surgeon General that delineated the nation's mental health inadequacies, identified prison and postrelease services as essential links in filling a crucial gap in our mental health service delivery system (New Freedom

Commission on Mental Health, 2003). Many of the New Freedom Commission's findings and recommendations in this area were reflected in the 2004 passage of the *Mentally Ill Offender Treatment and Crime Reduction Act (S. 1194)*, which allocated federal funds to support the implementation of evidence-based practices in the diversion, treatment, and reentry of offenders with mental illness.

In another pivotal development, state and federal justice agencies have attended to the growing proportion of women in the prison population and its ramifications for correctional practices. Traditional correctional practices, which evolved with a primarily "male-centric" orientation, are being replaced steadily by the development and promotion of gender-responsive prison programming that addresses the specific issues faced by women offenders (Bloom, Owen, & Covington, 2005). Notably, growing attention has been directed at programs that emphasize sensitivity to trauma, empowerment strategies, community integration, parenting skills, and child welfare complexities.

Finally, policymakers and correctional administrators increasingly have recognized the importance of prisoner reentry in achieving broader public safety goals as well as the inextricable link between correctional institutions and broader systems of community services (Council of State Governments, 2005). Particularly in the case of women offenders, critical pieces of the reentry picture are parenting and family reunification efforts that attempt to ameliorate the intergenerational effects of incarceration on children, families, and communities. The intersection of these three areas of policy attention—mental illness in correctional settings, the unique needs of women offenders, and prisoner reentry and reintegration—provide the foundation for the gender-responsive and community-focused program practices that we describe in this chapter.

## STANDARDS OF CARE

In the present policy context, correctional systems have been called on to evaluate and improve their systems of care for women with mental illness. Whereas many have invested considerably in improved systems of care and treatment, national surveys have found significant variation in the quality of services among institutions, with a small subset of prisons providing substantially augmented services and others struggling to meet even minimal requirements of care (Manderscheid, Gravesande, & Goldstrom, 2004).

Illustrating this cross-jurisdictional variation, standards of service can be viewed as a three-tiered hierarchy—a legal baseline that contains core constitutional requirements that all systems must meet, a second tier based on "voluntary" standards set forth by accrediting and professional bodies and capturing industry-accepted best practices, and a third tier that moves beyond core standards in pursuit of evidence-based practices. This hierarchy, illustrated in Figure 11.1, serves as the focal point for the remainder of this chapter.

### LEGAL PARAMETERS

Contemporary legal standards governing correctional-based health and mental health treatment generally stem from the U.S. Supreme Court's ruling in *Estelle v. Gamble* (1976).

**FIGURE 11.1** Standards of Service Hierarchy

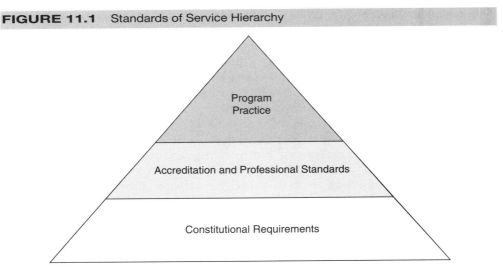

With its focus on the adequacy of health care in the Texas prison system, *Estelle v. Gamble* established that "deliberate indifference" to the health care needs of inmates represented a violation of the 8th Amendment's protections against cruel and unusual punishment.[1]

Applying the *Estelle v. Gamble* standard to mental health treatment, *Ruiz v. Estelle* (503 P. Supp. 1265.1323 [1980]), enumerated six major elements of a minimally adequate mental health treatment program:

- Systematic screening and evaluation.
- Assurance that treatment is more than mere seclusion or supervision.
- Treatment participation by trained mental health professionals.
- Accurate and confidential record-keeping procedures.
- Safeguards against inappropriate use of psychotropic medications.
- Suicide prevention programs.

Although fairly minimalist in its requirements, the *Ruiz* decision paved the way for subsequent federal court rulings regarding the quality of treatment in specific states. Major system reforms have been launched through consent decrees or settlement agreements that stemmed, in part, from the *Ruiz* standards in such states as Ohio (*Dunn v. Voinovich*, 1993), New Jersey (*D. M. v. Terhune, 1999*), California (*Coleman v. Wilson*, 1995), and Alabama (*Bradley v. Haley*, 2001; *Laube v. Haley*, 2002).

In addition to litigation over the adequacy of treatment programs, a significant body of case law has developed about the duties and limitations of correctional systems in their management of inmates with serious mental illness. Certain areas of correctional practice have attracted particular attention, including the placement of inmates with mental illness into disciplinary or administrative segregation units

---

[1]Beyond the 8th Amendment protections, case law regarding the right to treatment in jail settings has also cited 14th Amendment due process protections for pretrial detainees.

(*Jones'El v. Berge*, 2001; *Madrid v. Gomez*, 1995; *Ruiz v. Johnson*, 1999), custodial precautions to prevent inmate suicide,[2] and correctional departments' obligation to provide discharge planning services (*Brad H. v. City of New York*, 2000).

## PROFESSIONAL AND ACCREDITATION STANDARDS

Major legal challenges to the adequacy of prison mental health services have resulted in fairly detailed and prescriptive settlement agreements or consent decrees. However, the core *Ruiz* guidelines remain open to a wide variety of interpretations and also are variable in implementation. The next tier of standards—those set forth by accrediting bodies and professional organizations—provide additional guidance on the design of effective prison-based mental health services. These include accreditation standards from the National Commission on Correctional Health Care (National Commission on Correctional Health Care [NCCHC], 2003) and the American Correctional Association (American Correctional Association, 2002), as well as professional standards and guidelines from such organizations as the American Psychiatric Association (APA) (Weinstein, 2000) and the American Association of Correctional Psychologists (Althouse, 2000).

The NCCHC currently accredits approximately 135 prison facilities in the United States under its Standards for Prison Health, revised in 2003.[3] The specific mental health section of the standards is limited. Instead, the delivery of mental health services is covered under the broader rubric of health care standards that involve such issues as governance, service access, staffing adequacy, and patient confidentiality. Pursuant to the revision of its standards in 2003, the Commission published a guide to mental health services that prescribes a range of basic service components, including:

- Procedures for screening and identifying mentally ill prisoners.
- A continuum of mental health treatment services, including appropriate medication and other therapeutic interventions.
- A sufficient number of mental health professionals to provide effective services to all prisoners suffering from serious mental disorders.
- Detailed and confidential clinical records.
- Provisions for identifying and treating suicidal prisoners.
- Protocols to ensure that prisoners have timely access to necessary mental health services.
- Differentiated levels of care, including emergency crisis intervention services, inpatient capacity, intermediate care in specialized housing units, and general population (i.e., "outpatient") services.

The *APA Guidelines for Psychiatric Services in Prisons* (Weinstein, 2000) set forth mental health provisions related to three main areas:

- *Identification:* Initial screening and referral, brief mental health assessments, and comprehensive mental health evaluations.

---

[2]Dozens of such cases have been filed over the years; for listings and summaries of these cases, see Collins, 1995.

[3]Personal communication with Judith Stanley, NCCHC Director of Accreditation, January 2007.

- *Mental Health Treatment:* Levels of care, mental health coverage, treatment planning, psychotropic medications, and custodial staff training.
- *Discharge Planning:* Coordination with community providers, medication renewals, and continuity or care.

The APA also briefly enumerates the distinguishing features of female-centered services, such as specialized screening and programming for post-traumatic stress disorder, staff training associated with the characteristic aspects of symptom presentation among women, and considerations related to the use of seclusion and restraints.

## ELEMENTS OF EFFECTIVE PROGRAMMING

Legal, accreditation, and professional standards undoubtedly provide a solid framework for the development and management of effective service systems in prisons; nonetheless, in certain critical respects they remain limited. Although the standards recommend the fundamentals of quality prison-based mental health programs, they tend to be relatively nonspecific in terms of training curricula for staff, staffing levels, and operating procedures. Portions of these standards refer to women's services; however, most guidelines have been designed for "gender-neutral" application and, as such, only partially meet the mental health needs of female inmates. In light of these limitations, we focus our attention on program practices, emphasizing approaches that appear to be most effective in improving functioning and outcomes for women with serious mental illness. We base this review on five unifying principles:

- Integration with community-based systems of care.
- Effective systems of screening, assessment, and referral.
- Coordinated treatment planning and case management.
- A comprehensive collection of gender-responsive clinical treatment services.
- Postrelease planning and service capacity.

### INTEGRATION WITH COMMUNITY SYSTEMS OF CARE

Blitz, Wolff, and Paap (2006) found that a substantial proportion of women who entered prison needing psychiatric treatment reported that they had been unable to access community treatment before their incarceration. These findings speak directly to the interdependence between the correctional and public mental health systems on various critical levels. The study reinforces the demand for more effective systems of community-based outreach and greater overall service capacity, particularly for women whose life circumstances place them at a high risk of incarceration, such as co-occurring substance use and psychiatric disorders, previous involvement with the criminal justice system, and chronic homelessness. The profound gaps in our nation's public behavioral health care systems demand more effective prevention and diversion programs, as discussed elsewhere in this book.

The findings of Blitz and colleagues also underscore the vital role of prison-based behavioral health services in ameliorating fundamental community-based service inadequacies. Notably, the study found evidence that incarceration significantly improved access to needed services for many women, with services more readily available in prison than in the community. Most women with serious mental illness are never incarcerated. Those who are incarcerated tend to have the most complex range of problems—serious mental illness that is often combined with co-morbid personality and substance use disorders, homelessness, histories of trauma, and complex medical ailments, such as HIV, hepatitis C, and sexually transmitted diseases. Hence, prison-based behavioral health is far from a self-contained service system with isolated objectives; rather, it is best viewed as a critical point of intervention for women who often present the mental health system with its most complex and intractable service challenges.

Beyond the walls of the institution, coordination with community-based systems of care is highlighted by the fact that the vast majority of women entering prison will eventually return to their communities. Therefore, as we describe in this chapter, effective models of intersystem communication and investment in community-based resources in order to facilitate successful reentry are sorely needed.

In summary, prison-based programming for female offenders must recognize that the public health and correctional systems share fundamental goals. The public safety imperatives of the criminal justice system complement the public mental health system's mandate to improve the lives of individuals with mental illness. Meeting these mutual goals entails a coordinated three-pronged strategy: "front-end" prevention-oriented community services, effective prison-based care in accordance with the practices highlighted in this chapter, and "back end" strategies that ensure effective postrelease services in a manner that will forestall future involvement in the legal system and the reincarceration of women with serious mental illness and co-occurring disorders.

## EFFECTIVE SYSTEMS OF SCREENING, ASSESSMENT, AND REFERRAL

The front door of the prison system is a critical juncture for the identification and referral of women whose history or presenting problems indicate the need for mental health intervention. Accordingly, prisons must be equipped both to identify immediate signs and symptoms that might be associated with elevated suicide risk or psychiatric crisis and to establish a plan for ongoing mental health interventions during the period of incarceration. In contrast to jail-based screening systems, which place greater emphasis on identifying and treating acute distress and informing short-term treatment goals, prison-based systems must set the stage for more comprehensive clinical interventions during the period of incarceration.

NCCHC prison standards recommend a two-stage process, with general mental health issues evaluated as part of a "receiving screening" on system admission and before housing assignments, and a more comprehensive initial mental health screening conducted by a mental health professional within the first 14 days of admission (National Commission on Correctional Health Care, 2003). The primary purpose of the receiving screening process is to identify cases requiring immediate or priority service referrals, including individuals in crisis or otherwise requiring immediate mental health referrals, such as those with indicators of potential suicidality, prior hospitalizations, and current use of psychiatric medications. Of particular concern for women inmates is the identification of case characteristics that could complicate adjustment to the correctional environment, such as trauma history and separation from children.

Although researchers have found gender-neutral instruments, such as the Referral Decision Scale and the Suicide Checklist, to be effective means of screening new female inmates (Earthrowl & McCully, 2002), others have suggested that instruments validated for male inmate populations might prove problematic when applied to women (Steadman, Scott, Osher, Agnese, & Robbins, 2005). Recognizing this, the authors of the recently piloted Correctional Mental Health Screen have developed distinct instruments for men and women, with the eight-item female-focused instrument emphasizing factors such as responses to trauma and depression (Ford & Trestman, 2005).[4]

The second phase of the assessment process is the completion of a more specialized and focused mental health screening aimed at identifying women in need of ongoing treatment or intervention. Service standards and guidelines differ in terminology and prescribed processes.[5] Nonetheless, the components of these assessments generally include mental health history, previous treatment, medication history, psychosocial history (i.e., family, social, legal, relationships), a functional assessment, evaluation of current situational stressors, a mental status examination, and considerations of current diagnosis and relevant medical diagnoses, current medications, and substance use status (Council of State Governments, 2002).

A primary "output" of the initial mental health screen is the decision of whether to refer the inmate to a specialized mental health caseload. Although our emphasis in this chapter is on the care and management of women meeting the criteria for serious mental illness, we note that a substantial portion of women might not meet such criteria but nonetheless could manifest a broad range of conditions that warrant psychiatric treatment and specialized case management. In addition to suffering from preexisting, chronic disorders, such as dysthymia (chronic, low-grade depressed mood), many women who are incarcerated find that incarceration itself and the prison environment can produce a significant adjustment disorder with symptoms of anxiety, depression, and suicidality—conditions that can be exacerbated by factors such as separation from children. Combined with the generally higher rates of serious mental illness within the female prison population, these problems are common in the specialized mental health caseloads in women's prisons and are more than double those found in men's prisons. Several jurisdictions report that, at any given time, as many as half of the women housed in prison facilities are being monitored on a specialized mental health caseload (Beck & Maruschak, 2001).

## COORDINATED TREATMENT PLANNING AND CASE MANAGEMENT

After a woman inmate with mental illness is referred for ongoing mental health services and assigned a primary case manager, the next major system challenge is developing a treatment plan to serve as a "blueprint" for ongoing case management efforts. Most treatment plans are developed jointly between the case manager and the client with input from a multidisciplinary treatment team that sets specific goals for each client, along with strategies and time frames for meeting them. Treatment plans are dynamic and intended to be regularly updated and readjusted.

---

[4]Instrument available at http://www.asca.net/public/MH%20Screen%20-%20Women%20082806.pdf

[5]For example, the APA guidelines reflect a more comprehensive, multifaceted approach than that set forth by the NCCHC.

As previously stated, the mental health problems of incarcerated women are multifaceted and complicated, including major psychiatric problems, post-traumatic stress disorder, substance use disorders, separation from children and families, and histories of self-inflicted and intimate violence. From a treatment planning and case management standpoint, these conditions should never be viewed as distinct problems; they are highly interdependent and must to be handled in a coordinated manner (Henderson, Schaeffer, & Brown, 1998; Hills, Siegfried, & Ickowitz, 2004).

The importance of service coordination for people with serious mental illness is hardly endemic to correctional settings; service fragmentation has been recognized as a major challenge to systems of community mental health (Office of the Surgeon General, 1999). Yet these deficiencies are especially pronounced in prisons, where women can interact with a variety of providers, including medical staff, mental health professionals, correctional personnel, substance abuse treatment staff, and specialized program staff in areas such as domestic violence counseling, education and employment, and prenatal and parenting services. These programs often operate in tandem; they pursue independent treatment objectives, are managed under separate contractual arrangements and lines of accountability, and operate in the absence of integrated information systems.

In the realm of treatment planning, service coordination is therefore critical. For example:

- Women with co-occurring substance use disorders require treatment plans that recognize mental illness and substance abuse as one condition rather than independent problems.[6]
- Women with co-morbid medical conditions, such as HIV, hepatitis C, and chronic diseases, need coordinated medical and psychiatric care—elements of service that are often bifurcated in correctional settings.
- Women exhibiting ongoing behavioral problems—often attributable to borderline personality disorders or related conditions—require case management plans that are developed by correctional administrators and mental health professionals.

These large overlapping service needs underscore the imperative of coordinated treatment planning and case management efforts. Furthermore, they highlight the demand for streamlined systems of services and provider accountability, properly aligned incentives for providers and clients, and effective means of communication and information sharing among providers.

## GENDER-RESPONSIVE CLINICAL TREATMENT SERVICES

Most core guidelines and standards for effective mental health services apply equally to both male and female inmates. There are, however, distinguishing factors that should be paramount in the delivery of gender-responsive clinical care for women inmates. In an addendum to its guidelines, the APA noted that the higher prevalence

---

[6]From an organizational perspective, it is common for correctional agencies to manage substance abuse and mental health services under separate contractual arrangements. Although this generally permits jails and prisons to draw on specialized expertise, it encourages a bifurcated approach to treatment in the absence of extraordinary systems of cross-provider communication and collaboration.

of mental illness among women inmates, and the increased willingness of women inmates to accept treatment, require mental health staffing levels greater than those found in male prison facilities. Citing the higher prevalence of major depression, anxiety disorders, and post-traumatic stress disorders among female inmates, the APA suggested that clinical programs be designed in a manner that responds to critical gender differences in symptom presentation. Finally, the APA indicated that patient seclusion and restraint—while matters of concern in all psychiatric settings—require special attention in the case of women inmates, considering the significant role of trauma in many of their lives (Weinstein, 2000).

Beyond these factors, correctional managers and program staff also must address other gender-focused clinical issues, including systems of management for women with severe behavioral disturbances or patterns of self-destructive behaviors, coordinated care for women with co-occurring substance abuse, and the special needs of mothers who have been separated from their children. Clinical programs for women with serious mental disorders involve a range of service components; however, for purposes of our review, we distinguish the provision of psychiatric medications from the implementation of rehabilitative services at different levels of care.

## PSYCHIATRIC MEDICATION MANAGEMENT

The provision of psychotropic medications in correctional settings has long been characterized by an implicit tension between the imperative to control inappropriate (excessive) use and the demand to ensure access to needed medications (Vaughn, 1997). *Ruiz v. Estelle* (1982) identified the need of correctional administrators to safeguard against the inappropriate use of psychotropic medication as one of the core elements of constitutionally guaranteed and appropriate psychiatric services for prison inmates. The court's concern stemmed in part from the use of such medications as a means of behavioral control, in the absence of nonpharmacological therapies, and without appropriate medical supervision. Women inmates might be especially susceptible to overmedication, in light of societal responses to deviant behavior among women. In other words, rule-breaking among women inmates might be viewed as more serious than it is among men inmates and therefore more likely to be subject to disciplinary action, including medication to control behavior (Auerhahn & Leonard, 2000).

Another potential abuse of psychotropic medications involves inmates who seek out prescriptions for certain medications (for example, those with sedative effects) simply to experience their psychoactive properties or to use the substances as "currency" in the prison economy. This misuse of medications might be particularly pronounced among women inmates, considering the high rates of substance dependence within this inmate population.

Correctional systems often have been criticized for withholding potentially effective medications from inmates (Human Rights Watch, 2003). APA standards suggest that a "full range" of psychotropic medications be readily available in accordance with community standards of care. However, with pharmacy costs constituting a growing proportion of correctional budgets and with psychiatric medications—particularly the newer class of atypical antipsychotic agents, which are among the more costly—prison administrators face significant pressures to contain costs and limit the use of such medications.

In light of these factors, the provision of psychotropic medications in female prisons must follow fundamental practice guidelines. Prison systems must ensure that sufficient psychiatric resources are allocated to account for the higher rates of psychotropic medication use among women. Accordingly, most women's facilities require lower psychiatrist-to-inmate ratios to ensure that medication regimens are appropriately administered and overseen.

Clinical staff in women's facilities must be particularly wary of the potential for polypharmacy. Compared with men inmates, women inmates exhibit higher rates of disease, particularly communicable diseases, including hepatitis C, HIV, and sexually transmitted diseases, many of which involve extended and complex medication regimens. The comparatively high rates of psychotropic medication use among women prisoners and the substantial number of women on multiple medications increase the dangers of adverse drug reactions or interactions.

The high rates of co-occurring psychiatric and substance use disorders among women should discourage prison psychiatric practitioners from (although not preclude) the use of medications that might be prone to abuse. These include drugs that are widely prescribed in noncorrectional settings such as anti-anxiety medications and sedative-hypnotics (Metzner, 1998).

## DIFFERENTIATED LEVELS OF CARE

Consistent with treatment planning demands and custodial requirements, differentiated levels of care are now being implemented in prison with respect to varying behavioral profiles, levels of acuity, and the service needs of incarcerated women with mental illness. The level of care concept is based on the notion that, during incarceration, women can proceed through different phases of treatment, depending on the intensity and frequency of their symptoms.

According to APA guidelines, these levels of care consist of four options: (a) outpatient services provided in the general population; (b) acute care services (equivalent to psychiatric inpatient hospitalization) provided to individuals whose symptoms involve significant functional impairment; (c) chronic care services, involving residential care and treatment and provided to those individuals who do not meet the criteria for acute inpatient care but who encounter difficulties coping in the general population; and (d) crisis intervention services provided to individuals who are in immediate psychiatric crisis and require short-term stabilization. For our purposes, we examine services in three key areas: (a) ambulatory services provided in the general population; (b) acute care services delivered in the context of inpatient treatment and specialized crisis stabilization beds; and (c) residential treatment services, designed to expand treatment alternatives for women who do not meet the criteria for acute-level care but require services beyond those available in the general inmate population.

In the past several decades, the locus of public mental health care has shifted dramatically from large institutions to community-based models of care. Driven by clinical, political, civil libertarian, and fiscal considerations, the paradigm of treatment for mental illness has been predicated on a "least restrictive environment" standard that makes community integration its primary goal.

In prison, as in the community, the majority of women with mental health problems receive their services on an "outpatient" basis. Indeed, more intensive levels of care are designed to provide women with coping skills and help them control their symptoms so they can be managed in the ambulatory/outpatient domain. Hence, programs that involve special housing—inpatient, crisis stabilization, or residential treatments—are defined as time-limited interventions. Although a restricted number of chronic patients require extended stays in specialized housing, the ultimate goal for most mentally ill women inmates is to return to the general population.

The prison model closely mirrors community practice, but its application in the prison environment is complicated. Whereas patients in the community often view the transition to an ambulatory setting as a desirable step in the direction of independence and self-sufficiency, women returning to the general prison population face a potentially threatening environment in which their personal freedoms are curtailed. Moreover, the prison environment requires women to comply with rigid standards of conduct. Failure to comply with such standards can lead to disciplinary action.

Recognizing these factors, systems of ambulatory care must take into account the realities of prison life and the reluctance of women to leave the relative safety of the residential units for the general population. Therefore, intensive levels of services should facilitate adjustment to prison life as well as become a "safety valve" that will administer interventions before women decompensate to the point of needing more intensive services. Consistent with these goals, outpatient services combine group and individual counseling services as specified in the treatment plan. In accordance with the general principles of gender-responsive treatment, ambulatory mental health services should include:

- Therapeutic group activities that emphasize the centrality of relationships in women's lives.
- Rehabilitative services that focus on skill development and economic and social empowerment.
- Therapeutic activities that recognize the role of trauma in women's lives.
- Case management strategies that coordinate and integrate all services.

Correctional mental health systems also require treatment for people in acute psychiatric distress or with significantly impaired functioning. Under the rubric of "acute care" are crisis stabilization services, which are provided in the correctional environment, and inpatient services, which are typically provided under alternative facility arrangements.

Crisis stabilization services closely monitor and clinically manage women at risk of suicidal behaviors. As a rule, crisis services are delivered in designated housing areas, often located in a medical infirmary to permit continual supervision by nursing staff. In contrast to other ongoing, rehabilitation-focused therapeutic interventions, crisis services are geared toward meeting immediate clinical needs rather than effectuating significant behavioral change.

In contrast, inpatient care involves substantially higher levels of psychiatric staffing and intensive rehabilitation services than those provided in crisis intervention settings and are reserved for women experiencing acute and significant psychiatric distress that stems from serious mental illness. The goals of inpatient care are to develop or re-establish a stable care regimen that lays the foundation for continued rehabilitative services in a less intensive service environment and an ultimate return to the correctional institution. Although organizational structures for the provision of inpatient care and treatment for women inmates vary among institutions, the most common program model involves the management of treatment through mental health authorities that enter into interagency agreements with correctional authorities.

Regardless of the arrangement, both systems must contend with a complex constellation of issues regarding continuity of care, utilization management, and the balancing of therapeutic and correctional management objectives. Prominent among these issues is the environmental disparity between the relatively "safe and secure" inpatient setting and the significantly more demanding and threatening prison environment. This disparity, if not adequately reduced, can contribute to a "revolving door" phenomenon in which women discharged from inpatient care rapidly decompensate after they return to prison.

As prisons struggle with growing numbers of incarcerated inmates with serious mental illness, many have recognized the limitations of a bidimensional service model that consists solely of ambulatory and acute-level care. These systems have created specialized residential treatment programs intended to provide a "subacute" level of psychiatric care and rehabilitation. In contrast to inpatient units, which often are operated in psychiatric facilities, residential treatment programs operate in prisons under the authority of correctional policies and procedures. Thus, the unit's clinical activities must be closely coordinated with those of correctional staff. The officers assigned to these units are critical members of the multidisciplinary team. Such correctional involvement is vital to the success of both male and female residential treatment programs (Appelbaum, Hickey, & Packer, 2001; Dvoskin & Spiers, 2004). Nonetheless, prison staff working on women's units must be specifically attuned to the special needs of women offenders with serious mental illness, which as we already have noted here, include histories of trauma, suicidality, and separation from children.

Residential treatment programs are designed to provide time-limited treatment and rehabilitation services to women with such serious Axis I psychiatric disorders as schizophrenia, major depression, and bipolar disorder. Their mental conditions do not warrant inpatient hospitalization, but they are otherwise unable to function in the general prison population. Treatment of underlying mental disorders is a critical element of the work of residential programs, which also emphasize the acquisition of skills and capacities that will permit more effective functioning in the general population. A critical facet of most residential treatment programs is the provision of intensive psychosocial rehabilitation services that improve the inmate's capacity to manage in the general population and, ultimately, in the community. Residential treatment programs often are structured as therapeutic communities in which clients progress through a series of phases defined by specific treatment goals. New York's Intermediate Care Program, for example, has four phases:

- An evaluation phase (Step I) in which clients are oriented to the unit and to program norms and expectations.
- A core curriculum phase (Step II) involving immersion in the community's therapeutic regime and the increasing roles and responsibilities on the unit.
- A transitional phase (Step III) involving a gradual introduction to the general population while continuing to participate in unit activities.
- A follow-up phase (Step IV) in which clients are monitored and managed within the general population for a six-week period following unit release. (New York State Office of Mental Health, 2003)

Another example of residential treatment programming is the Correctional Services of Canada's Structured Living Environments (SLEs), located in Canada's four regional women's prisons. The SLEs provide 24-hour services that are delivered by a multidisciplinary staff with specialized correctional, psychosocial rehabilitation, and mental health backgrounds (Laishes, 2002).

As residential programs have evolved, correctional systems have recognized that women with serious mental disorders might be unsuitable for the core residential treatment model. For example, women struggling with co-occurring substance use disorders or those presenting significant behavioral management challenges require multifarious therapeutic interventions. One model of residential treatment involves units for women with profound behavioral problems or patterns of self-inflicted harm. These units have become more common as correctional systems struggle with how best to manage women with persistent patterns of disruptive behaviors that result in recurrent violations of prison rules.

Prevailing correctional practices respond to rule violations through the use of disciplinary segregation, in which inmates are isolated in a cell for 23 hours per day for a period of time commensurate with the severity of the infraction. This practice has received growing attention from representatives of the clinical, legal, and advocacy communities, who have cited both the pernicious mental health consequences of prolonged segregation and the disproportionate representation of inmates with mental illness in segregation units. For women with mental illness, the effects of segregation can result in severe psychiatric decompensation and dramatically increased potential for suicide and other forms of self-harm.

Women who exhibit chronic disruptive behaviors in prison commonly exhibit "Axis II" personality disorders, particularly borderline personalities associated with volatile, aggressive, and self-injurious behaviors. This constellation of behavioral symptoms, often involving co-occurring Axis I diagnoses, generally make these inmates unsuitable candidates for typical intermediate care programs. At the same time, their psychological vulnerability places them at considerable risk of self-harm if they are placed in isolation.

In response, some prison-based mental health systems have pursued alternatives to segregation that administer intensive treatments that attempt to change dysfunctional behaviors. Because these programs emphasize the management of disruptive behaviors, most embrace a strong system of behavioral reinforcement in which privileges are earned through program progress. Although evidence of the effectiveness of specific elements of these programs is still being collected, potentially promising models have received favorable attention from correctional mental health experts. One such model is the New York State Therapeutic Behavioral Management Program (TBM), jointly operated by the State's Office of Mental Health and Department of Correctional Services at the Bedford Hills Correctional Facility. The TBM is based on four phases of graduated privileges, in which women begin their time on the unit with significant restrictions and gradually earn the right to participate in recreational and therapeutic activities if they maintain good behavior.

Throughout their time on the unit, women meet regularly with their assigned case managers in order to implement their treatment plans (New York State Office of Mental Health, 2006). Citing the effectiveness of the unit and facing an increase in the number of women requiring TBM services, the state has indicated its intention to eventually double the size of the unit to 32 beds (New York State Office of Mental Health, 2005).

Another approach that has been applied in correctional settings with promising results is Dialectical Behavioral Therapy (DBT), a skill-based program that focuses on four key areas: core mindfulness skills, interpersonal effectiveness, emotional modulation, and distress tolerance (Linehan, 1993). Applying many of the principles of cognitive behavioral therapy, DBT focuses on the psychosocial forces underlying self-destructive behaviors, such as self-mutilation and attempted suicide. Although research on the effectiveness of DBT in women's prison settings has been limited by methodological factors (e.g., low sample size), initial research has indicated that the intervention might prove effective in reducing self-injurious behaviors (Nee & Farman, 2005). Preliminary qualitative research on DBT, conducted in the Canadian correctional system, has generated positive feedback from staff and clients and also identified critical implementation issues in such areas as resources, staff training, and client engagement (Sly & Taylor, 2003).

## POSTRELEASE PLANNING AND CAPACITY

The vast majority of women in state and federal prisons are eventually released to the community. Relatively few gender-focused prison reentry programs have been implemented, compared with the number of innovative program models for women with mental illness who are released from jail. Although many of the core components of jail-based discharge planning (e.g., mental health treatment, housing, medication, benefit eligibility, and family and support services) are applicable to prisoner reentry, women leaving prison face particularly pronounced community reintegration challenges.

With approximately 95% of women prisoners being incarcerated for longer than a year (Harrison & Beck, 2006), release planning can be construed as a "back-end" service to be initiated at pending release from correctional custody. Yet considering that the vast majority of women sent to prison will eventually be released to their communities, effective practice demands that the reentry planning process begin immediately on admission into the correctional system. In the case of women with serious mental illness, this is imperative. Although mental health treatment goals must certainly promote the safety and well-being of women during incarceration, these services must focus on the long-term goals of encouraging recovery and self-sufficiency on community reentry.

Promoting effective reentry practices for women with mental illness requires looking beyond mental health treatment and toward a complex and interdependent array of needs related to economic self-sufficiency, housing, family and social supports, and ongoing community supervision. As an extension of the aforementioned demand for collaborative treatment planning and case management during incarceration, effective reentry programming demands a significant coordination of effort among service providers.

Successful community reintegration requires the development of resources in the community that target the complex and unique challenges faced by women offenders with mental illness. The long-range effectiveness of even the most exemplary prison-based programs will be constrained by the capacity of community resources to respond to these challenges.

The provision of such capacity requires that policymakers and program planners recognize the singular burdens carried by women with offender status, mental illness, substance dependence, and minor children. For example, offender status can preclude eligibility for certain financial benefits, including federal housing subsidies, or a lapse into substance use can render women ineligible for supported housing programs that might otherwise help them manage their mental illness.

Considering these factors, targeted capacity development, such as that envisioned by the 2004 Mentally Ill Offender Treatment and Crime Reduction Act, is a linchpin for any comprehensive strategy to meet the needs of incarcerated women with mental illness. The elements of postrelease services for these women should include, at a minimum:

- A continuum of family-centric housing options, including residential treatment, supported housing, and independent living alternatives.
- Linkages to community-based treatment and ongoing case management, including integrated treatment for co-occurring disorders, sustained medication access and monitoring, streamlined access to crisis intervention services, and community-based support services, including psychosocial rehabilitation, education, vocational training, and peer support.
- Intensive child welfare case management services that promote family reunification while maintaining the priority of child safety.
- Responsive systems of postrelease community supervision, including systems of "graduated sanctions" and communication mechanisms that facilitate coordinated case management and collaboration among parole, social services, and mental health case management staff.

## SUMMARY AND CONCLUSIONS

This chapter has reviewed the key provisions for developing effective prison-based programming for women with serious mental illness. These provisions must look beyond core legal requirements and "gender-neutral" service standards and toward the specific needs of incarcerated women both in prison and upon their eventual return to the community.

As noted by the numerous studies and commissions that have investigated the mentally ill in the criminal justice system, cross-system collaboration is a characteristic of virtually all successful programs. With correctional facilities serving as a vital link in the broader mental health service continuum, information-sharing protocols and consistent standards of practice in correctional institutions and the community are the essential ingredients of best practices. In addition, coordination of service provision among providers in the prison environment is critical in meeting the multifaceted needs of women with serious mental illness and entails coordinated case management and treatment planning for care in prison and beyond.

Clinical services for women with mental illness must extend past symptom management and move toward a whole-life approach that recognizes the significant range of continuing problems and issues that will face women following their release. Coordinated program approaches must integrate psycho-pharmaceutical interventions with differentiated, gender-responsive approaches that integrate the themes of trauma, family, empowerment, and relationships.

Effective prison-based practice must focus on reentry, recognizing that community reintegration begins at the front door of the prison. Correctional systems certainly must respond to immediate needs, but it is equally critical that they remain focused on the "light at the end of the tunnel." Along these lines, success rests on the extent of the community-based capacity to overcome the complex range of challenges faced by women offenders with mental illness through the implementation of integrated systems of treatment, supervision, and coordinated community supports.

The implementation of many of the programmatic provisions discussed in this chapter requires significant investments in staffing, training, physical facilities, information infrastructure, and program development. Although common sense suggests that some of these costs can be offset by reduced correctional expenditures (e.g., operational costs associated with responding to adverse incidents), correctional institutions committed to improving the care of women with mental illness must inevitably invest additional program funds, either through the procurement of new dollars or reallocation of current departmental resources.

From a cost-benefit perspective, policymakers must look beyond facility walls to the broader system of correctional mental health. In the public safety realm, effective prison-based services are pivotal to reducing future criminal involvement. From the perspective of public behavioral health, prisons must be seen for what they are: crucial points of intervention for some of the most challenged and vulnerable individuals under the care of the public mental health system.

## References

Althouse, R. (2000). Standards for psychological services in jails, prisons, correctional facilities, and agencies. *Criminal Justice and Behavior*, *27*, 433–494.

American Correctional Association. (2002). *Performance-based standards for correctional health care in adult correctional institutions*. Lanham, MD: American Correctional Association, Department of Standards and Accreditation.

Appelbaum, K. L., Hickey, J. M., & Packer, I. (2001). The role of correctional officers in multidisciplinary mental health care in prisons. *Psychiatric Services*, *52*, 1343–1347.

Auerhahn, K., & Leonard, E. D. (2000). Docile bodies? Chemical restraints and the female inmate. *Journal of Criminal Law and Criminology*, *90*, 634.

Beck, A. J., & Harrison, P. M. (2001). *Prisoners in 2000*. Washington, DC: U.S. Department of Justice, Government Printing Office.

Beck, A. J., & Maruschak, L. M. (2001). *Mental health treatment in state prisons, 2000*. Washington, DC: U.S. Department of Justice, Government Printing Office.

Blitz, C. L., Wolff, N., & Paap, K. (2006). Availability of behavioral health treatment for women in prison. *Psychiatric Services*, *57*, 360.

Bloom, B., Owen, B., & Covington, S. (2005). *Gender-responsive strategies for women offenders*. Longmont, CO: National Institute of Corrections.

*Brad H. v. City of New York*, 712 336 (Supreme Court of New York 2000).

*Bradley v. Haley* (USDC Middle District of Alabama 2001).

*Coleman v. Wilson*, 912 1282 (Eastern District of California 1995).

Collins, W. C. (1995) The courts' role in shaping prison suicide policy. In L. M. Hayes (Ed.), *Prison suicide: An overview and guide to prevention*. Longmont, CO: National Institute of Corrections.

Council of State Governments. (2002). *Criminal justice/mental health consensus project*. New York: Council of State Governments Eastern Regional Conference.

Council of State Governments. (2005). *Report of the Reentry Policy Council: Charting the safe and successful return of prisoners to the community*. New York: Council of State Governments.

*D. M. v. Terhune*, 67 401 (D.N.J. 1999).

*Dunn v. Voinovich* C1-93-0166 (S.D. Ohio, 1995).

Dvoskin, J. A., & Spiers, E. M. (2004). On the role of correctional officers in prison mental health. *Psychiatric Quarterly*, 75, 41–59.

Earthrowl, M., & McCully, R. (2002). Screening new inmates in a female prison. *Journal of Forensic Psychiatry*, 13, 439.

Ford, J., & Trestman, R. (2005). *Evidence-based enhancement of the detection, prevention, and treatment of mental illness in correctional systems: Final report*. Retrieved January 13, 2007, from http://www.ncjrs.org/pdffiles1/nij/grants/210829.pdf

Greer, K. (2000). The changing nature of interpersonal relationships in a women's prison. *Prison Journal*, 80, 442–468.

Harlow, C. (1999). *Prior abuse reported by inmates and probationers*. Washington, DC: U.S. Department of Justice, Government Printing Office.

Harrison, P. M., & Beck, A. J. (2002). *Prisoners in 2001*. Washington, DC: U.S. Department of Justice, Government Printing Office.

Harrison, P. M., & Beck, A. J. (2003). *Prisoners in 2002*. Washington, DC: U.S. Department of Justice, Government Printing Office.

Harrison, P. M., & Beck, A. J. (2006). *Prisoners in 2005*. Washington, DC: U.S. Department of Justice, Government Printing Office.

Henderson, D., Schaeffer, J., & Brown, L. C. (1998). Gender-appropriate mental health services for incarcerated women: Issues and challenges. *Family and Community Health, 21,* 42–53.

Hills, H., Siegfried, C., & Ickowitz, A. (2004). *Effective prison mental health services: Guidelines to expand and improve treatment*. Longmont, CO: National Institute of Corrections.

Human Rights Watch. (2003). *Ill equipped: U.S. prisons and offenders with mental illness*. New York: Human Rights Watch.

James, D. J., & Glaze, L. E. (2006). *Mental health problems of prison and jail*. Washington, DC: U.S. Department of Justice, Government Printing Office.

*Jones v. Berge*, 164 1096 (Western District, Wisconsin 2001).

Laishes, J. (2002). *The 2002 mental health strategy for women offenders*. Ottawa, CN: Correctional Service of Canada.

*Laube v. Haley*, 234 1227 (M.D. Ala. 2002).

*Madrid v. Gomez*, 889 1146 (Northern District, California 1995).

Manderscheid, R. W., Gravesande, A., & Goldstrom, I. D. (2004). Growth of mental health services in state adult correctional facilities, 1988 to 2000. *Psychiatric Services*, 55, 869–872.

Mauer, M., & Chesney-Lind, M. (2001). *Invisible punishments: The collateral consequences of mass imprisonment*. New York: The Free Press.

Metzner, J. L. (1998). An introduction to correctional psychiatry: Part III. *Journal of the American Academy of Psychiatry and the Law*, 26, 115.

Mumola, C. (2000). *Incarcerated parents and their children*. Washington, DC: U.S. Department of Justice, Government Printing Office.

Mumola, C. (2006). *Drug use and dependence: State and federal prisoners, 2004*. Washington, DC: U.S. Department of Justice, Government Printing Office.

National Commission on Correctional Health Care. (2003). *Standards for health services in prisons*. Chicago: National Commission on Correctional Health Care.

Nee, C., & Farman, S. (2005). Female prisoners with borderline personality disorder: Some promising treatment developments. *Criminal Behavior and Mental Health*, 15, 2–16.

New Freedom Commission on Mental Health. (2003). *Achieving the promise: transforming mental health care in America: Final report*. Rockville, MD: President's New Freedom Commission on Mental Health.

New York State Office of Mental Health. (2003). *Intermediate care program manual.* Albany: New York State Office of Mental Health: New York State Department of Correctional Services.

New York State Office of Mental Health. (2005). *2005–2009 Statewide comprehensive plans for mental health services—Chapter 7: Forensic services.* Retrieved March 2007 from http://www.omh.state.ny.us/omhweb/statewideplan/2005/chapter7.htm

New York State Office of Mental Health. (2006). *Therapeutic behavioral management unit program manual.* Albany: New York State Office of Mental Health/New York State Department of Correctional Services.

Office of the Surgeon General. (1999). *Mental health: A report of the Surgeon General.* Rockville, MD: Department of Health and Human Services: U.S. Public Health Service.

Pollock, J. M. (2002). *Women, prison, and crime.* Belmont, CA: Wadsworth.

*Ruiz v. Johnson*, 37 856 (Southern District, Texas 1999).

Sharp, S. (2003). *The incarcerated woman.* Upper Saddle River, NJ: Prentice Hall.

Sly, A., & Taylor, K. (2003). *Preliminary evaluation of dialectical behavioral therapy within a women's structured living environment.* Ottawa, CN: Research Branch, Correctional Services of Canada.

Steadman, H. J., Scott, J. E., Osher, F., Agnese, T. K., & Robbins, P. C. (2005). Validation of the Brief Jail Mental Health Screen. *Psychiatric Services, 56*, 822.

Stinchcomb, J. B., & Fox, V. B. (1999). *Introduction to corrections.* Englewood Cliffs, NJ: Prentice Hall.

Vaughn, M. (1997). Civil liability against prison officials for prescribing and dispensing medication and drugs to prison inmates. *Journal of Legal Medicine, 18*, 315–344.

Veysey, B., & Bichler-Robertson, G. (2002). Prevalence estimates of psychiatric disorders in correctional settings. In *Health status of soon-to-be-released inmates: A report to Congress* (Vol. 2, pp. 57–80). Chicago: National Commission on Correctional Health Care.

Weinstein, H. C. (2000). *Psychiatric services in jails and prisons: A task force report of the American Psychiatric Association* (2nd ed.). Washington, DC: American Psychiatric Association.

# CHAPTER 12
# REENTRY NEEDS OF FEMALE MENTALLY ILL OFFENDERS

**Stephanie Hartwell**

**Karin Orr**

## ABSTRACT

Recent criminal justice policies have increased the rates of incarceration, and, although little is known how reentry experiences vary by gender, the number of females in state and federal prisons has also increased. A literature is emerging that suggests female inmates are distinct in their substance abuse histories and treatment needs, trauma histories, employment challenges, healthcare needs and problems, experience of postrelease supervision, social support networks and family relationships, and housing needs. The data presented in this chapter updates previous research on gender differences of mentally ill offenders. The data analysis presents that significant differences across gender continue across demographic, clinical, criminal history, service, and outcome variables. Female offenders are viewed as distinct from their male counterparts by psychiatric and criminal justice professionals as evidenced by their unique mental health service histories, diagnoses, and criminal justice dispositions. This research concludes that gender is, and will continue to be, a significant variable associated with mentally ill offenders' community reintegration and contingent services needed both before and postprison release. Reentry services, whether they are transitional, involve intensive case management, or diversionary, should be gender-specific.

## MENTALLY ILL OFFENDERS

Individuals with psychiatric disabilities are disproportionately represented in the criminal justice system. In her survey of inmates in Cook County jails, Teplin (1990) found four times the rate of mental illness than found in comparable members of the general population (Teplin 1990). Other reports indicate that anywhere from a quarter to nearly half of all individuals with major mental illness become involved with the criminal justice system over their lives and that prisons house three times as many mentally ill persons as hospitals (President's New Freedom Commission on Mental Health, 2002). The American Psychiatric Association reports that 1 in 5 inmates are seriously mentally ill, and 20% of all incarcerated individuals receive some form of psychiatric intervention while incarcerated (Metzner et al., 1998; American Psychiatric Association, 2000).

The appearance of individuals with psychiatric disabilities in the criminal justice system is the result of institutional change including deinstitutionalization of state mental hospitals and the Community Mental Health Center Act of nearly 40 years ago (see, e.g., Fisher, 2003). It was expected that decreasing the use of institutional settings and the use of coercive admissions as a means of controlling deviance exhibited by persons with mental illness would be offset by an expansion of community-based mental health services and advances in psychotropic medications (Hartwell, Fisher, & Davis, 2007). However, current trends working against community-based mental health services include declining reimbursements for psychiatric services as a result of behavioral managed care, reduced Medicare payments, and limited spending on mental health units associated with hospitals (Applebaum, 2002). These fiscal trends and continued deinstitutionalization have resulted in increased numbers of persons with mental illness residing in the community, unable to access treatment.

While individuals with complex and multiple problems confront barriers to hospitalization and services, they are left vulnerable to criminal justice violations in the community, more frequent contact with police, and ultimately criminalization (Draine, 2006; Teplin, McClelland, Abram, & Weiner, 2005). Additionally, in the 1980s and early 1990s, "tough on crime" criminal justice policies were introduced, including mandatory sentencing and three strikes laws that resulted in longer terms of incarceration (Morris & Tony, 1990). These systemic, policy, and psychopharmacologic changes resulted in the presence of more individuals with major mental illness in the community, more individuals in the community coming into contact with the criminal justice system, and, consequently, increased numbers of individuals with mental illness involved with the criminal justice system.

## REENTRY PROGRAMS AND CHALLENGES

Recent criminal justice policies have increased the overall rates of incarceration (Lurigio, Rollins, & Fallon, 2004; Morris & Tony, 1990). For instance, the number of females in state and federal prisons has increased from nearly 12,300 in 1980 to 107,500 (Bureau of Justice Statistics, 2006). Nearly 600,000 individuals are released annually (Roman & Travis, 2005). Given the current estimates, nearly 50,000 of these releases are females (Bureau of Justice Statistics, 2006). Reentry can be hazardous, manifested in the fact that two-thirds of ex-inmates return to the criminal justice system within 3 years of release, and these rates may be elevated for females (McKean & Ransford, 2004). Langan and colleagues (2002) tracked ex-inmates for 3 years after release in 15 states and found 67.5% were rearrested, 46.9% were reconvicted, 25% were resentenced for a new crime, and 52% returned to prison for a new crime or technical violation (Langan & Levin, 2002). Whether returned to correctional custody on a technical violation of parole/probation or for a new offense, this rebounding or recidivating to the criminal justice system is consequential and costly.

Variables cited to reduce recidivism among the general population of ex-inmates include stable housing, substance abuse treatment, educational programming, and employment (McKean & Ransford, 2004; Roman & Travis, 2004). However, released inmates often return to disadvantaged communities with few resources. For instance, nearly 30% have a history of homelessness. For individuals who lack family connections and finances, there are few viable housing alternatives to shelters post-release (Roman & Travis, 2004).

The Urban Institute conducted a four-state study focusing on the experiences of inmates postrelease from state correctional facilities (Travis, 2005). In interviews with male clients pre- and postrelease in Texas, Illinois, Maryland, and Ohio, a range of reentry challenges were highlighted as factors associated with postrelease success or failure. These factors included managing substance abuse histories and problems, finding gainful employment, having positive attitudes and beliefs about reentry, receiving health care benefits to deal with elevated rates of health problems, supervised release programs to monitor prosocial engagement including substance abuse treatment and employment, financial and housing support from families, and community environments with programs, mentoring, and housing (Travis, 2005; Visher & Courtney, 2006). The intent of this series of studies is to present the released prisoners' view on reentry and to highlight the necessity of particular programs and social supports that are essential to reentry postincarceration. However, little is known how these experiences vary by gender or for individuals with special needs such as major mental illness. A small body of literature on reentry programs for individuals with mental illness suggests that, without specialized services, mentally ill individuals who are released from correctional custody will fare poorly. Estimates run as high as two-thirds of mentally ill ex-inmates will be arrested and one-half will be hospitalized within 18 months of release if appropriate services are not provided (Feder, 1992; Hartwell, 2003).

## GENDER AND CORRECTIONAL REENTRY

Although females comprise approximately 7% of all inmates (Bureau of Justice Statistics, 2006), little is known about the extent to which they differ from their male counterparts in terms of their reentry needs. Nevertheless, a literature is emerging that suggests female inmates are distinct in their substance abuse histories and treatment needs, trauma histories, employment challenges, health care needs and problems, experience of postrelease supervision, social support networks and family relationships, and housing needs (Hartwell, 2001). To begin, female inmates are disproportionately more likely to commit nonviolent, drug, or property-related crimes (Andrews & Bonta, 1994; Broidy & Agnew, 1997; Bureau of Justice Statistics, 2006; Chesney-Lind, 1989; Daly & Chesney-Lind, 1988; Pajer, 1998; Teplin et al., 1996; Veysey, 1998). Nearly one-half report being physically and/or sexually abused during their lives, and although the rates are increasing, far fewer male inmates report the same victimization (Bureau of Justice Statistics, 1994; Bureau of Justice Statistics, 2006; Jacobson, 1989; Morash et al., 1998; Seiden, 1989). Thus, female inmates come to prison with distinct criminal profiles and backgrounds.

In terms of their behavioral health and social service needs, female inmates have elevated rates of mental illness and HIV (Bureau of Justice Statistics, 2006). Consistent with rates in the community, female inmates are more likely than male inmates to be diagnosed with a serious mental illness (Teplin et al., 1996). Estimates suggest that 16% of all males and 24% of all females in state prisons have a psychiatric disability, whereas 10% of male and 18% of female inmates are estimated to have an Axis I major disorder of thought or mood (Ditton, 1999; Pinta, 2001). Additionally, two-thirds are single parents and within that group, many lose custody of their children or are hoping to regain custody, raising specific social service needs and involvement. Finally, their histories of substance abuse, trauma, and health problems, as well as the constraints and challenges of being a mother, can interfere with consistent employment in the community, their social relationships, and their housing (Bureau of Justice Statistics, 2006; Pajer, 1998; Veysey, 1998).

In general, coping with the adjustment from prison to the community presents exceptional challenges for individuals with mental illness and criminal histories (Hartwell, 2003), and these challenges vary, in some part, based on gender. The reentry experiences of mentally ill females are worthy of exploration, but first their characteristics and service needs must be articulated.

## METHODS

The data presented updates previous research on gender differences of mentally ill offenders (Hartwell, 2001). It analyzes data on mentally ill offenders tracked for 3 months post-prison release by the Massachusetts Department of Mental Health, Forensic Transition Team program, since April 1, 1998. The data set has information on 1,145 mentally ill offenders, 228 or 20% of whom are female. Basic data categories include (a) demographic information(age, race, gender, ethnicity, and education); (b) clinical informationon primary diagnosis and mental health service history; (c) criminal history information including current criminal charge; (d) service information including housing and treatment needs such as substance abuse, sex offender, vocational training, and social club membership; and (e) outcome information on client dispositions postrelease such as engaged in community services, hospitalized, returned to prison, or disengaged from treatment. Simple cross-tabular and tests of significance were used to provide this comparison of male and female mentally ill offenders.

## FINDINGS

Significant differences across gender were found in each of the five data categories: (a) demographic information (age, region, and education), (b) clinical information (primary diagnosis and mental health service history), (c) criminal history information (current charge, violation of probationary status/parole), (d) service information (homelessness, substance abuse, sex offender treatment), and (e) outcome information (recidivism to the criminal justice system and hospitalization). Among the variables *not found* to differ by gender were race/ethnicity (approximately 65% White, 20% Black, and 14% Hispanic), rate of receiving probation (19%) or parole (9%) upon release, substance abuse (65%), and percentage of clients recidivating after 3 months of release (21%).

The remainder of this discussion focuses exclusively on the significant variables. In terms of demographics, females are less likely to be 45 years old or older (18% males vs. 10% of the females). In terms of education, the distribution by gender is bimodal: one-fifth (18%) of males and (19%) females had only grade school education. Females were less likely to complete high school or a GED (24% compared with 32% of the males), but *more likely* to have some college (25% vs. 11% of the men). This pattern breaks from the notion of female offenders having lower levels of education overall, in that for those who did complete high school have higher levels of educational attainment than their male counterparts. Perhaps age of illness onset or "first break" patterns manifest themselves in the lives of females and males at different times, or more likely, their different diagnoses influence levels of educational attainment to greater and lesser extents.

The males and females also vary in terms of the type of correctional setting from which they are released. Females in Massachusetts are more likely to be incarcerated in Framingham State Prison instead of a county house of correction regardless of whether they are serving a misdemeanor or felony sentence. This deficiency is an artifact of a corrections system that primarily held men for many years. A majority of this state's county corrections facilities still do not have the capacity to house women, and the vast majority of the beds for incarcerated females are concentrated at MCI Framingham.

This geographic variation has implications for services provided during incarceration including release planning as well as community relocation postrelease. For instance, correctional treatment services provided to those serving "county sentences" at the women's prison are abbreviated, and postrelease service planning is a priority. Thus, the needs of females serving county sentences must be identified at the state facility for optimal release and relocation plans including transportation upon release. Men serving time for misdemeanors are housed in the county system (61%), and those serving longer sentences for more severe felony crimes are incarcerated in Massachusetts Correctional Institutions (MCI) prison facilities located across the state (39%).

Because females comprise such a small percentage of all inmates, each state's arrangement for the incarceration of females often differs from men and has differing implications at time of release. Although consolidated in a single institution in Massachusetts, females have distinct patterns of reentry in terms of communities or areas they return to. They are more likely to return to urban and suburban areas rather than rural areas, perhaps due to social networks including family or their history of service linkages. They are also less likely than their male counterparts to be immediately homeless at release (21% vs. 28% of the males), but the quality of their living arrangements may cause them to be at risk, reflecting their higher rates of recidivism in the 3 months following release (this is discussed further in later sections of this chapter).

Similar to other female offenders, mentally ill females are more likely to serve sentences for property and public order crimes (46% female vs. 41% men) than person-related crimes (37% female vs. 48% men). They are also more likely than men to commit drug-defined crimes (15% female vs. 9% men). Although they are no more likely to receive parole or probation as a portion of their sentence than their male counterparts (19%), females are more likely to violate probation and parole (at a rate of

**TABLE 12.1** Significant differences between female and male mentally ill offenders[a]

| Variable | Male (n = 595) | | Female (n = 151) | | X2 | df | significance |
|---|---|---|---|---|---|---|---|
| | n | % | n | % | | | |
| **Demographics** | | | | | | | |
| Age (<46) | 755 | 82 | 205 | 90 | 12.04 | 2 | ** |
| Education (some college) | 36 | 11 | 26 | 25 | 16.87 | 7 | * |
| **Clinical Features** | | | | | | | |
| Primary Disorder | | | | | 66.83 | 4 | *** |
| Thought | 512 | 59 | 68 | 31 | | | |
| Mood | 311 | 36 | 121 | 56 | | | |
| Personality | 25 | 3 | 23 | 11 | | | |
| Service History | 659 | 72 | 190 | 83 | 12.53 | 1 | *** |
| **Criminal History** | | | | | | | |
| Charge (person related) | 419 | 48 | 79 | 37 | 29.45 | 7 | *** |
| Technical Violation (parole/probation) | 143 | 16 | 61 | 27 | 16.14 | 1 | *** |
| **Service Needs** | | | | | | | |
| Housing/Homeless | 258 | 28 | 47 | 21 | 5.29 | 1 | ** |
| Sex Offender Treatment | 128 | 14 | 9 | 4 | 17.37 | 1 | *** |
| Violence Assessment | 135 | 15 | 19 | 8 | 6.43 | 1 | ** |
| **Outcome** | | | | | 13.08 | 6 | * |
| Engaged | 376 | 41 | 100 | 44 | | | |
| Lost | 114 | 12 | 33 | 15 | | | |
| Hospitalized | 217 | 24 | 36 | 15 | | | |
| Recidivate | 141 | 15 | 44 | 20 | | | |

[a]Totals and percentages may not add up due to missing data or variables removed for analysis.

All variables in tables are statistically significant.

**P<.01

*P<.05

***P<.001

27% vs. 16% of the males). This higher rate of violating correctional oversight while in the community is suggestive of the difficulties females have in finding opportunities to remove themselves from their criminal lifestyles/networks (see Table 12.1).

In terms of postrelease services for the mentally ill offender, although there are no differences in substance abuse treatment need (65%) by gender, females are more likely to be involved in drug dealing activities and public order offenses suggestive of a lower level criminality involving the drug dealing, prostitution nexus. This nexus can be found in the areas females return to postrelease and results in patterns of probation/parole violations (for individuals receiving parole/probation), re-arrest, and reincarceration. Thus, substance abuse and addiction among the females forces them into a distinct pattern of criminality. Females are also more likely to have a history of service use including mental health services (83% vs. 72% of the males), which may help many females overcome negative social networks with more pro-social supports. Still, it seems for females that these patterns of criminality, substance abuse, and post-release communal returns do not vary from females who lack diagnostic mental illnesses. Consistent with diagnostic patterns in the community, the female offenders who have Axis I diagnoses are more likely to have a primary diagnosis of mood disorder (56% vs. 36% of males) and personality disorder (11% vs. 3% of males), but both disorders are more likely to go undetected in the context of substance abuse.

Finally, short-term 3-month postrelease outcomes vary by gender. It seems the female offenders with mental illness are more likely than their male counterparts to be engaged in services postrelease. This could be due to their relatively short sentences given the nature of their offenses and their connection or reconnection with their pre-existing service network. However, they are also more likely to be lost to follow-up (15% vs. 12%) and recidivate to prison on a technical violation or new charge (20% vs. 15%). Conversely, the males are more likely to be hospitalized (24% vs. 15%), probably due to the nature of their criminality and their clinical diagnosis. Males are more likely to be thought disordered rather than mood disordered. Individuals with mood disorders appear to be perceived as being easier to manage in the community than individuals with schizophrenia. Nevertheless, females are more likely than men to recidivate to the criminal justice system (20% females vs. 15% men). Perhaps a history of service need and reliance coupled with the shorter sentences females receive for public order and property crimes cycles them through the criminal justice system at a faster rate. For instance, prostitution and drug-related crimes—frequently in conjunction—are a means to make money and survive, and attenuated work and family relationships can make finding the support to live in the community difficult and criminal activity more compelling.

## SERVICE NEEDS

Given that the female mentally ill offenders in Massachusetts transitioned to date are not predatory offenders or murderers, diversion from the criminal justice system seems appropriate and arguably necessary to address their low level criminality ranging from nuisances to public order, property, and drug dealing related crimes. Mental health and substance abuse services may also provide support to maintain these individuals in the community rather than a hospital setting or the revolving door of the criminal justice system where they often fail in community correction programs violating conditions of probation or parole. Cross-training is necessary among probation and parole officers regarding their performance under correctional surveillance to understand that although females are less peripheral to the crime problem, their needs are often interrelated, and they are more likely to be imprisoned for lesser offenses or technical violations.

Female offenders differ in significant ways from their male counterparts. Prior to incarceration and upon release, they return to a community where they have distinct social roles. They are also viewed as distinct from their male counterparts by psychiatric and criminal justice professionals, as evidenced by their significantly different mental health service histories, diagnoses, and criminal justice dispositions—all social constructions. They are viewed as a decreased public safety risk and often forced to engage in alternative community survival strategies due to their social roles (single, unemployed mother with criminal history and psychiatric problems), including but not limited to social service use and low-level criminality. Thus, gender is and will continue to be a significant variable associated with mentally ill offenders' community reintegration and contingent services needed prior to and post-prison release, and reentry services, whether they are transitional, involve intensive case management, or diversionary, should be gender-specific.

In response to this need, the Massachusetts Department of Correction began funding the Women's Transition Program (initiated in 2003), a reentry program for females recently released from correctional custody or who are on probation or parole. The primary program objective is to reduce criminal recidivism by facilitating access to each female's specific needs upon release to the community. The program was explicitly funded to work with females who were not otherwise eligible for state services due to their higher level of psychiatric functioning, but who, nevertheless, had multiple needs upon community reentry. Program staff provide case management with assessment and engagement beginning prior to release from incarceration. Females in the program work with a case manager who assists them in developing an individualized service plan to help them meet their postrelease goals such as locating stable housing, participating in substance abuse, medical and mental health treatment, improving their parenting skills, and finding gainful employment. Programs such as the Massachusetts' Women's Transition Program are articulated to address the needs of females reentering the community postincarceration identified in the research data presented above.

## CONCLUSIONS

Draine and colleagues (2005) developed a conceptual framework for considering reentry for offenders with special needs—the "shared responsibility and interdependent model." This framework suggests that community reintegration for ex-offenders with mental illness is typically complex due to the social environments they return to, their limited social capital, and their individual characteristics. This framework focuses on the social dynamics of reentry that impact the flow of resources between individuals and their communities (Draine, Wolff, Jacoby, Hartwell, & Duclos, 2005). It proposes that successful community reentry is an interdependent process between the individual (personal history) and environment (social context). Furthermore, it identifies features like treatment availability and social processes as factors that influence the flow of resources between individuals and their communities, thereby providing the context for reentry. Community features such as public and private resources in employment, housing, and health services and treatment (substance abuse, mental health, and specialty services) subsume individual features highlighted here including age, education, service histories, diagnostic and criminal profiles, homelessness, and short-term outcomes. Thus, this framework is useful in thinking about reentry in general and may be particularly useful in working with female mentally ill offenders given the complexity of their needs, social histories of more formal service supports, and their varied ability to access or effectively utilize resources.

Draine and colleagues (2005) argue for the necessity of *the interaction* of individuals and service systems in the context of community settings, and emphasize the importance of community context stating, "to help meet the needs of individuals with mental illness leaving prison, communities will have to devote substantial, varied innovative resources to this purpose and reduce barriers to accessing those resources" (Draine et al., 2005, p. 705). Practically, this means emphasizing community involvement in promoting women's reentry, including encouraging relationships between community members, mentors, and program staff to strengthen any reentry initiative. And perhaps most critically for female reentry programming is the provision of case management services to stabilize family and parenting issues. As this research shows, females are distinct from their male counterparts in clinical and criminal features and in their needs on return to their communities. Appropriate identification of their needs and assistance with access to appropriate services can significantly affect the success of their reentry after release from incarceration.

## References

American Psychiatric Association. (2000). Introduction. In American Psychiatric Association (Ed.), *Psychiatric services in jails and prison* (2nd ed.). Washington, DC: American Psychiatric Association.

Andrews, D. A., & Bonta, J. (1994). *The psychology of criminal conduct*. Cincinnati, OH: Anderson.

Appelbaum, P. S. (2002). Starving in the midst of plenty: The mental health care crisis in America. *Psychiatric Services, 53*, 247–252.

Broidy, L., & Agnew, R. (1997). Gender and crime: A general strain theory perspective. *Journal of Research in Crime and Delinquency, 34*, 275–306.

Bureau of Justice Statistics, U.S. Department of Justice. (1994). *Special report: Women in prison* (NCJ 145321). Washington, DC: U.S. Government Printing Office.

Bureau of Justice Statistics, U.S. Department of Justice. (2006). *Factsheet: Women in prison*. Washington, DC: U.S. Government Printing Office.

Chesney-Lind, M. (1989). Girls, crime and a woman's place: Toward a feminist model of female delinquency. *Crime and Delinquency, 35*, 5–29.

Daly, K., & Chesney-Lind, M. (1988). Feminism in criminology. *Justice Quarterly, 5*, 497–535.

Ditton, P. M. (1999). *Mental health and treatment of inmates and probationers* (NCJ 174463). Washington, DC: U.S. Department of Justice, Bureau of Justice Statistics.

Draine, J. (2003). Where is the illness in the criminalization of the mentally ill? In W. H. Fisher (Ed.), *Community-based interventions for criminal offenders with severe mental illness* (pp. 9–24). New York: Elsevier.

Draine, J., Wolff, N., Jacoby, J., Hartwell, S., & Duclos, C. (2005). Understanding community reentry among former prisoners with mental illness: A conceptual model to move new research. *Behavioral Sciences & the Law, 23*, 689–707.

Feder, L. (1991). A comparison of the community adjustment of mentally ill offenders with those from the general population. *Law and Human Behavior, 15*, 477–493.

Fisher, W. H. (Ed.). (2003). *Community based interventions for criminal offenders with severe mental illness*. New York: Elsevier.

Freudenberg, N. (2004). Adverse effects of U.S. jail and prison policies on the health and well-being of women of color. *American Journal of Public Health, 92*, 1895–1899.

Freudenberg, N., Daniels, J., Crum, M., Perkins, T., & Richie, B. E. (2005). Coming home from jail: The social and health consequences of community reentry for women, male adolescents, and their families and communities. *American Journal of Public Health, 95*, 1725–1736.

Harrison, P., & Beck, A. (2005). *Prisoners in 2004* (NCJ 210677). Washington, DC: U.S. Department of Justice, Bureau of Justice Statistics.

Hartwell, S. (2001). Female mentally ill offenders and their community reintegration needs: An initial examination. *International Journal of Law and Psychiatry, 24*, 1–11.

Hartwell, S. (2003). Short term outcomes for offenders with mental illness released from incarceration. *International Journal of Offender Therapy and Comparative Criminology, 47,* 145–158.

Jacobson, A. (1989). Physical and sexual histories among psychiatric outpatients. *American Journal of Psychiatry, 146,* 755–758.

Langan, P. A., & Levin, D. J. (2002). *Recidivism of prisoners released in 1994.* (NCJ 193427). Washington, DC: U.S. Department of Justice, Bureau of Justice Statistics.

Lurigio, A. J., Rollins, A., & Fallon, J. (2004). The effects of serious mental illness on offender reentry. *Federal Probation, 68,* 2. Retrieved January 28, 2008, from http://www.uscourts.gov/fedprob/September_2004/illness.html

Metzner, J., Cohen, F., Grossman, L. S., & Wettstein, R. M. (1998). Treatment in jails and prisons. In R. M. Wettstein (Ed.), *Treatment of offenders with mental disorders* (pp. 211–264). New York: The Guilford Press.

McKean, L., & Ransford, C. (2004). Current strategies for reducing recidivism. Chicago: Center for Impact Research. Retrieved January 25, 2007, from http://www.issuelab.com/downloads/8764recidivismfullreport.pdf

Morash, M., Bynum, T. S., & Koons, B. A. (1998). *Women offenders: Programming needs and promising approaches.* Washington, DC: National Institute of Justice.

Morris, N., & Tonry, M. (1990). *Between prison and probation: Intermediate punishments in a rational sentencing system.* New York: Oxford University Press.

Pajer, K. A. (1998). What happens to "bad" girls? A review of the adult outcomes of antisocial adolescent girls. *American Journal of Psychiatry, 155,* 862–870.

Pinta, E. (2001). The prevalence of serious mental disorders among U.S. prisoners. In G. Landsberg & A. Smiley (Eds.), *Forensic mental health: Working with offenders with mental illness.* Kingston, NJ: Civic Research Institute.

President's New Freedom Commission on Mental Health. (2002, October 29). *Interim Report of the President's New Freedom Commission on Mental Health.* Washington, DC: Author.

Roman, C. G., & Travis, J. (2004). *Taking stock: Housing, homelessness and prisoner reentry.* Washington, DC: The Urban Institute. Retrieved January 28, 2008, from http://www.urban.org/url.cfm?ID=411096

Teplin, L. A. (1990). The prevalence of severe mental disorder among male urban jail detainees: Comparison with the epidemiologic catchment area program. *American Journal of Public Health, 80,* 663–669.

Teplin, L. A., Abram, K. M., & McClelland, G. M. (1996). Prevalence of psychiatric disorders among incarcerated women. *Archives of General Psychiatry, 53,* 505–512.

Teplin, L. A., McClelland, G., Abram, K. M., & Weiner, D. (2005). Crime victimization in adults with severe mental illness: Comparison with the national crime victimization survey. *Archives of General Psychiatry, 62,* 911–921.

Travis, J. (2005). *But they all come back: Facing the challenges of prisoner reentry.* Washington, DC: Urban Institute Press.

Veysey, B. M. (1998). Specific needs of women diagnosed with mental illness in U.S. jails. In B. L. Levin, A. K. Blanch, & A. Jennings (Eds.), *Women's mental health services: A public health perspective* (pp. 368–389). Thousand Oaks, CA: Sage.

Visher, C., & Courtney, S. M. E. (2006). *Cleveland prisoners' experiences returning home.* Washington, DC: The Urban Institute.

# CHAPTER 13

# BUILDING "PERSON-FIRST" REENTRY STRATEGIES FOR WOMEN LEAVING PRISON FROM THE PERSPECTIVES OF THE END USERS

## The Returning Women

### Nancy Wolff

## ABSTRACT

Reentry planning is a systematic and active effort to assist incarcerated persons to reintegrate into the community postincarceration. These plans work best when they reflect an accurate understanding of the returning person's strengths, needs, risks, and concerns, as well as the community's reluctance to respond to the person in ways that affirm and support their successful transition to independence and prosocial living. Herein we describe a person-focused strategy for empowering successful reintegration and recovery of women. The chapter has two objectives. The first is to profile the women inside prison and their needs and risks as they enter and leave the institution. The focus is on characteristics of incarcerated women that shape and challenge their reentry experience. The second objective is to respond to their strengths and challenges through a reentry strategy that has three separate but overlapping parts: empowerment, reintegration, and recovery, each with elements of information, skill building, resources, and support. The chapter concludes with recommendations for getting reentry right for women leaving prison. "Getting reentry right" means designing, implementing, and funding a person- and healing-focused, community-based reentry program that gives women the best chance to embrace their latent potential to be healthy and productive women of deliberate choice.

*Support for the research was provided by the Center for Mental Health Services & Criminal Justice Research (Grant #P20 MH66170).*

> The data are very clear concerning the distinguishing aspects of female and male offenders. They come into the criminal justice via different pathways; . . . exhibit differences in terms of substance abuse trauma, mental illness, parenting responsibilities, and employment histories; and represent different levels of risk. . . . (Bloom, Owen, & Covington, 2003)

Women account for approximately 7% of the prison population (Harrison & Beck, 2005). Although small in number, their ranks are growing. Each year since 1990, the number of women in prison has increased, often at a rate that exceeds their male counterparts (Beck & Harrison, 2001; Greenfeld & Snell, 1999; Harrison & Beck, 2005). As their numbers have grown, attention has centered on whether incarcerated women are different and, if so, what the implications are of these differences in terms of their needs inside prison and upon release to the community (Petersilia, 2003; Richie, 2001). Most often incarcerated women have been differentiated by type of crime, which, compared to their male counterparts, is typically less violent, and more related to drugs and directed at their intimates (Snell, 1994). The incarcerated woman also has been distinguished by her relationship history, responsibilities, and needs. The preponderance of incarcerated women have mental health problems (James & Glaze, 2006); histories of sexual, physical, and emotional abuse (Browne, Miller, & Maguin, 1999; Curry, 2001; Ditton, 1999); children for whom they have primary responsibility; and a desire for supportive relationships (Wagaman, 2003).

The growing recognition that women's pathways to prison and the challenges that they bring with them are gendered (Belknap, 2001; Fruedenberg et al., 2005; Richie, 2001; Tonkin et al., 2004; Wald, 2001) is beginning to inform the development of services that respond to their needs during incarceration and upon release to the community. Indeed, the first guiding principle in the National Institute of Correction's monograph entitled *Gender-Responsive Strategies* is to "acknowledge that gender makes a difference" (Bloom, Owen, & Covington, 2003). Accordingly, pressures have mounted to develop and provide gender-specific programming in prison settings (American Correctional Association, 1995; Bloom, Owen, & Covington, 2003; Morash & Bynum, 1999; Sharp, 2006). Although best-practice evidence is lacking here, there is an abundance of evidence showing that the vast majority of women inside prison have "wounds" associated with being survivors of extreme and sustained neglect, cruelty, personal disregard, and poverty (Ferraro, 2006; Ferraro & Moe, 2003; Girshick, 2003). The wounds of incarcerated women have their origins in place and in context of intimate relationships that together inform (and misinform) their sense of worth and behavior (Ferraro, 2006). Incarcerated women, because they are drawn disproportionately from impoverished communities (Rose & Clear, 1998; Sampson, Morenoff, & Gannon-Rowley, 2002), have literacy; vocational, life, parenting, social, and interpersonal skills; and a health status that reflect the social geography of impoverished neighborhoods—the substandard housing and schools, inadequate access to health care, and high rates of unemployment, crime, drug use, and violence. Inexplicably, the social history of their wounds often gets lost in the process of repair, especially in prison environments where healing and recovery are not primary functions or goals.

Focusing on the individual wounds (e.g., mental health problems, substance abuse, lack of vocational skills) of incarcerated women in isolation, separate from their history and social geography, or as separable and independent units, has quick-fix appeal in ways analogous to using *Botox* injections to erase the evidence of aging. In both cases, with an injection, the evidence of the unwanted disappears but, with time, the process generating that which is unwanted persists and regenerates itself, requiring yet another injection—creating a revolving door for episodic repair. Quick fixes, although easily marketed to policy makers and oft-times lucrative for provider agencies, fail in the long run because they do not understand (or acknowledge) and work with the process creating the wounds, a process that is central to healing and recovery. Building programs that focus on a specific "wound" and its need to be repaired in lieu of the causal and complicated process within the whole person is hazardous to the well-being of the woman, her family, and society, even if measured narrowly by rates of recidivism (Kubrin & Stewart, 2006) and mortality postrelease from prison (Binswanger et al., 2007).

Person-focused, healing approaches are recommended for people with co-occurring wounds (Wilson & Draine, 2006) in part because they see the woman as a whole, autonomous person who is responsible, with support, for her recovery. The goal of such approaches is to marshal the woman's strengths and cooperation in a process through which she is empowered to accept and manage effectively the constellation of needs, challenges, and risks that characterize her life and define, at least in part, who she is now and who she wants to be in the future. In empowering women, it is vital that those developing interventions and coaching their implementation understand that the constellation of needs-challenges-risks varies within the population (i.e., there is not a single constellation that describes all women; each has her own) and that these constellations are themselves dynamic, shifting with situation and circumstances, and uniquely interdependent, with contagions of reactions instigated within a constellation and across constellations by a single change—an event, word, action, or inaction.

Herein we describe a person-focused strategy for empowering the successful reintegration and recovery of women leaving prison. This chapter has two objectives. The first is to profile the women inside prison and their needs and strengths as they enter and leave the institution. The focus is on the characteristics of incarcerated women that shape and challenge their reentry experience. The second objective is to respond to their strengths, needs, challenges, and risks through a reentry strategy that has three separate but overlapping parts: empowerment, reintegration, and recovery. This strategy is informed by two research studies that focused on women and reentry. One study conducted by the author was based in New Jersey and addressed the needs and risks of women with mental health disorders (ranging from schizophrenia to anxiety disorder), most often with co-occurring substance use disorder (Wolff, 2005). The second study was a "first person" investigation into reentry from the perspective of 100 incarcerated women who were 6 months or less from release and resided in prisons located in six states. These women were engaged in discussions about their reentry concerns, needs, and risks, and in the design of a reentry program that was responsive to their articulated concerns, needs, and risks. The chapter concludes with recommendations for getting reentry right for women leaving prison. "Getting reentry right" means designing, implementing, and funding a person- and healing-focused, community-based reentry program that gives women the best chance to embrace their latent potential to be healthy and productive women of deliberate choice.

## THE PROFILE OF WOMEN INSIDE PRISON

Women represent the fastest-growing component of the correctional population (Greenfeld & Snell, 1999; Harrison & Beck, 2005). Like their male counterparts, these women are disproportionately African-American and Hispanic (Harrison & Beck, 2005). Compared to men, however, incarcerated women are younger and considerably more likely to be the sole or primary parent of young children (Fletcher, Shaver, & Moon, 1993; Morash, Haar, & Rucker, 1994; Richie, 2001). It is estimated that incarcerated women are mothers of 1.3 million minor children (Greenfeld & Snell, 1999). Most often their children are displaced while the women are incarcerated (Mumola, 2000).

Upon release from prison, returning women face significant barriers associated with their criminal convictions that affect their ability to qualify for public benefits, public housing, and jobs (Legal Action Center, 2004; Richie, 2001). Restrictions are greatest for women with prior drug and/or violent convictions (Allard, 2002). Roughly one-third of women in prison have convictions for drug possession or distribution (Blitz, Wolff, Pan, & Pogorzelski, 2005; Greenfeld & Snell, 1999). These individuals are permanently prohibited from enrolling in welfare reform programs in some states and conditionally limited in many other states (Pogorzelski, Wolff, Pan, & Blitz, 2005). Drug convictions often result in the suspension of a driver's license for 6 to 24 months, and additionally limits access to public housing, even as a short-term guest of a family member (Fishman, 2003; Legal Action Center, 2004). Gaining employment can be particularly challenging for women released from prison. Incarcerated women are less prepared for the workforce than their male counterparts: they are less likely to have had prior legal employment or to have marketable trade-based job skills (Blitz, 2006). Federal and state statutes also impose legal barriers on ex-offenders that bar employment in daycare and health care areas, common sectors employing women. Returning women also face the challenge of regaining custody of their children and finding the means to assume these responsibilities, as well as handling the financial and emotional issues surrounding reunification if it occurs, or conversely dealing with the loss of custody (Richie, 2001).

As described in earlier chapters, incarcerated women have a constellation of "wounds" that are likely to challenge their ability to reintegrate into the community because they create special needs (e.g., specialized and expensive behavioral health treatment that may require insurance, transportation, coordination, and motivation) or risks (e.g., employment restrictions, addictions, child care responsibilities, or limited vocational abilities to make money legally). It is especially important to understand that these needs and risks are compounding—they are likely to work together to limit the woman's access to housing, jobs, treatment, people, and communities. The following vignettes of women inside prison illustrate the range of problems they take with them into the community upon release.

*Woman A is in her early 20s and has been diagnosed with depressive disorder and substance abuse. She has no prior history of psychiatric hospitalization or suicide attempts. Her involvement with outpatient mental health treatment began at age 12 for behavioral difficulties at home. She has a moderate drug problem and poor anger management. This is her first prison sentence. She is serving time for drug distribution and a parole violation. Her institutional adjustment has been average and treatment compliance is fair.*

*Woman B, in her late 30s, is being treated for an adjustment disorder with depressed mood. She has a history of moderate drug use. She has no known psychiatric hospitalizations, suicide attempts, or outpatient mental health treatment. She has been incarcerated most of her adult life on drug-related charges and is currently serving a 4-year sentence for drug possession. She has no prior parole violation or convictions for violence. She has had good compliance with mental health treatment while in prison and has had no institutional infractions. Her risk for reoffending is high should she become involved with drugs again.*

*Woman C is in her late 30s and has been diagnosed with major depression, anxiety disorder, antisocial personality disorder, anger control problems, and polysubstance abuse. She has mood swings that arise when distressed. She has a long history of aggression and assaultiveness even while involved in community programs. She has no prior admissions to psychiatric hospitals or history of harming self. She has a long criminal record beginning as a juvenile that includes over 70 arrests. She supports her drug habit by prostitution and robbery. She has been incarcerated multiple times. Her most recent conviction is for a violent crime that carries a 10-year sentence. Her institutional adjustment has been rated as poor. She has spent time in administrative segregation for refusing to obey.*

*Woman D, in her mid 20s, has been diagnosed with bipolar disorder, borderline personality, substance abuse, learning disability, and an eating disorder. She reports hearing voices that berate her and has a history of more than two psychiatric hospitalizations and harming herself. She has been involved with mental health programs in the past, including at the time of her last arrest. She has failed to complete a drug treatment program. In prison she has been inconsistent with medication compliance, frequently stopping her medication. Her offense risk is high if she were to use drugs again. She has spent more than 6 years in prison and has violated parole. She is currently serving a 3-year sentence for drug convictions. While in prison she has had no disciplinary infractions.*

A more general view of the complex of mental disorders and criminal histories of incarcerated women is shown in Tables 13.1 and 13.2, respectively.[1] Approximately 37% of the women incarcerated in New Jersey prisons were identified as special needs, more than two times higher than the percentage of New Jersey male inmates with special needs (16%). The majority of the female special needs population was African-American (59.1%) and between the ages of 25 and 39 (62.0%).

For the purposes of comparative analysis, the incarcerated women with special needs were divided into two groups: those with and those without serious mental illness. The group of women categorized with serious mental illness was diagnosed with one or more of the following: schizophrenia or other psychotic or cognitive disorders, major depression or mood disorder, and bipolar disorder (McAlpine & Mechanic, 2000; Swanson et al., 2002).

Of the total female special-needs population, the majority (62.9%, $n = 298$) were diagnosed with serious mental illness (SMI) (see Table 13.1). Approximately 14% of

---

[1]The study population includes all adult female inmates identified with special needs who were confined in the New Jersey state prison system on August 10, 2002. Of the 1,267 incarcerated women in New Jersey, 37% ($n = 474$) were identified as having special needs. The New Jersey Department of Corrections classifies inmates as "special needs" if they are identified by prison clinical staff (i.e., psychiatrist, psychologist, or master's level social worker) as having a DSM Axis I diagnosis and "who need or receive mental health treatment of some type" (Cevasco & Moratti, 2001, p. 166).

**TABLE 13.1** Mental and behavioral health history for female inmates with special needs in the New Jersey prison system, August 10, 2002

| | | | | | | |
|---|---|---|---|---|---|---|
| | | | *Female inmates with special needs* | | | |
| *Mental health history* | *Total (n = 474)* | | *Serious mental illness (n = 298)* | | *Nonserious mental illness (n = 176)* | |
| *Most serious Axis I diagnosis* | N | % | N | % | N | % |
| Schizophrenia, psychosis, delusions, dementia, cognitive disorder | 78 | 16.5 | 78 | 26.2 | 0 | 0.0 |
| Major depression, bipolar, major mood disorder | 220 | 46.4 | 220 | 73.8 | 0 | 0.0 |
| Depressive disorder, dysthmia, adjustment disorder, PTSD, anxiety, panic, dissociative identity | 176 | 37.2 | 0 | 0.0 | 70 | 39.8 |
| *Other behavioral health characteristics* | | | | | | |
| Personality disorder | 65 | 13.7 | 40 | 13.4 | 25 | 14.2 |
| Mental retardation | 4 | 0.8 | 2 | 0.7 | 2 | 1.0 |
| Alcohol/substance dependence or abuse[1] | 302 | 63.7 | 207 | 69.5 | 95 | 54.0 |

[1]$\chi^2 = 11.48, \text{df} = 1, p < .01$

the female special needs inmates were diagnosed with a personality disorder. The majority (63.7%) of female inmates had a substance abuse or dependence problem. However, female inmates with a serious mental illness were significantly more likely to have an alcohol or drug abuse problem than their nonseriously mentally ill counterparts ($\chi^2 = 11.48, \text{df} = 1, p = .001$).

Generally speaking, incarcerated women with special needs were serving their first prison sentence and serving time for a nonviolent offense (see Table 13.2). Although about one-third (35.7%) of the female population had a violent offense conviction, very few were convicted of arson (1.7%) or sexual offenses (1.1%). Roughly one-third of female inmates with special needs was serving a prison term for a drug-related conviction. Although the SMI group had a higher prevalence of substance-related disorders (70%) compared to the non-SMI group (54%), a drug conviction was more likely among the female inmates with special needs and a nonserious mental illness, compared to those with a serious mental illness ($\chi^2 = 12.53, \text{df} = 1, p = .000$). Interestingly, most of the women who comprised the special-needs population (58%) were back in prison because of a parole violation. More than half of the parole violations were for the possession, distribution, or manufacture of controlled and dangerous substances (32.7%) or stealing (20.7%).

In addition to mental and substance use disorders, the majority of women in prison have histories of interpersonal violence. Although prior victimization is not a standard question in the management information systems of the New Jersey Department of

**TABLE 13.2**  Criminal history for female inmates with special needs in the New Jersey prison system, August 20, 2002

| Criminal history characteristics | Total (*n = 474*) | | Female inmates with special needs | | | |
|---|---|---|---|---|---|---|
| | | | Serious mental illness (*n = 298*) | | Nonserious mental illness (*n = 176*) | |
| | N | % | N | % | N | % |
| Incarcerated two or more times | 135 | 28.5 | 80 | 26.8 | 55 | 31.3 |
| Current sentence longer than 5 years[1] | 214 | 45.1 | 123 | 41.3 | 91 | 51.7 |
| Convicted of arson | 8 | 1.7 | 7 | 2.3 | 1 | 0.6 |
| Convicted of a violent offense | 169 | 35.7 | 111 | 37.2 | 64 | 33.0 |
| Convicted of a sex offense | 5 | 1.1 | 2 | 0.7 | 3 | 1.7 |
| Convicted of a drug offense[2] | 145 | 30.6 | 74 | 24.8 | 71 | 40.3 |
| Rearrested on a parole violation | 275 | 58.0 | 169 | 56.7 | 106 | 60.2 |

[1]$\chi^2 = 4.29$, df $= 1$, $p = .027$
[2]$\chi^2 = 12.53$, df $= 1$, $p = .000$

Corrections, individual interviews were conducted with a representative sample of women with special needs ($n = 55$), and during this interview they were asked questions about prior victimization. As shown in Table 13.3, prior victimization was common among incarcerated women with special needs. The majority of the SMI group (71.4%) and the non-SMI group (69.2%) reported a history of physical or sexual abuse. A history of sexual abuse victimization was twice as prevalent among the SMI group (61.9%) compared to the non-SMI group (38.5%). Relative to the non-SMI group, female inmates with serious mental illness were significantly more likely to report a history of thinking that others would harm them ($\chi^2 = 5.43$, df $= 1$, $p = .02$).

These statistics on victimization are consistent with extant research showing that at least three-quarters of incarcerated women have experienced at least one traumatic event in their lifetime (Bloom, Owen, & Covington, 2003). Childhood abuse is reported by 25% to 50% of incarcerated women (Brown, Miller, & Maguin, 1999; Snell, 1994). Prior victimization has been shown to be positively related to adult criminality (Falshaw, Browne, & Hollin, 1996; Widom, 1989, 1996), a wide array of mental health problems (Brown, 1998; Johnson, Kotch, Catellier, Winsor, Dufort, Hunter, & Amaya-Jackson, 2002; Kessler & Magee, 1994; Malinosky-Rummell & Hansen, 1993; Scarpa, Fikeretoglu, Bowser, Hurley, Pappert, Romero, & Van Voorhees, 2002; Wise, Zierler, & Harlow, 2001), and alcohol and drug addiction (Anderson, 2002; DATA, 2003; Mehrabian, 2001).

Interpersonal violence also continues inside prison. Wolff and colleagues estimated 6-month prevalence rates of inmate-on-inmate and staff-on-inmate sexual victimization at, respectively, 21.2% and 7.6% (Wolff, Blitz, Shi, Bachman, & Siegel, 2006). Female inmates with mental illness had significantly higher rates of any sexual

**TABLE 13.3** Victimization characteristics of a convenience sample of female inmates with special needs within 6 months of release from the New Jersey prison system, August 2002

| | Convenience sample of female inmates with special needs (n = 55) | | | |
|---|---|---|---|---|
| | Serious mental illness (n = 42) | | Nonserious mental illness (n = 13) | |
| Victimization characteristics | N | % | N | % |
| Physical and/or sexual abuse, history | 30 | 71.4 | 9 | 69.2 |
| Physical abuse, history | 26 | 61.9 | 8 | 61.5 |
| Sexual abuse, history | 26 | 61.9 | 5 | 38.5 |
| Physical and/or sexual abuse, 6 months prior to arrest | 14 | 33.3 | 4 | 30.8 |
| Physical abuse, 6 months prior to arrest | 13 | 31.0 | 2 | 16.7 |
| Sexual abuse, 6 months prior to arrest | 6 | 14.6 | 2 | 15.4 |
| Thinking others will harm you, history[1] | 18 | 42.9 | 1 | 7.7 |
| Thinking others will harm you, 6 months prior to arrest | 15 | 35.7 | 1 | 7.7 |

[1]$X^2 = 5.43$, df $= 1, p = .020$

victimization, ranging from 1.6 times higher (African-American) to 2.4 times higher (non-Hispanic White) (Wolff, Shi, & Blitz, 2007). The risk of victimization between inmates doubled for female inmates who experienced sexual abuse prior to age 18 (Wolff, Shi, Blitz, & Siegel, 2007).

Gender-responsive reentry strategies must take into account the women's life experiences and needs as they enter and leave prison, as well as the limitations placed on their access to resources on the outside by social policies (Bloom, Owen, & Covington, 2003). Focusing on "building up" the person is especially important for people who have experienced interpersonal trauma and have developed coping strategies that include self-medication with drugs and alcohol and other self-harming behaviors. Life in the community after prison is stressful and overwhelming and, as such, can trigger relapse and elevate the risk of returning to prison. Building skills is, therefore, critical prerelease: skills that address impulsivity and the capacity to cope effectively with life's stressors; draw connections among trauma and other life experiences, behaviors, and treatment; and empower women to gain control by managing their choices in ways that improve the quality of their lives.

## GETTING REENTRY PROGRAMMING RIGHT FOR WOMEN: WHAT DO WOMEN WANT?

To get reentry programming "right" for women, it is critical to begin with accurate and reliable information about what reentering women need and want, and more importantly what concerns them (Hartwell, 2001). They must be engaged and given voice in the design process if only because they are the end users. In this section, we draw on the qualitative responses of 100 incarcerated women who were 6 months or less from their release date. These women resided in prisons located in Missouri, New Jersey, Oklahoma, Oregon, Pennsylvania, and South Carolina. In groups of six to ten, they were asked in one 90-minute session what they saw as the goals, needs, and risks associated with returning to the community and in a second 90-minute session to design a reentry program for returning women using a worksheet divided into prerelease, transition period, and postrelease.

### THE GENERAL CONCERNS OF WOMEN

What concerned this group of incarcerated women most consistently was uncertainty—uncertainty about their immediate futures and their lack of information, practice, money, and social support to respond to it. Their frustration and fears are best described through the words of a woman who was 6 months away from leaving prison after having served 25 years. She said:

> I want to give you the real case scenario if you don't have anything, ok. Alright, I don't have any family. I don't have any support. The Department of Corrections is not makin' me go to a halfway house. They're gonna take me to the bus station and put me out. That's it. They're not gonna give me a dollar in my pocket. They're gonna give me a set of clothes that somebody's donated and they're gonna put me out at the bus station. That's all. That's all they're gonna do. Ok, so what do I do? Where am I supposed to go? The first thing I gotta try to do is try to find somewhere to lie down. I don't have a dime in my pocket to find me a bed to lay in, ok. So, I don't know what to do. Ok, now I've gotta look for a job. Maybe somebody will hire me and give me a job and a meal and maybe I can talk to somebody there that'll help me find me a place to lay down at night. Ok. That's the next best thing I can do. I don't know. Or, we're gonna do what we know how to do. We're gonna go out there and we're gonna turn into a prostitute. We're guaranteed that's money. Or we're gonna go back to call the nearest dope dealer that we know because we're guaranteed that's money. We don't know. Ok, let's—we find an apartment. We find somewhere, we've managed to get a job and they gave us a little-bit-a money and we found an apartment, ok. How do I get the lights turned on? I don't know. Who'm I supposed to call? I don't have credit, so I—there's nothin' for you to rely on to look at to see that I can pay this bill. Ok, what am I supposed to do—I can't get it up. I have nobody to cosign. I can't get a phone turned on. I don't know how. I can't go to the car lot and buy a car. I don't know how. I don't know how to fill out the paperwork, I don't know what this stuff means, ok. Um, insurance—I don't know. What do I need? Do I need collision? Do I need liability, what do I need? I don't know. None of these things were taught to us. We don't know. I've been in prison for 25 years . . . I don't know anymore what I'm supposed to do. Therefore, I would do the very best that I could and what I did know is what I'd have to go to—in order to survive. Because once the Department of Corrections is through with you that's what they do. They put you out at that bus station and nobody cares.

**TABLE 13.4** Conceptualization of Reentry Planning

| Elements of Reentry Planning | Strategic Areas of Reentry Planning | | |
|---|---|---|---|
| | *Empowerment* | *Reintegration* | *Recovery* |
| **Information** | Identification<br>Opportunities<br>Restrictions | Identification<br>Directions/schedules<br>Active benefit eligibility | Reliable<br>Accurate<br>Accessible |
| **Skill building** | Life<br>Social<br>Parenting<br>Giving back | Booster Sessions ⟶ | |
| **Resources** | Identification of<br>assets, needs, risks,<br>and options | Transportation<br>Safe housing<br>Treatment<br>Education<br>Job training | Coordination<br>Consistency<br>Structure<br>Accountability |
| **Support** | Community coach<br>Mentoring<br>Role models<br>In-Service groups | Community coach<br>Parole officer<br>Church<br>Peer-Support groups | Trust<br>Respectfulness<br>Empathy<br>Understanding<br>Professionalism<br>Fairness |

This woman, like the others, wanted a reentry plan that reduced her uncertainty about her life after prison and that gave her a sense of security, safety, and social support. This, in their view, should be the goal of reentry planning. Like any "planning" strategy, it seeks to reduce uncertainty through making arrangements in advance that provide structure and support to a situation that is ill-defined in ways that are central to living safely and prosocially in the community.

In interpreting the words of the woman above, the elements of reentry planning must include: information, skills, resources, and social support, which are clustered within strategic areas of empowerment, reintegration, and recovery (see Table 13.4). *Empowerment* builds *competencies*—the ability of women to exert control over and manage their lives, decisions, and experiences—and requires *practice*. *Reintegration* focuses on the *instrumental* aspects of reentry—getting identification, identifying resources, and having a social network. *Recovery* refers to the *procedural* attributes (e.g., quality of the information, coordination of the resources, and professionalism and fairness of the agencies and their representatives) defining the process of reentry and their ability to affirm and encourage the reconstruction and regeneration of a responsible, productive, and healthy woman. Table 13.4 describes the elements related to each of these three strategic areas.

## INFORMATION

Elemental to reentry is information. Rational, deliberate decision making and action requires information. For empowerment, women described the need for generalized information about functioning in the community, as well as information that would help them to identify the needs, opportunities, risks, and restrictions that will be present there. They needed information that would allow them to "get real" with living in the community. This included information about the importance of personal identification and the process for getting proof-based identification. It also required information about how incarceration, felony convictions, and parole supervision would likely affect their eligibility for public benefits, housing options and conditions, and types of employment. Accurate, reliable, and accessible information about application processes and fee arrangements, as well as opportunities and restrictions, will facilitate effective and efficient decision making in areas that are central to reintegration, particularly regarding obtaining personal identification, applying for public benefits, and making these arrangement either prior to release or immediately following release. Providing information that is inaccurate, incomplete, or inaccessible indirectly suggests that the person is not worth any better and foments frustration. Because people inside prison do not have access to the Internet, they are deprived of the most efficient venue for gaining access to application forms, information about public benefits, and access to resources. As long as institutional policies and practices control the flow of information into the prison, it is the prison administration's responsibility to ensure that the information needed for strategic reentry planning is available and equal in quality to what would be available to people outside the facility making similar decisions.

## SKILL BUILDING

Incarceration creates a way of living that breeds dependency; residents follow rules and a daily structure set by the institution. They comply mindlessly with decisions made by other adults on their behalf and without their involvement. Incarceration by design takes away the individual's decision-making authority, erodes her ability to act with volition and using the daily living skills required of adults, and encourages her passive compliance. It is a process of mass deskilling that stretches over years. In addition, by isolating the person from the community and technological advances, the individual becomes frozen in the skills of the past and, when she returns to society, she returns a foreigner to her community. Her skills are particularly obsolete in areas of banking, electronic job searching and processing, and public transportation. Also, the language, rules, and customs of the community were replaced with those of the total institution. Incarceration institutionalizes the person and makes them a stranger of the community and its ways. One person in our study reported that a "human upgrade" was required before an incarcerated person is released to the community. Not knowing how to do something or to do basic functions in the community, as indicated by the quote above, is intimidating, frustrating, demoralizing, disempowering, and a natural consequence of incarceration. For this reason, skill building—life skills (i.e., knowing how to use an ATM machine, submit an electronic job application, manage money and time), social skills (i.e., knowing how to talk to and engage people and cope with disappointment), parenting (i.e., knowing how to reconnect and care for children), and give back—(i.e., knowing how to reciprocate and give back to family and community) must be taught, practiced, and encouraged in the months prior to release to give the woman confidence in her ability to solve problems and function normally, followed by "booster sessions" to reinforce, guide, and encourage autonomy and healthy and prosocial decision making in the community.

## RESOURCES

Knowing how to access resources and gaining access to resources is central to reentry. It begins with the woman taking stock of what she has, what she needs, and what puts her at risk. A guided process is needed here to help the woman think over the past and project into the future. It requires having information but also the ability to strategize, problem solve, and contingency plan. It requires being able to learn from past experience and to guard against them in the future. For example, not having safe and affordable housing; money for food, clothing, toiletries, and medications; insurance coverage or access to free medical treatment; and reliable and affordable transportation are risk factors to empowerment, reintegration, and recovery. Yet to have them requires strategic planning prior to release and follow-through postrelease. During empowerment, the women must identify resource goals around needs, risks, and options, with assets inventoried to encourage positive thinking. Reintegration will be successful if goals and plans are designed in advance and access to these resources are structured and coordinated in user-friendly ways, are consistently available in ways that are nondiscriminatory and nonstigmatizing, and where providers are held accountable to professional performance standards that include procedural attributes of respect, integrity, and courtesy. Making it bureaucratically difficult and frustrating to access resources for which the woman is entitled defeats the goals of reentry planning and the resources allocated to that process.

## SUPPORT

A consistent theme among the incarcerated women was the need for community support throughout the entire reentry process. As an element of empowerment, support was described in terms of spending time with community residents. This time served many purposes; it was seen as a way to learn about the community, to get comfortable with the communication style of the outside world, to feel accepted by people from the outside, and to gain mentoring and help about how to live and work in the community. They also stressed the need for guidance from women "like them" who had succeeded. Everyday, the women say, released women return. They described how demoralizing it was to see women return, especially those they thought would "make good." What frustrated them most was never seeing successfully recovered women from whom they could model and find their hope. Although family support is typically highlighted in traditional reentry planning, most of the women with family connections stressed their reluctance to rely on family for support. Their reasons ranged from feeling as if they had already burdened their family enough during their incarceration to considering their family as a risk factor in terms of stress and negative habits. There was a strong sense among the women that they needed support from "strangers" who represented the good will of the community. They were looking for "ambassadors" who would help them feel comfortable in and with the community that felt so foreign and frightening to them. Empowering support was seen as "glue" during reintegration. The ambassadors would continue to coach and mentor the returning woman while she worked to connect with resources in her effort to make a place for herself and her children in the community. The role of ambassadors during reintegration was described analogously to AA/NA sponsors, in which the person was there to help with decision making, to encourage, and to listen. Although some traditional reentry initiatives offer "hotlines" for 24/7 support, this was not the type of support that the women described. They wanted someone they trusted and knew them as people to be the person they reached out to for support and encouragement. It was the personal caring and connection that was so important to them. The support "glue" was vital for recovery. It served the function of affirming the person and her place in the community. Support that was trustworthy, empathic, understanding, fair, and reflected professionalism conveyed a sense that the person existed, was worthy of humanity, and was welcome. By contrast, social or professional interactions that are discourteous, judgmental, disrespectful, and inconsiderate of the woman's feeling or time communicates directly and indirectly disdain and disregard for the person, her situation, and her feeling. It conveys that she is inadequate and unworthy of fair treatment, working against the reconstruction and regeneration of a responsible, productive, and healthy woman.

The women were clear about what was needed to get them ready for the community and to be successful there. What they needed was similar to what young adults need as they transition from high school and home to a university environment. Developmentally, it is a time in which the young person moves from supported living to living independently, where many things about the new environment and independence are uncertain, creating feelings of fear and intimidation, and where there are many opportunities to make good and bad decisions. Parents endeavor to empower the transitioning young person with information, skills, resources, and support, which are matched by the university to smooth the reintegration process. The process of entering the university is characterized by user-friendly information for the young adults (and parents), is efficiently coordinated and structured to facilitate reintegration with performance accountability built in to residence halls and academic programs, and is cognizant of the anxiety of the transitioning student and responds with standards of professionalism that are personalized and affirmative. Together, the parents and university representatives empower, coach, and support the young person's transition into independence. This is exactly the process that the returning women were describing when they thought about their return to the community and to their independence there.

## THE GENERAL PROBLEMS OF THE SYSTEMS

The correctional and community-based public systems have much to learn from the university system in terms of facilitating transition into adult independence. The first significant problem with transitional processing for incarcerated women is the lack of "working together" by the constitute systems (Wolff, 1998). It is customary to respond to the needs and risks of incarcerated women incrementally, with different systems responding to the different parts: the mental health system (or contractor) responding to mental disorders, the substance abuse treatment system (or contractor) to substance use disorders, and the criminal justice system to criminal deviance. Each of these systems (contractors) is funded separately and defines its mission uniquely (Wolff, 1998), creating systematic incentives to parse the person into unique problems and, in so doing, ignoring the interdependence among the problems. Because of their organizational independence, these systems have no incentive to work together in their response to the woman (Wolff, 2002). Similarly, they have no incentive to "heal" her because their payment depends not on healing but on treating—adding systematic momentum to the revolving door of relapse and recidivism.

Systematic fragmentation, and the parallel fragmentation of the woman, is one of the biggest challenges of reentry planning and explains in part why it is so needed by women leaving prison. If women are to have an even chance of living productively and prosocially in the community postincarceration, reentry planning must begin with a person-focused approach. The woman must be integrated holistically, not fragmented into individual parts in which her "unique" wounds are isolated from their etiology, other distally related wounds, and the regenerative strengths of the person. The woman's success depends fundamentally on working with all her parts together as a system.

Such an integrated approach is challenging because it requires assessing and responding to the heterogeneity of incarcerated women in terms of their variation and severity of behavioral health wounds, criminal histories, and abilities to take control of their lives and their well-being. Variation in therapeutic and developmental needs, criminality, and regenerative strengths within the incarcerated female population requires tailoring responses to the individual, which is not consistent with the "one-size-fits-all" approach that characterizes publicly funded programs. Moreover, it requires developing assessment capacities within the prison that can effectively identify the diversity of needs, risks, and strengths of women and then match them in a systematic way to the most appropriate specialized services in the community. These services, whether integrated internally by program design or externally by case management, would need the capacity to respond to a constellation of comorbid mental health and addiction problems, relational/family issues, anger/impulsivity, and homelessness, that have etiologies grounded in social history and geography.

## TOWARD GENDER-RESPONSIVE INTEGRATED STRATEGIES FOR WOMEN LEAVING PRISON

Effective gender-responsive treatment and reentry strategies for women must take into account their life experiences and their needs, risks, and concerns as they enter and leave prison, measured against their restricted access to resources and support on the outside by social policies (Bloom, Owen, & Covington, 2003). Focusing on "building up" the person is especially important for people who have mental and substance use disorders and experienced interpersonal trauma pre- and postincarceration, as well as mass deskilling as a result of institutionalization. Although there is little clear evidence on how best to respond to the needs and risks of incarcerated women, there are some general principles.

First, *integrated treatment* for co-morbid conditions is considered optimal, compared to parallel, sequential, or single treatment models (Harris & Fallot, 2001; Mueser et al., 2005). Second, *trauma-related difficulties are best treated in stages* (Herman, 1992), with the first stage focusing on safety through recognition, education, and skill (i.e., cognitive, behavioral, and interpersonal) building geared toward helping the women develop coping and life skills that replace the use of drugs or alcohol or other self-harming behaviors. Later stages of trauma recovery focus on addressing or processing the trauma directly after the person has achieved stable functioning. Third, *interventions must be sensitive to environment.* Trauma processing treatments such as exposure therapy or cognitive restructuring, although efficacious, require environments that are healing and supportive (Harris & Fallot, 2001). Correctional settings are not healing; they often have characteristics reminiscent of environments where trauma occurred in the past or where trauma has occurred or is occurring (Bowker, 1980; Toch, 1977). Providing trauma-focused therapy inside prison would be analogous to providing this therapy to military personnel while in a war zone. Moreover, prisons, like war zones, are not environments that accommodate the supportive needs of people who may be especially vulnerable during trauma-focused therapy (e.g., exposure). Interventions must be matched to settings in ways that support their therapeutic potential and goals of recovery. Fourth, *continuity of care is critical* to maintaining health and preventing relapse toward behaviors that are self-harming, such as substance use and criminality (Drake, Wallach, & McGovern, 2005; Rosenberg, Mueser, Friedman, & Gorman, 2001). Life in the community after prison is stressful and overwhelming and, as such, can trigger relapse and elevate the risk of returning to prison. Building skills is, therefore, critical prerelease—to address impulsivity and the capacity to cope effectively with life's stressors; draw connections among trauma experiences, behaviors, and treatment; and empower women to gain control by managing their choices in ways that improve the quality of their lives.

In conclusion, reentry planning is a systematic and active effort to assist the returning person reintegrate into the community postincarceration (Petersilia, 2003). These plans work best when they reflect an accurate understanding of the person's needs, risks, concerns, and strength, as well as the community's reluctance to respond to the person in ways that affirm and support their successful transition to independence and prosocial living. How the person is treated along the way matters in ways that are vitally important to their reintegration and recovery. It is not just about having a place to live or a job; it is about the messages conveyed to the person during the process about their value. Treating returning people with disdain and disrespect while giving them a housing voucher to a homeless shelter or a single room in a welfare hotel is not consistent with recovery. Reentry dollars will be less effective toward goals if the attributes of the procedures and resources convey meanings of worthlessness to the person, and if the process disregards the need to address uncertainty associated with "not knowing how" to do what is expected. Reentry planning is all about the person, the community, and the effort to build a social bond between the two. Failure to address the "person" and the "interpersonal" context and nuances of the transitional process will feed the dysfunction within the public systems with dollars, without producing anything of value for the end users: the returning woman, or the intended downstream benefactors, taxpayers. To be successful, we need to listen to the voices of the women and empower them with information, skills, access to resources, and support to become women of deliberate and responsible choice.

## References

Allard, P. (2002). *Life sentences: Denying welfare benefits to women convicted of drug offenses*. Retrieved March 3, 2007, from http://www.sentencingproject.org/pdfs/9088.pdf

American Correctional Association. (1995). *Public correctional policy on female offender services*. Lanham, MD: American Correctional Association.

Anderson, K. L. (2002). Perpetrator or victim? Relationships between intimate partner violence and well-being. *Journal of Marriage and Family, 64,* 851–863.

Beck, A. J., & Harrison, P. M. (2001). *Bureau of Justice Statistics bulletin: Prisoners in 2000*. Washington, DC: Bureau of Justice Statistics, Office of Justice Programs, U.S. Department of Justice; NCJ 188207.

Belknap, J. (2001). *The invisible woman: Gender, crime, and justice*. Belmont, CA: Wadsworth.

Binswanger, I. A., Stern, M. F., Deyo, R.A., et al. (2007). Release from prison—A high risk of death for former inmates. *New England Journal of Medicine, 356,* 157–165.

Blitz, C. L. (2006). Predictors of stable employment among female inmates in New Jersey: Implications for successful reintegration. *Journal of Offender Rehabilitation, 43,* 1–22.

Blitz, C. L., Wolff, N., Pan, K., & Pogorzelski, W. (2005). Gender-specific behavioral health and community release patterns among New Jersey prison inmates: Implications for treatment and community reentry. *American Journal of Public Health, 95,* 1741–1746.

Bloom, B., Owen, B., & Covington, S. (2003). *Gender-responsible strategies: Research, practice, & guiding principles for women offenders.* Washington, DC: National Institute of Corrections.

Bowker, L. (1980). *Prison victimization.* New York: Elsevier North Holland.

*Brad H. vs. City of New York,* 2001, 188 Misc. 2d 470; 729 N.Y.S.2d 348; 2001 N.Y. Misc. LEXIS 221 (2001).

Brown, G. W. (1998). Genetic and population perspectives on life events and depression. *Social Psychiatry and Psychiatric Epidemiology, 33,* 363–372.

Brown, A., Miller, A., & Maguin, E. (1999). Prevalence and severity of lifetime physical and sexual victimization among incarcerated women. *International Journal of Law and Psychiatry, 22,* 301–322.

Cevasco, R., & Moratti, D. (2001). New Jersey's mental health program. In American Correctional Association (Ed.), *The state of corrections, proceedings, American Correctional Association annual conferences, 2000* (pp. 159–168). Lanham, MD: American Correctional Association.

Curry, L. (2001). Tougher sentencing, economic hardships, and rising violence. *Corrections Today, 63,* 74–76.

DATA. (2003, January). Major depression related to course of substance dependence. *The Brown University Digest of Addiction Theory & Application, 22*(1), 1–3.

Ditton, P. M. (1999, July). Mental health and treatment of inmates and probationers. *U.S. Department of Justice Special Report* (NCJ-174463). Washington DC: U.S. Department of Justice, Bureau of Justice Statistics.

Drake, R. E., Wallach, M. A., & McGovern, M. P. (2005). Special section on relapse prevention: Future directions in preventing relapse to substance abuse among clients with severe mental illnesses. *Psychiatric Services, 56,* 1297–1302.

Falshaw, L., Browne, K. D., & Hollin, C. R. (1996). Victim to offender: A review. *Aggression and Violent Behavior, 1,* 389–404.

Ferraro, K. J. (2006). *Neither angels nor demons: Women, crime, and victimization.* Lebanon, NH: Northeastern University Press.

Ferraro, K. J., & Moe, A. M. (2003). Women's stories of survival and resistance. In B. H. Zaitzow & J. Thomas (Eds.), *Women in prison, Gender and social control* (pp. 65–94). Boulder, CO: Lynne Rienner.

Fishman, N. (2003). *Briefing paper: Legal barriers to prisoner reentry in New Jersey.* Prepared for the New Jersey Reentry Roundtable by the New Jersey Institute for Social Justice.

Fletcher, B. R., Shaver, L. D., & Moon, D. G. (1993). *Women prisoners: A forgotten population.* Portsmouth, NH: Greenwood Publishing Group.

Fruedenberg, N., Daniels, J., Crum, M., Perkins, T., & Richie, B. E. (2005). Coming home from jail: The social and health consequences of community reentry for women, male adolescents, and their families and communities. *American Journal of Public Health, 95*(1), 725–1736.

Girshick, L. B. (2003). Abused women and incarceration. In B. H. Zaitzow & J. Thomas (Eds.), *Women in prison, Gender and social control* (pp. 95–118). Boulder, CO: Lynne Rienner.

Greenfeld, L. A., & Snell, T. L. (1999). Women offenders. *Bureau of Justice Statistics Special Report* (NCJ 175688). Washington, DC: United States Department of Justice, Bureau of Justice Statistics.

Harris, M., & Fallot, R. D. (2001). Designing trauma-informed addictions services. *New Direction in Mental Health Services, 89,* 57–73.

Harrison, P. M., & Beck, A. J. (2005, October). *Bureau of Justice Statistics bulletin: Prisoners in 2004.* Washington, DC: Bureau of Justice Statistics, Office of Justice Programs, U.S. Department of Justice, NCJ 210677.

Hartwell, S. W. (2001). Female mentally ill offenders and their community reintegration needs: An initial examination. *International Journal of Law and Psychiatry, 24,* 1–11.

Herman, J. L. (1992). *Trauma and recovery: The aftermath of violence—from domestic abuse to political terror.* New York: Basic Books

James, D. J., & Glaze, L. E. (2006). *Bureau of Justice Statistics special report: Mental health problems of prison and jail inmates.* Washington, DC: Bureau of Justice Statistics, Office of Justice Programs, U.S. Department of Justice, NCJ 213600.

Johnson, R. M., Kotch, J. B., Catellier, D. J., Winsor, J. R., Dufort, V., Hunter, W., & Amaya-Jackson, L. (2002). Adverse behavioral and emotional outcomes from child abuse and witnessed violence. *Child Maltreatment, 7*(3), 179–186.

Kessler, R. C., & Magee, W. J. (1994). Childhood family violence and adult recurrent depression. *Journal of Health & Social Behavior, 35*(1), 13–28.

Kubrin, C. E., & Stewart, E. A. (2006). Predicting who reoffends: The neglected role of neighborhood context in recidivism studies. *Criminology, 44,* 165–195.

Legal Action Center. (2004). *After prison: Roadblocks to reentry, A report on state legal barriers facing people with criminal records.* New York: Author.

Malinosky-Rummell, R., & Hansen, D. J. (1993). Long-term consequences of childhood physical abuse. *Psychological Bulletin, 114,* 68–79.

McAlpine, D. D., & Mechanic, D. (2000). Utilization of specialty mental health care among persons with severe mental illness: The roles of demographics, need, insurance, and risk. *Health Services Research, 35*(1), 277–292.

Mehrabian, A. (2001). Gender relations among drug use, alcohol use, and major indexes of psychopathology. *The Journal of Psychology, 135*(1), 71–86.

Morash, M., & Bynum, T. (1999). *The mental health supplement to the National Study of Innovative and Promising Programs for Women Offenders.* Washington, DC: National Institute of Justice, U.S. Department of Justice.

Morash, M., Haar, R., & Rucker, L. A. (1994). Comparison of programming for women and men in U.S. prisons in the 1980's. *Crime & Delinquency, 40,* 197–221.

Mueser, K. T., Drake, R. E., Sigmon, S. C., & Brunette, M. F. (2005). Psychosocial interventions for adults with severe mental illnesses and co-occurring substance use disorders: A review of specific interventions. *Journal of Dual Disorders, 1,* 57–82.

Mumola, C. J. (2000). *Incarcerated parents and their children.* Washington, DC: U.S. Department of Justice, Bureau of Justice Statistics.

Petersilia, J. (2003). *When prisoners come home: Parole and prisoner reentry.* New York: Oxford University Press.

Pogorzelski, W., Wolff, N., Pan, K., & Blitz, C. L. (2005). Behavioral health problems, ex-offender reentry policies, and the "Second Chance Act." *American Journal of Public Health, 95,* 1718–1724.

Richie, B. (2001). Challenges incarcerated women face as they return to their communities: Findings from life history interviews. *Crime & Delinquency, 47,* 291–131.

Rose, D. R., & Clear, T. R. (1998). Incarceration, social capital, and crime: Implications for social disorganization theory. *Criminology, 36,* 441–479.

Rosenberg, S. D., Mueser, K. T., Friedman, M. J., & Gorman, P. G. (2001). Developing effective treatments for post-traumatic disorder among people with severe mental illness. *Psychiatric Services, 52,* 1453–1461.

Sampson, R. J., Morenoff, J. D., & Gannon-Rowley, T. (2002). Assessing neighborhood effects: Social processes and new directions in research. *Annual Review of Sociology, 28,* 443–478.

Scarpa, A., Fikretoglu, D., Bowser, F., Hurley, J. D., Pappert, C. A., Romero, N., & Van Voorhees, E. (2002). Community violence exposure in university students: A replication and extension. *Journal of Interpersonal Violence, 17*(3), 253–273.

Sharp, S. F. (2006). It's not just men anymore: The criminal justice system and women in the 21st century. *The Criminologist, 31,* 2–5.

Snell, T. (1994). Women in prison: A survey of state prison inmates, 1991. *Bureau of Justice Statistics special report.* Washington, DC: U.S. Department of Justice, Bureau of Justice Statistics.

Swanson, J. W., Swartz, M. S., Essock, S. M., Osher, F. C., Wagner, R., Goodman, L. A., Rosenberg, S. D., & Meador, K. G. (2002). The social-environment context of violent behavior in persons treated for severe mental illness. *American Journal of Public Health, 92*(9), 1523–1531.

Toch, H. (1977). *Living in prison: The ecology of survival.* New York: Free Press.

Tonkin, P., Dickie, J., Alemagno, S., & Grove, W. (2004). Women in jail: "Soft skills" and barriers to employment. *Journal of Offender Rehabilitation, 38,* 51–71.

Wagaman, G. L. (2003). Managing and treating female offenders. In T. J. Fagan & R. K. Ax (Eds.), *Correctional mental health handbook.* Thousand Oaks, CA: Sage.

Wald, P. M. (2001). Why focus on women offenders? *Criminal Justice, 16,* 10–16.

Widom, C. (1989). Child abuse, neglect, and violent criminal behavior. *Criminology, 27,* 251–271.

Widom, C. (1996). Childhood sexual abuse and its criminal consequences. *Society, 3,* 47–53.

Wilson, A. B., & Draine, J. (2006). Collaborations between criminal justice and mental health systems for prisoner reentry. *Psychiatric Services, 57*(6), 875–878.

Wise, L. A., Zierler, S. K., Krieger, N., & Harlow, B. L. (2001, September 15). Adult onset of major depressive disorder in relation to early life violent victimization: A case-control study. *Lancet, 358,* 881–888.

Wolff, N. (1998). Interactions between mental health and law enforcement systems: Problems and prospects for cooperation. *Journal of Health Politics, Policy and Law, 23*(1), 133–174.

Wolff, N. (2002). (New) public management of mentally disordered offenders: Part I. A cautionary tale. *International Journal of Law and Psychiatry, 2*(1), 15–28.

Wolff, N. (2002). Courts as therapeutic agents: Thinking past the novelty of mental health courts. *Journal of the American Academy of Psychiatry and Law, 30,* 431–437.

Wolff, N. (2005). Community reintegration of prisoners with mental illness: A social investment perspective. *International Journal of Law and Psychiatry, 28*(1), 43–58.

Wolff, N., Blitz, C. L., & Shi, J. (2007). Rates of sexual victimization inside prison for people with and without mental disorder. *Psychiatric Services, 58*(8), 1087–1094.

Wolff, N., Blitz, C. L., Shi, J., Bachman., R., & Siegel, J. (2006). Sexual violence inside prisons: Rates of victimization. *Journal of Urban Health, 83,* 835–848.

Wolff, N., Shi, J., Blitz, C., & Siegel, J. (2007). Understanding sexual victimization inside prisons: Factors that predict risk. *Criminology & Public Policy, 6*(3), 535–564.

# CHAPTER 14

# ETHICS, FEMALE OFFENDERS, AND PSYCHIATRIC ILLNESS

## How the Justice and Mental Health Systems Fail and Abandon Women

## Kristie R. Blevins
## Bruce A. Arrigo

### ABSTRACT

The experience of female offenders with psychological disorders presents unique prevention, custody, treatment, rehabilitation, and reentry concerns for this criminal subgroup. But are the very systems in place to assist them adequately designed and reasonably equipped to accommodate their pressing and manifold needs? This chapter presents data on the type and degree of problems female incarcerates with psychiatric illnesses routinely face. At issue here is the extent to which both the justice and mental health systems function to maximize (or not) desistance from crime and community reintegration efforts. As we suggest, each phase of intervention enumerated above demonstrates a lack of programming based on the gendered interests of women. As such, we sketch the ethical limits of such programming, arguing that both failure and abandonment more aptly characterize systemic strategies in place to assist female offenders with mental health issues. Several policy implications stemming from our analysis related to reentry and reintegration for this criminal population are provisionally delineated.

## INTRODUCTION

Historically, research on crime and criminality has focused principally on males. It was not until the 1970s that researchers began to examine female criminality. Before this time, women were generally not seen as a threat to society because their crimes were typically nonviolent. Although females still primarily commit nonviolent offenses, the number of violent and nonviolent crimes perpetrated by women has been increasing. Consequently, the number of females in all divisions of the criminal justice system is growing at a faster rate than their male counterparts (Bloom, Owen, & Covington, 2003; Federal Bureau of Investigation, 2005).

Although we are only beginning to understand the causes of female criminality, a plethora of empirical studies has consistently revealed that many female offenders, both adult and juvenile, suffer from mental illness (Acoca, 1998; Lederman, Dakof, Larre, & Li, 2004; Shelton, 2001). Additionally, psychological disorders are found at a higher rate among female criminals as compared with male offenders (Chamberlain & Moore, 2003; Espelage, Cauffman, Broidy, Piquero, Mazerolle, & Steiner, 2003; Kataoka, Zima, Dupre, Moreno, Yang, & McGarvey, 2001; National Mental Health Association, 2006; Teplin, Abrams, McClelland, Dulcan, & Mericle, 2002; Timmons-Mitchell, Brown, Schulz, Webster, Underwood, & Semple, 1997). In part because of the desinstitutionalization movement and the punitive, "get tough," attitude of society, many mentally ill female offenders are managed in the correctional rather than the mental health system (Arrigo, 2002, 2006; Draine, Solomon, & Meyerson, 1994; Hoffman, 1990; Lamb & Weinberger, 1998; Miller, 1992). In fact, more persons with psychiatric disorders are currently housed in U.S. jails and prisons than in all state mental health hospitals combined (Arrigo, 2004; Jones & Connelly, 2002).

Once in the correctional system, society is obligated to meet the basic needs — including physical and mental health care — of these incarcerates (Arrigo, 2002). Moreover, rehabilitation efforts are necessary in order to prepare these citizens for eventual release from correctional supervision (Kupers, 1999). However, evidence to date suggests that we are not succeeding in identifying, treating, and providing resources for female offenders with mental illness. Correctional institutions and programs have predominantly been designed to serve the male offender population, and they have not addressed the unique and multidimensional problems women face, including mental health issues (Austin, Bloom, & Donahue, 1992; National Mental Health Association, 2006).

Realizing that our criminal justice system is failing to meet the needs of mentally ill female offenders, it is important to think about some ethical issues surrounding their treatment or lack of therapeutic assistance. Accordingly, we first pose to you an ethical question that is not easily answered:

## HOW DO WE DEFINE FEMALE OFFENDERS WITH MENTAL ILLNESS?

It is important to understand that how we, as a society, define a group of offenders is significant on many levels. The criminal justice system in this country is set up in such a way that public opinion does, in fact, matter. Over the last 30 years, American society has demanded harsher punishments for offenders. Consequently, we have experienced a philosophical shift from rehabilitation to retribution. Consequently, if we define mentally ill female offenders as "monsters" or violent predators that seek to harm others, this type of public fear is likely to be translated into punitive sentences (Reiman, 2004). Alternatively, if we define these women as suffering from a disease—a debilitating psychiatric illness—that can be managed with appropriate interventions, then they might be handled very differently as they move throughout the system (Arrigo, 2001). Specifically, the focus would most likely be on providing treatment, not punishment. Ethically speaking, this is a strategy that humanizes the offender while de-mythologizing illness, in an effort to promote the goals of rehabilitation, restoration, and reintegration (Williams & Arrigo, 2008).

As you think about this issue, consider the case of Aileen Wuornos. She was convicted of murdering seven men and was ultimately executed by the state of Florida. Knowing only that Ms. Wuornos took the lives of seven human beings, it is probable that many would concur that Aileen got what she deserved. Before jumping to that conclusion, however, we should consider the circumstances in Ms. Wuornos' life, circumstances that contributed to her becoming a serial murderess.

To briefly summarize some of the junctures in a very complicated life, we should start by mentioning that Aileen Wuornos was raised by her maternal grandparents. There is evidence that she suffered from neglect and was physically, emotionally, and possibly sexually abused by her grandfather throughout her childhood years (Shipley & Arrigo, 2004). By the time she was a teenager, Aileen did not socialize well and had angry outbursts. She also spent time in detention after running away from home. Further, Aileen was pregnant at age 14, at which time she was sent to a group home where she had to give up her child for adoption. Ms. Wuornos was forced to leave her grandparents' home, dropped out of high school, and was prostituting herself at the age of 15. She was also committing other types of crime from an early age. For example, Aileen was involved in fights, she used alcohol and drugs, and she shoplifted. Eventually, Ms. Wournos was arrested for assaulting her first husband, and she spent time in prison for robbing a convenience store. It should also be noted that Ms. Wuornos claimed to have been raped nine times throughout her life, and she was eventually diagnosed as suffering from antisocial personality disorder (ASPD), also commonly known as psychopathy (Arrigo & Griffin, 2004; Shipley & Arrigo, 2004).

Psychopathy is a complicated mental disorder that may begin with a lack of parental love during infancy (Gabbard, 1990; Gacono, 2001). Factors that may affect the development of this disorder include neglect, childhood abuse, and exposure to violence (Widom, 1998). We should mention that most female offenders, even the violent ones, do not suffer from ASPD. This particular psychiatric condition is relatively rare, especially among females (Gacono, 2001). However, there is a wide array of mental illnesses that are more common among female offenders. Examples of these psychiatric conditions include depression, post-traumatic stress disorder, bipolar disorders, schizoaffective disorders, attention deficit disorder, obsessive-compulsive disorder, and mood disorders (Arrigo, 2006; Van Voorhis, Braswell, & Lester, 2000). Although these psychiatric illnesses may have very different symptoms, most of them have a number of core features. First, these psychological disorders can have deleterious effects on behavior, including crime. Second, environmental factors can affect their development and severity.

We do not maintain that experiencing a psychological disorder excuses the actions of Ms. Wuornos nor any other offender. However, we do want readers to understand that there are factors outside of individual offenders that contribute to mental illness and ultimately to their behavior. Further, we need to reexamine the case of Ms. Wuornos in order to assess whether something could have been done to help her. That is, did society miss an opportunity to treat her during her frequent contact with the criminal justice system?

Could society have intervened in some way that would have prevented Aileen from killing her victims? This brings us to our second ethical question:

## WHAT ARE WE DOING TO IDENTIFY MENTAL ILLNESS AMONG FEMALE OFFENDERS?

Although most people with psychiatric disorders are not arrested for violent behavior, there is evidence of a causal association between mental illness and violence (Arrigo & Shipley, 2001; Flowers, 1994; Hodgins, Mednick, Brennan, Schulsinger, & Engberg, 1996; Junginger, 1996; Lamb & Weinberger, 1998; Link, Andrews, & Cullen, 1992; Link & Stueve, 1995; Marzuk, 1996; Monahan, 1992; Swanson, Estroff, Swartz, Borum, Lachiotte, Zimmer, & Wagner, 1997; Torrey, 1994). For example, studies have shown that violence is more common among people with mental illness as compared with the general population (Ditton, 1999; Link et al., 1992; Fulwiler, Grossman, Forbes, & Ruthazer, 1997; Hodgins, 1992; Swanson, Holzer, Ganju, & Jono, 1990), and that rates of psychopathology are higher for offenders than for nonoffenders (Dixon, Howie, & Starling, 2004). The link between psychiatric illness and risk for violence appears particularly strong when a co-occurring disorder (e.g., substance abuse) is noted (Mulvey, 1994), even when demographic and contextual variables are taken into account (Bullock & Arrigo, 2006; Silver, 2000). This research leaves little doubt that mental illness is common among offenders. As a result, screening arrestees for psychological disorders would seem commonplace. Regrettably, that is not the case.

Many first-time female offenders are not considered dangerous and are released from the criminal justice system without ever having been screened, much less treated, for psychiatric illness. Moreover, as several researchers have noted, mental health screenings for offenders are perceived by correctional administrators as expensive, time consuming, and often unnecessary (Morash, Bynum, & Koons, 1998; Vitale, Smith, Brinkley, & Newman, 2002). Therefore, some argue that both taxpayers and already overloaded criminal justice personnel benefit by omitting such evaluations.

Although some mental health screenings are expensive and time consuming, validated standardized assessment instruments presently exist for both adults and juveniles that can be completed by trained criminal justice staff in a timely manner. These instruments can be used to effectively identify symptoms of mental illness (Cauffman, 2004; Grisso, Barnum, Fletcher, Cauggman, & Peuschold, 2001; Timmons-Mitchell et al., 1997). Examples of these screening tools include the Level of Service Inventory – Revised, Symptom Checklist – 90 – Revised, Massachusetts Youth Screening Instrument – Second Version, Millon Adolescent Clinical Inventory, Youth Self-Report, and Diagnostic Interview Schedule for Children. Moreover, such assessments do not have to be conducted on every offender. Current practices can be improved by training criminal justice employees to recognize signs of mental illness such as depression, anxiety, and psychotic disorders (Timons-Mitchell et al., 1997). Further, it has been established that certain previous experiences—especially physical, emotional, or sexual abuse—are associated with some mental illnesses such as anxiety, depression, and post-traumatic stress disorder (Bloom et al., 2003; Mulder, Beautrais, Joyce, & Fergusson, 1998). Therefore, if criminal justice officials recognize that offenders exhibit signs of mental illness, or if offenders report having experienced factors known to be associated with a debilitating mental health condition, they can then be referred for psychiatric screenings.

We cannot even begin to treat an individual with mental illness if we do not first identify it. Still, there are cases in which female offenders are diagnosed with psychiatric disorders but continue through the correctional system with little, if any, palliative care and treatment. That is, assessments or evaluations are conducted but never used. Sometimes evaluation results and clinical profiles show indications of mental illness; however, these warnings are somehow filed away or disregarded. In these cases, the women are eventually released with the same, or worse, psychological issues they experienced when they were initially brought into the system. Too often it becomes evident after-the-fact that some female offenders, even first-time violators, *are* a threat to society if left untreated. This was the tragic situation with Aileen Wuornos.

As discussed previously, Aileen had multiple behavioral problems and contacts with the criminal justice system. In her case, psychological assessments *were* conducted on some occasions. She was even evaluated by a counselor at her school. During the evaluation, the counselor realized that Ms. Wuornos needed mental health treatment. To be precise, the counselor wrote, "It is vital for this girl to receive counseling immediately" (Russell, 1992, p. 42). At that time, no counseling was provided for Ms. Wuornos. Later, while in prison for armed robbery, another psychological evaluation was conducted on her. Results indicated that she was not psychotic, but that she was unstable. Ms. Wuornos still received no treatment. Even evaluations conducted during her stays at medical centers and inpatient facilities (for alcohol use) recognized that she exhibited signs of mental illness and the potential for violence. Still, no psychiatric treatment or care was provided to Ms. Wuornos (Shipley & Arrigo, 2004).

Whereas most female offenders will not go on to become serial murderesses, those with mental illness tend to have high rates of recidivism (Sigurdson, 2000). Accordingly, it is vitally important that we identify those offenders who need treatment *and* use that information to devise a sentence and treatment strategy aimed at rehabilitating them. Indeed, ethically speaking, it is a waste of time, resources, and money to conduct assessments on offenders if we do not (properly) use that information for therapeutic purposes (Loza, Neo, Shahinfar, & Loza-Fanous, 2005).

Individualized mental health treatment plans can be designed for female offenders whether they are sentenced to prison or sentenced to a community corrections sanction. We should point out that the majority of female offenders are still handled in the community. More females receive a sentence of probation than any other type of sentence (Latessa & Allen, 2003). Still, more and more females are being sent to prisons as a result of their crime(s) or technical violation(s). We will return to the issue of treatment in the community later in this chapter. For now, though, we present our third ethical issue:

## IS PRISON THE BEST SOLUTION FOR MENTALLY ILL FEMALE OFFENDERS?

Punitive public attitudes, along with "get tough" initiatives such as the War on Drugs, Three Strikes Laws, and mandatory minimum sentences have resulted in large numbers of females being sentenced to prison. As a matter of fact, females are being incarcerated at a faster rate than males, although their crimes are generally nonviolent such as larceny or otherwise drug-related (Bureau of Justice Statistics, 2006). Among the reasons cited for this increase in female incarceration are (a) harsher punishment through retribution or "just desserts" and (b) crime reduction through deterrence and incapacitation. If society's only goal is to inflict pain on these offenders, or to give them retributive punishment, then perhaps prison is the answer. However, the other justifications for imprisoning females are not being achieved through the increased use of prisons. Research has shown that incapacitation and deterrence do little to reduce crime (Latessa & Allen, 2003; Petersilia, 1992). Therefore, money spent on incarcerating these women could be more effectively utilized by providing services that improve their lives and prevent them from committing future acts of criminality.

If our ultimate goal is to reduce recidivism, we must consider the circumstances surrounding the offender's criminal act at the time of the offense. Once we identify these causal factors, we can attempt to rehabilitate the inmate by targeting these issues. Numerous factors have been shown to be precursors of crime, and mental illness often emerges as one of the more significant (Hodgins, 1992). In fact, research has shown that mental illness among prisoners occurs at a rate at least five times that of the general population (The Sentencing Project, 2002), and about 25% of female inmates in the United States have been identified as mentally ill (Ditton, 1999). Bearing in mind that as many as one in four female incarcerates is mentally ill, one would imagine that treatment would be readily available in prisons. Unfortunately, this is not the case. Although some female correctional institutions do offer mental health programming and treatment (Morash, Haarr, & Rucker, 1994), many facilities do not provide adequate, if *any*, mental health services for women in prison (Bureau of Justice Statistics, 2001; Kanapaux, 2004).

Aside from the fact that psychological services are not available to many female incarcerates, we should also consider the effects that incarceration itself can have on women suffering from psychiatric disorders. The act of imprisoning females with mental illness may exacerbate the problems they already experience (Arrigo & Takahashi, 2007). Many of these women have minor children that are taken from their custody when they are convicted or incarcerated. Additionally, most states have only one prison for females, which is often miles from their homes. The distance alone can cause the women to lose touch with their families and other prosocial networks. Further, most prisons in the United States are set up in such a way that inmates feel very isolated. They are also "tracked" by number, resulting in a loss of personal identity (Snyder, 2001). In essence, they often become just another prisoner, and they begin to define themselves as such. The loss of family relationships, along with isolation and loss of identity, can aggravate existing mental disturbances (Van Voorhis et al., 2000), which might affect future behavior.

There are certainly some female offenders that need to be incapacitated to prevent them from harming others. After Ms. Wuornos was arrested for murder, she claimed that she would commit her crimes all over again if she had the opportunity (Shipley & Arrigo, 2004). At this point in her life, her ASPD was fully developed, and she would have been extremely difficult to treat. Therefore, incapacitating her was probably beneficial to society. We can only speculate whether the result would have been the same had she been treated earlier in her criminal career (Arrigo & Griffin, 2004).

We reiterate that the vast majority of female offenders have not committed personal crimes and will therefore eventually be released back into the community. Indeed, some of these women will complete their sentences and simply be released into the community unsupervised; however, the majority will be released under some type of correctional supervision, typically parole. Whether female offenders are reentering the community after incarceration or whether they are entering the community under a community corrections sanction without incarceration, we have to consider the following ethical question:

## ARE MENTALLY ILL FEMALE OFFENDERS RECEIVING THE SUPPORT THEY NEED TO MEET THEIR BASIC NEEDS WHEN THEY RETURN TO THE COMMUNITY?

When returning to the community after being convicted of a crime (and sometimes serving a prison sentence), female offenders face many of the same burdens as male offenders. In addition, they also face problems that are unique to females (Bloom et al., 2003). For example, many female offenders are single mothers with either no employment or a low-paying job (Arrigo & Takahashi, 2007; Radosh, 2002). Unfortunately, most female offenders, especially those with mental illness, already have decreased economic potential because of low educational levels and a lack of vocational skills. Therefore, it is difficult for them to find and keep a job that will generate enough money to make them self-sufficient and to provide them with proper childcare during workdays. Without stable employment, it is not likely that these women can meet their basic needs and/or those of their families (Radosh, 2002).

Even for female offenders without children, maintaining stable employment can be difficult (Wagman, 2003). They often have to report to multiple agencies if they are still under the care of the correctional system. In other words, for example, in addition to meeting with probation or parole officers on a regular basis, these women might be ordered to attend counseling, drug and alcohol treatment, educational training, or other court-ordered programs. Of course, the extent of these responsibilities will vary considerably according to the resources and correctional programming available in the area. Still, meeting these obligations alone may make it difficult to secure and maintain a job (Bloom et al., 2003).

Another factor that can make it difficult for mentally ill female offenders to obtain a job is the stigma associated with (a) having mental illness and (b) having been convicted of a crime. The general public has a limited tolerance for both "convicts" and mentally ill individuals in the community (Arrigo, 2002; Lamb, Weinberger, & Reston-Parham, 1996; Miller, 1992; Rogers & Bagby, 1992). We have already discussed how societal opinion affects laws and philosophies of punishment but, perhaps more importantly, public sentiment can greatly influence how a female offender is able to function in the community.

Fear and poor opinion of offenders, especially those with mental illness, can affect their ability to adapt to the community. Many individuals do not want their families (or themselves) to be exposed to persons with psychiatric illnesses, making it difficult for these offenders to gain employment or to secure a residence (Link,

Cullen, Frank, & Wozniak, 1987; Link & Stueve, 1995). Even the offenders' own families sometime have little (or no) tolerance for their troubled son/daughter, eventually ostracizing, rejecting, or otherwise abandoning their offspring. Regrettably, this was the case with Aileen Wuornos (Shipley & Arrigo, 2004). Under these circumstances, society's unwillingness to provide even the most basic of opportunities to these women only adds to their litany of problems, exacerbates their situations and, worse, contributes to their psychological decompensation and social deterioration (Arrigo & Griffin, 2004).

Ironically, retaining a job, achieving financial stability, and establishing a modicum of independence are often conditions of a community corrections sentence. To be precise, female offenders with these types of conditions will be guilty of committing a technical violation of their sentence if they fail to comply with these requirements. Moreover, if an offender misses a compulsory appointment with a criminal justice or treatment official—even if it is because she fears missing work—the individual's noncompliance represents a violation. These types of technical infractions can result in the community sanction being revoked and the offender subsequently being sent to prison. Not surprisingly, female offenders are more likely to be arrested on these kinds of probation and parole violations than males (Wolff, 2003).

Given the problems that these female offenders already confront in meeting the demands imposed on them by the courts (e.g., employment, financial stability), are decarcerated women with psychiatric conditions set up to experience failure? On the one hand, many women want to adjust to life after being convicted of a crime while in the community. On the other hand, society places incredible requirements on these ex-offenders, and they are often in situations in which they have no support from the community or even their families. For some decarcerated women, these demands are simply impossible to attain, especially given the limited resources available to them. This brings us to our fifth ethical issue:

## DOES SOCIETY PROVIDE ADEQUATE TREATMENT RESOURCES FOR MENTALLY ILL FEMALE OFFENDERS IN THE COMMUNITY?

Mentally ill female offenders are at a high risk for committing additional crimes (Prescott, 1998). Unfortunately, many of them do not have access to psychiatric treatment services. Some jurisdictions, especially in rural areas, have no locally available mental health treatment (Staton, Leukefeld, & Webster, 2003). More commonly, mental health services do exist but these offenders are unable to take advantage of the programs. In some cases, the offenders are offered treatment under the condition that they are financially responsible for the services they receive. Of course, most of these women cannot even afford to meet their basic needs, so they are not able to afford what may be seen as "unnecessary" treatment (Radosh, 2002; Wagaman, 2003). Other times, mental health facilities are available but will not accept clients that have been convicted of committing a crime (Draine et al., 1994; Jemelka, Trupin, & Chiles, 1989; Kanapaux, 2004).

Some individuals argue that the lack of treatment is not a problem because rehabilitation is ineffective and, hence, a waste of resources. They may even claim that "nothing works" to rehabilitate offenders (Martinson, 1974). However, empirical research has indicated that certain rehabilitative programs do work to improve the lives of offenders and to reduce recidivism (Latessa & Allen, 2003). Therefore, the lack of appropriate mental health treatment for female offenders is a problem (Singer, Bussey, Song, & Lunghofer, 1995; Staton, Leukefeld, & Webster, 2003; Teplin, Abram, & McClelland, 1996).

Even when treatment is available, there is a great deal of disagreement concerning what types of intervention offenders should receive. As with many other strategies in the criminal justice system, most treatment services have been designed for male offenders. Few programs have been tailored to fit the specific needs of women (Bloom et al., 2003). Although we are only beginning to understand the pathways to female criminality, we do know that, during treatment, we should target dynamic risk factors that are related to recidivism (Harris & Rice, 1997). These factors include certain environmental variables, such as criminal peer groups, as well as psychological factors including mental illness and substance abuse (Staton, Leukefeld, & Webster, 2003).

Among the most effective treatments for mentally ill female offenders are behavioral strategies. These are interventions in which the women are made aware of the consequences of their actions (Chemtob, Nocaco, Hamada, & Gross, 1997; Foxx, Bittle, & Faw, 1999; Harris & Rice, 1997). In these programs, offenders earn rewards when they act in a pro-social manner, and they are punished (often by losing rewards they have gained) when they act aggressively. Still, depending on the particular psychological disorder, behavior modification alone is not enough. Sometimes pharmacological therapies are also necessary, particularly among those with active psychosis (Falloon, Boyd, McGill, Razani, Moss, & Giderman, 1982). For example, nadolol, which can affect reactions to stress by blocking the effects of adrenaline, has been shown to reduce aggression among the mentally ill (Ratey, Sorgi, O'Driscoll, Sands, Daehler, Fletcher, et al., 1992). Another potentially helpful medication is clozapine, an atypical antipsychotic medication sometimes used to treat personality disorders such as schizophrenia. It has been used successfully in combination with behavioral programs (Menditto, Beck, Stuve, Fisher, Stacy, Logue, et. al., 1996). Although these are just two examples of several medications that may effectively be used to treat mentally ill female offenders, we must be cautious not to believe that society can change these women simply by writing them a prescription and sending them on their way. In truth, many of these individuals will not take their medications as prescribed if they do not have the support of treatment providers or other caring professionals in the community (Link & Stueve, 1995).

For effective recovery and rehabilitation, research indicates that female offenders need to have an ongoing relationship with treatment providers even after their sentences are complete or therapeutic assistance has ended (Latessa & Allen, 2003). Most female offenders are not able to maintain the progress they made during treatment if they do not have aftercare and support (Austin et al., 1992). Indeed, the most effective programs provide aftercare and life-planning for clients once the basic treatment program has been completed (Petersilia, 2003; Travis, 2005). Unfortunately, many existing programs do not offer ample follow-up or aftercare with clients (Latessa & Allen, 2003).

   Too often, offenders are simply released to fend for themselves and expected to continue practicing the strategies they learned in treatment (Travis & Visher, 2005). When this is the case, even the women that demonstrated excellent coping or adjustment during treatment in prison are likely to have subsequent problems. The offenders themselves often recognize the lack of aftercare and believe they would have been more successful following treatment had they received continuing community support (Maruna, 2001; Maruna, Immarigeon, & LeBel, 2004).

## WHERE DO WE GO FROM HERE? HOW CAN WE IMPROVE THE WAY THE CRIMINAL JUSTICE SYSTEM DEALS WITH MENTALLY ILL FEMALE OFFENDERS?

Clearly, there is a lack of effective treatment available for the more than one million female offenders under correctional care in the United States. If the research is correct, approximately 250,000 mentally ill offenders are already in the system. Many of these women have had multiple prior contacts with criminal justice agencies, but were not identified as psychiatrically disordered and/or given appropriate treatment for their problems. Again, some researchers, politicians, and policy analysts maintain that the systemic responsibility is to punish these women for their crimes, or to give them their just desserts. However, we contend that the systemic obligation is not simply to punish but to provide palliative rehabilitation and treatment services. This is the ethically sound and prudent response as it balances the demands of society and the needs of the individual (Williams & Arrigo, 2008). We recognize that ecological and contextual factors contribute to the development of psychiatric disorders and, in the long run, crime. However, if we are able to reduce recidivism through mental health intervention, these services will serve to benefit both the offenders and the public at large. Without therapeutic assistance, removing offenders from society for a period of incarceration will not curb recidivism when these citizens return to society (Maruna, 2001; Petersilia, 2003; Travis, 2005).

   Based on the evidence presented, we may certainly claim that the system is failing, and sometimes abandoning, mentally ill female offenders by not providing adequate treatment opportunities. Still, there is a larger ethical issue at hand: If we relinquish our responsibility to identify and treat these women, are we not contributing to their future criminality and, consequently to the problem of crime in this country? We are quick to hold offenders accountable for their actions. Should we not similarly hold society accountable when it neglects to help offenders when opportunities arise? Although our inaction in these instances might not result in direct and proximate injury to others, it might be the reason that some psychologically disturbed female offenders go on to commit interpersonal violence. In that way, we *are* indirectly contributing to crime. If the criminal justice or mental health systems had intervened in the life of Aileen Wuornos when warning signs were recognized, would she have gone on to take the lives of seven men? If her own family, as well as society in general, had not abandoned her, would she still have committed murder? Put differently, if Ms. Wuornos had connections to at least some members of her family, the community, or social welfare institutions in place to assist her, would she have had the necessary and sufficient incentive to change? We will never be able to definitively answer these questions; however, we speculate that the outcome would have been very different.

It is imperative that the criminal justice system take steps to assess and provide services for mentally ill female offenders. The first step must be to identify those offenders in need of treatment. Quite simply, without detection of mental illness, there is no chance to intervene. It is recommended that upon conviction, female offenders be routinely screened for mental illness. At the very least, criminal justice personnel should be trained to recognize signs of mental disorders so that the offenders can be referred for psychiatric assessments. To that end, it is important that trained mental health experts be accessible for evaluations at the request of the courts (Lamb & Weinberger, 1998). Further, identification is vital to early intervention, which is especially important for more severe mental disturbances. For example, if we are able to detect the early risk factors of psychopathy (or ASPD), more effective interventions can be implemented (Shipley & Arrigo, 2004).

Second, if a female offender is identified as suffering from mental illness, we should do everything possible to keep her out of prison. As discussed previously, incarceration can have detrimental effects on mentally ill female offenders, sometimes exacerbating their psychiatric disorder. Further, increased use of prisons has not had an appreciable effect on recidivism. That being said, we must ask ourselves what advantages society gains by confining offenders who could be handled more effectively in the community (Arrigo, 2002). Again, those who endorse retribution would argue that the offender deserves prison as punishment. We ask you to consider whether knowing that someone received the punishment she "deserves" is enough. Does this "just dessert" undo the wrong that was done to the victim or help society in any way? From our perspective, it is difficult to identify the benefits of imprisoning women suffering from mental illness (Kupers, 1999; Snyder, 2001).

Perhaps retribution is not the best guiding philosophy for the criminal justice system. An alternate philosophy to consider is the restorative justice approach. This model of justice does not concentrate on punishment. Rather, the focus is on restoring the offender, as well as the victim and the community (Bazemore & Shiff, 2001; Braithwaite, 1998). This philosophy seeks to rehabilitate the criminal, while helping to repair the harm to the victim and to the community (Sullivan & Tifft, 2005). As a result, the offender is more easily reintegrated into the community, because the community is more apt to provide support and opportunities to both the offender and the victim.

We realize that the correctional philosophy of this country will not be easily changed. This notwithstanding, we recommend that whenever possible female offenders be diverted for treatment to the mental health system (Lamb & Weinberger, 1998). Some will need residential placement during treatment; however, most can be handled on an outpatient basis in the community. Keeping these offenders in the community will allow them to utilize existing pro-social networks and give them a better chance at preserving employment.

Of course, keeping mentally ill female offenders in the community will not help in our endeavors to rehabilitate them or to reduce recidivism if treatment resources remain unavailable. Whether the treatment is voluntary or court-ordered, studies repeatedly have shown that some mental health interventions are effective in reducing re-arrests, violence, and recidivism in general (Hoffman, 1990; Lamb et al., 1996). Without question, some forms of treatment are more effective than others; however, therapeutic assistance is almost always superior to no treatment (Arrigo, 2006; Latessa & Allen, 2003). It is not likely that criminal justice funding will ever be ample enough to provide adequate treatment for all mentally disordered offenders (Wolff, 2003); however, we must strive to provide at least basic mental health services to offenders in all jurisdictions. Indeed, many transgressors might not have engaged in criminal behavior had the appropriate therapeutic care and assistance been made available to them (Dvoskin & Steadman, 1994).

We also need to ask ourselves why correctional assessments and rehabilitation programs primarily designed around male offenders are still used for women (Plotch, Hahn, & Reis, 1996). We have learned that female criminality is complicated; however, we are not necessarily using this knowledge effectively. In short, very few gender-responsive programs are available, despite the fact that effective treatment strategies for male offenders will not necessarily work for incarcerated women (Bloom et al., 2003). Female offending has been escalating over the past 20 years (Bureau of Justice Statistics, 1999), and it is time to recognize that women now account for a significant amount of crime. Therefore, we must consider and target the causal factors that contribute to female criminality and understand that these women will likely need several types of services to meet their wide-ranging needs. Treatment-relevant factors for women include, but are not limited to: abuse history, trauma, substance abuse, and mental illness (Bloom et al., 2003; Morash, Bynum, & Koons, 1998). However, they also need other comprehensive services to address their basic needs. For example, these women often require help with childcare, transportation, and even housing (Arrigo & Takahashi, 2007). They also need to access treatment personnel beyond normal business hours (Richie, 2001) and to maintain a sustained relationship with treatment providers (Latessa & Allen, 1993).

If we hope to reduce the recidivism of female offenders through rehabilitation, it is time to design and implement treatment programs specifically targeted to meet the dynamic and manifold mental health issues of women. As such, psychological treatment should be a priority for female offenders. As Link and Stueve (1995) maintain, if we can improve the availability and type of treatment services for psychiatrically disordered offenders, we eventually might be able to assert that "people with mental illness pose no more of a crime threat than do other members of the general population" (p. 180). Indeed, in the final analysis, if the criminal justice system is to confront fully its neglect and abandonment of female offenders with psychiatric disorders, then the ethical dilemmas we have identified must be cogently reviewed, strategically addressed, and systematically eradicated.

# References

Acoca, L. (1998). Outside/inside: The violation of American girls at home, on the streets, and in the juvenile justice system. *Crime and Delinquency, 44,* 561–589.

Arrigo, B. A. (2001). Transcarceration: A constitutive ethnography of mentally ill offenders. *The Prison Journal, 81,* 162–186.

Arrigo, B. A. (2002). *Punishing the mentally ill: A critical analysis of law and psychiatry.* Albany: SUNY Press.

Arrigo, B. A. (2004). *Psychological jurisprudence: Critical explorations in law, crime, and society.* Albany: SUNY Press.

Arrigo, B. A. (2006). *Criminal behavior: A systems approach.* Upper Saddle River, NJ: Prentice Hall.

Arrigo, B. A., & Griffin, A. (2004). Serial murder and the case of Aileen Wuornos: Attachment theory, psychopathy, and predatory aggression. *Behavioral Sciences and the Law, 22*, 375–393.

Arrigo, B. A., & Shipley, S. L. (2001). The confusion over psychopathy I: Historical considerations. *International Journal of Offender Therapy and Comparative Criminology, 45*, 325–344.

Arrigo, B. A., & Takahashi, Y. (2007). Theorizing community reentry for male incarcerates and confined mothers: Lessons learned from housing the homeless. *Journal of Offender Rehabilitation, 46*(1/2).

Austin, J., Bloom, B., & Donahue, T. (1992). *Female offenders in the community.* San Francisco: National Council on Crime and Delinquency.

Bazemore, G., & Shiff, M. (Eds.). (2001). *Restorative community justice: Repairing harm and transforming communities.* Cincinnati, OH: Anderson Publishing.

Bloom, B., Owen, B., & Covington, S. (2003). *Gender-responsive strategies: Research, practice, and guiding principles for women offenders.* Washington, DC: National Institute of Corrections.

Braithwaite, J. (1998). Restorative justice. In M. Tonry (Ed.), *The handbook of crime and punishment* (pp. 323–344). New York: Oxford University Press.

Bullock, J. L., & Arrigo, B. A. (2006). The myth that mental illness causes crime. In J. Walker & R. Bohm (Eds.), *Demystifying crime, and criminal justice* (pp. 12–19). Los Angeles, CA: Roxbury Publishing Company.

Bureau of Justice Statistics. (1999). *Special report: Women offenders.* Washington, DC: U.S. Department of Justice.

Bureau of Justice Statistics. (2001). *Mental health treatment in state prisons, 2000.* Washington, DC: U.S. Department of Justice.

Bureau of Justice Statistics. (2006). *Prisoners in 2005.* Washington, DC: U.S. Department of Justice.

Cauffman, E. (2004). A statewide screening of mental health symptoms among juvenile offenders in detention. *Journal of the American Academy of Child & Adolescent Psychiatry, 43*, 430–439.

Chamberlain, P., & Moore, K. (2003). Chaos and trauma in the lives of adolescent females with antisocial behavior and delinquency. *Journal of Aggression, Maltreatment and Trauma, 6*, 79–108.

Chemtob, C. M., Novaco, R. W., Hamada, R. S., & Gross, D. M. (1997). Cognitive-behavioral treatment for severe anger in posttraumatic stress disorder. *Journal of Consulting and Clinical Psychology, 65*, 184–189.

Ditton, P. (1999). *Mental health treatment of inmates and probationers.* Washington, DC: Bureau of Justice Statistics.

Dixon, A., Howie, P., & Starling, J. (2004). Psychopathology in female juvenile offenders. *Journal of Child Psychology and Psychiatry, 45*, 1150–1158.

Draine, J., Solomon, P., & Meyerson, A. T. (1994). Predictors of reincarceration among patients who received psychiatrics services in jail. *Hospital and Community Psychiatry, 45*, 163–167.

Dvoskin, J. A., & Steadman, H. J. (1994). Using intensive case management to reduce violence by mentally ill persons in the community. *Hospital and Community Psychiatry, 45*, 679–684.

Espelage, D. L., Cauffman, E., Broidy, L., Piquero, A. R., Mazerolle, P., & Steiner, H. (2003). A cluster-analytic investigation of MMPI profiles of serious male and female juvenile offenders. *Journal of the American Academy of Child and Adolescent Psychiatry, 7,* 770–778.

Falloon, I. R., Boyd, J. L., McGill, C. W., Razani, J., Moss, H. B., & Giderman, A. M. (1982). Family management in the prevention of exacerbations of schizophrenia: A controlled study. *New England Journal of Medicine, 306,* 1437–1440.

Federal Bureau of Investigation. (2005). *Crime in the United States 2004.* Washington, DC: Federal Bureau of Investigation.

Flowers, R. B. (1994). *Female criminals, crimes, and cellmates.* Westport, CT: Greenwood Press.

Fox, R. M., Bittle, R. G., & Faw, G. D. (1989). A maintenance strategy for discontinuing aversive procedures: A 52-month follow-up of the treatment of aggression. *American Journal on Mental Retardation, 94,* 27–36.

Fulwiler, C., Grossman, H., Forbes, C., & Ruthazer, R. (1997). Early-onset substance abuse and community violence by outpatients with chronic mental illness. *Psychiatric Services, 48,* 1181–1185.

Gabbard, G. O. (1990). *Psychodynamic psychiatry in clinical practice.* Washington, DC: American Psychiatric Press.

Gacono, C. B. (Ed.). (2001). *The clinical and forensic assessment of psychopathy.* Mahwah, NJ: Erlbaum.

Grisso, T., Barnum, R., Fletcher, K. E., Cauggman, E., & Peuschold, D. (2001). Massachusetts Youth Screening Instrument for mental health needs of juvenile justice youths. *Journal of the American Academy of Child & Adolescent Psychiatry, 40,* 541–548.

Harris, G. T., Rice, M. E., & Quinsey, V. L. (1993). Violent recidivism of mentally disordered offenders: The development of a statistical prediction instrument. *Criminal Justice and Behavior, 20,* 315–355.

Hodgins, S. (1992). Mental disorder, intellectual deficiency, and crime. *Archives of General Psychiatry, 49,* 476–483.

Hodgins, S., Mednick, S. A., Brennan, P. A., Schulsinger, F., & Engberg, M. (1996). Mental disorder and crime: Evidence from a Danish birth cohort. *Archives of General Psychiatry, 53,* 89–496.

Hoffman, B. F. (1990). The criminalization of the mentally ill. *Canadian Journal of Psychiatry, 35,* 166–169.

Jemelka, R. P., Trupin, E. W., & Chiles, J. A. (1989). The mentally ill in prisons: A review. *Hospital and Community Psychiatry, 40,* 481–491.

Jones, G., & Connelly, M. (2002). *Mentally ill offenders and mental health care issues: An overview of the research.* College Park, MD: State Commission on Criminal Sentencing Policy.

Junginger, J. (1996). Psychosis and violence: The case for a content analysis of psychotic experience. *Schizophrenia Bulletin, 22,* 91–103.

Kanapaux, W. (2004). Guilty of mental illness. *Psychiatric Times, 21,* 1–6.

Kataoka, S. H., Zima, B. T., Dupre, D. A., Moreno, K. A., Yang, X., & McGarvey, E. L. (2001). Mental health problems and service use among female juvenile offenders: Their relationship to criminal history. *Journal of the American Academy of Child and Adolescent Psychiatry, 40,* 549–555.

Kupers, T. (1999). *Prison madness: The mental health crisis behind bars and what we must do about it.* San Francisco, CA: Jossey-Bass.

Lamb, H. R., & Weinberger, L. E. (1998). Persons with severe mental illness in jails and prisons: A review. *Psychiatric Services, 48,* 1307–1310.

Lamb, H. R., Weinberger, L. E., & Reston-Parham, C. (1996). Court intervention to address the mental health needs of mentally ill offenders. *Psychiatric Services, 47,* 275–281.

Latessa, E. J., & Allen, H. E. (2003). *Corrections in the community* (3rd ed.). Cincinnati, OH: Anderson Publishing.

Lederman, C. S., Dakof, G. A., Larre, M. A., & Li, H. (2004). Characteristics of adolescent girls in juvenile detention. *International Journal of Law and Psychiatry, 27,* 321–337.

Link, B. G., Andrews, H., & Cullen, F. T. (1992). The violent and illegal behavior of mental patients reconsidered. *American Psychological Review, 57,* 275–292.

Link, B. G., Cullen, F. T., Frank, J., & Wozniak, J. F. (1987). The social rejection of former mental patients: Understanding why labels matter. *American Journal of Sociology, 92,* 1462–1500.

Link, B. G., & Stueve, A. (1995). Evidence bearing on mental illness as a possible cause of violent behavior. *Epidemiological Review, 172,* 17–181.

Loza, W., Neo, L. H., Shahinfar, A., & Loza-Fanous, A. (2005). Cross-validation of the self-appraisal questionnaire: A tool for assessing violent and non-violent recidivism among female offenders. *International Journal of Offender Therapy and Comparative Criminology, 49,* 547–560.

Martinson, R. (1974). What works? Questions and answers about prison reform. *The Public Interest, 35,* 22–53.

Maruna, S. (2001). *Making good: How ex-convicts reform and rebuild their lives.* Washington, DC: American Psychological Association.

Maruna, S., Immarigeon, R., & LeBel, T. P. (2004). Ex-offender reintegration: Theory and practice. In S. Maruna & R. Immarigeon (Eds.), *After crime and punishment: Pathways to offender reintegration* (pp. 3–26). Cullompton, UK: Willan Press.

Marzuk, P. M. (1996). Violence, crime, and mental illness: How strong a link? *Archives of General Psychiatry, 53,* 481–486.

Menditto, A. A., Beck, N. C., Stuve, P., Fisher, J. A., Stacy, M., Logue, M. B., et al. (1996). Effectiveness of clozapine and a social learning program for severely disabled psychiatric inpatients. *Psychiatric Services, 47,* 46–51.

Miller, R. D. (1992). Economic factors leading to diversion of the mentally disordered from the civil to the criminal commitment systems. *International Journal of Law and Psychiatry, 15,* 1–12.

Monahan, J. (1992). Mental disorder and violent behavior. *American Psychologist, 47,* 511–521.

Morash, M., Bynum, T., & Koons, B. (1998). *Women offenders: Programming needs and promising approaches.* National Institute of Justice Research in Brief. Washington, DC: Office of Justice Programs.

Morash, M., Haarr, R. N., & Rucker, L. (1994). A comparison of programming for women and men in U.S. prisons in the 1980s. *Crime & Delinquency, 40,* 197–221.

Mulder, R. T., Beautrais, A. L., Joyce, P. R., & Fergusson, D. M. (1998). Relationships between dissociation, childhood sexual abuse, childhood physical abuse, and mental illness in a general population sample. *American Journal of Psychiatry, 155,* 806–811.

Mulvey, E. P. (1994). Assessing the evidence of a link between mental illness and violence. *Hospital and Community Psychiatry, 45,* 663–668.

National Mental Health Association. (2006). *Mental health and adolescent girls in the justice system.* Alexandria, VA: National Mental Health Association.

Petersilia, J. (1992). California's prison policy: Causes, costs, and consequences. *The Prison Journal, 72,* 8–36.

Petersilia, J. (2003). *When prisoners come home: Parole and prisoner re-entry.* New York: Oxford University Press.

Plotch, A., Hahn, J., & Reis, S. (1996). *Prevention and parity: Girls in juvenile justice.* Washington, DC: U.S. Department of Justice.

Prescott, L. (1998). *Improving policy and practice for adolescent girls with co-occurring disorders in the juvenile justice system.* Delmar, NY: The GAINS Center.

Quinsey, V. L. (1988). Assessments of the treatability of forensic patients. *Behavioral Sciences and Law, 6,* 443–452.

Radosh, P. F. (2002). Reflections on women's crime and mothers in prison: A peacemaking approach, *Crime and Delinquency, 48*(2), 300–315.

Ratey, J. J., Sorgi, P., O'Driscoll, G. A., Sands, S., Daehler, M., Fletcher J., et al. (1992). Nadolol to treat aggression and psychiatric symptomatology in chronic psychiatric inpatients: A double-blind, placebo-controlled study. *Journal of Clinical Psychiatry, 53,* 41–46.

Reiman, J. (2004). *The rich get richer and the poor get prison: Ideology, class, and criminal justice* (7th ed.). Boston: Allyn & Bacon.

Richie, B. (2001). Challenges incarcerated women face as they return to their communities: Findings from life history interviews. *Crime & Delinquency, 47,* 368–389.

Rogers, R., & Bagby, R. M. (1992). Diversion of mentally disordered offenders: A legitimate role for clinicians? *Behavioral Sciences and the Law, 10,* 407–418.

Russell, S. (1992). *Damsel of death.* London: BCA.

The Sentencing Project. (2002). *Mentally ill offenders in the criminal justice system: An analysis and prescription.* Washington, DC: The Sentencing Project.

Shelton, D. (2001). Emotional disorders in young offenders. *Journal of Nursing Scholarship, 33,* 259–263.

Shipley, S. L., & Arrigo, B. A. (2004). *The female homicide offender: Serial murder and the case of Aileen Wuornos.* Upper Saddle River, NJ: Pearson Education.

Sigurdson, C. (2000). The mad, the bad and the abandoned: The mentally ill in prisons and jails. *Corrections Today, 62,* 70–78.

Silver, E. (2000). Race, neighborhood disadvantage, and violence among persons with mental disorders: The importance of contextual measurement. *Law & Human Behavior, 24,* 449–456.

Singer, M., Bussey, J., Song, L., & Lunghofer, L. (1995). The psychological issues of women serving time in jail. *Social Work, 40,* 103–113.

Snyder, T. R. (2001). *The protestant ethic and the spirit of punishment.* Grand Rapids, MI: William B. Eerdmans Publishing Company.

Staton, M., Leukefeld, C., & Webster, J. M. (2003). Substance use, health, and mental health: Problems and service utilization among incarcerated women. *International Journal of Offender Therapy and Comparative Criminology, 47,* 224–239.

Swanson, J., Estroff, S., Swartz, M., Borum, R., Lachicotte, W., Zimmer, C., & Wagner, R. (1997). Violence and severe mental disorder in clinical and community populations: The effects of psychotic symptoms, comorbidity, and lack of treatment. *Psychiatry, 60,* 1–22.

Swanson, J., Holzer, C., Ganju, V., & Jono, R. (1990). Violence and psychiatric disorder in the community: Evidence from the epidemiologic catchment area surveys. *Hospital and Community Psychiatry, 41,* 761–770.

Teplin, L. A., Abram, K. M., & McClelland, G. M. (1996). Prevalence of psychiatric disorders among incarcerated women. *Archives of General Psychiatry, 53,* 505–512.

Teplin, L. A., Abram, K. M., McClelland, G. M, Dulcan, M. K., & Mericle, A. A. (2002). Psychiatric disorders in youth in juvenile detention. *Archives of General Psychiatry, 59,* 1133–1143.

Sullivan, D., & Tifft, L. (2005). *Restorative justice: Healing the foundations of our everyday lives* (2nd ed.). Monsey, NY: Criminal Justice Press.

Timmons-Mitchell, J., Brown, C., Schulz, C., Webster, S. E., Underwood, L. A., & Semple, W. E. (1997). Comparing the mental health needs of female and male juvenile delinquents. *Behavioral Sciences and the Law,* 195–202.

Torrey, E. F. (1994). Violent behavior by individuals with serious mental illness. *Hospital and Community Psychiatry, 45,* 653–662.

Travis, J. (2005). *But they all come back: Facing the challenges of prisoner reentry.* New York: Urban Institute Press.

Travis, J., & Visher, C. (Eds.). (2005). *Prisoner reentry and crime in America.* New York: Cambridge University Press.

Van Voorhis, P., Braswell, M., & Lester, D. (2000). *Correctional counseling and rehabilitation* (4th ed.). Cincinnati, OH: Anderson Publishing.

Vitale, J. E., Smith, S. S., Brinkley, C. A., & Newman, J. P. (2002). The reliability and validity of the psychopathy checklist—revised in a sample of female offenders. *Criminal Justice and Behavior, 29,* 202–231.

Wagaman, G. L. (2003). Managing and treating female offenders. In T. J. Fagan & R. K. Ax (Eds.), *Correctional mental health handbook* (pp. 123–143). Thousand Oaks, CA: Sage.

Widom, J. (1998). Child abuse, neglect, and witnessing violence. In D. M. Stoff, J. Breiling, & J. D. Maser (Eds.), *Handbook of antisocial behavior* (pp. 159–170). New York: Wiley.

Williams, C. R., & Arrigo, B. A. (2008). *Ethics, crime, and criminal justice.* Upper Saddle River, NJ: Prentice Hall.

Wolff, N. (2003). *Investing in health and justice outcomes: An investment strategy for offenders with mental health problems in New Jersey.* Newark, NJ: New Jersey Institute for Social Justice.

# INDEX

ॐ